D1757716

Introduction to Software Testing

Extensively class tested, this text takes an innovative approach to software testing: it defines testing as the process of applying a few well-defined, general-purpose test criteria to a structure or model of the software. The structure of the text directly reflects the pedagogical approach and incorporates the latest innovations in testing, including modern types of software such as OO, Web applications, and embedded software. The book contains numerous examples throughout. An instructor's solution manual, PowerPoint slides, sample syllabi, additional examples and updates, testing tools for students, and example software programs in Java are available on an extensive Web site at www.introsoftwaretesting.com.

Paul Ammann, PhD, is an Associate Professor of software engineering at George Mason University. He received an outstanding teaching award in 2007 from the Volgenau School of Information Technology and Engineering. Dr. Ammann earned an AB degree in computer science from Dartmouth College and MS and PhD degrees in computer science from the University of Virginia.

Jeff Offutt, PhD, is a Professor of software engineering at George Mason University. He is editor-in-chief of the *Journal of Software Testing, Verification and Reliability*; chair of the steering committee for the IEEE International Conference on Software Testing, Verification, and Validation; and on the editorial boards for several journals. He received the outstanding teacher award from the Volgenau School of Information Technology and Engineering in 2003. Dr. Offutt earned a BS degree in mathematics and data processing from Morehead State University and MS and PhD degrees in computer science from the Georgia Institute of Technology.

INTRODUCTION TO SOFTWARE TESTING

Paul Ammann
George Mason University

Jeff Offutt
George Mason University

CAMBRIDGE
UNIVERSITY PRESS

CAMBRIDGE UNIVERSITY PRESS
Cambridge, New York, Melbourne, Madrid, Cape Town, Singapore, São Paulo, Delhi

Cambridge University Press
32 Avenue of the Americas, New York, NY 10013-2473, USA

www.cambridge.org
Information on this title: www.cambridge.org/9780521880381

© Paul Ammann and Jeff Offutt 2008

This publication is in copyright. Subject to statutory exception
and to the provisions of relevant collective licensing agreements,
no reproduction of any part may take place without
the written permission of Cambridge University Press.

First published 2008

Printed in the United States of America

A catalog record for this publication is available from the British Library.

Library of Congress Cataloging in Publication Data

Ammann, Paul, 1961–
Introduction to software testing / Paul Ammann, Jeff Offutt.
   p.   cm.
Includes bibliographical references and index.
ISBN 978-0-521-88038-1 (hardback)
1. Computer software – Testing.   I. Offutt, Jeff, 1961–   II. Title.
QA76.76.T48A56   2008
004.2′4–dc22   2007035077

ISBN   978-0-521-88038-1 hardback

Cambridge University Press has no responsibility for
the persistence or accuracy of URLs for external or
third-party Internet Web sites referred to in this publication
and does not guarantee that any content on such
Web sites is, or will remain, accurate or appropriate.

Contents

List of Figures

List of Tables

Preface

This book presents software testing as a practical engineering activity, essential to producing high-quality software. It is designed to be used as the primary textbook in either an undergraduate or graduate course on software testing, as a supplement to a general course on software engineering or data structures, and as a resource for software test engineers and developers. This book has a number of unique features:

- It organizes the complex and confusing landscape of test coverage criteria with a novel and extremely simple structure. At a technical level, software testing is based on satisfying coverage criteria. The book's central observation is that there are few truly different coverage criteria, each of which fits easily into one of four categories: graphs, logical expressions, input space, and syntax structures. This not only simplifies testing, but it also allows a convenient and direct theoretical treatment of each category. This approach contrasts strongly with the traditional view of testing, which treats testing at each phase in the development process differently.
- It is designed and written to be a textbook. The writing style is direct, it builds the concepts from the ground up with a minimum of required background, and it includes lots of examples, homework problems, and teaching materials. It provides a balance of theory and practical application, presenting testing as a collection of objective, quantitative activities that can be measured and repeated. The theoretical concepts are presented when needed to support the practical activities that test engineers follow.
- It assumes that testing is part of a mental discipline that helps all IT professionals develop higher-quality software. Testing is not an anti-engineering activity, and it is not an inherently destructive process. Neither is it only for testing specialists or domain experts who know little about programming or math.
- It is designed with modular, interconnecting pieces; thus it can be used in multiple courses. Most of the book requires only basic discrete math and introductory programming, and the parts that need more background are clearly marked. By

using the appropriate sections, this book can support several classes, as described later in the preface.
- It assumes the reader is learning to be an engineer whose goal is to produce the best possible software with the lowest possible cost. The concepts in this book are well grounded in theory, are practical, and most are currently in use.

WHY SHOULD THIS BOOK BE USED?

Not very long ago, software development companies could afford to employ programmers who could not test and testers who could not program. For most of the industry, it was not necessary for either group to know the technical principles behind software testing or even software development. Software testing in industry historically has been a nontechnical activity. Industry viewed testing primarily from the managerial and process perspective and had limited expectations of practitioners' technical training.

As the software engineering profession matures, and as software becomes more pervasive in everyday life, there are increasingly stringent requirements for software reliability, maintainability, and security. Industry must respond to these changes by, among other things, improving the way software is tested. This requires increased technical expertise on the part of test engineers, as well as increased emphasis on testing by software developers. The good news is that the knowledge and technology are available and based on over 30 years of research and practice. This book puts that knowledge into a form that students, test engineers, test managers, and developers can access.

At the same time, it is relatively rare to find courses that teach testing in universities. Only a few undergraduate courses exist, almost no masters degree programs in computer science or software engineering require a course in software testing, and only a few dozen have an elective course. Not only is testing not covered as an essential part of undergraduate computer science education, most computer science students either never gain any knowledge about testing, or see only a few lectures as part of a general course in software engineering.

The authors of this book have been teaching software testing to software engineering and computer science students for more than 15 years. Over that time we somewhat reluctantly came to the conclusion that no one was going to write the book we wanted to use. Rather, to get the book we wanted, we would have to write it.

Previous testing books have presented software testing as a relatively simple subject that relies more on process than technical understanding of how software is constructed, as a complicated and fractured subject that requires detailed understanding of numerous software development technologies, or as a completely theoretical subject that can be mastered only by mathematicians and theoretical computer scientists. Most books on software testing are organized around the phases in a typical software development lifecycle, an approach that has the unfortunate side effect of obscuring common testing themes. Finally, most testing books are written as reference books, not textbooks. As a result, only instructors with prior expertise in software testing can easily teach the subject. **This book is accessible to instructors who are not already testing experts**.

This book differs from other books on software testing in other important ways. Many books address managing the testing process. While this is important, it is equally important to give testers specific techniques grounded in basic theory. This book provides a balance of theory and practical application. This is important information that software companies must have; however, this book focuses specifically on the technical nuts-and-bolts issues of designing and creating tests. Other testing books currently on the market focus on specific techniques or activities, such as system testing or unit testing. This book is intended to be comprehensive over the entire software development process and to cover as many techniques as possible.

As stated previously, the motivation for this book is to support courses in software testing. Our first target was our own software testing course in our Software Engineering MS program at George Mason University. This popular elective is taught to about 30 computer science and software engineering students every semester. We also teach PhD seminars in software testing, industry short courses on specialized aspects, and lectures on software testing in various undergraduate courses. Although few undergraduate courses on software testing exist, we believe that they should exist, and we expect they will in the near future. Most testing books are not designed for classroom use. We specifically wrote this book to support our classroom activities, and it is no accident that the syllabus for our testing course, available on the book's Web site (www.introsoftwaretesting.com), closely follows the table of contents for this book.

This book includes numerous carefully worked examples to help students and teachers alike learn the sometimes complicated concepts. The instructor's resources include high-quality powerpoint slides, presentation hints, solutions to exercises, and working software. Our philosophy is that we are doing more than writing a book; we are offering our course to the community. One of our goals was to write material that is scholarly and true to the published research literature, but that is also accessible to nonresearchers. Although the presentation in the book is quite a bit different from the research papers that the material is derived from, the essential ideas are true to the literature. To make the text flow more smoothly, we have removed the references from the presentation. For those interested in the research genealogy, each chapter closes with a bibliographic notes section that summarizes where the concepts come from.

WHO SHOULD READ THIS BOOK?

Students who read and use this book will learn the fundamental principles behind software testing, and how to apply these principles to produce better software, faster. They will not only become better programmers, they will also be prepared to carry out high-quality testing activities for their future employers. *Instructors* will be able to use this book in the classroom, even without prior practical expertise in software testing. The numerous exercises and thought-provoking problems, classroom-ready and classroom-tested slides, and suggested outside activities make this material teachable by instructors who are not already experts in software testing. *Research students* such as beginning PhD students will find this book to be an invaluable resource as a starting point to the field. The theory is sound and clearly presented, the practical applications reveal what is useful and what is not, and the advanced reading and bibliographic notes provide pointers into the literature. Although the set of research students in software testing is a relatively small audience, we believe it is a key audience, because a common, easily achievable baseline would reduce the effort required for research students to join the community of testing researchers. *Researchers* who are already familiar with the field will find the criteria-approach to be novel and interesting. Some may disagree with the pedagogical approach, but we have found that the view that testing is an application of only a few criteria to a very few software structures to be very helpful to our research. We hope that testing research in the future will draw away from searches for more criteria to novel uses and evaluations of existing criteria.

Testers in the industry will find this book to be an invaluable collection of techniques that will help improve their testing, no matter what their current process is. The criteria presented here are intended to be used as a "toolbox" of tricks that can be used to find faults. *Developers* who read this book will find numerous ways to improve their own software. Their self-testing activities can become more efficient and effective, and the discussions of software faults that test engineers search for will help developers avoid them. To paraphrase a famous parable, if you want to teach a person to be a better fisherman, explain how and where the fish swim. Finally, *managers* will find this book to be a useful explanation of how clever test engineers do their job, and of how test tools work. They will be able to make more effective decisions regarding hiring, promotions, and purchasing tools.

HOW CAN THIS BOOK BE USED?

A major advantage of the structure of this book is that it can be easily used for several different courses. Most of the book depends on material that is taught very early in college and some high schools: basic concepts from data structures and discrete math. The sections are organized so that the early material in each chapter is accessible to less advanced students, and material that requires more advanced knowledge is clearly marked.

Specifically, the book defines six separate sets of chapter sections that form *streams* through the book:

1. A module within a CS II course
2. A sophomore-level course on software testing
3. A module in a general software engineering course
4. A senior-level course on software testing
5. A first-year MS level course on software testing
6. An advanced graduate research-oriented course on software testing
7. Industry practioner relevant sections

The stream approach is illustrated in the abbreviated table of contents in the figure shown on pp. xix–xx. Each chapter section is marked with which stream it belongs too. Of course, individual instructors, students, and readers may prefer to adapt the stream to their own interests or purposes. We suggest that the first two sections of Chapter 1 and the first two sections of Chapter 6 are appropriate reading for a module in a data structures (CS II) class, to be followed by a simple

Stream 1: Module in a CS II course.

Stream 2: Sophomore-level course on software testing.

Stream 3: Module in a general software engineering course.

Stream 4: Senior-level course on software testing.

Stream 5: First-year MS course on software testing.

Stream 6: Advanced graduate research-oriented course on software testing.

Stream 7: Industry practitioner relevant sections

Stream 1: Module in a CS II course.

Stream 2: Sophomore-level course on software testing.

Stream 3: Module in a general software engineering course.

Stream 4: Senior-level course on software testing.

Stream 5: First-year MS course on software testing.

Stream 6: Advanced graduate research-oriented course on software testing.

Stream 7: Industry practitioner relevant sections

	STREAMS						
	1	2	3	4	5	6	7
Part III: Applying Criteria in Practice							
Chapter 6. Practical Considerations	■	■	■	■	■	■	■
6.1 Regression Testing	■	■	■	■	■	■	■
6.2 Integration and Testing	■	■	■	■	■	■	■
6.3 Test Process				■	■	■	■
6.4 Test Plans				■	■	■	■
6.5 Identifying Correct Outputs		■	■	■	■	■	
6.5 Bibliographic Notes						■	
Chapter 7. Engineering Criteria for Technologies				■	■	■	■
7.1 Testing Object-Oriented Software				■	■	■	■
7.2 Testing Web Applications and Web Services					■	■	■
7.3 Testing Graphical User Interfaces					■	■	■
7.4 Real-Time Software and Embedded Software					■	■	■
7.5 Bibliographic Notes						■	
Chapter 8. Building Testing Tools					■	■	■
8.1 Instrumentation for Graph and Logical Expression Criteria					■	■	■
8.2 Building Mutation Testing Tools						■	
8.3 Bibliographic Notes						■	
Chapter 9. Challenges in Testing Software					■	■	■
9.1 Testing for Emergent Properties: Safety and Security					■	■	■
9.2 Software Testability					■	■	■
9.3 Test Criteria and the Future of Software Testing					■	■	
9.4 Bibliographic Notes						■	

assignment. Our favorite is to ask the students to retrieve one of their previously graded programs and satisfy some simple test criterion like branch coverage. We offer points for every fault found, driving home two concepts: an "A" grade doesn't mean the program always works, and finding faults is a good thing.

The sophomore-level course on software testing (stream 2) is designed to immediately follow a data structures course (CS II). The marked sections contain material that depends only on data structures and discrete math.

A module in a general software engineering course (stream 3) could augment the survey material typical in such courses. The sections marked provide basic literacy in software testing.

The senior-level course on software testing (stream 4) is the primary target for this text. It adds material that requires a little more sophistication in terms of software development than the sophomore stream. This includes sections in Chapter 2 on data flow testing, sections that involve integration testing of multiple modules, and sections that rely on grammars or finite state machines. Most senior computer science students will have seen this material in their other courses. Most of the sections that appear in stream 4 but not stream 2 could be added to stream 2 with appropriate short introductions. It is important to note that a test engineer does not need to know all the theory of parsing to use data flow testing or all the theory on finite state machines to use statecharts for testing.

The graduate-level course on software testing (stream 5) adds some additional sections that rely on a broader context and that require more theoretical maturity. For example, these sections use knowledge of elementary formal methods, polymorphism, and some of the UML diagrams. Some of the more advanced topics and the entire chapter on building testing tools are also intended for a graduate audience. This chapter could form the basis for a good project, for example, to implement a simple coverage analyzer.

An advanced graduate course in software testing with a research emphasis such as a PhD seminar (stream 6) includes issues that are still unproven and research in nature. The bibliographic notes are recommended only for these students as indicators for future in-depth reading.

Finally, sections that are reasonably widely used in industry, especially those that have commercial tool support, are marked for stream 7. These sections have a minimum of theory and omit criteria that are still of questionable usefulness.

Extensive supplementary materials, including sample syllabuses, PowerPoint slides, presentation hints, solutions to exercises, working software, and errata are available on the book's companion Web site.

ACKNOWLEDGMENTS

Many people helped us write this book. Not only have the students in our Software Testing classes at George Mason been remarkably tolerant of using a work in progress, they have enthusiastically provided feedback on how to improve the text. We cannot acknowledge all by name (ten semesters worth of students have used it!), but the following have made especially large contributions: Aynur Abdurazik, Muhammad Abdulla, Yuquin Ding, Jyothi Chinman, Blaine Donley, Patrick Emery, Brian Geary, Mark Hinkle, Justin Hollingsworth, John King, Yuelan Li, Xiaojuan Liu, Chris Magrin, Jyothi Reddy, Raimi Rufai, Jeremy Schneider, Bill Shelton, Frank Shukis, Quansheng Xiao, and Linzhen Xue. We especially appreciate those who generously provided extensive comments on the entire book: Guillermo Calderon-Meza, Becky Hartley, Gary Kaminski, and Andrew J. Offutt. We gratefully acknowledge the feedback of early adopters at other educational institutions: Roger Alexander, Jane Hayes, Ling Liu, Darko Marinov, Arthur Reyes, Michael Shin, and Tao Xie. We also want to acknowledge several people who provided material for the book: Roger Alexander, Mats Grindal, Hong Huang, Gary Kaminski, Robert Nilsson, Greg Williams, Wuzhi Xu. We were lucky to receive excellent suggestion from Lionel Briand, Renée Bryce, Kim King, Sharon Ritchey, Bo Sanden, and Steve Schach. We are grateful to our editor, Heather Bergman, for providing unwavering support and enforcing the occasional deadline to move the project along, as well as Kerry Cahill from Cambridge University Press for very strong support on this project.

We also acknowledge George Mason University for supporting both of us on sabbaticals and for providing GTA support at crucial times. Our department Chair, Hassan Gomaa, has enthusiastically supported this effort.

Finally, of course none of this is possible without the support of our families. Thanks to Becky, Jian, Steffi, Matt, Joyce, and Andrew for keeping us grounded in reality and helping keep us happy for the past five years.

Just as all programs contain faults, all texts contain errors. Our text is no different. And, as responsibility for software faults rests with the developers, responsibility for errors in this text rests with us, the authors. In particular, the bibliographic notes sections reflect our perspective of the testing field, a body of work we readily acknowledge as large and complex. We apologize in advance for omissions, and invite pointers to relevant citations.

Paul Ammann
Jeff Offutt

PART 1

Overview

1

Introduction

The ideas and techniques of software testing have become essential knowledge for all software developers. A software developer can expect to use the concepts presented in this book many times during his or her career. This chapter introduces the subject of software testing by describing the activities of a test engineer, defining a number of key terms, and then explaining the central notion of test coverage.

Software is a key ingredient in many of the devices and systems that pervade our society. Software defines the behavior of network routers, financial networks, telephone switching networks, the Web, and other infrastructure of modern life. Software is an essential component of embedded applications that control exotic applications such as airplanes, spaceships, and air traffic control systems, as well as mundane appliances such as watches, ovens, cars, DVD players, garage door openers, cell phones, and remote controllers. Modern households have over 50 processors, and some new cars have over 100; all of them running software that optimistic consumers assume will never fail! Although many factors affect the engineering of reliable software, including, of course, careful design and sound process management, testing is the primary method that the industry uses to evaluate software under development. Fortunately, a few basic software testing concepts can be used to design tests for a large variety of software applications. A goal of this book is to present these concepts in such a way that the student or practicing engineer can easily apply them to any software testing situation.

This textbook differs from other software testing books in several respects. The most important difference is in how it views testing techniques. In his landmark book *Software Testing Techniques*, Beizer wrote that testing is simple – all a tester needs to do is "find a graph and cover it." Thanks to Beizer's insight, it became evident to us that the myriad testing techniques present in the literature have much more in common than is obvious at first glance. Testing techniques typically are presented in the context of a particular software artifact (for example, a requirements document or code) or a particular phase of the lifecycle (for example, requirements analysis or implementation). Unfortunately, such a presentation obscures the underlying similarities between techniques. This book clarifies these similarities.

It turns out that graphs do not characterize all testing techniques well; other abstract models are necessary. Much to our surprise, we have found that a small number of abstract models suffice: graphs, logical expressions, input domain characterizations, and syntactic descriptions. The main contribution of this book is to simplify testing by classifying coverage criteria into these four categories, and this is why Part II of this book has exactly four chapters.

This book provides a balance of theory and practical application, thereby presenting testing as a collection of objective, quantitative activities that can be measured and repeated. The theory is based on the published literature, and presented without excessive formalism. Most importantly, the theoretical concepts are presented when needed to support the practical activities that test engineers follow. That is, this book is intended for software developers.

1.1 ACTIVITIES OF A TEST ENGINEER

In this book, a *test engineer* is an information technology (IT) professional who is in charge of one or more technical test activities, including designing test inputs, producing test case values, running test scripts, analyzing results, and reporting results to developers and managers. Although we cast the description in terms of test engineers, every engineer involved in software development should realize that he or she sometimes wears the hat of a test engineer. The reason is that each software artifact produced over the course of a product's development has, or should have, an associated set of test cases, and the person best positioned to define these test cases is often the designer of the artifact. A *test manager* is in charge of one or more test engineers. Test managers set test policies and processes, interact with other managers on the project, and otherwise help the engineers do their work.

Figure 1.1 shows some of the major activities of test engineers. A test engineer must design tests by creating test requirements. These requirements are then

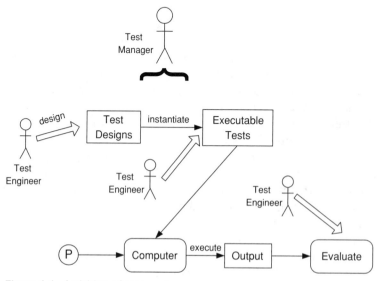

Figure 1.1. Activities of test engineers.

transformed into actual values and scripts that are ready for execution. These executable tests are run against the software, denoted P in the figure, and the results are evaluated to determine if the tests reveal a fault in the software. These activities may be carried out by one person or by several, and the process is monitored by a test manager.

One of a test engineer's most powerful tools is a formal coverage criterion. Formal coverage criteria give test engineers ways to decide what test inputs to use during testing, making it more likely that the tester will find problems in the program and providing greater assurance that the software is of high quality and reliability. Coverage criteria also provide stopping rules for the test engineers. The technical core of this book presents the coverage criteria that are available, describes how they are supported by tools (commercial and otherwise), explains how they can best be applied, and suggests how they can be integrated into the overall development process.

Software testing activities have long been categorized into levels, and two kinds of levels have traditionally been used. The most often used level categorization is based on traditional software process steps. Although most types of tests can only be run after some part of the software is implemented, tests can be designed and constructed during all software development steps. The most time-consuming parts of testing are actually the test design and construction, so test activities can and should be carried out throughout development. The second-level categorization is based on the attitude and thinking of the testers.

1.1.1 Testing Levels Based on Software Activity

Tests can be derived from requirements and specifications, design artifacts, or the source code. A different level of testing accompanies each distinct software development activity:

- Acceptance Testing – assess software with respect to requirements.
- System Testing – assess software with respect to architectural design.
- Integration Testing – assess software with respect to subsystem design.
- Module Testing – assess software with respect to detailed design.
- Unit Testing – assess software with respect to implementation.

Figure 1.2 illustrates a typical scenario for testing levels and how they relate to software development activities by isolating each step. Information for each test level is typically derived from the associated development activity. Indeed, standard advice is to design the tests concurrently with each development activity, even though the software will not be in an executable form until the implementation phase. The reason for this advice is that the mere process of explicitly articulating tests can identify defects in design decisions that otherwise appear reasonable. Early identification of defects is by far the best means of reducing their ultimate cost. Note that this diagram is **not** intended to imply a waterfall process. The synthesis and analysis activities generically apply to any development process.

The *requirements analysis* phase of software development captures the customer's needs. *Acceptance testing* is designed to determine whether the completed software in fact meets these needs. In other words, acceptance testing probes

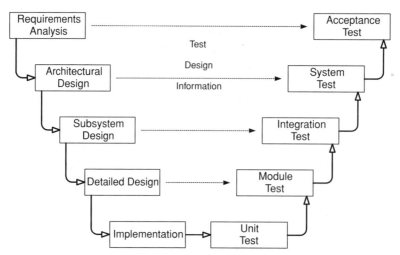

Figure 1.2. Software development activities and testing levels – the "V Model".

whether the software does what the users want. Acceptance testing must involve users or other individuals who have strong domain knowledge.

The *architectural design* phase of software development chooses components and connectors that together realize a system whose specification is intended to meet the previously identified requirements. *System testing* is designed to determine whether the assembled system meets its specifications. It assumes that the pieces work individually, and asks if the system works as a whole. This level of testing usually looks for design and specification problems. It is a very expensive place to find lower-level faults and is usually not done by the programmers, but by a separate testing team.

The *subsystem design* phase of software development specifies the structure and behavior of subsystems, each of which is intended to satisfy some function in the overall architecture. Often, the subsystems are adaptations of previously developed software. *Integration testing* is designed to assess whether the interfaces between modules (defined below) in a given subsystem have consistent assumptions and communicate correctly. Integration testing must assume that modules work correctly. Some testing literature uses the terms integration testing and system testing interchangeably; in this book, integration testing does **not** refer to testing the integrated system or subsystem. Integration testing is usually the responsibility of members of the development team.

The *detailed design* phase of software development determines the structure and behavior of individual modules. A program *unit*, or procedure, is one or more contiguous program statements, with a name that other parts of the software use to call it. Units are called functions in C and C++, procedures or functions in Ada, methods in Java, and subroutines in Fortran. A *module* is a collection of related units that are assembled in a file, package, or class. This corresponds to a file in C, a package in Ada, and a class in C++ and Java. *Module testing* is designed to assess individual modules in isolation, including how the component units interact with each other and their associated data structures. Most software development organizations make module testing the responsibility of the programmer.

Implementation is the phase of software development that actually produces code. *Unit testing* is designed to assess the units produced by the implementation phase and is the "lowest" level of testing. In some cases, such as when building general-purpose library modules, unit testing is done without knowledge of the encapsulating software application. As with module testing, most software development organizations make unit testing the responsibility of the programmer. It is straightforward to package unit tests together with the corresponding code through the use of tools such as *JUnit* for Java classes.

Not shown in Figure 1.2 is regression testing, a standard part of the maintenance phase of software development. *Regression testing* is testing that is done after changes are made to the software, and its purpose is to help ensure that the updated software still possesses the functionality it had before the updates.

Mistakes in requirements and high-level design wind up being implemented as faults in the program; thus testing can reveal them. Unfortunately, the software faults that come from requirements and design mistakes are visible only through testing months or years after the original mistake. The effects of the mistake tend to be dispersed throughout multiple software components; hence such faults are usually difficult to pin down and expensive to correct. On the positive side, even if tests cannot be executed, the very process of defining tests can identify a significant fraction of the mistakes in requirements and design. Hence, it is important for test planning to proceed concurrently with requirements analysis and design and not be put off until late in a project. Fortunately, through techniques such as use-case analysis, test planning is becoming better integrated with requirements analysis in standard software practice.

Although most of the literature emphasizes these levels in terms of **when** they are applied, a more important distinction is on the **types of faults** that we are looking for. The faults are based on the software **artifact** that we are testing, and the software **artifact** that we derive the tests from. For example, unit and module tests are derived to test units and modules, and we usually try to find faults that can be found when executing the units and modules individually.

One of the best examples of the differences between unit testing and system testing can be illustrated in the context of the infamous Pentium bug. In 1994, Intel introduced its Pentium microprocessor, and a few months later, Thomas Nicely, a mathematician at Lynchburg College in Virginia, found that the chip gave incorrect answers to certain floating-point division calculations.

The chip was slightly inaccurate for a few pairs of numbers; Intel claimed (probably correctly) that only one in nine billion division operations would exhibit reduced precision. The fault was the omission of five entries in a table of 1,066 values (part of the chip's circuitry) used by a division algorithm. The five entries should have contained the constant +2, but the entries were not initialized and contained zero instead. The MIT mathematician Edelman claimed that "the bug in the Pentium was an easy mistake to make, and a difficult one to catch," an analysis that misses one of the essential points. This was a very difficult mistake to find during system testing, and indeed, Intel claimed to have run millions of tests using this table. But the table entries were left empty because a loop termination condition was incorrect; that is, the loop stopped storing numbers before it was finished. This turns out to be a very simple fault to find during unit testing; indeed analysis showed that almost any unit level coverage criterion would have found this multimillion dollar mistake.

The Pentium bug not only illustrates the difference in testing levels, but it is also one of the best arguments for paying more attention to unit testing. There are no shortcuts – all aspects of software need to be tested.

On the other hand, some faults can only be found at the system level. One dramatic example was the launch failure of the first Ariane 5 rocket, which exploded 37 seconds after liftoff on June 4, 1996. The low-level cause was an unhandled floating-point conversion exception in an internal guidance system function. It turned out that the guidance system could never encounter the unhandled exception when used on the Ariane 4 rocket. In other words, the guidance system function is correct for Ariane 4. The developers of the Ariane 5 quite reasonably wanted to reuse the successful inertial guidance system from the Ariane 4, but no one reanalyzed the software in light of the substantially different flight trajectory of Ariane 5. Furthermore, the system tests that would have found the problem were technically difficult to execute, and so were not performed. The result was spectacular – and expensive!

Another public failure was the Mars lander of September 1999, which crashed due to a misunderstanding in the units of measure used by two modules created by separate software groups. One module computed thruster data in English units and forwarded the data to a module that expected data in metric units. This is a very typical integration fault (but in this case enormously expensive, both in terms of money and prestige).

One final note is that object-oriented (OO) software changes the testing levels. OO software blurs the distinction between units and modules, so the OO software testing literature has developed a slight variation of these levels. *Intramethod testing* is when tests are constructed for individual methods. *Intermethod testing* is when pairs of methods within the same class are tested in concert. *Intraclass testing* is when tests are constructed for a single entire class, usually as sequences of calls to methods within the class. Finally, *interclass testing* is when more than one class is tested at the same time. The first three are variations of unit and module testing, whereas interclass testing is a type of integration testing.

1.1.2 Beizer's Testing Levels Based on Test Process Maturity

Another categorization of levels is based on the test process maturity level of an organization. Each level is characterized by the goal of the test engineers. The following material is adapted from Beizer [29].

Level 0 There's no difference between testing and debugging.
Level 1 The purpose of testing is to show that the software works.
Level 2 The purpose of testing is to show that the software doesn't work.
Level 3 The purpose of testing is not to prove anything specific, but to reduce the risk of using the software.
Level 4 Testing is a mental discipline that helps all IT professionals develop higher quality software.

Level 0 is the view that testing is the same as debugging. This is the view that is naturally adopted by many undergraduate computer science majors. In most CS programming classes, the students get their programs to compile, then debug the programs with a few inputs chosen either arbitrarily or provided by the professor.

This model does not distinguish between a program's incorrect behavior and a mistake within the program, and does very little to help develop software that is reliable or safe.

In **Level 1** testing, the purpose is to show correctness. While a significant step up from the naive level 0, this has the unfortunate problem that in any but the most trivial of programs, correctness is virtually impossible to either achieve or demonstrate. Suppose we run a collection of tests and find no failures. What do we know? Should we assume that we have good software or just bad tests? Since the goal of correctness is impossible, test engineers usually have no strict goal, real stopping rule, or formal test technique. If a development manager asks how much testing remains to be done, the test manager has no way to answer the question. In fact, test managers are in a powerless position because they have no way to quantitatively express or evaluate their work.

In **Level 2** testing, the purpose is to show failures. Although looking for failures is certainly a valid goal, it is also a negative goal. Testers may enjoy finding the problem, but the developers never want to find problems – they want the software to work (level 1 thinking is natural for the developers). Thus, level 2 testing puts testers and developers into an adversarial relationship, which can be bad for team morale. Beyond that, when our primary goal is to look for failures, we are still left wondering what to do if no failures are found. Is our work done? Is our software very good, or is the testing weak? Having confidence in when testing is complete is an important goal for all testers.

The thinking that leads to **Level 3** testing starts with the realization that testing can show the presence, but not the absence, of failures. This lets us accept the fact that whenever we use software, we incur some risk. The risk may be small and the consequences unimportant, or the risk may be great and the consequences catastrophic, but risk is always there. This allows us to realize that the entire development team wants the same thing – to reduce the risk of using the software. In level 3 testing, both testers and developers work together to reduce risk.

Once the testers and developers are on the same "team," an organization can progress to real **Level 4** testing. Level 4 thinking defines testing as *a mental discipline that increases quality*. Various ways exist to increase quality, of which creating tests that cause the software to fail is only one. Adopting this mindset, test engineers can become the technical leaders of the project (as is common in many other engineering disciplines). They have the primary responsibility of measuring and improving software quality, and their expertise should help the developers. An analogy that Beizer used is that of a spell checker. We often think that the purpose of a spell checker is to find misspelled words, but in fact, the best purpose of a spell checker is to improve our ability to spell. Every time the spell checker finds an incorrectly spelled word, we have the opportunity to learn how to spell the word correctly. The spell checker is the "expert" on spelling quality. In the same way, level 4 testing means that the purpose of testing is to improve the ability of the developers to produce high quality software. The testers should train your developers.

As a reader of this book, you probably start at level 0, 1, or 2. Most software developers go through these levels at some stage in their careers. If you work in software development, you might pause to reflect on which testing level describes your company or team. The rest of this chapter should help you move to level 2 thinking, and to understand the importance of level 3. Subsequent chapters will give you the knowledge, skills, and tools to be able to work at level 3. The ultimate goal of this book is to provide a philosophical basis that will allow readers to become "change agents" in their organizations for level 4 thinking, and test engineers to become **software quality experts**.

1.1.3 Automation of Test Activities

Software testing is expensive and labor intensive. Software testing requires up to 50% of software development costs, and even more for safety-critical applications. One of the goals of software testing is to automate as much as possible, thereby significantly reducing its cost, minimizing human error, and making regression testing easier.

Software engineers sometimes distinguish *revenue tasks*, which contribute directly to the solution of a problem, from *excise* tasks, which do not. For example, compiling a Java class is a classic excise task because, although necessary for the class to become executable, compilation contributes nothing to the particular behavior of that class. In contrast, determining which methods are appropriate to define a given data abstraction as a Java class is a revenue task. Excise tasks are candidates for automation; revenue tasks are not. Software testing probably has more excise tasks than any other aspect of software development. Maintaining test scripts, re-running tests, and comparing expected results with actual results are all common excise tasks that routinely consume large chunks of test engineer's time. Automating excise tasks serves the test engineer in many ways. First, eliminating excise tasks eliminates drudgery, thereby making the test engineers job more satisfying. Second, automation frees up time to focus on the fun and challenging parts of testing, namely the revenue tasks. Third, automation can help eliminate errors of omission, such as failing to update all the relevant files with the new set of expected results. Fourth, automation eliminates some of the variance in test quality caused by differences in individual's abilities.

Many testing tasks that defied automation in the past are now candidates for such treatment due to advances in technology. For example, generating test cases that satisfy given test requirements is typically a hard problem that requires intervention from the test engineer. However, there are tools, both research and commercial, that automate this task to varying degrees.

EXERCISES

Section 1.1.

1. What are some of the factors that would help a development organization move from Beizer's testing level 2 (*testing is to show errors*) to testing level 4 (*a mental discipline that increases quality*)?
2. The following exercise is intended to encourage you to think of testing in a more rigorous way than you may be used to. The exercise also hints at the strong relationship between specification clarity, faults, and test cases.[1]
   (a) Write a Java method with the signature
      public static Vector union (Vector a, Vector b)
         The method should return a Vector of objects that are in either of the two argument Vectors.

(b) Upon reflection, you may discover a variety of defects and ambiguities in the given assignment. In other words, ample opportunities for faults exist. Identify as many possible faults as you can. (*Note:* Vector *is a Java* Collection *class. If you are using another language, interpret* Vector *as a list.*)

(c) Create a set of test cases that you think would have a reasonable chance of revealing the faults you identified above. Document a rationale for each test in your test set. If possible, characterize all of your rationales in some concise summary. Run your tests against your implementation.

(d) Rewrite the method signature to be precise enough to clarify the defects and ambiguities identified earlier. You might wish to illustrate your specification with examples drawn from your test cases.

1.2 SOFTWARE TESTING LIMITATIONS AND TERMINOLOGY

As said in the previous section, one of the most important limitations of software testing is that testing can show only the presence of failures, not their absence. This is a fundamental, theoretical limitation; generally speaking, the problem of finding all failures in a program is undecidable. Testers often call a successful (or effective) test one that finds an error. While this is an example of level 2 thinking, it is also a characterization that is often useful and that we will use later in this book.

The rest of this section presents a number of terms that are important in software testing and that will be used later in this book. Most of these are taken from standards documents, and although the phrasing is ours, we try to be consistent with the standards. Useful standards for reading in more detail are the IEEE Standard Glossary of Software Engineering Terminology, DOD-STD-2167A and MIL-STD-498 from the US Department of Defense, and the British Computer Society's Standard for Software Component Testing.

One of the most important distinctions to make is between validation and verification.

Definition 1.1 Validation: The process of evaluating software at the end of software development to ensure compliance with intended usage.

Definition 1.2 Verification: The process of determining whether the products of a given phase of the software development process fulfill the requirements established during the previous phase.

Verification is usually a more technical activity that uses knowledge about the individual software artifacts, requirements, and specifications. Validation usually depends on domain knowledge; that is, knowledge of the application for which the software is written. For example, validation of software for an airplane requires knowledge from aerospace engineers and pilots.

The acronym "IV&V" stands for "independent verification and validation," where "independent" means that the evaluation is done by nondevelopers. Sometimes the IV&V team is within the same project, sometimes the same company, and sometimes it is entirely an external entity. In part because of the independent nature of IV&V, the process often is not started until the software is complete and is often done by people whose expertise is in the application domain rather than software development. This can sometimes mean that validation is given more weight than verification.

Two terms that we have already used are fault and failure. Understanding this distinction is the first step in moving from level 0 thinking to level 1 thinking. We adopt the definition of software fault, error, and failure from the dependability community.

Definition 1.3 Software Fault: A static defect in the software.

Definition 1.4 Software Error: An incorrect internal state that is the manifestation of some fault.

Definition 1.5 Software Failure: External, incorrect behavior with respect to the requirements or other description of the expected behavior.

Consider a medical doctor making a diagnosis for a patient. The patient enters the doctor's office with a list of *failures* (that is, *symptoms*). The doctor then must discover the *fault*, or root cause of the symptom. To aid in the diagnosis, a doctor may order tests that look for anomalous internal conditions, such as high blood pressure, an irregular heartbeat, high levels of blood glucose, or high cholesterol. In our terminology, these anomalous internal conditions correspond to *errors*.

While this analogy may help the student clarify his or her thinking about faults, errors, and failures, software testing and a doctor's diagnosis differ in one crucial way. Specifically, faults in software are *design mistakes*. They do not appear spontaneously, but rather exist as a result of some (unfortunate) decision by a human. Medical problems (as well as faults in computer system hardware), on the other hand, are often a result of physical degradation. This distinction is important because it explains the limits on the extent to which any process can hope to control software faults. Specifically, since no foolproof way exists to catch arbitrary mistakes made by humans, we cannot eliminate all faults from software. In colloquial terms, we can make software development foolproof, but we cannot, and should not attempt to, make it damn-foolproof.

For a more technical example of the definitions of fault, error, and failure, consider the following Java method:

```java
public static int numZero (int[] x) {
  // Effects: if x == null throw NullPointerException
  //     else return the number of occurrences of 0 in x
  int count = 0;
  for (int i = 1; i < x.length; i++)
  {
    if (x[i] == 0)
    {
      count++;
    }
  }
  return count;
}
```

The fault in this program is that it starts looking for zeroes at index 1 instead of index 0, as is necessary for arrays in Java. For example, numZero ([2, 7, 0]) correctly evaluates to 1, while numZero ([0, 7, 2]) incorrectly evaluates to 0. In both of these cases the fault is executed. Although both of these cases result in an error, only the second case results in failure. To understand the error states, we need to identify the state for the program. The state for numZero consists of values for the variables x, count, i, and the program counter (denoted PC). For the first example given above, the state at the if statement on the very first iteration of the loop is $(x = [2, 7, 0], count = 0, i = 1, PC = if)$. Notice that this state is in error precisely because the value of i should be zero on the first iteration. However, since the value of count is coincidentally correct, the error state does not propagate to the output, and hence the software does not fail. In other words, a state is in error simply if it is not the expected state, even if all of the values in the state, considered in isolation, are acceptable. More generally, if the required sequence of states is $s_0, s_1, s_2, \ldots$, and the actual sequence of states is $s_0, s_2, s_3, \ldots$, then state s_2 is in error in the second sequence.

In the second case the corresponding (error) state is $(x = [0, 7, 2], count = 0, i = 1, PC = if)$. In this case, the error propagates to the variable count and is present in the return value of the method. Hence a failure results.

The definitions of fault and failure allow us to distinguish testing from debugging.

Definition 1.6 Testing: Evaluating software by observing its execution.

Definition 1.7 Test Failure: Execution that results in a failure.

Definition 1.8 Debugging: The process of finding a fault given a failure.

Of course the central issue is that for a given fault, not all inputs will "trigger" the fault into creating incorrect output (a failure). Also, it is often very difficult to relate a failure to the associated fault. Analyzing these ideas leads to the fault/failure model, which states that three conditions must be present for a failure to be observed.

1. The location or locations in the program that contain the fault must be reached (*Reachability*).
2. After executing the location, the state of the program must be incorrect (*Infection*).
3. The infected state must propagate to cause some output of the program to be incorrect (*Propagation*).

This "RIP" model is very important for coverage criteria such as mutation (Chapter 5) and for automatic test data generation. It is important to note that the RIP model applies even in the case of faults of omission. In particular, when execution traverses the missing code, the program counter, which is part of the internal state, necessarily has the wrong value.

The next definitions are less standardized and the literature varies widely. The definitions are our own but are consistent with common usage. A test engineer must recognize that tests include more than just input values, but are actually multipart software artifacts. The piece of a test case that is referred to the most often is what we call the test case value.

Definition 1.9 Test Case Values: The input values necessary to complete some execution of the software under test.

Note that the definition of test case values is quite broad. In a traditional batch environment, the definition is extremely clear. In a Web application, a complete execution might be as small as the generation of part of a simple Web page, or it might be as complex as the completion of a set of commercial transactions. In a real-time system such as an avionics application, a complete execution might be a single frame, or it might be an entire flight.

Test case values are the inputs to the program that test engineers typically focus on during testing. They really define what sort of testing we will achieve. However, test case values are not enough. In addition to test case values, other inputs are often needed to run a test. These inputs may depend on the source of the tests, and may be commands, user inputs, or a software method to call with values for its parameters. In order to evaluate the results of a test, we must know what output a correct version of the program would produce for that test.

Definition 1.10 Expected Results: The result that will be produced when executing the test if and only if the program satisfies its intended behavior.

Two common practical problems associated with software testing are how to provide the right values to the software and observing details of the software's behavior. These two ideas are used to refine the definition of a test case.

Definition 1.11 Software Observability: How easy it is to observe the behavior of a program in terms of its outputs, effects on the environment, and other hardware and software components.

Definition 1.12 Software Controllability: How easy it is to provide a program with the needed inputs, in terms of values, operations, and behaviors.

These ideas are easily illustrated in the context of embedded software. Embedded software often does not produce output for human consumption, but affects the behavior of some piece of hardware. Thus, observability will be quite low. Likewise, software for which all inputs are values entered from a keyboard is easy to control. But an embedded program that gets its inputs from hardware sensors is more difficult to control and some inputs may be difficult, dangerous or impossible to supply (for example, how does the automatic pilot behave when a train jumps off-track). Many observability and controllability problems can be addressed with simulation, by extra software built to "bypass" the hardware or software components that interfere with testing. Other applications that sometimes have low observability and controllability include component-based software, distributed software and Web applications.

Depending on the software, the level of testing, and the source of the tests, the tester may need to supply other inputs to the software to affect controllability or observability. For example, if we are testing software for a mobile telephone, the test case values may be long distance phone numbers. We may also need to turn the phone on to put it in the appropriate state and then we may need to press "talk" and "end" buttons to view the results of the test case values and terminate the test. These ideas are formalized as follows.

Definition 1.13 Prefix Values: Any inputs necessary to put the software into the appropriate state to receive the test case values.

Definition 1.14 Postfix Values: Any inputs that need to be sent to the software after the test case values are sent.

Postfix values can be subdivided into two types.

Definition 1.15 Verification Values: Values necessary to see the results of the test case values.

Definition 1.16 Exit Commands: Values needed to terminate the program or otherwise return it to a stable state.

A test case is the combination of all these components (test case values, expected results, prefix values, and postfix values). When it is clear from context, however, we will follow tradition and use the term "test case" in place of "test case values."

Definition 1.17 Test Case: A test case is composed of the test case values, expected results, prefix values, and postfix values necessary for a complete execution and evaluation of the software under test.

We provide an explicit definition for a test set to emphasize that coverage is a property of a set of test cases, rather than a property of a single test case.

Definition 1.18 Test Set: A test set is simply a set of test cases.

Finally, wise test engineers automate as many test activities as possible. A crucial way to automate testing is to prepare the test inputs as executable tests for the software. This may be done as Unix shell scripts, input files, or through the use of a tool that can control the software or software component being tested. Ideally, the execution should be complete in the sense of running the software with the test case values, getting the results, comparing the results with the expected results, and preparing a clear report for the test engineer.

Definition 1.19 Executable Test Script: A test case that is prepared in a form to be executed automatically on the test software and produce a report.

The only time a test engineer would not want to automate is if the cost of automation outweighs the benefits. For example, this may happen if we are sure the test will only be used once or if the automation requires knowledge or skills that the test engineer does not have.

EXERCISES
Section 1.2.

1. For what do testers use automation? What are the limitations of automation?
2. How are faults and failures related to testing and debugging?

3. Below are four faulty programs. Each includes a test case that results in failure. Answer the following questions about each program.

```
public int findLast (int[] x, int y) {
//Effects: If x==null throw NullPointerException
//   else return the index of the last element
//   in x that equals y.
//   If no such element exists, return -1
    for (int i=x.length-1; i > 0; i--)
    {
        if (x[i] == y)
        {
            return i;
        }
    }
    return -1;
}
    // test:  x=[2, 3, 5]; y = 2
    //        Expected = 0
```

```
public static int lastZero (int[] x) {
//Effects: if x==null throw NullPointerException
//   else return the index of the LAST 0 in x.
//   Return -1 if 0 does not occur in x

    for (int i = 0; i < x.length; i++)
    {
        if (x[i] == 0)
        {
            return i;
        }
    }
    return -1;
}
    // test:  x=[0, 1, 0]
    //        Expected = 2
```

```
public int countPositive (int[] x) {
//Effects: If x==null throw NullPointerException
//   else return the number of
//     positive elements in x.
    int count = 0;
    for (int i=0; i < x.length; i++)
    {
        if (x[i] >= 0)
        {
            count++;
        }
    }
    return count;
}
    // test:  x=[-4, 2, 0, 2]
    //        Expected = 2
```

```
public static int oddOrPos(int[] x) {
//Effects: if x==null throw NullPointerException
// else return the number of elements in x that
//     are either odd or positive (or both)
    int count = 0;
    for (int i = 0; i < x.length; i++)
    {
        if (x[i]% 2 == 1 || x[i] > 0)
        {
            count++;
        }
    }
    return count;
}
    // test:  x=[-3, -2, 0, 1, 4]
    //        Expected = 3
```

(a) Identify the fault.

(b) If possible, identify a test case that does **not** execute the fault.

(c) If possible, identify a test case that executes the fault, but does **not** result in an error state.

(d) If possible identify a test case that results in an error, but **not** a failure. Hint: Don't forget about the program counter.

(e) For the given test case, identify the first error state. Be sure to describe the complete state.

(f) Fix the fault and verify that the given test now produces the expected output.

1.3 COVERAGE CRITERIA FOR TESTING

Some ill-defined terms occasionally used in testing are "complete testing," "exhaustive testing," and "full coverage." These terms are poorly defined because of a fundamental theoretical limitation of software. Specifically, the number of potential inputs for most programs is so large as to be effectively infinite. Consider a Java compiler – the number of potential inputs to the compiler is not just all Java programs, or even all almost correct Java programs, but all strings. The only limitation is the size of the file that can be read by the parser. Therefore, the number of inputs is effectively infinite and cannot be explicitly enumerated.

This is where formal coverage criteria come in. Since we cannot test with all inputs, coverage criteria are used to decide which test inputs to use. The software testing community believes that effective use of coverage criteria makes it more likely that test engineers will find faults in a program and provides informal assurance that the software is of high quality and reliability. While this is, perhaps, more an article of faith than a scientifically supported proposition, it is, in our view, the best option currently available. From a practical perspective, coverage criteria provide useful rules for when to stop testing.

This book defines coverage criteria in terms of test requirements. The basic idea is that we want our set of test cases to have various properties, each of which is provided (or not) by an individual test case.[2]

Definition 1.20 Test Requirement: A test requirement is a specific element of a software artifact that a test case must satisfy or cover.

Test requirements usually come in sets, and we use the abbreviation *TR* to denote a set of test requirements.

Test requirements can be described with respect to a variety of software artifacts, including the source code, design components, specification modeling elements, or even descriptions of the input space. Later in this book, test requirements will be generated from all of these.

Let's begin with a non-software example. Suppose we are given the enviable task of testing bags of jelly beans. We need to come up with ways to sample from the bags. Suppose these jelly beans have the following six flavors and come in four colors: Lemon (colored Yellow), Pistachio (Green), Cantaloupe (Orange), Pear (White), Tangerine (also Orange), and Apricot (also Yellow). A simple approach to testing might be to test one jelly bean of each flavor. Then we have six test requirements, one for each flavor. We satisfy the test requirement "Lemon" by selecting and, of course, tasting a Lemon jelly bean from a bag of jelly beans. The reader might wish to ponder how to decide, prior to the tasting step, if a given Yellow jelly bean is Lemon or Apricot. This dilemma illustrates a classic controllability issue.

As a more software-oriented example, if the goal is to cover all decisions in the program (branch coverage), then each decision leads to two test requirements, one for the decision to evaluate to false, and one for the decision to evaluate to true. If every method must be called at least once (call coverage), each method leads to one test requirement.

A coverage criterion is simply a recipe for generating test requirements in a systematic way:

Definition 1.21 Coverage Criterion: A coverage criterion is a rule or collection of rules that impose test requirements on a test set.

That is, the criterion describes the test requirements in a complete and unambiguous manner. The "flavor criterion" yields a simple strategy for selecting jelly beans. In this case, the set of test requirements, *TR*, can be formally written out as

$$TR = \{flavor = Lemon, \ flavor = Pistachio, \ flavor = Cantaloupe,$$
$$flavor = Pear, \ flavor = Tangerine, \ flavor = Apricot\}$$

Test engineers need to know how good a collection of tests is, so we measure test sets against a criterion in terms of coverage.

Definition 1.22 Coverage: Given a set of test requirements TR for a coverage criterion C, a test set T satisfies C if and only if for every test requirement tr in TR, at least one test t in T exists such that t satisfies tr.

To continue the example, a test set T with 12 beans: three Lemon, one Pistachio, two Cantaloupe, one Pear, one Tangerine, and four Apricot satisfies the "flavor criterion." Notice that it is perfectly acceptable to satisfy a given test requirement with more than one test.

Coverage is important for two reasons. First, it is sometimes expensive to satisfy a coverage criterion, so we want to compromise by trying to achieve a certain coverage level.

Definition 1.23 Coverage Level: Given a set of test requirements TR and a test set T, the coverage level is simply the ratio of the number of test requirements satisfied by T to the size of TR.

Second, and more importantly, some requirements cannot be satisfied. Suppose Tangerine jelly beans are rare, some bags may not contain any, or it may simply be too difficult to find a Tangerine bean. In this case, the flavor criterion cannot be 100% satisfied, and the maximum coverage level possible is 5/6 or 83%. It often makes sense to drop unsatisfiable test requirements from the set TR – or to replace them with less stringent test requirements.

Test requirements that cannot be satisfied are called *infeasible*. Formally, no test case values exist that meet the test requirements. Examples for specific software criteria will be shown throughout the book, but some may already be familiar. Dead code results in infeasible test requirements because the statements cannot be reached. The detection of infeasible test requirements is formally undecidable for most coverage criteria, and even though some researchers have tried to find partial solutions, they have had only limited success. Thus, 100% coverage is impossible in practice.

Coverage criteria are traditionally used in one of two ways. One method is to directly generate test case values to satisfy a given criterion. This method is often assumed by the research community and is the most obvious way to use criteria. It is also very hard in some cases, particularly if we do not have enough automated tools to support test case value generation. The other method is to generate test case values externally (by hand or using a pseudo-random tool, for example) and then measure the tests against the criterion in terms of their coverage. This method is usually favored by industry practitioners, because generating tests to directly satisfy the criterion is too hard. Unfortunately, this use is sometimes misleading. If our tests do not reach 100% coverage, what does that mean? We really have no data on how much, say, 99% coverage is worse than 100% coverage, or 90%, or even 75%. Because of this use of the criteria to evaluate existing test sets, coverage criteria are sometimes called *metrics*.

This distinction actually has a strong theoretical basis. A *generator* is a procedure that automatically generates values to satisfy a criterion, and a *recognizer* is a procedure that decides whether a given set of test case values satisfies a criterion. Theoretically, both problems are provably undecidable in the general case for most criteria. In practice, however, it is possible to recognize whether test cases satisfy a criterion far more often than it is possible to generate tests that satisfy the criterion. The primary problem with recognition is infeasible test requirements; if no infeasible test requirements are present then the problem becomes decidable.

In practical terms of commercial automated test tools, a generator corresponds to a tool that automatically creates test case values. A recognizer is a coverage analysis tool. Coverage analysis tools are quite plentiful, both as commercial products and freeware.

It is important to appreciate that the set TR depends on the specific artifact under test. In the jelly bean example, the test requirement $color = Purple$ doesn't make sense because we assumed that the factory does not make Purple jelly beans. In the software context, consider statement coverage. The test requirement "Execute statement 42" makes sense only if the program under test does indeed have a statement 42. A good way to think of this issue is that the test engineer starts with a given software artifact and then chooses a particular coverage criterion. Combining the artifact with the criterion yields the specific set TR that is relevant to the test engineer's task.

Coverage criteria are often related to one another, and compared in terms of subsumption. Recall that the "flavor criterion" requires that every flavor be tried once. We could also define a "color criterion," which requires that we try one jelly bean of each color {*yellow, green, orange, white*}. If we satisfy the flavor criterion, then we have also implicitly satisfied the color criterion. This is the essence of subsumption; that satisfying one criterion will guarantee that another one is satisfied.

Definition 1.24 Criteria Subsumption: A coverage criterion C_1 subsumes C_2 if and only if every test set that satisfies criterion C_1 also satisfies C_2.

Note that this has to be true for **every** test set, not just some sets. Subsumption has a strong similarity with set subset relationships, but it is not exactly the same. Generally, a criterion C_1 can subsume another C_2 in one of two ways. The simpler way is if the test requirements for C_1 always form a superset of the requirements for C_2. For example, another jelly bean criterion may be to try all flavors whose name begins with the letter 'C'. This would result in the test requirements {*Cantaloupe*}, which is a subset of the requirements for the flavor criterion: {*Lemon, Pistachio, Cantaloupe, Pear, Tangerine, Apricot*}. Thus, the flavor criterion subsumes the "starts-with-C" criterion.

The relationship between the flavor and the color criteria illustrate the other way that subsumption can be shown. Since every flavor has a specific color, and every color is represented by at least one flavor, if we satisfy the flavor criterion we will also satisfy the color criterion. Formally, a many-to-one mapping exists between the requirements for the flavor criterion and the requirements for the color criterion. Thus, the flavor criterion subsumes the color criterion. (If a one-to-one mapping exists between requirements from two criteria, then they would subsume each other.)

For a more realistic software-oriented example, consider branch and statement coverage. (These should already be familiar, at least intuitively, and will be defined formally in Chapter 2.) If a test set has covered every branch in a program (satisfied branch coverage), then the test set is guaranteed to have covered every statement as well. Thus, the branch coverage criterion subsumes the statement coverage criterion. We will return to subsumption with more rigor and more examples in subsequent chapters.

1.3.1 Infeasibility and Subsumption

A subtle relationship exists between infeasibility and subsumption. Specifically, sometimes a criterion C_1 will subsume another criterion C_2 if and only if all test requirements are feasible. If some test requirements in C_1 are infeasible, however, C_1 may not subsume C_2.

Infeasible test requirements are common and occur quite naturally. Suppose we partition the jelly beans into *Fruits* and *Nuts*.[3] Now, consider the *Interaction Criterion*, where each flavor of bean is sampled in conjunction with some other flavor in the same block. Such a criterion has a useful counterpart in the software domain in cases where feature interactions are a source of concern. So, for example, we might try Lemon with Pear or Tangerine, but we would not try Lemon with itself or with Pistachio. We might think that the Interaction Criterion subsumes the Flavor criterion, since every flavor is tried in conjunction with some other flavor. Unfortunately, in our example, Pistachio is the only member of the *Nuts* block, and hence the test requirement to try it with some other flavor in the *Nuts* block is infeasible.

One possible strategy to reestablish subsumption is to replace each infeasible test requirement for the Interaction Criterion with the corresponding one from the Flavor criterion. In this example, we would simply taste Pistachio nuts by themselves. In general, it is desirable to define coverage criteria so that they are robust with respect to subsumption in the face of infeasible test requirements. This is not commonly done in the testing literature, but we make an effort to do so in this book.

That said, this problem is mainly theoretical and should not overly concern practical testers. Theoretically, sometimes a coverage criterion C_1 will subsume another C_2 if we assume that C_1 has **no** infeasible test requirements, but if C_1 does create an infeasible test requirement for a program, a test suite that satisfies C_1 while skipping the infeasible test requirements might also "skip" some test requirements from C_2 that are satisfiable. In practice, only a few test requirements for C_1 are infeasible for any given program, and if some are, it is often true that corresponding test requirements in C_2 will also be infeasible. If not, the few test cases that are lost will **probably** not make a difference in the test results.

1.3.2 Characteristics of a Good Coverage Criterion

Given the above discussion, an interesting question is "what makes a coverage criterion good?" Certainly, no definitive answers exist to this question, a fact that may partly explain why so many coverage criteria have been designed. However, three important issues can affect the use of coverage criteria.

1. The difficulty of computing test requirements
2. The difficulty of generating tests
3. How well the tests reveal faults

Subsumption is at best a very rough way to compare criteria. Our intuition may tell us that if one criterion subsumes another, then it should reveal more faults. However, no theoretical guarantee exists and the experimental studies have usually not been convincing and are far from complete. Nevertheless, the research community has reasonably wide agreement on relationships among some criteria. The difficulty of computing test requirements will depend on the artifact being used as well as the criterion. The fact that the difficulty of generating tests can be directly related to how well the tests reveal faults should not be surprising. A software tester must strive for balance and choose criteria that have the right cost / benefit tradeoffs for the software under test.

EXERCISES
Section 1.3.

1. Suppose that coverage criterion C_1 subsumes coverage criterion C_2. Further suppose that test set T_1 satisfies C_1 and on program P test set T_2 satisfies C_2, also on P.
   (a) Does T_1 necessarily satisfy C_2? Explain.
   (b) Does T_2 necessarily satisfy C_1? Explain.
   (c) If P contains a fault, and T_2 reveals the fault, T_1 does **not** necessarily also reveal the fault. Explain.[4]
2. How else could we compare test criteria besides subsumption?

1.4 OLDER SOFTWARE TESTING TERMINOLOGY

The testing research community has been very active in the past two decades, and some of our fundamental views of what and how to test have changed. This section presents some of the terminology that has been in use for many years, but for various reasons has become dated. Despite the fact that they are not as relevant now as they were at one time, these terms are still used and it is important that testing students and professionals be familiar with them.

From an abstract perspective, black-box and white-box testing are very similar. In this book in particular, we present testing as proceeding from abstract models of the software such as graphs, which can as easily be derived from a black-box view or a white-box view. Thus, one of the most obvious effects of the unique philosophical structure of this book is that these two terms become obsolete.

Definition 1.25 Black-box testing: Deriving tests from external descriptions of the software, including specifications, requirements, and design.

Definition 1.26 White-box testing: Deriving tests from the source code internals of the software, specifically including branches, individual conditions, and statements.

In the early 1980s, a discussion took place over whether testing should proceed from the top down or from the bottom up. This was an echo of a previous discussion over how to develop software. This distinction has pretty much disappeared as we first learned that top-down testing is impractical, then OO design pretty much made the distinction obsolete. The following pair of definitions assumes that software can be viewed as a tree of software procedures, where the edges represent calls and the root of the tree is the main procedure.

Definition 1.27 Top-Down Testing: Test the main procedure, then go down through procedures it calls, and so on.

Definition 1.28 Bottom-Up Testing: Test the leaves in the tree (procedures that make no calls), and move up to the root. Each procedure is tested only if all of its children have been tested.

OO software leads to a more general problem. The relationships among classes can be formulated as general graphs with cycles, requiring test engineers to make the difficult choice of what order to test the classes in. This problem is discussed in Chapter 6.

Some parts of the literature separate static and dynamic testing as follows:

Definition 1.29 Static Testing: Testing without executing the program. This includes software inspections and some forms of analysis.

Definition 1.30 Dynamic Testing: Testing by executing the program with real inputs.

Most of the literature currently uses "testing" to refer to dynamic testing and "static testing" is called "verification activities." We follow that use in this book and it should be pointed out that this book is only concerned with dynamic or *execution-based* testing.

One last term bears mentioning because of the lack of definition. *Test Strategy* has been used to mean a variety of things, including coverage criterion, test process, and technologies used. We will avoid using it.

1.5 BIBLIOGRAPHIC NOTES

All books on software testing and all researchers owe major thanks to the landmark books in 1979 by Myers [249], in 1990 by Beizer [29], and in 2000 by Binder [33]. Some excellent overviews of unit testing criteria have also been published, including one by White [349] and more recently by Zhu, Hall, and May [367]. The statement that software testing requires up to 50 percent of software development costs is from Myers and Sommerville [249, 316]. The recent text from Pezze and Young [289] reports relevant processes, principles, and techniques from the testing literature, and includes many useful classroom materials. The Pezze and Young text presents coverage criteria in the traditional lifecycle-based manner, and does not organize criteria into the four abstract models discussed in this chapter.

Numerous other software testing books were not intended as textbooks, or do not offer general coverage for classroom use. Beizer's *Software System Testing and Quality Assurance* [28] and Hetzel's *The Complete Guide to Software Testing* [160] cover various aspects of management and process for software testing. Several books cover specific aspects of testing [169, 227, 301]. The STEP project at Georgia

Institute of Technology resulted in a comprehensive survey of the practice of software testing by Department of Defense contractors in the 1980s [100].

The definition of *unit* is from Stevens, Myers and Constantine [318], and the definition of *module* is from Sommerville [316]. The definition of *integration testing* is from Beizer [29]. The clarification for OO testing levels with the terms *intra-method*, *inter-method*, and *intra-class* testing is from Harrold and Rothermel [152] and *inter-class* testing is from Gallagher, Offutt and Cincotta [132].

The information for the Pentium bug and Mars lander was taken from several sources, including by Edelman, Moler, Nuseibeh, Knutson, and Peterson [111, 189, 244, 259, 286]. The accident report [209] is the best source for understanding the details of the Ariane 5 Flight 501 Failure.

The testing levels in Section 1.1.2 were first defined by Beizer [29].

The elementary result that finding all failures in a program is undecidable is due to Howden [165].

Most of the terminology in testing is from standards documents, including the IEEE Standard Glossary of Software Engineering Terminology [175], the US Department of Defense [260, 261], the US Federal Aviation Administration FAA-DO178B, and the British Computer Society's Standard for Software Component Testing [317]. The definitions for observability and controllability come from Freedman [129]. Similar definitions were also given in Binder's book *Testing Object-Oriented Systems* [33].

The fault/failure model was developed independently by Offutt and Morell in their dissertations [101, 246, 247, 262]. Morell used the terms execution, infection, and propagation [247, 246], and Offutt used reachability, sufficiency, and necessity [101, 262]. This book merges the two sets of terms by using what we consider to be the most descriptive terms.

The multiple parts of the test case that we use are based on research in test case specifications [23, 319].

One of the first discussions of infeasibility from other than a purely theoretical view was by Frankl and Weyuker [128]. The problem was shown to be undecidable by Goldberg et al. [136] and DeMillo and Offutt [101]. Some partial solutions have been presented [132, 136, 177, 273].

Budd and Angluin [51] analyzed the theoretical distinctions between generators and recognizers from a testing viewpoint. They showed that both problems are formally undecidable, and discussed tradeoffs in approximating the two.

Subsumption has been widely used as a way to analytically compare testing techniques. We follow Weiss [340] and Frankl and Weyuker [128] for our definition of subsumption. Frankl and Weyuker actually used the term *includes*. The term subsumption was defined by Clarke et al.: A criterion C_1 *subsumes* a criterion C_2 if and only if every set of execution paths P that satisfies C_1 also satisfies C_2 [81]. The term *subsumption* is currently the more widely used and the two definitions are equivalent; this book follows Weiss's suggestion to use the term *subsumes* to refer to Frankl and Weyuker's definition.

The descriptions of excise and revenue tasks were taken from Cooper [89].

Although this book does not focus heavily on the theoretical underpinnings of software testing, students interested in research should study such topics more in depth. A number of the papers are quite old and often do not appear in current literature, and their ideas are beginning to disappear. The authors encourage the study of the older papers. Among those are truly seminal papers in the 1970s by Goodenough and Gerhart [138] and Howden [165], and Demillo, Lipton, Sayward, and Perlis [98, 99]. These papers were followed up and refined by Weyuker and Ostrand [343], Hamlet [147], Budd and Angluin [51], Gourlay [139], Prather [293], Howden [168], and Cherniavsky and Smith [67]. Later theoretical papers were contributed by Morell [247], Zhu [366], and Wah [335, 336]. Every PhD student's adviser will certainly have his or her own favorite theoretical papers, but this list should provide a good starting point.

NOTES

1 Liskov's *Program Development in Java*, especially chapters 9 and 10, is a great source for students who wish to pursue this direction further.
2 While this is a good general rule, exceptions exist. For example, test requirements for some logic coverage criteria demand pairs of related test cases instead of individual test cases.
3 The reader might wonder whether we need an *Other* category to ensure that we have a partition. In our example, we are ok, but in general, one would need such a category to handle jelly beans such as Potato, Spinach, or Ear Wax.
4 Correctly answering this question goes a long way towards understanding the weakness of the subsumption relation.

PART 2

Coverage Criteria

2

Graph Coverage

This chapter introduces the major test coverage criteria in use today. It starts out in a very theoretical way, but a firm grasp of the theoretical aspects of graphs and graph coverage makes the remainder of the chapter simpler. We first emphasize a generic view of a graph without regard to the graph's source. After this model is established, the rest of the chapter turns to practical applications by demonstrating how graphs can be obtained from various software artifacts and how the generic versions of the criteria are adapted to those graphs.

2.1 OVERVIEW

Directed graphs form the foundation for many coverage criteria. Given an artifact under test, the idea is to obtain a graph abstraction of that artifact. For example, the most common graph abstraction for source code maps code to a control flow graph. It is important to understand that the graph is not the same as the artifact, and that, indeed, artifacts typically have several useful, but nonetheless quite different, graph abstractions. The same abstraction that produces the graph from the artifact also maps test cases for the artifact to paths in the graph. Accordingly, a graph-based coverage criterion evaluates a test set for an artifact in terms of how the paths corresponding to the test cases "cover" the artifact's graph abstraction.

We give our basic notion of a graph below and will add additional structures later in the chapter when needed. A graph G formally is

- a set N ot *nodes*
- a set N_0 of *initial nodes*, where $N_0 \subseteq N$
- a set N_f of *final nodes*, where $N_f \subseteq N$
- a set E of *edges*, where E is a subset of $N \times N$

For a graph to be useful for generating tests, it is necessary for N, N_0, and N_f to contain at least one node each. Sometimes, it is helpful to consider only part of a graph. A *subgraph* of a graph is also a graph and is defined by a subset of N, along with the corresponding subsets of N_0, N_f, and E. Specifically, if N_{sub} is a subset of

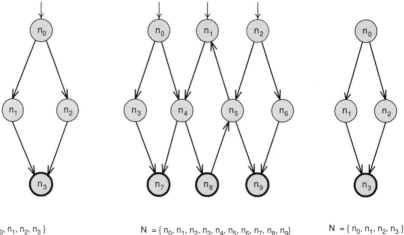

$N = \{ n_0, n_1, n_2, n_3 \}$
$N_0 = \{ n_0 \}$
$E = \{ (n_0, n_1), (n_0, n_2), (n_1, n_3), (n_2, n_3) \}$

$N = \{ n_0, n_1, n_2, n_3, n_4, n_5, n_6, n_7, n_8, n_9 \}$
$N_0 = \{ n_0, n_1, n_2 \}$
$|E| = 12$

$N = \{ n_0, n_1, n_2, n_3 \}$
$|E| = 4$

(a) A graph with a single initial node   (b) A graph with mutiple initial nodes   (c) A graph with no initial node

Figure 2.1. Graph (a) has a single initial node, graph (b) multiple initial nodes, and graph (c) (rejected) with no initial nodes.

N, then for the subgraph defined by N_{sub}, the set of initial nodes is $N_{sub} \cap N_0$, the set of final nodes is $N_{sub} \cap N_f$, and the set of edges is $(N_{sub} \times N_{sub}) \cap E$.

Note that more than one initial node can be present; that is, N_0 is a set. Having multiple initial nodes is necessary for some software artifacts, for example, if a class has multiple entry points, but sometimes we will restrict the graph to having one initial node. Edges are considered to be *from* one node and *to* another and written as (n_i, n_j). The edge's initial node n_i is sometimes called the *predecessor* and n_j is called the *successor*.

We always identify final nodes, and there must be at least one final node. The reason is that every test must start in some initial node and end in some final node. The concept of a final node depends on the kind of software artifact the graph represents. Some test criteria require tests to end in a particular final node. Other test criteria are satisfied with any node for a final node, in which case the set N_f is the same as the set N.

The term *node* has various synonyms. Graph theory texts sometimes call a node a *vertex*, and testing texts typically identify a node with the structure it represents, often a statement or a basic block. Similarly, graph theory texts sometimes call an edge an *arc*, and testing texts typically identify an edge with the structure it represents, often a branch. This section discusses graph criteria in a generic way; thus we stick to general graph terms.

Graphs are often drawn with bubbles and arrows. Figure 2.1 shows three example graphs. The nodes with incoming edges but no predecessor nodes are the initial nodes. The nodes with heavy borders are final nodes. Figure 2.1(a) has a single initial node and no cycles. Figure 2.1(b) has three initial nodes, as well as a cycle ($[n_1, n_4, n_8, n_5, n_1]$). Figure 2.1(c) has no initial nodes, and so is not useful for generating test cases.

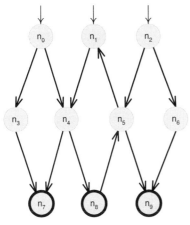

Path Examples	
1	n_0, n_3, n_7
2	n_1, n_4, n_8, n_5, n_1
3	n_2, n_6, n_9

Invalid Path Examples	
1	n_0, n_7
2	n_3, n_4
3	n_2, n_6, n_8

(a) Path examples

	Reachability Examples
1	$reach\ (n_0) = N - \{\, n_2, n_6\,\}$
2	$reach\ (n_0, n_1, n_2) = N$
3	$reach\ (n_4) = \{\, n_1, n_4, n_5, n_7, n_8, n_9\,\}$
4	$reach\ ([n_6, n_9]) = \{\, n_6, n_9\,\}$

(b) Reachability examples

Figure 2.2. Example of paths.

A *path* is a sequence $[n_1, n_2, \ldots, n_M]$ of nodes, where each pair of adjacent nodes, (n_i, n_{i+1}), $1 \leq i < M$, is in the set E of edges. The length of a path is defined as the number of edges it contains. We sometimes consider paths and subpaths of length zero. A *subpath* of a path p is a subsequence of p (possibly p itself). Following the notation for edges, we say a path is *from* the first node in the path and *to* the last node in the path. It is also useful to be able to say that a path is *from* (or *to*) an edge e, which simply means that e is the first (or last) edge in the path.

Figure 2.2 shows a graph along with several example paths, and several examples that are not paths. For instance, the sequence $[n_0, n_7]$ is not a path because the two nodes are not connected by an edge.

Many test criteria require inputs that start at one node and end at another. This is only possible if those nodes are connected by a path. When we apply these criteria on specific graphs, we sometimes find that we have asked for a path that for some reason cannot be executed. For example, a path may demand that a loop be executed zero times in a situation where the program always executes the loop at least once. This kind of problem is based on the **semantics** of the software artifact that the graph represents. For now, we emphasize that we are looking only at the **syntax** of the graph.

We say that a node n (or an edge e) is *syntactically reachable* from node n_i if there exists a path from node n_i to n (or edge e). A node n (or edge e) is also *semantically reachable* if it is possible to execute at least one of the paths with some input. We can define the function $reach_G(x)$ as the portion of a graph that is syntactically reachable from the parameter x. The parameter for $reach_G()$ can be a node, an edge, or a set of nodes or edges. Then $reach_G(n_i)$ is the subgraph of G that is syntactically reachable from node n_i, $reach_G(N_0)$ is the subgraph of G that is syntactically reachable from any initial node, $reach_G(e)$ is the subgraph of G syntactically reachable from edge e, and so on. In our use, $reach_G()$ includes the starting nodes. For example, both $reach_G(n_i)$ and $reach_G([n_i, n_j])$ always include n_i, and $reach_G([n_i, n_j])$ includes edge $([n_i, n_j])$. Some graphs have nodes or starting edges that cannot be syntactically reached from any of the initial nodes N_0. These graphs frustrate attempts to satisfy a coverage criterion, so we typically restrict our attention to $reach_G(N_0)$.[1]

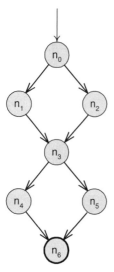

Figure 2.3. A single entry single exit graph.

Consider the examples in Figure 2.2. From n_0, it is possible to reach all nodes except n_2 and n_6. From the entire set of initial nodes $\{n_0, n_1, n_2\}$, it is possible to reach all nodes. If we start at n_4, it is possible to reach all nodes except n_0, n_2, n_3, and n_6. If we start at edge (n_6, n_9), it is possible to reach only n_6, n_9 and edge (n_6, n_9). In addition, some graphs (such as finite state machines) have explicit edges from a node to itself, that is, (n_i, n_i).

Basic graph algorithms, usually given in standard data structures texts, can be used to compute syntactic reachability.

A test path represents the execution of a test case. The reason test paths must start in N_0 is that test cases always begin from an initial node. It is important to note that a single test path may correspond to a very large number of test cases on the software. It is also possible that a test path may correspond to zero test cases if the test path is infeasible. We return to the crucial but theoretical issue of infeasibility later, in Section 2.2.1.

Definition 2.31 Test path: A path p, possibly of length zero, that starts at some node in N_0 and ends at some node in N_f.

For some graphs, all test paths start at one node and end at a single node. We call these *single entry/single exit* or *SESE* graphs. For SESE graphs, the set N_0 has exactly one node, called n_0, and the set N_f also has exactly one node, called n_f, which may be the same as n_0. We require that n_f be syntactically reachable from every node in N, and that no node in N (except n_f) be syntactically reachable from n_f (unless n_0 and n_f are the same node). In other words, no edges start at n_f, except when n_0 and n_f happen to be the same node.

Figure 2.3 is an example of a SESE graph. This particular structure is sometimes called a "double-diamond" graph and corresponds to the control flow graph for a sequence of two if-then-else statements. The initial node, n_0, is designated with an incoming arrow (remember we only have one initial node), and the final

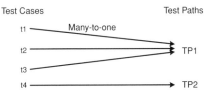

In deterministic software, a many-to-one relationship exists between test cases and test paths.

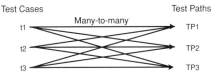

For nondeterministic software, a many-to-many relationship exists between test cases and test paths.

Figure 2.4. Test case mappings to test paths.

node, n_6, is designated with a thick circle. Exactly four test paths exist in the double-diamond graph: $[n_0, n_1, n_3, n_4, n_6]$, $[n_0, n_1, n_3, n_5, n_6]$, $[n_0, n_2, n_3, n_4, n_6]$, and $[n_0, n_2, n_3, n_5, n_6]$.

We need some terminology to express the notion of nodes, edges, and subpaths that appear in test paths, and choose familiar terminology from traveling. A test path p is said to *visit* node n if n is in p. Test path p is said to *visit* edge e if e is in p. The term visit applies well to single nodes and edges, but sometimes we want to turn our attention to subpaths. For subpaths, we use the term **tour**. Test path p is said to *tour* subpath q if q is a subpath of p. The first path of Figure 2.3, $[n_0, n_1, n_3, n_4, n_6]$, visits nodes n_0 and n_1, visits edges (n_0, n_1) and (n_3, n_4), and tours the subpath $[n_1, n_3, n_4]$ (among others, these lists are not complete). Since the subpath relationship is reflexive, the tour relationship is also reflexive. That is, any given path p always tours itself.

We define a mapping $path_G$ for tests, so for a test case t, $path_G(t)$ is the test path in graph G that is executed by t. Since it is usually obvious which graph we are discussing, we omit the subscript G. We also define the set of paths toured by a set of tests. For a test set T, $path(T)$ is the set of test paths that are executed by the tests in T: $path_G(T) = \{ path_G(t) | t \in T \}$.

Except for nondeterministic structures, which we do not consider until Chapter 7, each test case will tour exactly one test path in graph G. Figure 2.4 illustrates the difference with respect to test case/test path mapping for deterministic vs. nondeterministic software.

Figure 2.5 illustrates a set of test cases and corresponding test paths on a SESE graph with the final node $n_f = n_2$. Some edges are annotated with predicates that describe the conditions under which that edge is traversed. (This notion is formalized later in this chapter.) So, in the example, if a is less than b, the only path is from n_0 to n_1 and then on to n_3 and n_2. This book describes all of the graph coverage criteria in terms of relationships of test paths to the graph in question, but it is important to realize that testing is carried out with test cases, and that the test path is simply a model of the test case in the abstraction captured by the graph.

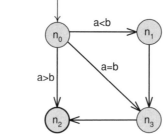

(a) Graph for testing the case with input integers
a, b and output (a+b)

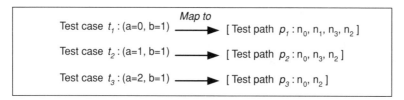

(b) Mapping between test cases and test paths

Figure 2.5. A set of test cases and corresponding test paths.

EXERCISES

Section 2.1.

1. Give the sets N, N_0, N_f, and E for the graph in Figure 2.2.
2. Give a path that is not a test path in Figure 2.2.
3. List all test paths in Figure 2.2.
4. In Figure 2.5, find test case inputs such that the corresponding test path visits edge (n_1, n_3).

2.2 GRAPH COVERAGE CRITERIA

The structure in Section 2.1 is adequate to define coverage on graphs. As is usual in the testing literature, we divide these criteria into two types. The first are usually referred to as *control flow coverage* criteria. Because we generalize this situation, we call them *structural graph coverage criteria*. The other criteria are based on the flow of data through the software artifact represented by the graph and are called *data flow coverage* criteria. Following the discussion in Chapter 1, we identify the appropriate test requirements and then define each criterion in terms of the test requirements. In general, for any graph-based coverage criterion, the idea is to identify the test requirements in terms of various structures in the graph.

For graphs, coverage criteria define test requirements, TR, in terms of properties of test paths in a graph G. A typical test requirement is *met* by *visiting* a particular node or edge or by *touring* a particular path. The definitions we have given so far for a *visit* are adequate, but the notion of a *tour* requires more development. We return to the issue of touring later in this chapter and then refine it further in the context of data flow criteria. The following definition is a refinement of the definition of *coverage* given in Chapter 1:

> *Definition 2.32 Graph Coverage:* Given a set TR of test requirements for a graph criterion C, a test set T satisfies C on graph G if and only if for every test requirement tr in TR, there is at least one test path p in $path(T)$ such that p meets tr.

This is a very general statement that must be refined for individual cases.

2.2.1 Structural Coverage Criteria

We specify graph coverage criteria by specifying a set of test requirements, TR. We will start by defining criteria to visit every node and then every edge in a graph. The first criterion is probably familiar and is based on the old notion of executing every statement in a program. This concept has variously been called "statement coverage," "block coverage," "state coverage," and "node coverage." We use the general graph term "node coverage." Although this concept is familiar and simple, we introduce some additional notation. The notation initially seems to complicate the criterion, but ultimately has the effect of making subsequent criteria cleaner and mathematically precise, avoiding confusion with more complicated situations.

The requirements that are produced by a graph criterion are technically predicates that can have either the value true (the requirement has been met) or false (the requirement has **not** been met). For the double-diamond graph in Figure 2.3, the test requirements for node coverage are: $TR = \{$ visit n_0, visit n_1, visit n_2, visit n_3, visit n_4, visit n_5, visit $n_6\}$. That is, we must satisfy a predicate for each node, where the predicate asks whether the node has been visited or not. With this in mind, the formal definition of node coverage is as follows[2]:

> *Definition 2.33 Node Coverage (Formal Definition):* For each node $n \in reach_G(N_0)$, TR contains the predicate "*visit n.*"

This notation, although mathematically precise, is too cumbersome for practical use. Thus we choose to introduce a simpler version of the definition that abstracts the issue of predicates in the test requirements.

CRITERION **2.1 Node Coverage (NC):** *TR contains each reachable node in G.*

With this definition, it is left as understood that the term "contains" actually means "contains the predicate $visit_n$." This simplification allows us to simplify the writing of the test requirements for Figure 2.3 to only contain the nodes: $TR = \{n_0, n_1, n_2, n_3, n_4, n_5, n_6\}$. Test path $p_1 = [n_0, n_1, n_3, n_4, n_6]$ meets the first, second, fourth, fifth, and seventh test requirements, and test path $p_2 = [n_0, n_2, n_3, n_5, n_6]$ meets the first, third, fourth, sixth, and seventh. Therefore, if a test set T contains $\{t_1, t_2\}$, where $path(t_1) = p_1$ and $path(t_2) = p_2$, then T satisfies node coverage on G.

The usual definition of node coverage omits the intermediate step of explicitly identifying the test requirements, and is often stated as given below. Notice the economy of the form used above with respect to the standard definition. Several

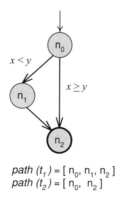

$$path\ (t_1) = [\ n_0,\ n_1,\ n_2\ ]$$
$$path\ (t_2) = [\ n_0,\ n_2\ ]$$

$T_1 = \{\ t_1\ \}$ $T_2 = \{\ t_1,\ t_2\ \}$
T_1 satisfies node coverage on the graph T_2 satisfies edge coverage on the graph

(a) Node Coverage   (b) Edge Coverage

Figure 2.6. A graph showing node coverage and edge coverage.

of the exercises emphasize this point by directing the student to recast other criteria in the standard form.

> *Definition 2.34 Node Coverage (NC) (Standard Definition):* Test set T satisfies node coverage on graph G if and only if for every syntactically reachable node n in N, there is some path p in $path(T)$ such that p visits n.

The exercises at the end of the section have the reader reformulate the definitions of some of the remaining coverage criteria in both the formal way and the standard way. We choose the intermediate definition because it is more compact, avoids the extra verbiage in a standard coverage definition, and focuses just on the part of the definition of coverage that changes from criterion to criterion.

Node coverage is implemented in many commercial testing tools, most often in the form of statement coverage. So is the next common criterion of edge coverage, usually implemented as branch coverage:

CRITERION **2.2 Edge Coverage (EC):** *TR contains each reachable path of length up to 1, inclusive, in G.*

The reader might wonder why the test requirements for edge coverage also explicitly include the test requirements for node coverage – that is, why the phrase "up to" is included in the definition. In fact, all the graph coverage criteria are developed like this. The motivation is subsumption for graphs that do not contain more complex structures. For example, consider a graph with a node that has no edges. Without the "up to" clause in the definition, edge coverage would not cover that node. Intuitively, we would like edge testing to be at least as demanding as node testing. This style of definition is the best way to achieve this property. To make our TR sets readable, we list only the maximal length paths.

Figure 2.6 illustrates the difference between node and edge coverage. In program statement terms, this is a graph of the common "if-else" structure.

Other coverage criteria use only the graph definitions introduced so far. For example, one requirement is that each path of length (up to) two be toured by some test path. With this context, node coverage could be redefined to contain each path of length zero. Clearly, this idea can be extended to paths of any length, although possibly with diminishing returns. We formally define one of these criteria; others are left as exercises for the interested reader.

CRITERION **2.3 Edge-Pair Coverage (EPC):** *TR contains each reachable path of length up to 2, inclusive, in G.*

One useful testing criterion is to start the software in some state (that is, a node in the finite state machine) and then follow transitions (that is, edges) so that the last state is the same as the start state. This type of testing is used to verify that the system is not changed by certain inputs. Shortly we will formalize this notion as round trip coverage.

Before defining round trip coverage, we need a few more definitions. A path from n_i to n_j is *simple* if no node appears more than once in the path, with the exception that the first and last nodes may be identical. That is, simple paths have no internal loops, although the entire path itself may wind up being a loop. One useful aspect of simple paths is that any path can be created by composing simple paths.

Even fairly small programs may have a very large number of simple paths. Most of these simple paths aren't worth addressing explicitly since they are subpaths of other simple paths. For a coverage criterion for simple paths we would like to avoid enumerating the entire set of simple paths. To this end we list only maximal length simple paths. To clarify this notion, we introduce a formal definition for a maximal length simple path, which we call a *prime path*, and we adopt the name "prime" for the criterion:

Definition 2.35 Prime Path: A path from n_i to n_j is a prime path if it is a simple path and it does not appear as a proper subpath of any other simple path.

CRITERION **2.4 Prime Path Coverage (PPC):** *TR contains each prime path in G.*

While this definition of prime path coverage has the practical advantage of keeping the number of test requirements down, it suffers from the problem that a given infeasible prime path may well incorporate many feasible simple paths. The solution is direct: replace the infeasible prime path with relevant feasible subpaths. For the purposes of this textbook, we choose not to include this aspect of prime path coverage formally in the definition, but we assume it in later theoretical characterizations of prime path coverage.

Prime path coverage has two special cases that we include below for historical reasons. From a practical perspective, it is usually better simply to adopt prime path coverage. Both special cases involve treatment of loops with "round trips."

A *round trip* path is a prime path of nonzero length that starts and ends at the same node. One type of round trip test coverage requires at least one round trip path to be taken for each node, and another requires all possible round trip paths.

CRITERION **2.5 Simple Round Trip Coverage (SRTC):** *T R contains at least one round-trip path for each reachable node in G that begins and ends a round-trip path.*

CRITERION **2.6 Complete Round Trip Coverage (CRTC):** *T R contains all round-trip paths for each reachable node in G.*

Next we turn to path coverage, which is traditional in the testing literature.

CRITERION **2.7 Complete Path Coverage (CPC):** *T R contains all paths in G.*

Sadly, complete path coverage is useless if a graph has a cycle, since this results in an infinite number of paths, and hence an infinite number of test requirements. A variant of this criterion is, however, useful. Suppose that instead of requiring all paths, we consider a specified set of paths. For example, these paths might be given by a customer in the form of usage scenarios.

CRITERION **2.8 Specified Path Coverage (SPC):** *T R contains a set S of test paths, where S is supplied as a parameter.*

Complete path coverage is not feasible for graphs with cycles; hence the reason for developing the other alternatives listed above. Figure 2.7 contrasts prime path coverage with complete path coverage. Part (a) of the figure shows the "diamond" graph, which contains no loops. Both complete path coverage and prime path coverage can be satisfied on this graph with the two paths shown. Part (b), however, includes a loop from n_1 to n_3 to n_4 to n_1, thus the graph has an infinite number of possible test paths, and complete path coverage is not possible. The requirements for prime path coverage, however, can be toured with two test paths, for example, $[n_0, n_1, n_2]$ and $[n_0, n_1, n_3, n_4, n_1, n_3, n_4, n_1, n_2]$.

Touring, Sidetrips, and Detours

An important but subtle point to note is that while simple paths do not have internal loops, we do **not** require the test paths that tour a simple path to have this property. That is, we distinguish between the path that **specifies** a test requirement and the portion of the test path that **meets** the requirement. The advantage of separating these two notions has to do with the issue of infeasible test requirements. Before describing this advantage, let us refine the notion of a tour.

We previously defined "visits" and "tours," and recall that using a path p to tour a subpath $[n_1, n_2, n_3]$ means that the subpath is a subpath of p. This is a rather strict definition because each node and edge in the subpath must be visited **exactly** in the order that they appear in the subpath. We would like to relax this a bit to allow

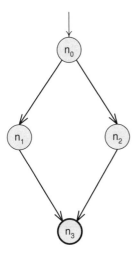 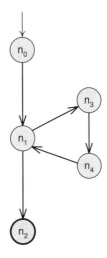

Prime Paths = { [n_0, n_1, n_3], [n_0, n_2, n_3] }
path (t$_1$) = [n_0, n_1, n_3]
path (t$_2$) = [n_0, n_2, n_3]
T_1 = {t_1, t_2}
T_1 satisfies prime path coverage on the graph

Prime Paths = { [n_0, n_1, n_2],
        [n_0, n_1, n_3, n_4], [n_1, n_3, n_4, n_1],
        [n_3, n_4, n_1, n_3], [n_4, n_1, n_3, n_4],
        [n_3, n_4, n_1, n_2] }
path (t$_3$) = [n_0, n_1, n_2]
path (t$_4$) = [n_0, n_1, n_3, n_4, n_1, n_3, n_4, n_1, n_2]
T_2 = {t_3, t_4}
T_2 satisfies prime path coverage on the graph

(a) Prime Path Coverage on a
    Graph with No Loops

(b) Prime Path Coverage on a
    Graph with Loops

Figure 2.7. Two graphs showing prime path coverage.

loops to be included in the tour. Consider the graph in Figure 2.8, which features a small loop from b to c and back.

If we are required to tour subpath $q = [a, b, d]$, the strict definition of tour prohibits us from meeting the requirement with any path that contains c, such as $p = [s_0, a, b, c, b, d, s_f]$, because we do not visit a, b, and d in exactly the same order. We relax the tour definition in two ways. The first allows the tour to include "sidetrips," where we can leave the path temporarily from a node and then return to the same node. The second allows the tour to include more general "detours" where we can leave the path from a node and then return to the **next** node on the

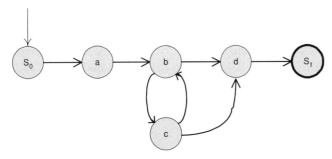

Figure 2.8. Graph with a loop.

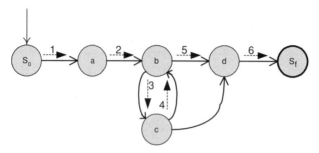

(a) Graph being toured with a sidetrip

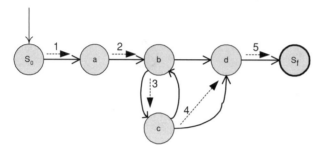

(b) Graph being toured with a detour

Figure 2.9. Tours, sidetrips, and detours in graph coverage.

path (skipping an edge). In the following definitions, q is a required subpath that is assumed to be simple.

Definition 2.36 Tour: Test path p is said to *tour* subpath q if and only if q is a subpath of p.

Definition 2.37 Tour with Sidetrips: Test path p is said to *tour* subpath q *with sidetrips* if and only if every **edge** in q is also in p in the same order.

Definition 2.38 Tour with Detours: Test path p is said to *tour* subpath q *with detours* if and only if every **node** in q is also in p in the same order.

The graphs in Figure 2.9 illustrate sidetrips and detours on the graph from Figure 2.8. In Figure 2.9(a), the dashed lines show the sequence of edges that are executed in a tour with a sidetrip. The numbers on the dashed lines indicate the order in which the edges are executed. In Figure 2.9(b), the dashed lines show the sequence of edges that are executed in a tour with a detour.

While these differences are rather small, they have far-reaching consequences. The difference between sidetrips and detours can be seen in Figure 2.9. The subpath $[b, c, b]$ is a **sidetrip** to $[a, b, d]$ because it leaves the subpath at node b and then returns to the subpath at node b. Thus, every edge in the subpath $[a, b, d]$ is executed in the same order. The subpath $[b, c, d]$ is a **detour** to $[a, b, d]$ because it leaves the subpath at node b and then returns to a node in the subpath at a later point, bypassing the edge (b, d). That is, every node $[a, b, d]$ is executed in the same order but every edge is not. Detours have the potential to drastically change the behavior of the intended test. That is, a test that takes the edge (c, d) may exhibit different behavior and test different aspects of the program than a test that takes the edge (b, d).

To use the notion of sidetrips and detours, one can "decorate" each appropriate graph coverage criterion with a choice of touring. For example, prime path coverage could be defined strictly in terms of tours, less strictly to allow sidetrips, or even less strictly to allow detours.

The position taken in this book is that sidetrips are a practical way to deal with infeasible test requirements, as described below. Hence we include them explicitly in our criteria. Detours seem less practical, and so we do not include them further.

Dealing with Infeasible Test Requirements

If sidetrips are not allowed, a large number of infeasible requirements can exist. Consider again the graph in Figure 2.9. In many programs it will be impossible to take the path from a to d without going through node c at least once because, for example, the loop body is written such that it cannot be skipped. If this happens, we need to allow sidetrips. That is, it may not be possible to tour the path $[a, b, d]$ without a sidetrip.

The argument above suggests dropping the strict notion of touring and simply allowing test requirements to be met with sidetrips. However, this is not always a good idea! Specifically, if a test requirement can be met without a sidetrip, then doing so is clearly superior to meeting the requirement with a sidetrip. Consider the loop example again. If the loop can be executed zero times, then the path $[a, b, d]$ should be toured without a sidetrip.

The argument above suggests a hybrid treatment with desirable practical and theoretical properties. The idea is to meet test requirements first with strict tours, and then allow sidetrips for unmet test requirements. Clearly, the argument could easily be extended to detours, but, as mentioned above, we elect not to do so.

> *Definition 2.39 Best Effort Touring:* Let TR_{tour} be the subset of test require-
> ments that can be toured and $TR_{sidetrip}$ be the subset of test requirements
> that can be toured with sidetrips. Note that $TR_{tour} \subseteq TR_{sidetrip}$. A set T of test
> paths achieves *best effort touring* if for every path p in TR_{tour}, some path in
> T tours p directly and for every path p in $TR_{sidetrip}$, some path in T tours p
> either directly or with a sidetrip.

Best-effort touring has the practical benefit that as many test requirements are met as possible, yet each test requirement is met in the strictest possible way. As we will see in Section 2.2.3 on subsumption, best effort touring has desirable theoretical properties with respect to subsumption.

Finding Prime Test Paths

It turns out to be relatively simple to find all prime paths in a graph, and test paths to tour the prime paths can be constructed in a mechanical manner. Consider the example graph in Figure 2.10. It has seven nodes and nine edges, including a loop and an edge from node n_4 to itself (sometimes called a "self-loop.")

Prime paths can be found by starting with paths of length 0, then extending to length 1, and so on. Such an algorithm collects all simple paths, whether prime or

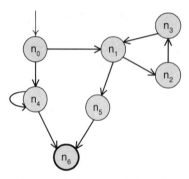

Figure 2.10. An example for prime
test paths.

not. The prime paths can be easily screened from this set. The set of paths of length 0 is simply the set of nodes, and the set of paths of length 1 is simply the set of edges. For simplicity, we simply list the node numbers in this example.

Simple paths of length 0 (7):

1) [0]
2) [1]
3) [2]
4) [3]
5) [4]
6) [5]
7) [6] !

The exclamation point on the path [6] tells us that this path cannot be extended. Specifically, the final node 6 has no outgoing edges, and so paths that end with 6 are not extended further.

Simple paths of length 1 (9):

8) [0, 1]
9) [0, 4]
10) [1, 2]
11) [1, 5]
12) [2, 3]
13) [3, 1]
14) [4, 4] *
15) [4, 6] !
16) [5, 6] !

The asterisk on the path [4, 4] tells us that path can go no further because the first node is the same as the last (it is already a cycle). For paths of length 2, we identify each path of length 1 that is not a cycle (marked with asterisks). We then extend the path with every node that can be reached from the final node in the path unless that node is already in the path and not the first node. The first path of length 1, [0, 1], is extended to [0, 1, 2] and [0, 1, 5]. The second, [0, 4], is extended to [0, 4, 6] but not [0, 4, 4], because node 4 is already in the path ([0, 4, 4] is not simple and thus is not prime).

Simple paths of length 2 (8):

17) [0, 1, 2]
18) [0, 1, 5]
19) [0, 4, 6] !
20) [1, 2, 3]
21) [1, 5, 6] !
22) [2, 3, 1]
23) [3, 1, 2]
24) [3, 1, 5]

Paths of length 3 are computed in a similar way.
Simple paths of length 3 (7):

25) [0, 1, 2, 3] !
26) [0, 1, 5, 6] !
27) [1, 2, 3, 1] *
28) [2, 3, 1, 2] *
29) [2, 3, 1, 5]
30) [3, 1, 2, 3] *
31) [3, 1, 5, 6] !

Finally, only one path of length 4 exists. Three paths of length 3 cannot be extended because they are cycles; two others end with node 6. Of the remaining two, the path that ends in node 3 cannot be extended because [0, 1, 2, 3, 1] is **not** simple and thus is not prime.
Prime paths of length 4 (1):

32) [2, 3, 1, 5, 6]!

The prime paths can be computed by eliminating any path that is a (proper) subpath of some other simple path. Note that every simple path without an exclamation mark or asterisk is eliminated as it can be extended and is thus a proper subpath of some other simple path. There are eight prime paths:

14) [4, 4] *
19) [0, 4, 6] !
25) [0, 1, 2, 3] !
26) [0, 1, 5, 6] !
27) [1, 2, 3, 1] *
28) [2, 3, 1, 2] *
30) [3, 1, 2, 3] *
32) [2, 3, 1, 5, 6]!

This process is guaranteed to terminate because the length of the longest possible prime path is the number of nodes. Although graphs often have many simple paths (32 in this example, of which 8 are prime), they can usually be toured with far fewer test paths. Many possible algorithms can find test paths to tour the prime paths. Observation will suffice with a graph as simple as in Figure 2.10. For example, it can be seen that the four test paths [0, 1, 5, 6], [0, 1, 2, 3, 1, 2, 3, 1, 5, 6], [0, 4, 6], and $[0, 4, 4, 6]$ are enough. This approach, however, is error-prone. The easiest thing to do is to tour the loop $[1, 2, 3]$ only once, which omits the prime paths $[2, 3, 1, 2]$ and $[3, 1, 2, 3]$.

With more complicated graphs, a mechanical approach is needed. We recommend starting with the longest prime paths and extending them to the beginning and end nodes in the graph. For our example, this results in the test path $[0, 1, 2, 3, 1, 5, 6]$. The test path $[0, 1, 2, 3, 1, 5, 6]$ tours 3 prime paths 25, 27, and 32.

The next test path is constructed by extending one of the longest remaining prime paths; we will continue to work backward and choose 30. The resulting test path is $[0, 1, 2, 3, 1, 2, 3, 1, 5, 6]$, which tours 2 prime paths, 28 and 30 (it also tours paths 25 and 27).

The next test path is constructed by using the prime path 26 $[0, 1, 5, 6]$. This test path tours only maximal prime path 26.

Continuing in this fashion yields two more test paths, $[0, 4, 6]$ for prime path 19, and $[0, 4, 4, 6]$ for prime path 14.

The complete set of test paths is then:

1) $[0, 1, 2, 3, 1, 5, 6]$
2) $[0, 1, 2, 3, 1, 2, 3, 1, 5, 6]$
3) $[0, 1, 5, 6]$
4) $[0, 4, 6]$
5) $[0, 4, 4, 6]$

This can be used as is, or optimized if the tester desires a smaller test set. It is clear that test path 2 tours the prime paths toured by test path 1, so 1 can be eliminated, leaving the four test paths identified informally earlier in this section. Simple algorithms can automate this process.

EXERCISES

Section 2.2.1.

1. Redefine *edge coverage* in the standard way (see the discussion for *node coverage*).
2. Redefine *complete path coverage* in the standard way (see the discussion for *node coverage*).
3. Subsumption has a significant weakness. Suppose criterion C_{strong} subsumes criterion C_{weak} and that test set T_{strong} satisfies C_{strong} and test set T_{weak} satisfies C_{weak}. It is not necessarily the case that T_{weak} is a subset of T_{strong}. It is also not necessarily the case that T_{strong} reveals a fault if T_{weak} reveals a fault. Explain these facts.
4. Answer questions (a)–(d) for the graph defined by the following sets:
   - $N = \{1, 2, 3, 4\}$
   - $N_0 = \{1\}$
   - $N_f = \{4\}$
   - $E = \{(1, 2), (2, 3), (3, 2), (2, 4)\}$

(a) Draw the graph.
(b) List test paths that achieve node coverage, but not edge coverage.
(c) List test paths that achieve edge coverage, but not edge Pair coverage.
(d) List test paths that achieve edge pair coverage.

5. Answer questions (a)–(g) for the graph defined by the following sets:
   ■ $N = \{1, 2, 3, 4, 5, 6, 7\}$
   ■ $N_0 = \{1\}$
   ■ $N_f = \{7\}$
   ■ $E = \{(1, 2), (1, 7), (2, 3), (2, 4), (3, 2), (4, 5), (4, 6), (5, 6), (6, 1)\}$
   Also consider the following (candidate) test paths:
   ■ $t_0 = [1, 2, 4, 5, 6, 1, 7]$
   ■ $t_1 = [1, 2, 3, 2, 4, 6, 1, 7]$
   (a) Draw the graph.
   (b) List the test requirements for edge-pair coverage. (Hint: You should get 12 requirements of length 2).
   (c) Does the given set of test paths satisfy edge-pair coverage? If not, identify what is missing.
   (d) Consider the simple path **[3, 2, 4, 5, 6]** and test path **[1, 2, 3, 2, 4, 6, 1, 2, 4, 5, 6, 1, 7]**. Does the test path tour the simple path directly? With a sidetrip? If so, identify the sidetrip.
   (e) List the test requirements for node coverage, edge coverage, and prime path coverage on the graph.
   (f) List test paths that achieve node coverage but not edge coverage on the graph.
   (g) List test paths that achieve edge coverage but not prime path coverage on the graph.

6. Answer questions (a)–(c) for the graph in Figure 2.2.
   (a) Enumerate the test requirements for node coverage, edge coverage, and prime path coverage on the graph.
   (b) List test paths that achieve node coverage but not edge coverage on the graph.
   (c) List test paths that achieve edge coverage but not prime path coverage on the graph.

7. Answer questions (a)–(d) for the graph defined by the following sets:
   ■ $N = \{0, 1, 2\}$
   ■ $N_0 = \{0\}$
   ■ $N_f = \{2\}$
   ■ $E = \{(0, 1), (0, 2), (1, 0), (1, 2), (2, 0)\}$
   Also consider the following (candidate) paths:
   ■ $p_0 = [0, 1, 2, 0]$
   ■ $p_1 = [0, 2, 0, 1, 2]$
   ■ $p_2 = [0, 1, 2, 0, 1, 0, 2]$
   ■ $p_3 = [1, 2, 0, 2]$
   ■ $p_4 = [0, 1, 2, 1, 2]$
   (a) Which of the listed paths are test paths? Explain the problem with any path that is not a test path.

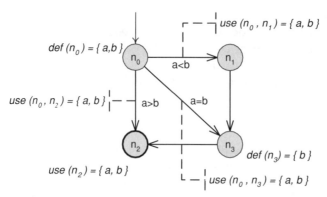

Figure 2.11. A graph showing variables, def sets and use sets.

(b) List the eight test requirements for edge-pair coverage (only the length two subpaths).

(c) Does the set of **test** paths (part a) above satisfy edge-pair coverage? If not, identify what is missing.

(d) Consider the prime path $[n_2, n_0, n_2]$ and path p_2. Does p_2 tour the prime path directly? With a sidetrip?

8. Design and implement a program that will compute all prime paths in a graph, then derive test paths to tour the prime paths. Although the user interface can be arbitrarily complicated, the simplest version will be to accept a graph as input by reading a list of nodes, initial nodes, final nodes, and edges.

2.2.2 Data Flow Criteria

The next few testing criteria are based on the assumption that to test a program adequately, we should focus on the flows of data values. Specifically, we should try to ensure that the values created at one point in the program are created and used correctly. This is done by focusing on definitions and uses of values. A *definition (def)* is a location where a value for a variable is stored into memory (assignment, input, etc.). A *use* is a location where a variable's value is accessed. Data flow testing criteria use the fact that values are carried from defs to uses. We call these *du-pairs* (they are also known as *definition-use*, *def-use*, and *du* associations in the testing literature). The idea of data flow criteria is to exercise du-pairs in various ways.

First we must integrate data flow into the existing graph model. Let V be a set of variables that are associated with the program artifact being modeled in the graph. Each node n and edge e is considered to define a subset of V; this set is called $def(n)$ or $def(e)$. (Although graphs from programs cannot have defs on edges, other software artifacts such as finite state machines can allow defs as side effects on edges.) Each node n and edge e is also considered to use a subset of V; this set is called $use(n)$ or $use(e)$.

Figure 2.11 gives an example of a graph annotated with defs and uses. All variables involved in a decision are assumed to be used on the associated edges, so a and b are in the use set of all three edges (n_0, n_1), (n_0, n_2), and (n_0, n_3).

An important concept when discussing data flow criteria is that a def of a variable may or may not reach a particular use. The most obvious reason that a def of a variable v at location l_i (a location could be a node or an edge) will not reach a use at location l_j is because no path goes from l_i to l_j. A more subtle reason is that the variable's value may be changed by another def before it reaches the use. Thus, a path from l_i to l_j is *def-clear* with respect to variable v if for every node n_k and every edge e_k on the path, $k \neq i$ and $k \neq j$, v is not in $def(n_k)$ or in $def(e_k)$. That is, no location between l_i and l_j changes the value. If a def-clear path goes from l_i to l_j with respect to v, we say that the def of v at l_i *reaches* the use at l_j.

For simplicity, we will refer to the start and end of a du-path as nodes, even if the definition or the use occurs on an edge. We discuss relaxing this convention later. Formally, a *du-path* with respect to a variable v is a simple path that is def-clear with respect to v from a node n_i for which v is in $def(n_i)$ to a node n_j for which v is in $use(n_j)$. We want the paths to be simple to ensure a reasonably small number of paths. Note that a du-path is always associated with a specific variable v, a du-path always has to be simple, and there may be intervening uses on the path.

Figure 2.12 gives an example of a graph annotated with defs and uses. Rather than displaying the actual sets, we show the full program statements that are associated with the nodes and edges. This is common and often more informative to a human, but the actual sets are simpler for automated tools to process. Note that the parameters (*subject* and *pattern*) are considered to be *explicitly defined* by the first node in the graph. That is, the def set of node 1 is $def(1) = \{subject, pattern\}$. Also note that decisions in the program (for example, *if subject[iSub] == pattern[0]*) result in uses of each of the associated variables for both edges in the decision. That is, $use(4, 10) \equiv use(4,5) \equiv \{subject, iSub, pattern\}$. The parameter *subject* is used at node 2 (with a reference to its *length* attribute) and at edges $(4, 5), (4, 10), (7, 8)$, and $(7, 9)$, thus du-paths exist from node 1 to node 2 and from node 1 to each of those four edges.

Figure 2.13 shows the same graph, but this time with the def and use sets explicitly marked on the graph.[3] Note that node 9 both defines and uses the variable *iPat*. This is because of the statement *iPat++*, which is equivalent to *iPat = iPat+1*. In this case, the use occurs before the def, so for example, a def-clear path goes from node 5 to node 9 with respect to *iPat*.

The test criteria for data flow will be defined as sets of du-paths. This makes the criteria quite simple, but first we need to categorize the du-paths into several *groups*.

The first grouping of du-paths is according to definitions. Specifically, consider all of the du-paths with respect to a given variable defined in a given node. Let the *def-path* set $du(n_i, v)$ be the set of du-paths with respect to variable v that start at node n_i. Once we have clarified the notion of touring for dataflow coverage, we will define the All-Defs criterion by simply asking that at least one du-path from each def-path set be toured. Because of the large number of nodes in a typical graph, and the potentially large number of variables defined at each node, the number of def-path sets can be quite large. Even so, the coverage criterion that arises from the def-path groupings tends to be quite weak.

Perhaps surprisingly, it is *not* helpful to group du-paths by uses, and so we will not provide a definition of "use-path" sets that parallels the definition of def-path sets given above.

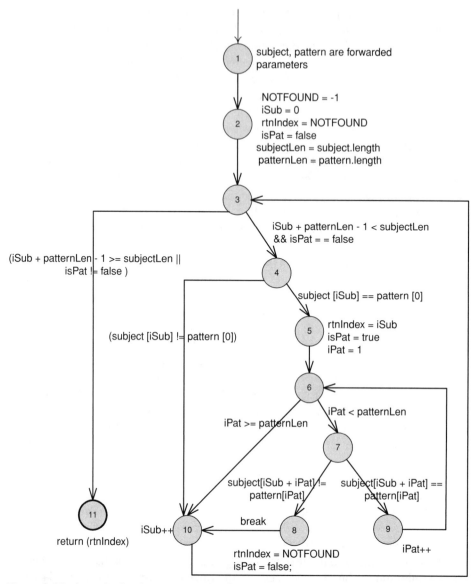

Figure 2.12. A graph showing an example of du-paths.

The second, and more important, grouping of du-paths is according to pairs of definitions and uses. We call this the *def-pair* set. After all, the heart of data flow testing is allowing definitions to flow to uses. Specifically, consider all of the du-paths with respect to a given variable that are defined in one node and used in another (possibly identical) node. Formally, let the *def-pair* set $du(n_i, n_j, v)$ be the set of du-paths with respect to variable v that start at node n_i and end at node n_j. Informally, a def-pair set collects together all the (simple) ways to get from a given definition to a given use. Once we have clarified the notion of touring for dataflow coverage, we will define the All-Uses criterion by simply asking that at least one du-path from

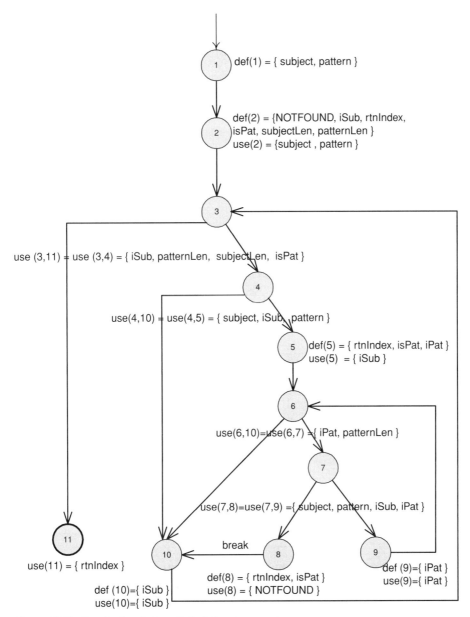

def(1) = { subject, pattern }

def(2) = {NOTFOUND, iSub, rtnIndex, isPat, subjectLen, patternLen }
use(2) = {subject , pattern }

use (3,11) = use (3,4) = { iSub, patternLen, subjectLen, isPat }

use(4,10) = use(4,5) = { subject, iSub , pattern }

def(5) = { rtnIndex, isPat, iPat }
use(5) = { iSub }

use(6,10)=use(6,7) ={ iPat, patternLen }

use(7,8)=use(7,9) ={ subject, pattern, iSub, iPat }

break

def(8) = { rtnIndex, isPat }
use(8) = { NOTFOUND }

def (9)={ iPat }
use(9)={ iPat }

use(11) = { rtnIndex }

def (10)={ iSub }
use(10)={ iSub }

Figure 2.13. Graph showing explicit def and use sets.

each def-pair set be toured. Since each definition can typically reach multiple uses, there are usually many more def-pair sets than def-path sets.

In fact, the def-path set for a def at node n_i is the union of all the def-pair sets for that def. More formally: $du(n_i, v) = \cup_{n_j} du(n_i, n_j, v)$.

To illustrate the notions of def-path sets and def-pair sets, consider du-paths with respect to the variable *iSub*, which has one of its definitions in node 10 in Figure 2.13. There are du-paths with respect to *iSub* from node 10 to nodes 5 and 10, and to edges (3, 4), (3, 11), (4, 5), (4, 10), (7, 8), and (7, 9).

The def-path set for the use of *isub* at node 10 is:

$$du(10, iSub) = \{[10, 3, 4], [10, 3, 4, 5], [10, 3, 4, 5, 6, 7, 8], [10, 3, 4, 5, 6, 7, 9],$$
$$[10, 3, 4, 5, 6, 10], [10, 3, 4, 5, 6, 7, 8, 10], [10, 3, 4, 10],$$
$$[10, 3, 11]\}$$

This def-path set can be broken up into the following def-pair sets:

$$du(10, 4, iSub) = \{[10, 3, 4]\}$$
$$du(10, 5, iSub) = \{[10, 3, 4, 5]\}$$
$$du(10, 8, iSub) = \{[10, 3, 4, 5, 6, 7, 8]\}$$
$$du(10, 9, iSub) = \{[10, 3, 4, 5, 6, 7, 9]\}$$
$$du(10, 10, iSub) = \{[10, 3, 4, 5, 6, 10], [10, 3, 4, 5, 6, 7, 8, 10], [10, 3, 4, 10]\}$$
$$du(10, 11, iSub) = \{[10, 3, 11]\}$$

Next, we extend the definition of *tour* to apply to du-paths. A test path p is said to *du tour* subpath d with respect to v if p tours d and the portion of p to which d corresponds is def-clear with respect to v. Depending on how one wishes to define the coverage criteria, one can either allow or disallow def-clear sidetrips with respect to v when touring a du-path. Because def-clear sidetrips make it possible to tour more du-paths, we define the dataflow coverage criteria given below to allow sidetrips where necessary.

Now we can define the primary data flow coverage criteria. The three most common are best understood informally. The first requires that each def reaches **at least one use**, the second requires that each def reaches **all possible uses**, and the third requires that each def reaches all possible uses through **all possible du-paths**. As mentioned in the development of def-path sets and def-pair sets, the formal definitions of the criteria are simply appropriate selections from the appropriate set. For each test criterion below, we assume best effort touring (see Section 2.2.1), where sidetrips are required to be def-clear with respect to the variable in question.

> CRITERION **2.9 All-Defs Coverage (ADC):** *For each def-path set $S = du(n, v)$, TR contains at least one path d in S.*

Remember that the def-path set $du(n, v)$ represents all def-clear simple paths from n to all uses of v. So All-Defs requires us to tour at least one path to at least one use.

> CRITERION **2.10 All-Uses Coverage (AUC):** *For each def-pair set $S = du(n_i, n_j, v)$, TR contains at least one path d in S.*

Remember that the def-pair set $du(n_i, n_j, v)$ represents all the def-clear simple paths from a def of v at n_i to a use of v at n_j. So All-Uses requires us to tour at least one path for every def-use pair.[4]

> CRITERION **2.11 All-du-Paths Coverage (ADUPC):** *For each def-pair set $S = du(n_i, n_j, v)$, TR contains every path d in S.*

The definition could also simply be written as "include every du-path." We chose the given formulation because it highlights that the key difference between All-Uses

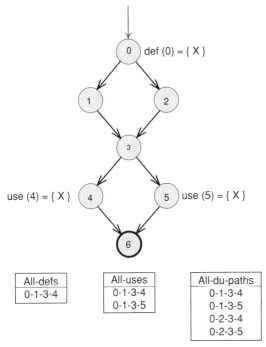

Figure 2.14. Example of the differences among the three data flow coverage criteria.

and All-du-Paths is a change in quantifier. Specifically, the "at least one du-path" directive in All-Uses is changed to "every path" in All-du-Paths. Thought of in terms of def-use pairs, All-Uses requires *some* def-clear simple path to each use, whereas All-du-Paths requires *all* def-clear simple paths to each use.

To simplify the development above, we assumed that definitions and uses occurred on nodes. Naturally, definitions and uses can occur on edges as well. It turns out that the development above also works for uses on edges, so data flow on program flow graphs can be easily defined (uses on program flow graph edges are sometimes called "p-uses"). However, the development above does not work if the graph has definitions on edges. The problem is that a du-path from an edge to an edge is no longer necessarily simple, since instead of simply having a common first and last *node*, such a du-path now might have a common first and last *edge*. It is possible to modify the definitions to explicitly mention definitions and uses on edges as well as nodes, but the definitions tend to get messier. The bibliographic notes contain pointers for this type of development.

Figure 2.14 illustrates the differences among the three data flow coverage criteria with the double-diamond graph. The graph has one def, so only one path is needed to satisfy all-defs. The def has two uses, so two paths are needed to satisfy all-uses. Since two paths go from the def to each use, four paths are needed to satisfy all-du-paths. Note that the definitions of the data flow criteria leave open the choice of touring. The literature uses various choices – in some cases demanding direct touring, and, in other cases, allowing def-clear sidetrips. Our recommendation is best-effort touring, a choice that, in contrast to the treatments in the literature, yields the desired subsumption relationships even in the case of infeasible test requirements. From a practical perspective, best-effort touring also makes sense – each test requirement is satisfied as rigorously as possible.

2.2.3 Subsumption Relationships among Graph Coverage Criteria

Recall from Chapter 1 that coverage criteria are often related to one another by *subsumption*. The first relation to note is that edge coverage subsumes node coverage. In most cases, this is because if we traverse every edge in a graph, we will visit every node. However, if a graph has a node with no incoming or outgoing edges, traversing every edge will not reach that node. Thus, edge coverage is defined to include every path of length **up to 1**, that is, of length 0 (all nodes) and length 1 (all edges). The subsumption does not hold in the reverse direction. Recall that Figure 2.6 gave an example test set that satisfied node coverage but not edge coverage. Hence, node coverage does not subsume edge coverage.

We have a variety of subsumption relations among the criteria. Where applicable, the structural coverage relations assume best-effort touring. Because best-effort Touring is assumed, the subsumption results hold even if some test requirements are infeasible.

The subsumption results for data flow criteria are based on three assumptions: (1) every use is preceded by a def, (2) every def reaches at least one use, and (3) for every node with multiple outgoing edges, at least one variable is used on each out edge, and the same variables are used on each out edge. If we satisfy All-Uses

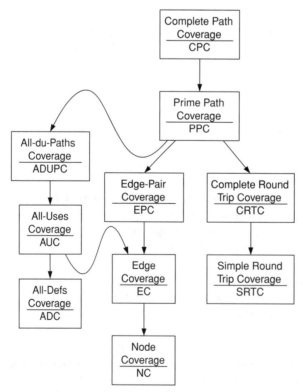

Figure 2.15. Subsumption relations among graph coverage criteria.

coverage, then we will have implicitly ensured that every def was used. Thus All-Defs is also satisfied and All-Uses subsumes All-Defs. Likewise, if we satisfy All-du-Paths coverage, then we will have implicitly ensured that every def reached every possible use. Thus All-Uses is also satisfied and All-du-Paths subsumes All-Uses. Additionally, each edge is based on the satisfaction of some predicate, so each edge has at least one use. Therefore All-Uses will guarantee that each edge is executed at least once, so All-Uses subsumes edge coverage.

Finally, each du-path is also a simple path, so prime path coverage subsumes All-du-Paths coverage.[5] This is a significant observation, since computing prime paths is considerably simpler than analyzing data flow relationships. Figure 2.15 shows the subsumption relationships among the structural and data flow coverage criteria.

EXERCISES

Section 2.2.3.

1. Below are four graphs, each of which is defined by the sets of nodes, initial nodes, final nodes, edges, and defs and uses. Each graph also contains a collection of test paths. Answer the following questions about each graph.

Graph I.
$N = \{0, 1, 2, 3, 4, 5, 6, 7\}$
$N_0 = \{0\}$
$N_f = \{7\}$
$E = \{(0, 1), (1, 2), (1, 7), (2, 3), (2, 4), (3, 2),$
$(4, 5), (4, 6), (5, 6), (6, 1)\}$
$def(0) = def(3) = use(5) = use(7) = \{x\}$
Test Paths:
$t1 = [0, 1, 7]$
$t2 = [0, 1, 2, 4, 6, 1, 7]$
$t3 = [0, 1, 2, 4, 5, 6, 1, 7]$
$t4 = [0, 1, 2, 3, 2, 4, 6, 1, 7]$
$t5 = [0, 1, 2, 3, 2, 3, 2, 4, 5, 6, 1, 7]$
$t6 = [0, 1, 2, 3, 2, 4, 6, 1, 2, 4, 5, 6, 1, 7]$

Graph II.
$N = \{1, 2, 3, 4, 5, 6\}$
$N_0 = \{1\}$
$N_f = \{6\}$
$E = \{(1, 2), (2, 3), (2, 6), (3, 4), (3, 5), (4, 5), (5, 2)\}$
$def(1) = def(3) = use(3) = use(6) = \{x\}$

Test Paths:
$t1 = [1, 2, 6]$
$t2 = [1, 2, 3, 4, 5, 2, 3, 5, 2, 6]$
$t3 = [1, 2, 3, 5, 2, 3, 4, 5, 2, 6]$
$t4 = [1, 2, 3, 5, 2, 6]$

Graph III.
$N = \{1, 2, 3, 4, 5, 6\}$
$N_0 = \{1\}$
$N_f = \{6\}$
$E = \{(1, 2), (2, 3), (3, 4), (3, 5), (4, 5), (5, 2), (2, 6)\}$
$def(1) = def(4) = use(3) = use(5) = use(6) = \{x\}$

Test Paths:
$t_1 = [1, 2, 3, 5, 2, 6]$
$t_2 = [1, 2, 3, 4, 5, 2, 6]$

Graph IV.
$N = \{1, 2, 3, 4, 5, 6\}$
$N_0 = \{1\}$
$N_f = \{6\}$
$E = \{(1, 2), (2, 3), (2, 6), (3, 4), (3, 5), (4, 5),$
$(5, 2)\}$
$def(1) = def(5) = use(5) = use(6) = \{x\}$
Test Paths:
$t1 = [1, 2, 6]$
$t2 = [1, 2, 3, 4, 5, 2, 3, 5, 2, 6]$
$t3 = [1, 2, 3, 5, 2, 3, 4, 5, 2, 6]$

(a) Draw the graph.
(b) List all of the du-paths with respect to x. (Note: Include all du-paths, even those that are subpaths of some other du-path).
(c) For each test path, determine which du-paths that test path tours. For this part of the exercise, you should consider both direct touring and sidetrips. Hint: A table is a convenient format for describing this relationship.
(d) List a minimal test set that satisfies *all-defs* coverage with respect to x. (Direct tours only.) Use the given test paths.
(e) List a minimal test set that satisfies *all-uses* coverage with respectto x.

```
if (x < y)
{
    y = 0;
    x = x + 1;
}
else
{
    x = y;
}
```

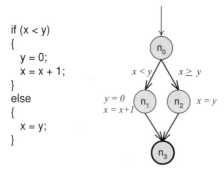

Figure 2.16. CFG fragment for the if-else structure.

       (Direct tours only.) Use the given test paths.

(f) List a minimal test set that satisfies *all-du-paths* coverage with respect to x. (Direct tours only.) Use the given test paths.

2.3 GRAPH COVERAGE FOR SOURCE CODE

Most of the graph coverage criteria were developed for source code, and these definitions match the definitions in Section 2.2 very closely. As in Section 2.2, we first consider structural coverage criteria and then data flow criteria.

2.3.1 Structural Graph Coverage for Source Code

The most widely used graph coverage criteria are defined on source code. Although precise details vary from one programming language to another, the basic pattern is the same for most common languages. To apply one of the graph criteria, the first step is to define the graph, and for source code, the most common graph is called a *control flow graph (CFG)*. Control flow graphs associate an edge with each possible branch in the program, and a node with sequences of statements. Formally, a *basic block* is a maximum sequence of program statements such that if any one statement of the block is executed, all statements in the block are executed. A basic block has only one entry point and one exit point. Our first example language structure is an if statement with an else clause, shown as Java code followed by the corresponding CFG in Figure 2.16. The if-else structure results in two basic blocks.

    Note that the two statements in the then part of the if statement both appear in the same node. Node n_0, which represents the conditional test x < y has more than one out-edge, and is called a *decision* node. Node n_3, which has more than one in-edge, is called a *junction* node.

    Next we turn to the degenerate case of an if statement without an else clause, shown in Figure 2.17. This is the same graph previously seen in Figure 2.6, but this time based on actual program statements.

    Note that the control flow graph for this structure has only three nodes. The reader should note that a test with $x < y$ traverses all of the nodes in this control flow graph, but not all of the edges.

    Representing loops is a little tricky because we have to include nodes that are not directly derived from program statements. The simplest kind of loop is a while loop with an initializing statement, as shown in Figure 2.18. (Assume that y has a

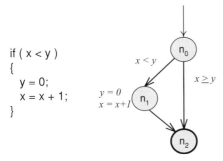

```
if ( x < y )
{
  y = 0;
  x = x + 1;
}
```

Figure 2.17. CFG fragment for the if structure without an else.

value defined at this point in the program.)

The graph for the while structure has a decision node, which is needed for the conditional test, and a single node for the body of the while loop. Node n_1 is sometimes called a "dummy node," because it does not represent any statements, but gives the iteration edge (n_2, n_1) somewhere to go. Node n_1 can also be thought of as representing a decision. A common mistake for beginners is to try to have the edge go to n_0; this is not correct because that would mean the initialization step is done each iteration of the loop. Note that the method call f(x,y) is not expanded in this particular graph; we return to this issue later.

Now, consider a for loop that is equivalent to the prior while loop. The graph becomes a little more complicated, as shown in Figure 2.19, essentially because the for structure is at a very high level of abstraction.

Although the initialization, test, and increment of the loop control variable x are all on the same line in the program, they need to be associated with different nodes in the graph. The control flow graph for the for loop is slightly different from that of the while loop. Specifically, we show the increment of x in a different node than the method call y = f(x,y). Technically speaking, this violates the definition of a basic block and the two nodes should be combined, but it is often easier to develop templates for the various possible program structures and then plug the control flow graph for the relevant code into the correct spot in the template. Commercial tools typically do this to make the graph generation simpler. In fact, commercial tools often do not follow the strict definition of the basic block and sometimes add seemingly random nodes. This can have trivial effects on the bookkeeping (for ex-

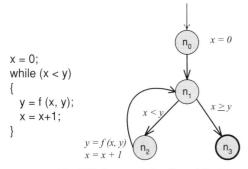

```
x = 0;
while (x < y)
{
  y = f (x, y);
  x = x+1;
}
```

Figure 2.18. CFG fragment for the while loop structure.

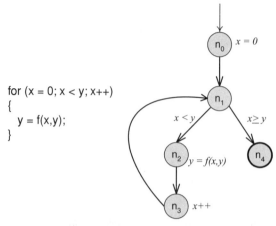

for (x = 0; x < y; x++)
{
    y = f(x,y);
}

Figure 2.19. CFG fragment for the for loop structure.

ample, we might cover 67 of 73 instead of 68 of 75), but is not really important for testing.

Our final language structure is the case statement, or switch in Java. The case structure can be graphed either as a single node with multi-way branching or as a series of if-then-else structures. We choose to illustrate the case structure with multi-way branching, as in Figure 2.20.

The coverage criteria from the previous section can now be applied to graphs from source code. The application is direct with only the names being changed. Node coverage is often called *statement coverage* or *basic block coverage*, and edge coverage is often called *branch coverage*.

2.3.2 Data Flow Graph Coverage for Source Code

This section applies the data flow criteria to the code examples given in the prior section. Before we can do this, we need to define what constitutes a *def* and what constitutes a *use*. A *def* is a location in the program where a value for a variable is stored into memory (assignment, input, etc.). A *use* is a location where a variable's

```
read (c);
switch (c)
{
case 'N':
    y = 25;
    break;
case 'Y':
    y = 50;
    break;
default:
    y = 0;
    break;
}
print (y);
```

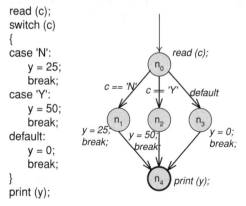

Figure 2.20. CFG fragment for the case structure.

value is accessed.

A def may occur for variable x in the following situations:

1. x appears on the left side of an assignment statement
2. x is an actual parameter in a call site and its value is changed within the method
3. x is a formal parameter of a method (an implicit def when the method begins execution)
4. x is an input to the program

Some features of programming languages greatly complicate this seemingly simple definition. For example, is a def of an array variable a def of the entire array, or of just the element being referenced? What about objects; should the def consider the entire object, or only a particular instance variable of the object? If two variables reference the same location, that is, the variables are aliases, how is the analysis done? What is the relationship between coverage of the original source code, coverage of the optimized source code, and coverage of the machine code? We omit these complicating issues in our presentation and refer advanced readers to the bibliographic notes.

If a variable has multiple definitions in a single basic block, the last definition is the only one that is relevant to data flow analysis.

A use may occur for variable x in the following situations:

1. x appears on the right side of an assignment statement
2. x appears in a conditional test (note that such a test is always associated with at least two edges)
3. x is an actual parameter to a method
4. x is an output of the program
5. x is an output of a method in a return statement or returned as a parameter

Not all uses are relevant for data flow analysis. Consider the following statements that reference local variables (ignoring concurrency):

```
y = z;
x = y + 2;
```

The use of y in the second statement is called a *local* use; it is impossible for a def in another basic block to reach the use in x = y + 2. The reason is that the definition of y in y = z; *always* overrides any definition of y from any other basic block. That is, no def-clear path goes from any other def to that use. In contrast, the use of z is called *global*, because the definition of z used in this basic block must originate in some other basic block. Data flow analysis only considers global uses.

The TestPat example in Figure 2.21 illustrates dataflow analysis for a simple string pattern matching program called TestPat written in Java.

The CFG for TestPat was previously shown in Figure 2.12, with the actual Java statements annotated on the nodes and edges.

The CFG for TestPat with def and use sets explicitly marked was shown in Figure 2.13. While numerous tools can create CFGs for programs, it helps students to

```
// Example program for pattern matching of two strings
class TestPat
{
  public static void main (String[] argv)
  {
   final int MAX = 100;
   char subject[] = new char[MAX];
   char pattern[] = new char[MAX];
   if (argv.length != 2)
   {
    System.out.println
    ("java TestPat String-Subject String-Pattern");
    return;
   }
   subject = argv[0].toCharArray();
   pattern = argv[1].toCharArray();
   TestPat testPat = new TestPat ();
   int n = 0;
   if ((n = testPat.pat (subject, pattern)) == -1)
     System.out.println
     ("Pattern string is not a substring of the subject string");
   else
     System.out.println
     ("Pattern string begins at the character " + n);
  }

  public TestPat ()
  { }

  public int pat (char[] subject, char[] pattern)
  {
  // Post: if pattern is not a substring of subject, return -1
  //       else return (zero-based) index where the pattern (first)
  //       starts in subject

   final int NOTFOUND = -1;
   int  iSub = 0, rtnIndex = NOTFOUND;
   boolean isPat  = false;
   int subjectLen = subject.length;
   int patternLen = pattern.length;

   while (isPat == false && iSub + patternLen - 1 < subjectLen)
   {
    if (subject [iSub] == pattern [0])
    {
     rtnIndex = iSub; // Starting at zero
     isPat = true;
     for (int iPat = 1; iPat < patternLen; iPat ++)
     {
      if (subject[iSub + iPat] != pattern[iPat])
      {
       rtnIndex = NOTFOUND;
       isPat = false;
       break;  // out of for loop
      }
     }
    }
    iSub ++;
   }
   return (rtnIndex);
  }
}
```

Figure 2.21. TestPat for data flow example.

create CFGs by hand. When doing so, a good habit is to draw the CFG first with the statements, then redraw it with the def and use sets.

Table 2.1 lists the defs and uses at each node in the CFG for TestPat This simply repeats the information in Figure 2.13, but in a convenient form. Table 2.2 contains the same information for edges. We suggest that beginning students check their

Table 2.1. Defs and uses at each node in the CFG for TestPat

node	def	use
1	{subject, pattern}	
2	{NOTFOUND, isPat, iSub, rtnIndex, subjectLen, patternLen}	{subject, pattern}
3		
4		
5	{rtnIndex, isPat, iPat}	{iSub}
6		
7		
8	{rtnIndex, isPat}	{NOTFOUND}
9	{iPat}	{iPat}
10	{iSub}	{iSub}
11		{rtnIndex}

understanding of these definitions by verifying that the contents of these two tables are correct.

Finally, we list the du-paths for each variable in TestPat followed by all the du-paths for each du-pair in Table 2.3. The first column gives the variable name, and the second gives the def node number and variable (that is, the left side of the formula that lists all the du-paths with respect to the variable, as defined in Section 2.2.2). The third column lists all the du-paths that start with that def. If a du-pair has more than one path to the same use, they are listed on multiple rows with subpaths that end with the same node number. The fourth column, "prefix?", is a notational convenience that is explained below. This information is extremely tedious to derive by hand, and testers tend to make many errors. This analysis is best done automatically.

Several def/use pairs have more than one du-path in TestPat. For example, the variable iSub is defined in node 2 and used in node 10. Three du-paths exist, [2,3,4,10](iSub), [2,3,4,5,6,10](iSub), and [2,3,4,5,6,7,8,10](iSub).

Table 2.2. Defs and uses at each edge in the CFG for TestPat.

edge	use
(1, 2)	
(2, 3)	
(3, 4)	{iSub, patternLen, subjectLen, isPat}
(3, 11)	{iSub, patternLen, subjectLen, IsPat}
(4, 5)	{subject, iSub, pattern}
(4, 10)	{subject, iSub, pattern}
(5, 6)	
(6, 7)	{iPat, patternLen}
(6, 10)	{iPat, patternLen}
(7, 8)	{subject, iSub, iPat, pattern}
(7, 9)	{subject, iSub, iPat, pattern}
(8, 10)	
(9, 6)	
(10, 3)	

Table 2.3. Du-path sets for each variable in TestPat

variable	du-path set	du-paths	prefix?
NOTFOUND	du (2, NOTFOUND)	[2,3,4,5,6,7,8]	
rtnIndex	du (2, rtnIndex)	[2,3,11]	
	du (5, rtnIndex)	[5,6,10,3,11]	
	du (8, rtnIndex)	[8,10,3,11]	
iSub	du (2, iSub)	[2,3,4]	Yes
		[2,3,4,5]	Yes
		[2,3,4,5,6,7,8]	Yes
		[2,3,4,5,6,7,9]	
		[2,3,4,5,6,10]	
		[2,3,4,5,6,7,8,10]	
		[2,3,4,10]	
		[2,3,11]	
	du (10, iSub)	[10,3,4]	Yes
		[10,3,4,5]	Yes
		[10,3,4,5,6,7,8]	Yes
		[10,3,4,5,6,7,9]	
		[10,3,4,5,6,10]	
		[10,3,4,5,6,7,8,10]	
		[10,3,4,10]	
		[10,3,11]	
iPat	du (5, iPat)	[5,6,7]	Yes
		[5,6,10]	
		[5,6,7,8]	
		[5,6,7,9]	
	du (9, iPat)	[9,6,7]	Yes
		[9,6,10]	
		[9,6,7,8]	
		[9,6,7,9]	
isPat	du (2, isPat)	[2,3,4]	
		[2,3,11]	
	du (5, isPat)	[5,6,10,3,4]	
		[5,6,10,3,11]	
	du (8, isPat)	[8,10,3,4]	
		[8,10,3,11]	
subject	du (1, subject)	[1,2]	Yes
		[1,2,3,4,5]	Yes
		[1,2,3,4,10]	
		[1,2,3,4,5,6,7,8]	
		[1,2,3,4,5,6,7,9]	
pattern	du (1, pattern)	[1,2]	Yes
		[1,2,3,4,5]	Yes
		[1,2,3,4,10]	
		[1,2,3,4,5,6,7,8]	
		[1,2,3,4,5,6,7,9]	
subjectLen	du (2, subjectLen)	[2,3,4]	
		[2,3,11]	
patternLen	du (2, patternLen)	[2,3,4]	Yes
		[2,3,11]	
		[2,3,4,5,6,7]	
		[2,3,4,5,6,10]	

Table 2.4. Test paths to satisfy all du-paths coverage on TestPat

test case (subject,pattern,output)	test path(t)
(a, bc, −1)	[1,2,3,11]
(ab, a, 0)	[1,2,3,4,5,6,10,3,11]
(ab, ab, 0)	[1,2,3,4,5,6,7,9,6,10,3,11]
(ab, ac, −1)	[1,2,3,4,5,6,7,8,10,3,11]
(ab, b, 1)	[1,2,3,4,10,3,4,5,6,10,3,11]
(ab, c, −1)	[1,2,3,4,10,3,4,10,3,11]
(abc, abc, 0)	[1,2,3,4,5,6,7,9,6,7,9,6,10,3,11]
(abc, abd, −1)	[1,2,3,4,5,6,7,9,6,7,8,10,3,11]
(abc, ac −1)	[1,2,3,4,5,6,7,8,10,3,4,10,3,11]
(abc, ba, −1)	[1,2,3,4,10,3,4,5,6,7,8,10,3,11]
(abc, bc, 1)	[1,2,3,4,10,3,4,5,6,7,9,6,10,3,11]

One optimization uses the fact that a du-path must be toured by any test that tours an extension of that du-path. These du-paths are marked with the annotation "Yes" in the prefix? column of the table. For example, [2,3,4](iSub) is necessarily toured by any test that tours the du-path [2,3,4,5,6,7,8](iSub), because [2,3,4] is a prefix of [2,3,4,5,6,7,8]. Thus, the path is not considered in the subsequent table that relates du-paths to test paths that tour them. One has to be a bit careful with this optimization, since the extended du-path may be infeasible even if the prefix is not.

Table 2.4 shows that a relatively small set of 11 test cases satisfies all du-paths coverage on this example. (One du-path is infeasible.) The reader may wish to evaluate this test set with the non-data flow graph coverage criteria.

Table 2.5 lists which du-paths are toured by each test case. For each test case in the first column, the test path that is executed by that test is shown in the second column, and the du-path that is toured by the test path is shown in the third column.

Table 2.5. Test paths and du-paths covered on TestPat.

test case (subject,pattern, output)	test path(t)	du-path toured
(ab, ac, −1)	[1,2,3,4,5,6,7,8,10,3,11]	[2,3,4,5,6,7,8](NOTFOUND)
(a, bc, −1)	[1,2,3,11]	[2,3,11](rtnIndex)
(ab, a, 0)	[1,2,3,4,5,6,10,3,11]	[5,6,10,3,11](rtnIndex)
(ab, ac, −1)	[1,2,3,4,5,6,7,8,10,3,11]	[8,10,3,11](rtnIndex)
(ab, ab, 0)	[1,2,3,4,5,6,7,9,6,10,3,11]	[2,3,4,5,6,7,9] (iSub)
(ab, a, 0)	[1,2,3,4,5,6,10,3,11]	[2,3,4,5,6,10](iSub)
(ab, ac, −1)	[1,2,3,4,5,6,7,8,10,3,11]	[2,3,4,5,6,7,8,10](iSub)
(ab, c, −1)	[1,2,3,4,10,3,4,10,3,11]	[2,3,4,10](iSub)
(a, bc, −1)	[1,2,3,11]	[2,3,11] (iSub)
(abc, bc, 1)	[1,2,3,4,10,3,4,5,6,7,9,6,10,3,11]	[10,3,4,5,6,7,9](iSub)
(ab, b, 1)	[1,2,3,4,10,3,4,5,6,10,3,11]	[10,3,4,5,6,10](iSub)
(abc, ba, −1)	[1,2,3,4,10,3,4,5,6,7,8,10,3,11]	[10,3,4,5,6,7,8,10](iSub)
(ab, c, −1)	[1,2,3,4,10,3,4,10,3,11]	[10,3,4,10](iSub)

Table 2.5. *Continued*

test case (subject,pattern, output)	test path(t)	du-path toured
(ab, a, 0)	[1,2,3,4,5,6,10,3,11]	[10,3,11](iSub)
(ab, a, 0)	[1,2,3,4,5,6,10,3,11]	[5,6,10](iPat)
(ab, ac, −1)	[1,2,3,4,5,6,7,8,10,3,11]	[5,6,7,8](iPat)
(ab, ab, 0)	[1,2,3,4,5,6,7,9,6,10,3,11]	[5,6,7,9](iPat)
(ab, ab, 0)	[1,2,3,4,5,6,7,9,6,10,3,11]	[9,6,10](iPat)
(abc, abd, −1)	[1,2,3,4,5,6,7,9,6,7,8,10,3,11]	[9,6,7,8](iPat)
(abc, abc, 0)	[1,2,3,4,5,6,7,9,6,7,9,6,10,3,11]	[9,6,7,9](iPat)
(ab, ac, −1)	[1,2,3,4,5,6,7,8,10,3,11]	[2,3,4](isPat)
(a, bc, −1)	[1,2,3,11]	[2,3,11](isPat)
No test case	Infeasible	[5,6,10,3,4](isPat)
(ab, a, 0)	[1,2,3,4,5,6,10,3,11]	[5,6,10,3,11](isPat)
(abc, ac −1)	[1,2,3,4,5,6,7,8,10,3,4,10,3,11]	[8,10,3,4](isPat)
(ab, ac, −1)	[1,2,3,4,5,6,7,8,10,3,11]	[8,10,3,11](isPat)
(ab, c, −1)	[1,2,3,4,10,3,4,10,3,11]	[1,2,3,4,10](subject)
(ab, ac, −1)	[1,2,3,4,5,6,7,8,10,3,11]	[1,2,3,4,5,6,7,8](subject)
(ab, ab, 0)	[1,2,3,4,5,6,7,9,6,10,3,11]	[1,2,3,4,5,6,7,9](subject)
(ab, c, −1)	[1,2,3,4,10,3,4,10,3,11]	[1,2,3,4,10](pattern)
(ab, ac, −1)	[1,2,3,4,5,6,7,8,10,3,11]	[1,2,3,4,5,6,7,8](pattern)
(ab, ab, 0)	[1,2,3,4,5,6,7,9,6,10,3,11]	[1,2,3,4,5,6,7,9](pattern)
(ab, c, −1)	[1,2,3,4,10,3,4,10,3,11]	[2,3,4](subjectLen)
(a, bc, −1)	[1,2,3,11]	[2,3,11](subjectLen)
(a, bc, −1)	[1,2,3,11]	[2,3,11](patternLen)
(ab, ac, −1)	[1,2,3,4,5,6,7,8,10,3,11]	[2,3,4,5,6,7](patternLen)
(ab, a, 0)	[1,2,3,4,5,6,10,3,11]	[2,3,4,5,6,10](patternLen)

EXERCISES
Section 2.3.

1. Use the following program fragment for questions (a)–(e) below.

```
w = x;        // node 1
if (m > 0)
{
  w++;        // node 2
}
else
{
  w=2*w;      // node 3
}
// node 4 (no executable statement)
if (y <= 10)
{
  x = 5*y;    // node 5
}
else
```

```
{
   x = 3*y+5;  // node 6
}
z = w + x;    // node 7
```

    (a) Draw a control flow graph for this program fragment. Use the node numbers given above.

    (b) Which nodes have defs for variable w?

    (c) Which nodes have uses for variable w?

    (d) Are there any du-paths with respect to variable w from node 1 to node 7? If not, explain why not. If any exist, show one.

    (e) Enumerate all of the du-paths for variables w and x.

2. Select a commercial coverage tool of your choice. Note that some have free trial evaluations. Choose a tool, download it, and run it on some software. You can use one of the examples from this text, software from your work environment, or software available over the Web. Write up a short summary report of your experience with the tool. Be sure to include any problems installing or using the tool. The main grading criterion is that you actually collect some coverage data for a reasonable set of tests on some program.

3. Consider the pattern matching example in Figure 2.21. Instrument the code so as to be able to produce the execution paths reported in the text for this example. That is, on a given test execution, your instrumentation program should compute and print the corresponding test path. Run the instrumented program on the test cases listed at the end of Section 2.3.

4. Consider the pattern matching example in Figure 2.21. In particular, consider the final table of tests in Section 2.3. Consider the variable *iSub*. Number the (unique) test cases, starting at 1, from the top of the *iSub* part of the table. For example, $(ab, c, -1)$, which appears twice in the *iSub* portion of the table, should be labeled test $t4$.

    (a) Give a minimal test set that satisfies *all defs* coverage. Use the test cases given.

    (b) Give a minimal test set that satisfies *all uses* coverage.

    (c) Give a minimal test set that satisfies *all du-paths* coverage.

5. Again consider the pattern matching example in Figure 2.21. Instrument the code so as to produce the execution paths reported in the text for this example. That is, on a given test execution, your tool should compute and print the corresponding test path. Run the following three test cases and answer questions (a)–(g) below:

    ■ *subject* = "brown owl" *pattern* = "wl" *expected output* = 7

    ■ *subject* = "brown fox" *pattern* = "dog" *expected output* = -1

    ■ *subject* = "fox" *pattern* = "brown" *expected output* = -1

    (a) Find the actual path followed by each test case.

    (b) For each path, give the du-paths that the path tours in the table at the end of Section 2.3. To reduce the scope of this exercise, consider only the following du-paths: *du (10, iSub)*, *du (2, isPat)*, *du (5, isPat)*, and *du (8, isPat)*.

    (c) Explain why the du-path [5, 6, 10, 3, 4] cannot be toured by any test path.

(d) Select tests from the table at the end of Section 2.3 to complete coverage of the (feasible) du-paths that are uncovered in question a.

(e) From the tests above, find a minimal set of tests that achieves All-Defs coverage with respect to the variable *isPat*.

(f) From the tests above, find a minimal set of tests that achieves All-Uses Coverage with respect to the variable *isPat*.

(g) Is there any difference between All-Uses coverage and all du-paths coverage with respect to the variable *isPat* in the *pat* method?

6. Use the following method **fmtRewrap()** for questions a–e below.

```
1. /** ****************************************************
2.  *  Rewraps the string (Similar to the Unix fmt).
3.  *  Given a string S, eliminate existing CRs and add CRs to the
4.  *  closest spaces before column N.  Two CRs in a row are considered to
5.  *  be "hard CRs" and are left alone.
7.  ***************************************************** /
6.
8. static final char CR = '\n';
9. static final int inWord       = 0;
10. static final int betweenWord = 1;
11. static final int lineBreak    = 2;
12. static final int crFound      = 3;
13. static private String fmtRewrap (String S, int N)
14. {
15.    int state = betweenWord;
16.    int lastSpace = -1;
17.    int col = 1;
18.    int i = 0;
19.    char c;
20.
21.    char SArr [] = S.toCharArray();
22.    while (i < S.length())
23.    {
24.      c = SArr[i];
25.      col++;
26.      if (col >= N)
27.         state = lineBreak;
28.      else if (c == CR)
29.         state = crFound;
30.      else if (c == ' ')
31.         state = betweenWord;
32.      else
33.         state = inWord;
34.      switch (state)
35.      {
36.      case betweenWord:
```

```
37.         lastSpace = i;
38.         break;
39.
40.     case lineBreak:
41.        SArr [lastSpace] = CR;
42.        col = i-lastSpace;
43.        break;
44.
45.     case crFound:
46.        if (i+1 < S.length() && SArr[i+1] == CR)
47.        {
48.           i++; // Two CRs => hard return
49.           col = 1;
50.        }
51.        else
52.           SArr[i] = ";
53.        break;
54.
55.     case inWord:
56.     default:
57.        break;
58.     } // end switch
59.     i++;
60.   } // end while
61.   S = new String (SArr) + CR;
62.   return (S);
63. }
```

(a) Draw the control flow graph for the **fmtRewrap()** method.
(b) For **fmtRewrap()**, find a test case such that the corresponding test path visits the edge that connects the beginning of the **while** statement to the **S = new String(SArr) + CR;** statement **without** going through the body of the while loop.
(c) Enumerate the test requirements for node coverage, edge coverage, and prime path coverage for the graph for **fmtRewrap()**.
(d) List test paths that achieve node coverage but not edge coverage on the graph.
(e) List test paths that achieve edge coverage but not prime path coverage on the graph.

7. Use the following method **printPrimes()** for questions a–f below.

```
1. /** **************************************************
2.  * Finds and prints n prime integers
3.  * Jeff Offutt, Spring 2003
4.  ************************************************** */
5. private static void printPrimes (int n)
6. {
```

```
7.   int curPrime;        // Value currently considered for primeness
8.   int numPrimes;       // Number of primes found so far.
9.   boolean isPrime;     // Is curPrime prime?
10.  int [] primes = new int [MAXPRIMES]; // The list of prime numbers.
11.
12.  // Initialize 2 into the list of primes.
13.  primes [0] = 2;
14.  numPrimes = 1;
15.  curPrime  = 2;
16.  while (numPrimes < n)
17.  {
18.    curPrime++; // next number to consider ...
19.    isPrime = true;
20.    for (int i = 0; i <= numPrimes-1; i++)
21.    { // for each previous prime.
22.      if (isDivisible (primes[i], curPrime))
23.        { // Found a divisor, curPrime is not prime.
24.          isPrime = false;
25.          break; // out of loop through primes.
26.        }
27.    }
28.    if (isPrime)
29.    { // save it!
30.        primes[numPrimes] = curPrime;
31.        numPrimes++;
32.    }
33.  } // End while
34.
35.  // Print all the primes out.
36.  for (int i = 0; i <= numPrimes-1; i++)
37.  {
38.    System.out.println ("Prime: " + primes[i]);
39.  }
40. } // end printPrimes
```

(a) Draw the control flow graph for the **printPrimes()** method.
(b) Consider test cases $t1 = (n = 3)$ and $t2 = (n = 5)$. Although these tour the same prime paths in *printPrimes()*, they do not necessarily find the same faults. Design a simple fault that $t2$ would be more likely to discover than $t1$ would.
(c) For *printPrimes()*, find a test case such that the corresponding test path visits the edge that connects the beginning of the **while** statement to the **for** statement **without** going through the body of the while loop.
(d) Enumerate the test requirements for node coverage, edge coverage, and prime path coverage for the graph for *printPrimes()*.

(e) List test paths that achieve node coverage but not edge coverage on the graph.

(f) List test paths that achieve edge coverage but not prime path coverage on the graph.

2.4 GRAPH COVERAGE FOR DESIGN ELEMENTS

Use of data abstraction and object-oriented software has led to an increased emphasis on modularity and reuse. This means that testing of software based on various parts of the design (*design elements*) is becoming more important than in the past. These activities are usually associated with integration testing. One of the benefits of modularity is that the software components can be tested independently, which is usually done by programmers during unit and module testing.

2.4.1 Structural Graph Coverage for Design Elements

Graph coverage for design elements usually starts by creating graphs that are based on couplings between software components. *Coupling* measures the dependency relations between two units by reflecting their interconnections; faults in one unit may affect the coupled unit. Coupling provides summary information about the design and the structure of the software. Most test criteria for design elements require that various connections among program components be visited.

The most common graph used for structural design coverage is the *call graph*. In a call graph, the nodes represent methods (or units) and the edges represent method calls. Figure 2.22 represents a small program that contains six methods. Method A calls B, C, and D, and C in turn calls E and F, and D also calls F.

The coverage criteria from Section 2.2.1 can be applied to call graphs. Node coverage requires that each method be called at least once and is also called *method coverage*. Edge coverage requires that each call be executed at least once and is also called *call coverage*. For the example in Figure 2.22, node coverage requires

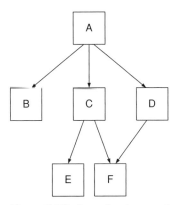

Figure 2.22. A simple call graph.

that each method be called at least once, whereas edge coverage requires that F be called at least twice, once from C and once from D.

Application to Modules

Recall from Chapter 1 that a module is a collection of related units, for example a class is Java's version of a module. As opposed to complete programs, the units in a class may not all call each other. Thus, instead of being able to obtain one connected call graph, we may generate several disconnected call graphs. In a simple degenerative case (such as for a simple stack), there may be no calls between units. In these cases, module testing with this technique is not appropriate. Techniques based on sequences of calls are needed.

Inheritance and Polymorphism

The object-oriented language features of inheritance and polymorphism introduce new abilities for designers and programmers, but also new problems for testers. As of this writing, it is still not clear how best to test these language features or what criteria are appropriate. This text introduces the current state of knowledge; the interested reader is encouraged to keep up with the literature for continuing results and techniques for testing OO software. The bibliographic notes give some current references, and further ideas are discussed in Chapter 7. The most obvious graph to create for testing these features (which we collectively call "the OO language features") is the inheritance hierarchy. Figure 2.23 represents a small inheritance hierarchy with four classes. Classes C and D inherit from B, and B in turn inherits from A.

The coverage criteria from Section 2.2.1 can be applied to inheritance hierarchies in ways that are superficially simple, but have some subtle problems. In OO programming, classes are not directly tested because they are not executable. In fact, the edges in the inheritance hierarchy do not represent execution flow at all, but rather inheritance dependencies. To apply any type of coverage, we first need a model for

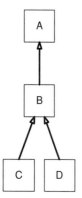

Figure 2.23. A simple inheritance hierarchy.

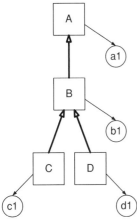

Figure 2.24. An   inheritance   hierarchy   with
objects instantiated.

what coverage means. The first step is to require that objects be instantiated for
some or all of the classes. Figure 2.24 shows the inheritance hierarchy from Figure
2.23 with one object instantiated for each class.

The most obvious interpretation of node coverage for this graph is to require
that at least one object be created for each class. However, this seems weak because
it says nothing about execution. The logical extension is to require that for each
object of each class, the call graph must be covered according to the call coverage
criterion above. Thus, the *OO call coverage* criterion can be called an "aggregation
criterion" because it requires call coverage to be applied on at least one object for
each class.

An extension of this is the *all object call* criterion, which requires that call coverage be satisfied for every object that is instantiated for every class.

2.4.2 Data Flow Graph Coverage for Design Elements

Control connections among design elements are simple and straightforward and
tests based on them are probably not very effective at finding faults. On the other
hand, data flow connections are often very complex and difficult to analyze. For
a tester, that should immediately suggest that they are a rich source for software
faults. The primary issue is where the defs and uses occur. When testing program
units, the defs and uses are in the same unit. During integration testing, defs and
uses are in different units. This section starts with some standard compiler/program
analysis terms.

A *caller* is a unit that invokes another unit, the *callee*. The statement that makes
the call is the *call site*. An *actual parameter* is in the caller; its value is assigned to
a *formal parameter* in the callee. The *interface* between two units is the mapping of
actual to formal parameters.

The underlying premise of the data flow testing criteria for design elements is
that to achieve confidence in the interfaces between integrated program units, it
must be ensured that variables defined in caller units be appropriately used in callee

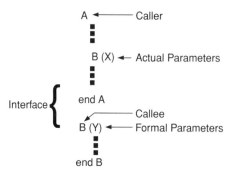

Figure 2.25. An example of parameter coupling.

units. This technique can be limited to the unit interfaces, allowing us to restrict our attention to the **last** definitions of variables just **before** calls to and returns from the called units, and the **first** uses of variables just **after** calls to and returns from the called unit.

Figure 2.25 illustrates the relationships that the data flow criteria will test. The criteria require execution from definitions of actual parameters through calls to uses of formal parameters.

Three types of data flow couplings have been identified. The most obvious is *parameter coupling*, where parameters are passed in calls. *Shared data coupling* occurs when two units access the same data object as a global or other non-local variable, and *external device coupling* occurs when two units access the same external medium such as a file. In the following, all examples and discussion will be in terms of parameters and it will be understood that the concepts apply equally to shared data and external device coupling. We use the general term *coupling variable* for variables that are defined in one unit and used in another.

This form of data flow is concerned only with last-defs before calls and returns and first-uses after calls and returns. That is, it is concerned only with defs and uses immediately surrounding the calls between methods. The last-defs before a call are locations with defs that reach uses at callsites and the last-defs before a return are locations with defs that reach a return statement. The following definitions assume a variable that is defined in either the caller or the callee, and used in the other.

> *Definition 2.40 Last-def:* The set of nodes that define a variable x for which there is a def-clear path from the node through the call site to a use in the other unit.

The variable can be passed as a parameter, a return value, or a shared variable reference. If the function has no return statement, an implicit return statement is assumed to exist at the last statement in the method.

The definition for first-use is complementary to that of last-def. It depends on paths that are not only def-clear, but also use-clear. A path from n_i to n_j is *use-clear* with respect to variable v if for every node n_k on the path, $k \neq i$ and $k \neq j$, v is not in $use(n_k)$. Assume that the variable y is used in one of the units after having been defined in the other. Assume that a variable y has received a value that has been

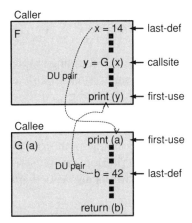

Figure 2.26. Coupling du-pairs.

passed from the other unit, either through parameter passing, a return statement, shared data, or other value passing.

> *Definition 2.41 First-use:* The set of nodes that have uses of *y* and for which there exists a path that is def-clear and use-clear from the entry point (if the use is in the callee) or the call site (if the use is in the caller) to the nodes.

Figure 2.26 shows a caller F() and a callee G(). The callsite has two du-pairs; x in F() is passed to a in G() and b in G() is returned and assigned to y in F(). Note that the assignment to y in F() is explicitly **not** the use, but considered to be part of the transfer. Its use is further down, in the print(y) statement.

This definition allows for one anomaly when a return value is not explicitly assigned to a variable, as in the statement print (f(x)). In this case, an implicit assignment is assumed and the first-use is in the print(y) statement.

Figure 2.27 illustrates last-defs and first-uses between two units with two partial CFGs. The unit on the left, the caller, calls the callee B, with one actual parameter, X, which is assigned to formal parameter y. X is defined at nodes 1, 2 and 3, but the def at node 1 cannot reach the call site at node 4, thus the last-defs for X is the set {2, 3}. The formal parameter y is used at nodes 11, 12, and 13, but no use-clear path goes from the entry point at node 10 to 13, so the first-uses for y is the set {11, 12}.

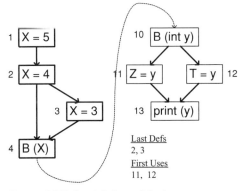

Figure 2.27. Last-defs and first-uses.

Recall that a du-path is a path from a def to a use in the same graph. This notion is refined to a *coupling du-path* with respect to a coupling variable x. A coupling du-path is a path from a last-def to a first-use.

The coverage criteria from Section 2.2.2 can now be applied to coupling graphs. All-Defs coverage requires that a path be executed from every last-def to at least one first-use. In this context, all-defs is called *All-Coupling-Def* coverage. All-Uses coverage requires that a path be executed from every last-def to every first-use. In this context, All-Uses is also called *All-Coupling-Use* coverage.

Finally, All-du-Paths coverage requires that we tour every simple path from every last-def to every first-use. As before, the All-du-Paths criterion can be satisfied by tours that include sidetrips. In this context, All-du-Paths is also called *All-Coupling-du-Paths* coverage.

Example

Now we will turn to an example to illustrate coupling data flow. Class Quadratic in Figure 2.28 computes the quadratic root of an equation, given three integer coefficients. The call to Root() on line 34 in main passes in three parameters. Each of the variables X, Y, and Z have three last-defs in the caller at lines 16, 17, 18, lines 23, 24, and 25, and lines 30, 31, and 32. They are mapped to formal parameters A, B, and C in Root(). All three variables have a first-use at line 47. The class variables Root1 and Root2 are defined in the callee and used in the caller. Their last-defs are at lines 53 and 54 and the first-use is at line 37.

The value of local variable Result is returned to the caller, with two possible last-defs at lines 50 and 55 and first-use at line 35.

The coupling du-pairs can be listed using pairs of triples. Each triple gives a unit name, variable name, and a line number. The first triple in a pair says where the variable is defined, and the second where it is used. The complete set of coupling du-pairs for class Quadratic is

```
(main(), X, 16) -- (Root(), A, 47)
(main(), Y, 17) -- (Root(), B, 47)
(main(), Z, 18) -- (Root(), C, 47)
(main(), X, 23) -- (Root(), A, 47)
(main(), Y, 24) -- (Root(), B, 47)
(main(), Z, 25) -- (Root(), C, 47)
(main(), X, 30) -- (Root(), A, 47)
(main(), Y, 31) -- (Root(), B, 47)
(main(), Z, 32) -- (Root(), C, 47)
(Root(), Root1, 53) -- (main(), Root1, 37)
(Root(), Root2, 54) -- (main(), Root2, 37)
(Root(), Result, 50) -- (main(), ok, 35)
(Root(), Result, 55) -- (main(), ok, 35)
```

A couple of notes are important to remember about coupling data flow. First, only variables that are used or defined in the callee are considered. That is, last-defs that have no corresponding first-uses are not useful for testing. Second, we must

```
 1  // Program to compute the quadratic root for two numbers
 2  import java.lang.Math;
 3
 4  class Quadratic
 5  {
 6  private static double Root1, Root2;
 7
 8  public static void main (String[] argv)
 9  {
10    int X, Y, Z;
11    boolean ok;
12    if (argv.length == 3)
13    {
14      try
15      {
16        X = Integer.parseInt (argv[0]);
17        Y = Integer.parseInt (argv[1]);
18        Z = Integer.parseInt (argv[2]);
19      }
20      catch (NumberFormatException e)
21      {
22        System.out.println ("Inputs not integers, using 8, 10, -33.");
23        X = 8;
24        Y = 10;
25        Z = -33;
26      }
27    }
28    else
29    {
30      X = 8;
31      Y = 10;
32      Z = -33;
33    }
34    ok = Root (X, Y, Z);
35    if (ok)
36      System.out.println
37         ("Quadratic: Root 1 = " + Root1 + ", Root 2 = " + Root2);
38    else
39      System.out.println ("No solution.");
40  }
41
42  // Finds the quadratic root, A must be non-zero
43  private static boolean Root (int A, int B, int C)
44  {
45    double D;
46    boolean Result;
47    D = (double)(B*B) - (double)(4.0*A*C);
48    if (D < 0.0)
49    {
50      Result = false;
51      return (Result);
52    }
53    Root1 = (double) ((-B + Math.sqrt(D)) / (2.0*A));
54    Root2 = (double) ((-B - Math.sqrt(D)) / (2.0*A));
55    Result = true;
56    return (Result);
57  } // End method Root
58
59  } // End class Quadratic
```

Figure 2.28. Quadratic root program.

remember implicit initialization of class and global variables. In some languages (such as Java and C), class and instance variables are given default values. These definitions can be modeled as occurring at the beginning of appropriate units. For example, class-level initializations may be considered to occur in the main() method or in constructors. Although other methods that access class variables may use the default values on the first call, it is also possible for such methods to use values written by other methods, and hence the normal coupling data flow analysis methods should

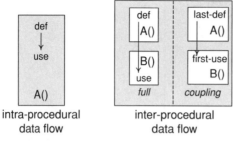

Figure 2.29. Def-use pairs under intra-procedural and inter-procedural data flow.

be employed. Also, this analysis is specifically not considering "transitive du-pairs." That is, if unit A calls B, and B calls C, last-defs in A do **not** reach first-uses in C. This type of analysis is prohibitively expensive with current technologies and of questionable value. Finally, data flow testing has traditionally taken an abstract view of array references. Identifying and keeping track of individual array references is an undecidable problem in general and very expensive even in finite cases. So, most tools consider a reference to one element of an array to be a reference to the entire array.

Inheritance and Polymorphism (*Advanced topic*)
The previous discussion covers the most commonly used form of data flow testing as applied beyond the method level. However, the flow of data along couplings between callers and callees is only one type of a very complicated set of data definition and use pairs. Consider Figure 2.29, which shows the types of du-pairs discussed so far. On the left is a method, A(), which contains a def and a use. (For this discussion we will omit the variable and assume that all du-pairs refer to the same variable.) The right illustrates that there are two types of inter-procedural du-pairs.

Full inter-procedural data flow identifies **all** du-pairs between a caller (A()) and a callee (B()). *Coupling inter-procedural* data flow is as described in Section 2.4.2; identifying du-pairs between last-defs and first-uses.

Figure 2.30 illustrates du-pairs in object-oriented software. DU pairs are usually based on the *class* or *state* variables defined for the class. The left picture in Figure 2.30 shows the "direct" case for OO du-pairs. A *coupling method*, F(), calls

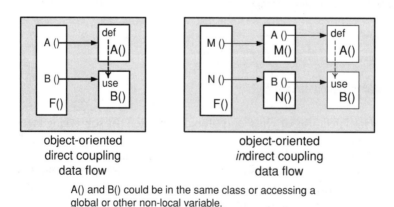

A() and B() could be in the same class or accessing a global or other non-local variable.

Figure 2.30. Def-use pairs in object-oriented software.

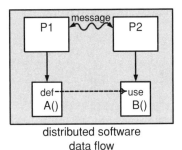

distributed software
data flow

"message" could be HTTP, RMI, or other mechanism.
A() and B() could be in the same class or accessing a
persistent variable such as in a Web session.

Figure 2.31. Def-use pairs in web applications
and other distributed software.

two methods, A() and B(). A() defines a variable and B() uses it. For the variable
reference to be the same, both A() and B() must be called through the same *instance
context*, or object reference. That is, if the calls are o.A() and o.B(), they are called
through the instance context of o. If the calls are not made through the same instance
context, the definition and use will be to different instances of the variable.

The right side of Figure 2.30 illustrates "indirect" du-pairs. In this scenario, the
coupling method F() calls two methods, M() and N(), which in turn call two other
methods, A() and B(). The def and use are in A() and B(), so the reference is indirect.
The analysis for indirect du-pairs is considerably more complicated than for direct
du-pairs. It should be obvious that there can be more than one call between the
coupling method and the methods with the def and use.

In OO data flow testing, the methods A() and B() could be in the same class, or
they could be in different classes and accessing the same global variables.

Finally, Figure 2.31 illustrates du-pairs in distributed software. P1 and P2 are two
processes, threads, or other distributed software components, and they call A() and
B(), which def and use the same variable. The distribution and communication could
use any of a number of methods, including HTTP (Web-based), remote method
invocation (RMI), or CORBA. A() and B() could be in the same class or could access
a persistent variable such as a Web session variable or permanent data store. While
this sort of "very loosely coupled" software can be expected to have far fewer du-
pairs, identifying them, finding def-clear paths between them, and designing test
cases to cover them is quite complicated.

EXERCISES

Section 2.4.

1. Use the class *Stutter* in Figures 2.34 and 2.35 in Section 2.5 to answer questions
   a–d below.
   (a) Draw a control flow graph for Stutter.
   (b) List all the call sites.
   (c) List all du-pairs for each call site.
   (d) Create test data to satisfy *All-Coupling-Use coverage* for Stutter.

2. Use the following program fragment for questions (a)–(e) below.

```
public static void f1 (int x, int y)
{
   if (x < y) { f2 (y); } else { f3 (y); };
}
public static void f2 (int a)
{
   if (a % 2 == 0) { f3 (2*a); };
}
public static void f3 (int b)
{
   if (b > 0) { f4(); } else { f5(); };
}
public static void f4() {... f6()....}
public static void f5() {... f6()....}
public static void f6() {...}
```

Use the following test inputs:
- $t1 = f1 (0, 0)$
- $t2 = f1 (1, 1)$
- $t3 = f1 (0, 1)$
- $t4 = f1 (3, 2)$
- $t5 = f1 (3, 4)$

(a) Draw the call graph for this program fragment.
(b) Give the path in the graph followed by each test.
(c) Find a minimal test set that achieves node coverage.
(d) Find a minimal test set that achieves edge coverage.
(e) Give the (maximal) prime paths in the graph. Give the maximal prime path that is not covered by any of the test paths above.

3. Use the following methods **trash()** and **takeOut()** to answer questions (a)–(c).

```
1 public void trash (int x)          15 public int takeOut (int a, int b)
2 {                                   16 {
3    int m, n;                        17    int d, e;
4                                     18
5    m = 0;                           19    d = 42*a;
6    if (x > 0)                       20    if (a > 0)
7       m = 4;                        21       e = 2*b+d;
8    if (x > 5)                       22    else
9       n = 3*m;                      23       e = b+d;
10   else                            24    return (e);
11      n = 4*m;                     25 }
12   int o = takeOut (m, n);
13   System.out.println ("o is: " + o);
14 }
```

(a) Give all call sites using the line numbers given.

(b) Give all pairs of *last-def*s and *first-use*s.

(c) Provide test inputs that satisfy *all-coupling-uses* (note that **trash()** only has one input).

2.5 GRAPH COVERAGE FOR SPECIFICATIONS

Testers can also use software specifications as sources for graphs. The literature presents many techniques for generating graphs and criteria for covering those graphs, but most of them are in fact very similar. We begin by looking at graphs based on *sequencing constraints* among methods in classes, then graphs that represent state behavior of software.

2.5.1 Testing Sequencing Constraints

We pointed out in Section 2.4.1 that call graphs for classes often wind up being disconnected, and in many cases, such as with small abstract data types (ADTs), methods in a class share no calls at all. However, the order of calls is almost always constrained by rules. For example, many ADTs must be initialized before being used, we cannot pop an element from a stack until something has been pushed onto it, and we cannot remove an element from a queue until an element has been put on it. These rules impose constraints on the order in which methods may be called. Generally, a *sequencing constraint* is a rule that imposes some restriction on the order in which certain methods may be called.

Sequencing constraints are sometimes explicitly expressed, sometimes implicitly expressed, and sometimes not expressed at all. Sometimes they are encoded as a precondition or other specification, but not directly as a sequencing condition. For example, consider the following precondition for DeQueue():

```
public int DeQueue ()
{
// Pre: At least one element must be on the queue.
.
:
public EnQueue (int e)
{
// Post: e is on the end of the queue.
```

Although it is not said explicitly, a wise programmer can infer that the only way an element can "be on the queue" is if EnQueue() has previously been called. Thus, an implicit sequencing constraint occurs between EnQueue() and DeQueue().

Of course, formal specifications can help make the relationships more precise. A wise tester will certainly use formal specifications when available, but a responsible tester must look for formal relationships even when they are not explicitly stated. Also, note that sequencing constraints do not capture all the behavior, but only abstract certain key aspects. The sequence constraint that EnQueue() must be called

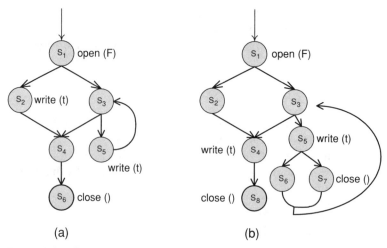

Figure 2.32. Control flow graph using the File ADT.

before DeQueue() does not capture the fact that if we only EnQueue() one item, and then try to DeQueue() two items, the queue will be empty. The precondition may capture this fact, but usually not in a formal way that automated tools can use. This kind of relationship is beyond the ability of a simple sequencing constraint but can be dealt with by some of the state behavior techniques in the next section.

This relationship is used in two places during testing. We illustrate them with a small example of a class that encapsulates operations on a file. Our class FileADT will have three methods:

- open (String fName) // Opens the file with the name fName
- close (String fName) // Closes the file and makes it unavailable for use
- write (String textLine) // Writes a line of text to the file

This class has several sequencing constraints. The statements use "must" and "should" in very specific ways. When "must" is used, it implies that violation of the constraint is a fault. When "should" is used, it implies that violation of the constraint is a potential fault, but not necessarily.

1. An open(F) must be executed before every write(t)
2. An open(F) must be executed before every close()
3. A write(t) must not be executed after a close() unless an open(F) appears in between
4. A write(t) should be executed before every close()
5. A close() must not be executed after a close() unless an open(F) appears in between
6. An open(F) must not be executed after an open(F) unless a close() appears in between

Constraints are used in testing in two ways to evaluate software that uses the class (a "client"), based on the CFG of Section 2.3.1. Consider the two (partial) CFGs in Figure 2.32, representing two units that use FileADT. We can use this graph to test the use of the FileADT class by checking for sequence violations. This can be done both statically and dynamically.

Static checks (not considered to be traditional testing) proceed by checking each constraint. First consider the write(t) statements at nodes 2 and 5 in graph (a). We can check to see whether paths exist from the open(F) at node 1 to nodes 2 and 5 (constraint 1). We can also check whether a path exists from the open(F) at node 1 to the close() at node 6 (constraint 2). For constraints 3 and 4, we can check to see if a path goes from the close() at node 6 to any of the write(t) statements, and see if a path exists from the open(F) to the close() that does not go through at least one write(t). This will uncover one possible problem, the path [1, 3, 4, 6] goes from an open(F) to a close() with no intervening write(t) calls.

For constraint 5, we can check if a path exists from a close() to a close() that does not go through an open(F). For constraint 6, we can check if a path exists from an open(F) to an open(F) that does not go through a close().

This process will find a more serious problem with graph (b) in 2.32. A path exists from the close() at node 7 to the write(t) at node 5 and to the write(t) at node 4. While this may seem simple enough not to require formalism for such small graphs, this process is quite difficult with large graphs containing dozens or hundreds of nodes.

Dynamic testing follows a slightly different approach. Consider the problem in graph (a) where no write() appears on the possible path [1, 3, 4, 6]. It is quite possible that the logic of the program dictates that the edge (3, 4) can *never* be taken unless the loop [3, 5, 3] is taken at least once. Because deciding whether the path [1, 3, 4, 6] can be taken or not is formally undecidable, this situation can be checked only by dynamic execution. Thus we generate test requirements to try to *violate* the sequencing constraints. For the FileADT class, we generate the following sets of test requirements:

1. Cover every path from the start node to every node that contains a write(t) such that the path does not go through a node containing an open(F).
2. Cover every path from the start node to every node that contains a close() such that the path does not go through a node containing an open(F).
3. Cover every path from every node that contains a close() to every node that contains a write(t) such that the path does not contain an open(F).
4. Cover every path from every node that contains an open(F) to every node that contains a close() such that the path does not go through a node containing a write(t).
5. Cover every path from every node that contains an open(F) to every node that contains an open(F).

Of course, all of these test requirements will be infeasible in well written programs. However, any tests created as a result of these requirements will almost certainly reveal a fault if one exists.

2.5.2 Testing State Behavior of Software

The other major method for using graphs based on specifications is to model state behavior of the software by developing some form of finite state machine (FSM). Over the last 25 years, many suggestions have been made for creating FSMs and how to test software based on the FSM. The topic of how to create, draw, and interpret a

FSM has filled entire textbooks, and authors have gone into great depth and effort to define what exactly goes into a state, what can go onto edges, and what causes transitions. Rather than using any particular notation, we choose to define a very generic model for FSMs that can be adapted to virtually any notation. These FSMs are essentially graphs, and the graph testing criteria already defined can be used to test software that is based on the FSM.

One of the advantages of basing tests on FSMs is that huge numbers of practical software applications are based on a FSM model or can be modeled as FSMs. Virtually all embedded software fits in this category, including software in remote controls, household appliances, watches, cars, cell phones, airplane flight guidance, traffic signals, railroad control systems, network routers, and factory automation. Indeed, most software can be modeled with FSMs, the primary limitation being the number of states needed to model the software. Word processors, for example, contain so many commands and states that modeling them as FSMs is probably impractical.

Creating FSMs often has great value. If the test engineer creates a FSM to describe existing software, he or she will almost certainly find faults in the software. Some would even argue the converse; if the designers created FSMs, the testers should not bother creating them because problems will be rare.

FSMs can be annotated with different types of actions, including actions on transitions, entry actions on nodes, and exit actions on nodes. Many languages are used to describe FSMs, including UML statecharts, finite automata, state tables (SCR), and petri nets. This book presents examples with basic features that are common to many languages. It is closest to UML statecharts, but not exactly the same.

A *finite state machine* is a graph whose nodes represent states in the execution behavior of the software and edges represent transitions among the states. A *state* represents a recognizable situation that remains in existence over some period of time. A state is defined by specific values for a set of variables; as long as those variables have those values the software is considered to be in that state. (Note that these variables are defined at the design modeling level and may not necessarily correspond to variables in the software.) A *transition* is thought of as occurring in zero time and usually represents a change to the values of one or more variables. When the variables change, the software is considered to move from the transition's *pre-state* (predecessor) to its *post-state* (successor). (If a transition's pre-state and post-state are the same, then values of state variables will not change.) FSMs often define *preconditions* or *guards* on transitions, which define values that specific variables must have for the transition to be enabled, and *triggering events*, which are changes in variable values that cause the transition to be taken. A triggering event "triggers" the change in state. For example, the modeling language SCR calls these WHEN conditions and triggering events. The values the triggering events have before the transition are called *before-values*, and the values after the transition are called *after-values*. When graphs are drawn, transitions are often annotated with the guards and the values that change.

Figure 2.33 illustrates this model with a simple transition that opens an elevator door. If the elevator button is pressed (the triggering event), the door opens only if the elevator is not moving (the precondition, *elevSpeed* = 0).

Given this type of graph, many of the previous criteria can be defined directly. Node coverage requires that each state in the FSM be visited at least once and is

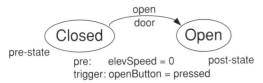

Figure 2.33. Elevator door open transition.

called *state coverage*. Edge coverage is applied by requiring that each transition in the FSM be visited at least once, which is called *transition coverage*. The edge-pair coverage criterion was originally defined for FSMs and is also called *transition-pair* and *two-trip*.

The data flow coverage criteria are a bit more troublesome for FSMs. In most formulations of FSMs, nodes are not allowed to have defs or uses of variables. That is, all of the action is on the transitions. Unlike with code-based graphs, different edges from the same node in a FSM need not have the same set of defs and uses. In addition, the semantics of the triggers imply that the effects of a change to the variables involved are felt immediately by taking a transition to the next state. That is, defs of triggering variables immediately reach uses.

Thus, the All-Defs and All-Uses criteria can only be applied meaningfully to variables involved in guards. This also brings out a more practical problem, which is that the FSMs do not always model assignment to all variables. That is, the uses are clearly marked in the FSM, but defs are not always easy to find. Because of these reasons, few attempts have been made to apply data flow criteria to FSMs.

Deriving Finite State Machine Graphs

One of the difficult parts of applying graph techniques to FSMs is deriving the FSM model of the software in the first place. As we said earlier, FSM models of the software may already exist, or may not. If not, the tester is likely to dramatically increase his or her understanding of the software by deriving the FSMs. However, it is not necessarily obvious how to go about deriving a FSM, so we offer some suggestions. This is not a complete tutorial on constructing FSMs; indeed, a number of complete texts exist on the subject and we recommend that the interested reader study these elsewhere.

This section offers some simple and straightforward suggestions to help readers who are unfamiliar with FSMs get started and avoid some of the more obvious mistakes. We offer the suggestions in terms of a running example, the class Stutter in Figures 2.34 and 2.35. Class Stutter checks each adjacent pair of words in a text file and prints a message if a pair is identical. The second author originally wrote it to edit his papers and find a common mistake mistake.

Class Stutter has a main method and three support methods. When left to their own devices, students will usually pick one of four strategies for generating FSMs from code. Each of these is discussed in turn.

1. Combining control flow graphs
2. Using the software structure
3. Modeling state variables
4. Using the implicit or explicit specifications

1. *Combining control flow graphs*: For programmers who have little or no knowledge of FSMs, this is often the most natural approach to deriving FSMs. Our experience

```
/** *********************************************************
// Stutter checks for repeat words in a text file.
// It prints a list of repeat words, by line number.
// Stutter will accept standard input or a list
// of file names.
// Jeff Offutt, June 1989 (in C), Java version March 2003
//********************************************************* */
class Stutter
{
  // Class variables used in multiple methods.
  private static boolean lastdelimit = true;
  private static String curWord = "", prevWord = "";
  private static char delimits [] =
      {" ,' ',' ',' ',' ','\t',' ','-','+','=','.',':','?',
       '&', '{', '}', '\\'}; // First char in list is a tab

  //*************************************************
  // main parses the arguments, decides if stdin
  // or a file name, and calls Stut().
  //*************************************************
  public static void main (String[] args) throws IOException
  {
    String fileName;
    FileReader myFile;
    BufferedReader inFile = null;

    if (args.length == 0)
    { // no file, use stdin
      inFile = new BufferedReader (new InputStreamReader (System.in));
    }
    else
    {
      fileName = args [0];
      if (fileName == null)
      { // no file name, use stdin
        inFile = new BufferedReader (new InputStreamReader (System.in));
      }
      else
      { // file name, open the file.
        myFile = new FileReader (fileName);
        inFile = new BufferedReader (myFile);
      }
    }

    stut (inFile);
  }

  //*************************************************
  // Stut() reads all lines in the input stream, and
  // finds words. Words are defined as being surrounded
  // by delimiters as defined in the delimits[] array.
  // Every time an end of word is found, checkDupes()
  // is called to see if it is the same as the
  // previous word.
  //*************************************************
  private static void stut (BufferedReader inFile) throws IOException
  {
    String inLine;
    char c;
    int linecnt = 1;
```

Figure 2.34. Stutter – Part A.

has been that the majority of students will use this approach if not guided away from it. A control flow graph-based FSM for class Stutter is given in Figure 2.36.

The graph in Figure 2.36 is **not** a FSM at all, and this is not the way to form graphs from software. This method has several problems, the first being that the nodes are not states. The methods must return to the appropriate callsites, which means that the graphs contain built-in nondeterminism. For example, in

```
      while ((inLine = inFile.readLine()) != null)
      { // For each line

        for (int i=0; i<inLine.length(); i++)
        { // for each character
          c = inLine.charAt(i);

          if (isDelimit (c))
          { // Found an end of a word.
            checkDupes (linecnt);
          }
          else
          {
            lastdelimit = false;
            curWord = curWord + c;
          }
        }
        linecnt++;
        checkDupes (linecnt);
      }
    } // end Stut

    //*************************************************
    // checkDupes() checks to see if the globally defined
    // curWord is the same as prevWord and prints a message
    // if they are the same.
    //^^^^^^^^^^^^^^^^^^^*****************************
    private static void checkDupes (int line)
    {
      if (lastdelimit)
        return; // already checked, keep skipping
      lastdelimit = true;
      if (curWord.equals(prevWord))
      {
        System.out.println ("Repeated word on line " + line + ": " +
                    prevWord+ " " + curWord);
      }
      else
      {
        prevWord = curWord;
      }
      curWord = "";
    } // end checkDupes

    //*************************************************
    // Checks to see if a character is a delimiter.
    //*************************************************
    private static boolean isDelimit (char C)
    {
      for (int i = 0; i < delimits.length; i++)
        if (C == delimits [i])
          return (true);
      return (false);
    }

  } // end class Stutter
```

Figure 2.35. Stutter   Part B.

Figure 2.36, there is an edge from node 2 in checkDupes() to node 6 in stut(), and also an edge from node 2 in checkDupes() to node 8 in stut(). Which edge is taken depends on whether the edge from node 6 in stut() was taken to enter checkDupes() or the edge from node 8 in stut() was taken to enter checkDupes(). Second, the implementation must be finished before the graph can be built; remember from Chapter 1 that one of our goals is to prepare tests as early as possible. Most importantly, however, this kind of graph does not scale to large software products. The graph is complicated enough with small Stutter and gets much worse with larger programs.

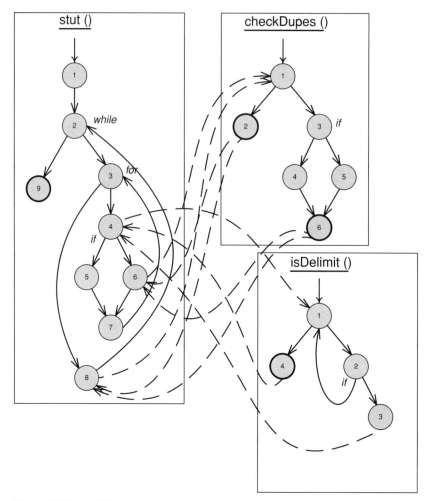

Figure 2.36. A FSM representing stutter, based on control flow graphs of the methods.

2. *Using the software structure*: A more experienced programmer may consider the overall flow of operations in the software. This might lead to something like the graph in Figure 2.37.

Although an improvement over the control flow graph, the kind of derivation shown in Figure 2.37 is very subjective. Different testers will draw different graphs, which introduces inconsistency in the testing. It also requires in-depth knowledge of the software, is not possible until at least the detailed design is ready, and is hard to scale to large programs.

3. *Modeling state variables*: A more mechanical method for deriving FSMs is to consider the values of the state variables in the program. These are usually defined early in design. The first step is to identify the state variables, then choose which ones are actually relevant to the FSM (for example, global and class variables). Class Stutter defines four state variables, lastdelimit, curWord, prevWord, and delimits. The variable delimits is defined at the class level for convenience, but should not

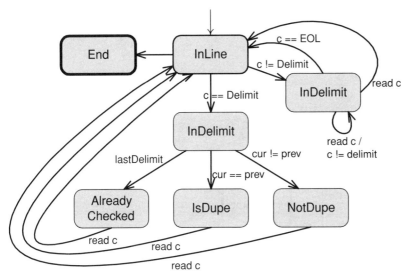

Figure 2.37. A FSM representing Stutter, based on the structure of the software.

really be considered part of the state. In fact, it is possible that it will not even be included in the design. However, lastdelimit, curWord, and prevWord are true state variables.

Theoretically, each combination of values for the three state variables defines a different state. In practice, however, this can result in an infinite number of states. For example, curWord and prevWord are strings and have an infinite number of values. Thus, it is common to identify values or ranges of values that should be represented as states. For class Stutter, the obvious approach is to consider the relationship between the two variables, yielding the following possible values:

curWord: undefined, word
prevWord: undefined, sameword, differentword
lastdelimit: true, false

where word is an arbitrary string. This combination of values leads to twelve possible states:

1. (undefined, undefined, true)
2. (undefined, undefined, false)
3. (undefined, sameword, true)
4. (undefined, sameword, false)
5. (undefined, differentword, true)
6. (undefined, differentword, false)
7. (word, undefined, true)
8. (word, undefined, false)
9. (word, sameword, true)
10. (word, sameword, false)

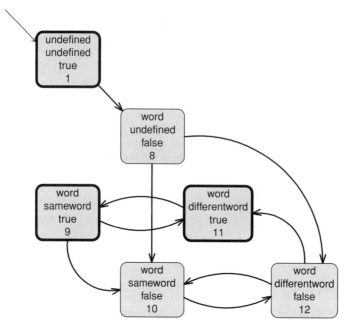

Figure 2.38. A FSM representing Stutter, based on modeling state variables.

11. (word, differentword, true)
12. (word, differentword, false)

Not every combination is possible. For example, curWord is given a value immediately and never becomes undefined thereafter. So the only possible state where curWord has the value undefined is state 1, which also happens to be the initial state. As soon as a character is read, curWord has value word and lastdelimit is set to false (state 8). When a delimiter is found, prevWord is either the same (sameword) or different (different word) from curWord (states 10 or 12). If the two words are the same, the next character read changes curWord, so the software transitions to (word, differentword, false), state 12. The complete state machine is derived in this way, by deciding all possible transitions from the states. The complete FSM for Stutter is shown in Figure 2.38. Note that it is impossible to get to state 7, so it is omitted from the FSM. Also, note that the program terminates at the end of a file, which is always just after a delimiter is found. So every state in which lastdelimit = true is a final state.

The mechanical process of this strategy is appealing because we can expect different testers to derive the same or similar FSMs. It is not yet possible at this time to completely automate this process because of the difficulty of determining transitions from the source and because the decision of which variables to model requires judgment. The software is not necessary for this diagram to be derived, but the design is needed. The FSMs that are derived by modeling state variables may not accurately reflect the software.

4. *Using the implicit or explicit specifications*: The last method for deriving FSMs relies on explicit requirements or formal specifications describing the software's behavior. A FSM for class Stutter based on this approach is shown in Figure 2.39.

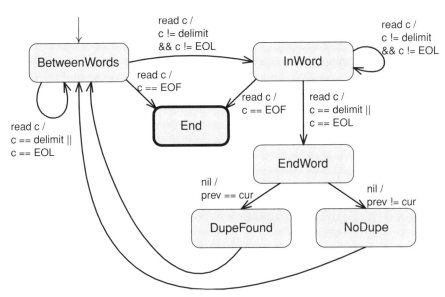

Figure 2.39. A FSM representing Stutter, based on the specifications.

This FSM looks a lot like the FSM based on the code, and this is to be expected. At the same time, FSMs based on specifications are usually cleaner and easier to understand. If the software is designed well, this type of FSM should contain the same information that UML state charts contain.

EXERCISES
Section 2.5.

1. Use the class **Queue** in Figure 2.40 for questions (a)–(f) below. The queue is managed in the usual circular fashion.
   Suppose we build a FSM where states are defined by the representation variables of **Queue**. That is, a state is a 4-tuple defined by the values for [*elements, size, front, back*]. For example, the initial state has the value [[*null, null*], 0, 0, 0], and the state that results from pushing an object *obj* onto the queue in its initial state is [[*obj, null*], 1, 0, 1].
   (a) We do not actually care which specific objects are in the queue. Consequently, there are really just four useful values for the variable *elements*. Enumerate them.
   (b) How many states are there?
   (c) How many of these states are reachable?
   (d) Show the reachable states in a drawing.
   (e) Add edges for the *enqueue*() and *dequeue*() methods. (For this assignment, ignore the exceptional returns, although you should observe that when exceptional returns are taken, none of the instance variables are modified.)
   (f) Define a small test set that achieves edge coverage. Implement and execute this test set. You might find it helpful to write a method that shows the internal variables at each call.

```
public class Queue
{ // Overview:  a Queue is a mutable, bounded FIFO data structure
  // of fixed size  (size is 2, for this exercise).
  // A typical Queue is [], [o1], or [o1, o2], where neither o1 nor o2
  // are ever null.  Older elements are listed before newer ones.
private Object[] elements;
private int size, front, back;
private static final int capacity = 2;

public Queue ()
{
  elements = new Object [capacity];
  size  = 0; front = 0; back  = 0;
}

public void enqueue (Object o)
    throws NullPointerException, IllegalStateException
{  // Modifies: this
   // Effects:  If argument is null throw NullPointerException
   // else if this is full, throw IllegalStateException,
   // else make o the newest element of this
   if (o == null)
     throw new NullPointerException ("Queue.enqueue");
   else if (size == capacity)
     throw new IllegalStateException ("Queue.enqueue");
   else
   {
     size++;
     elements [back] = o;
     back = (back+1) % capacity;
   }
}

public Object dequeue () throws IllegalStateException
{ // Modifies: this
  // Effects:   If queue is empty, throw IllegalStateException,
  // else remove and return oldest element of this

  if (size == 0)
    throw new IllegalStateException ("Queue.dequeue");
  else
  {
    size--;
    Object o = elements [ (front % capacity) ];
    elements [front] = null;
    front = (front+1) % capacity;
    return o;
  }
}

public boolean isEmpty() { return (size == 0); }
public boolean isFull() { return (size == capacity); }

public String toString()
{
  String result = "[";
  for (int i = 0; i < size; i++)
  {
    result += elements[ (front + i) % capacity ] . toString();
    if (i < size -1) {
      result += ", ";
    }
  }
  result += "]";
  return result;
}
}
```

Figure 2.40. Class Queue for exercises.

2. For the following questions (a)–(c), consider the method FSM for a (simplified) programmable thermostat. Suppose the variables that define the state and the methods that transition between states are:

partOfDay : {Wake, Sleep}
temp   : {Low, High}

// Initially "Wake" at "Low" temperature

// Effects: Advance to next part of day
public void advance();

// Effects: Make current temp higher, if possible
public void up();

// Effects: Make current temp lower, if possible
public void down();

   (a) How many states are there?
   (b) Draw and label the states (with variable values) and transitions (with method names). Notice that all of the methods are total.
   (c) A test case is simply a sequence of method calls. Provide a test set that satisfies edge coverage on your graph.

2.6 GRAPH COVERAGE FOR USE CASES

UML use cases are widely used to clarify and express software requirements. They are meant to describe sequences of actions that software performs as a result of inputs from the users; that is, they help express the **workflow** of a computer application. Because use cases are developed early in software development, they can be help the tester start testing activities early.

Many books and papers can help the reader develop use cases. As with FSMs, it is not the purpose of this book to explain how to develop use cases, but how to use them to create useful tests. The technique for using graph coverage criteria to develop tests from use cases is expressed with a simple example.

Figure 2.41 shows three simple use cases for an automated teller machine (ATM). In use cases, *actors* are humans or other software systems that use the software being modeled. They are drawn as simple stick figures. In Figure 2.41, the actor is an ATM customer who has three potential use cases; Withdraw Funds, Get Balance, and Transfer Funds.

While Figure 2.41 is technically a graph, it is not a very useful graph for testing. About the best we could do as a tester is to use node coverage, which amounts to "try each use case once." However, use cases are usually elaborated, or "documented" with a more detailed textual description. The description describes the details of operation and includes *alternatives*, which model choices or conditions during execution. The Withdraw Funds use case from Figure 2.41 can be described as follows:

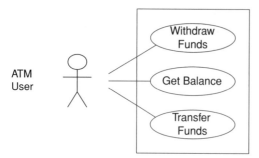

Figure 2.41. ATM actor and use cases.

Use Case Name: Withdraw Funds
Summary: Customer uses a valid card to withdraw funds from a valid bank account.
Actor: ATM Customer
Precondition: ATM is displaying the idle welcome message
Description:

1. Customer inserts an ATM Card into the ATM Card Reader.
2. If the system can recognize the card, it reads the card number.
3. System prompts the customer for a PIN.
4. Customer enters PIN.
5. System checks the expiration date and whether the card has been stolen or lost.
6. If card is valid, the system checks whether the PIN entered matches the card PIN.
7. If the PINs match, the system finds out what accounts the card can access.
8. System displays customer accounts and prompts the customer to choose a type of transaction. Three types of transactions are Withdraw Funds, Get Balance, and Transfer Funds. (The previous eight steps are part of all three use cases; the following steps are unique to the Withdraw Funds use case.)
9. Customer selects Withdraw Funds, selects account number, and enters the amount.
10. System checks that the account is valid, makes sure that the customer has enough funds in the account, makes sure that the daily limit has not been exceeded, and checks that the ATM has enough funds.
11. If all four checks are successful, the system dispenses the cash.
12. System prints a receipt with a transaction number, the transaction type, the amount withdrawn, and the new account balance.
13. System ejects card.
14. System displays the idle welcome message.

Alternatives:

- If the system cannot recognize the card, it is ejected and a welcome message is displayed.
- If the current date is past the card's expiration date, the card is confiscated and a welcome message is displayed.

- If the card has been reported lost or stolen, it is confiscated and a welcome message is displayed.
- If the customer entered PIN does not match the PIN for the card, the system prompts for a new PIN.
- If the customer enters an incorrect PIN three times, the card is confiscated and a welcome message is displayed.
- If the account number entered by the user is invalid, the system displays an error message, ejects the card, and a welcome message is displayed.
- If the request for withdrawal exceeds the maximum allowable daily withdrawal amount, the system displays an apology message, ejects the card, and a welcome message is displayed.
- If the request for withdrawal exceeds the amount of funds in the ATM, the system displays an apology message, ejects the card, and a welcome message is displayed.
- If the customer enters Cancel, the system cancels the transaction, ejects the card, and a welcome message is displayed.
- If the request for withdrawal exceeds the amount of funds in the account, the system displays an apology message, cancels the transaction, ejects the card, and a welcome message is displayed.

Postcondition: Funds have been withdrawn from the customer's account.

At this point, some testing students will be wondering why this discussion is included in a chapter on graph coverage. That is, there is little obvious relationship with graphs thus far. We want to reiterate the first phrase in Beizer's admonition: "testers find a graph, then cover it." In fact, there is a nice graph structure in the use case textual description, which may be up to the tester to express. This graph can be modeled as the transaction flow graphs in Beizer's Chapter 4, or can be drawn as a UML **Activity Diagram**.

An activity diagram shows the flow among activities. Activities can be used to model a variety of things, including state changes, returning values, and computations. We advocate using them to model use cases as graphs by considering activities as *user level steps*. Activity diagrams have two kinds of nodes, action states and sequential branches.[6]

We construct activity graphs as follows. The numeric items in the use case **Description** express steps that the actors undertake. These correspond to inputs to or outputs from the software and appear as **nodes** in the activity diagram as action states. The **Alternatives** in the use case represent decisions that the software or actors make and are represented as **nodes** in the activity diagram as sequential branches.

The activity diagram for the withdraw funds scenario is shown in Figure 2.42. Several things are **expected** but not **required** of activity diagrams constructed from use cases. First, they usually do not have many loops, and most loops they do contain are tightly bounded or determinate. For example, the graph in Figure 2.42 contains a three-iteration loop when the PIN is entered incorrectly. This means that complete path coverage is often feasible and sometimes reasonable. Second, it is very rare to see a complicated predicate that contains multiple clauses. This is because the use case is usually expressed in terms that the users can understand. This means that the logic coverage criteria in Chapter 3 are usually not useful. Third, there are no

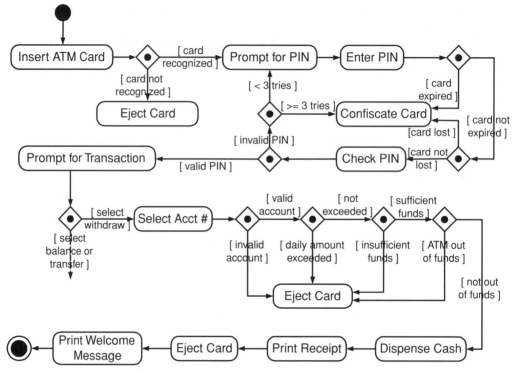

Figure 2.42. Activity graph for ATM withdraw funds.

obvious data definition-use pairs. This means that data flow coverage criteria are not applicable.

The two criteria that are most obviously applicable to use case graphs are node coverage and edge coverage. Test case values are derived from interpreting the nodes and predicates as inputs to the software. One other criterion for use case graphs is based on the notion of "scenarios."

2.6.1 Use Case Scenarios

A use case scenario is an *instance* of, or a complete path through, a use case. A scenario should make some sense semantically to the users and is often derived when the use cases are constructed. If the use case graph is finite (as is usually the case), then it is possible to list all possible scenarios. However, domain knowledge can be used to reduce the number of scenarios that are useful or interesting from either a modeling or test case perspective. Note that *specified path coverage*, defined at the beginning of this chapter, is exactly what we want here. The set *S* for specified path coverage is simply the set of all scenarios.

If the tester or requirements writer chooses all possible paths as scenarios, then specified path coverage is equivalent to complete path coverage. The scenarios are chosen by people and they depend on domain knowledge. Thus it is **not** guaranteed that specified path coverage subsumes edge coverage or node coverage. That is, it is possible to choose a set of scenarios that do not include every edge. This would probably be a mistake, however. So, in practical terms, specified path coverage can be expected to cover all edges.

EXERCISES

Section 2.6.

1. Construct two separate use cases and use case scenarios for interactions with a bank automated teller machine. Do not try to capture all the functionality of the ATM into one graph; think about two different people using the ATM and what each one might do.

   Design test cases for your scenarios.

2.7 REPRESENTING GRAPHS ALGEBRAICALLY

While we typically think of graphs as circles and arrows, they can be represented in various nonpictorial ways. One useful way is an algebraic representation, which can be manipulated using standard algebraic operations and converted to regular expressions. These operations can then be used as a basis for testing the software and to answer various questions about the graphs.

The first requirement is that each edge have a unique label or name. The edge names can come from labels that are already associated with the edges, or can be added specifically for the algebraic representation. This book assumes the labels are unique lower case letters. The multiplicative operator in graph algebra is concatenation; if edge a is followed by edge b, their product is ab (the operator '*' is not written explicitly). The additive operator is selection; if either edge a or edge b can be taken, their sum is $a + b$. Concatenating edges together forms a path, so a sequence of edges is called a *path product*. A *path expression* contains path products and zero or more '+' operators. Thus, every path product is a path expression. Note that an edge label is a special case of a path product with no multiplication, and a path product is a special case of a path expression with no addition. Path expressions are sometimes represented by upper case letters, for example, $A = ab$.

Figure 2.43 shows three example graphs drawn from the double-diamond graph, the loop touring graph, and the Stutter example from previous sections. Figure 2.43(a) has exactly four paths, all of which are shown. Figure 2.43(b) and (c) include loops, so not all paths are shown. In graph algebra, loops are best represented using exponents.

If an edge, path product, or path expression can be repeated, then it is labeled with an exponent. Therefore, $a^2 = aa$, $a^3 = aaa$, and $a^* = aa \cdots a$, that is, an arbitrary number of repetitions. As a special case, an empty, or zero length path, can be represented by $a^0 = \lambda$. This makes λ the multiplicative identity, so $a\lambda = a$, or more generally, $A\lambda = A$.

Representing paths or partial paths with upper case letters makes for convenient manipulation. For example, we can take some partial path expressions from Figure 2.43(b) above:

$$
\begin{aligned}
A &= ab \\
B &= eg \\
C &= cd \\
AB &= abeg \\
C^3 &= cdcdcd
\end{aligned}
$$

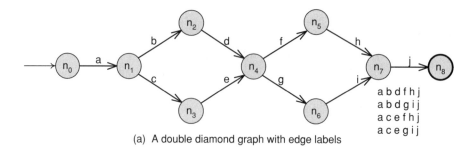

(a) A double diamond graph with edge labels

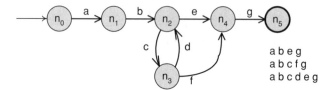

(b) A graph with a loop

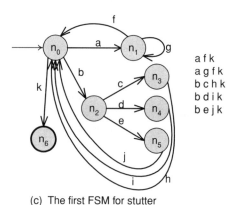

(c) The first FSM for stutter

Figure 2.43. Examples of path products.

$$AC^2B = ab(cd)^2eg$$
$$= abcdcdeg$$
$$D = be + bcf$$

Unlike standard algebra, path products are **not** commutative. That is, $AB \neq BA$. They are, however, associative, so $A(BC) = (AB)C = ABC$.

All paths in the graph in Figure 2.43(a) above can be represented by the expression: $abdfhj + abdgij + acefhj + acegij$. Paths that are summed can be considered to be independent or parallel paths. So path summation is both commutative and associative, that is, $A + B = B + A$, $(A + B) + C = A + (B + C) = A + B + C$.

With this basis, we can start applying standard algebraic laws. Both the distributive law and absorption rule can be applied.

$$A(B + C) = AB + AC \text{ (distributive)}$$
$$(B + C)D = BD + CD \text{ (distributive)}$$
$$A + A = A \text{ (absorption rule)}$$

We also have two more shorthand notations for repetition or loops. If a loop has to be taken at least once (for example, a repeat-until structure), then the '+' exponent is used. That is, $AA^* = A^+$. We can also put bounds on repetition if a loop has a definite bound (for example, a **for** loop). This is done with an underscore: $A^{\underline{3}} = A^0 + A^1 + A^2 + A^3$, or more generally, $A^{\underline{n}} = A^0 + A^1 + \cdots + A^n$. It is sometimes helpful to bound the number of iterations on both ends – that is, at least m and at most n iterations are possible. To do this, we introduce the notation $A^{\underline{m-n}} = A^m + A^{m+1} + \cdots + A^n$.

The absorption rule can be used to combine the exponent notations in several ways. This is used to simplify path expressions as follows:

$$
\begin{aligned}
A^{\underline{n}} + A^{\underline{m}} &= A^{\underline{max\ (n,m)}} \\
A^{\underline{n}} A^{\underline{m}} &= A^{\underline{n+m}} \\
A^{\underline{n}} A^* &= A^* A^{\underline{n}} = A^* \\
A^{\underline{n}} A^+ &= A^+ A^{\underline{n}} = A^+ \\
A^* A^+ &= A^+ A^* = A^+
\end{aligned}
$$

The multiplicative identity operator, λ, can also be used to simplify path expressions.

$$
\begin{aligned}
\lambda + \lambda &= \lambda \\
\lambda A &= A\lambda = A \\
\lambda^n &= \lambda^{\underline{n}} = \lambda^* = \lambda^+ = \lambda \\
\lambda^+ + \lambda &= \lambda^* = \lambda
\end{aligned}
$$

We also need an additive identity. We will use ϕ to represent the set of paths that contains no paths (not even the empty path λ). Mathematically, any path expression added to ϕ is just that path expression. The additive ϕ can be thought of as "blocking" the paths in the graph, therefore making a null path.

$$
\begin{aligned}
A + \phi &= \phi + A = A \\
A\phi &= \phi A = \phi \\
\phi^* &= \lambda + \phi + \phi^2 + \cdots = \lambda
\end{aligned}
$$

Figure 2.44 shows a small graph that has a null path. If we list all paths from node n_0 to n_3, we get the path expression $bc + a\phi = bc$.

A special case is the path expression $A + \lambda$. This situation is illustrated in Figure 2.45. The complete path expression is $(A + \lambda)B$, or $AB + \lambda B$, or $AB + B$. Thus, $A + \lambda$ cannot be reduced.

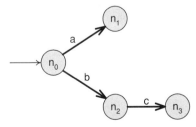

Figure 2.44. Null path that leads to additive identity ϕ.

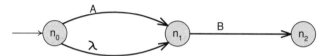

Figure 2.45. A or lambda.

2.7.1 Reducing Graphs to Path Expressions

Now that we have the basic tools, we can see how to go about reducing arbitrary graphs to path expressions. The process given here is not a strict algorithm as it requires some thought and decisions, but is good enough to be used by human testers. As far as we know, this process has not been automated and implemented in a tool; however, it is a special case of the common technique of constructing regular expressions from deterministic FSMs. The process is illustrated on the graph shown in Figure 2.46.

Step 1: First we combine all sequential edges, multiplying the edge labels. More formally, for any node that has only one incoming edge and one outgoing edge, eliminate the node, combine the two edges, and multiply their path expressions. Applying this step to the graph in Figure 2.46 combines edges h and i, giving the graph shown in Figure 2.47.

Step 2: Next combine all parallel edges, adding the edge labels. More formally, for any pair of edges that have the same source and target nodes, combine the edges into one edge, and add their path expressions. The graph in Figure 2.47 contains one such pair of edges, b and c, so they are combined to yield $b + c$, giving the graph shown in Figure 2.48.

Step 3: Remove self-loops (from a node to itself) by creating a new "dummy" node with an incoming edge that uses the exponent operator '*', then merging the three edges with multiplication. More formally, for any node n_1 that has an edge to itself with label X, and incoming edge A and outgoing edge B, remove the edge with label X, and add a new node n'_1 and an edge with label X^*. Then combine the three edges A, X^*, and B into one edge $A X^* B$ (eliminating nodes n_1 and n'_1). The graph in Figure 2.48 contains one self-loop on node n_3 with label e. The edge is first replaced with node n'_3 and an edge from n_3 to n'_3 with label e^* (as shown in Figure 2.49(a)), then the edges labeled d, e^* and f are combined, as shown in Figure 2.49(b).

Step 4: Now the tester starts choosing nodes to remove. Select a node that is not the initial or final node. Replace it by inserting edges from all predecessors to all successors, multiplying the path expressions from the incoming to the outgoing edges. Figure 2.50 illustrates this with a node that has two incoming and two outgoing edges.

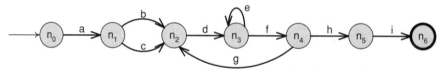

Figure 2.46. Example graph to show reduction to path expressions.

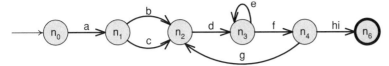

Figure 2.47. After step 1 in path expression reduction.

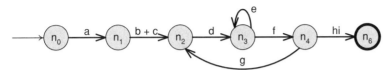

Figure 2.48. After step 2 in path expression reduction.

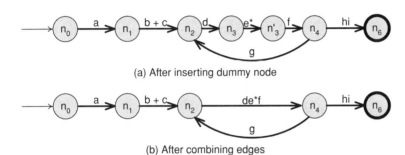

(a) After inserting dummy node

(b) After combining edges

Figure 2.49. After step 3 in path expression reduction.

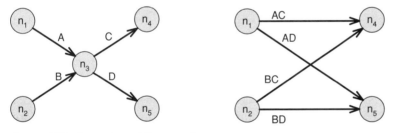

Figure 2.50. Removing arbitrary nodes.

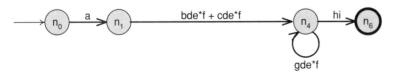

Figure 2.51. Eliminating node n_2.

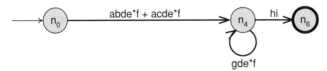

Figure 2.52. Removing sequential edges.

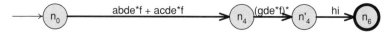

Figure 2.53. Removing self-loop edges.

Node n_2 in Figure 2.49(b) has two incoming edges and one outgoing edge. Edges (n_1, n_2) and (n_2, n_4) become edge (n_1, n_4), with the two path expressions multiplied, and edges (n_4, n_2) and (n_2, n_4) become a self-loop (n_4, n_4), with the two path expressions multiplied. The resulting graph is shown in Figure 2.51.

Steps 1 through 4 are repeated until only one edge remains in the graph. Applying step 1 (combining sequential edges) again to the graph in Figure 2.51 yields the graph shown in Figure 2.52.

Applying step 2 (combining parallel edges) again is skipped because the graph in Figure 2.52 has no parallel edges. Applying step 3 (removing self-loops) again to the graph in Figure 2.52 removes the self-loop on node n_4, yielding the graph shown in Figure 2.53. The final graph (and regular expression) in our example is shown in Figure 2.54.

2.7.2 Applications of Path Expressions

Now that the mathematical preliminaries are out of the way, it is fair to ask what do we do with these path expressions? Path expressions are abstract, formal representations of graphs. As such, they can be manipulated to give us information about the graphs they represent. This section presents several applications of path expressions.

2.7.3 Deriving Test Inputs

The most direct way to use path expression representations of graphs is to define covering test cases. Each path, that is, each path product, defined by the path expression should be executed, with an appropriate limitation on loops. This is a form of *specified path coverage (SPC)*. If an unbounded exponent ('*') appears in the path expression, it can be replaced with one or more reasonably chosen constant values, then a complete list of paths can be written out. This technique will ensure (that is, subsume) node coverage and edge coverage on the graph.

The final path expression for the example in Figures 2.46 through 2.54 is $abde^* f(gde^* f)^*hi + acde^* f(gde^* f)^*hi$. This expression has two separate path products, and the exponents can be replaced (arbitrarily) by the constant 5. This results in the following two test requirements: $abde^5 f(gde^5 f)^5hi$ and $acde^5 f(gde^5 f)^5hi$.

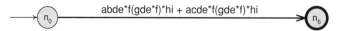

Figure 2.54. Final graph with one path expression.

2.7.4 Counting Paths in a Flow Graph and Determining Max Path Length

It is sometimes useful to know the number of paths in a graph. This can be used as a simplistic complexity measure or as a rough estimation of the number of tests needed to cover the graph. The path expressions allow this computation with straightforward arithmetic, yielding a reasonable approximation for the maximum number of paths.

As discussed earlier, whenever a graph has a cycle, theoretically the graph has an infinite number of paths. However, some graphs have no cycles, and domain knowledge can be used to put appropriate bounds on the number of iterations. The bound may be a true maximum number of iterations, or it may represent a tester's assumption that executing the loop "N times" is enough.

The first step is to label each edge with an *edge weight*. For most edges, the edge weight is one. If the edge represents an expensive operation, such as a method call or external process, the edge weight should be the approximate weight of that operation (for example, the number of paths in the method). If the edge represents a cycle, mark it with the maximum number of iterations possible (the *cycle weight*). It is possible that this number is infinite, which means the maximum number of paths in the graph is infinite. It is important that not all edges in a cycle be labeled with the cycle weight. Only one edge per each cycle should be labeled. Sometimes, which edge to label is obvious, other times the tester must choose an appropriate edge, taking care not to omit a cycle or label a cycle twice. Consider graphs (b) and (c) in Figure 2.43. It should be clear that the cycle weight should be placed on edge d in graph (b). Cycle weights should also be placed on edges h, i, and j in graph (c), and on both edges f and g. Edge f will always occur on any path that includes edge g, so it is easy to forget one of those cycle weights; however, they represent separate cycles.

Sometimes we want to separately annotate a loop to indicate how many times it can be taken. The notation "(0–10)" means that the loop can be taken 0 to 10 times inclusive. Note that this notation is **not** the same as the edge weight.

Next compute the path expression for the graph and substitute the weights into the path expression. The operators are used as one might expect. If the path expression is $A + B$, the substitution is $W_A + W_B$. If the path expression is AB, the substitution is $W_A * W_B$. If the path expression is A^n, the substitution is the summation $\sum_{i=0}^{n} W_A^i$. If the path expression is A^{m-n}, the substitution is the summation $\sum_{i=m}^{n} W_A^i$.

Figure 2.55 shows a simple graph with edge labels and edge weights. As indicated on edge d, the loop can be taken 0 to 2 times inclusive, and the edge weight for d is one. The resulting path expression is $a(b + c)(d(b + c))^{0-2}e$.

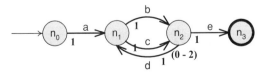

Figure 2.55. Graph example for computing maximum number of paths.

The maximum number of paths can then be calculated by substituting the appropriate value for each edge label into the path expression.

$$1 * (1+1) * (1 * (1+1))^{0-2} * 1$$
$$= 1 * 2 * 2^{0-2} * 1$$
$$= 2 * \sum_{i=0}^{2} 2^i * 1$$
$$= 2 * (2^0 + 2^1 + 2^2) * 1$$
$$= 2 * (1+2+4) * 1$$
$$= 2 * 7 * 1$$
$$= 14$$

The length of the longest path in the graph can also be found. If the path expression is $A + B$, the substitution is $max(W_A, W_B)$. If the path expression is AB, the substitution is $W_A + W_B$. If the path expression is A^n, the substitution is $n * W_A$. So the length of the longest path in the graph in Figure 2.55 is $1 + max(1, 1) + 2 * (1 + max(1, 1)) + 1 = 7$.

It is important to remember that these analyses do not include a feasibility analysis. Some paths may be infeasible, so this should be interpreted as an upper, or conservative, bound on the number of paths.

2.7.5 Minimum Number of Paths to Reach All Edges

A related question is how many paths have to be traversed to reach all edges. The process is very similar to counting the maximum number of paths and uses the same edge weights, but the computation is slightly different.

Specifically, if the path expression is $A + B$, the substitution is $W_A + W_B$. However, if the path expression is AB, the substitution is $max(W_A, W_B)$. If the path expression is A^n, the substitution requires some judgment from the tester and is either 1 or W_A. If it is reasonable to assume that all paths through the loop can be taken during one test case, the value should be 1. If not, however, the value should be the weight of the loop, W_A. The second assumption is more conservative and leads to a higher number.

Again consider the graph in Figure 2.55. Assume that if the edge d is taken, the same edge that preceded it must then be taken. That is, if b is taken, then d, the logic of the graph dictates that b must be taken again. This means that we must use the conservative estimate for the loop, yielding

$$1 * (2) * (1 * (2))^2 * 1$$
$$= 1 * (2) * (1 * 2) * 1$$
$$= max(1, 2, 1, 2, 1)$$
$$= 2$$

A visual inspection of the graph can confirm that all edges can be reached with two traversals of the graph.

2.7.6 Complementary Operations Analysis

The last application of path expressions is not a counting application, but an analysis that looks for anomalies that may lead to mistakes. It is based on the idea of "complementary operations." Two operations are *complementary* if their behaviors negate each other, or one must be done before the other. Examples include push

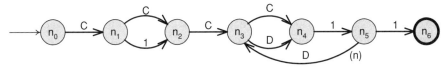

Figure 2.56. Graph example for complementary path analysis.

and pop in stacks, enqueue and dequeue in queues, get and dispose for memory, and open and close for files.

The process starts with the path expression for a graph, except instead of edge weights, each edge is marked with one of the following three labels:

1. C – Creator operation (push, enqueue, etc.)
2. D – Destructor operation (pop, dequeue, etc.)
3. 1 – Neither a creator nor a destructor

The path expression multiplicative and additive operators are replaced with the following two tables[7]:

*	C	D	1
C	C^2	1	C
D	DC	D^2	D
1	C	D	1

+	C	D	1
C	C	$C+D$	$C+1$
D	$D+C$	D	$D+1$
1	$1+C$	$1+D$	1

Note the differences from the usual algebra defined on integers. $C * D$ reduces to 1, $C + C$ reduces to C, and $D + D$ reduces to D.

Consider the graph in Figure 2.56. Edges are marked with C, D or 1, and its initial path expression is $C(C + 1)C(C + D)1(D(C + D)1)^n 1$. The algebraic rules are used to rewrite this as $(CCCC + CCCD + CCC + CCD)(DC + DD)^n$. The two tables above can be used to further reduce the path expression to $(CCCC + CC + CCC + C)(DC + DD)^n$.

The first question to ask of this path expression is "is it possible to have more destruct operations than creates?" The answer is yes, and some expressions are

$$CCCD(DD)^n, n > 1$$
$$CCD(DD)^n, n > 0$$
$$CCC(DDDCDD)$$

Another question is "is it possible to have more create operations than destructs?" Again, the answer is yes, and some expressions are:

$$CCCC$$
$$CCD(DC)^n, \forall n$$

Each yes answer represents a specification for a test that is likely to cause anomalous behavior.

EXERCISES
Section 2.7.

1. Derive and simplify the path expressions for the three graphs in Figure 2.43.
2. Derive and simplify the path expression for the flow graph in Figure 2.12. Assign reasonable cycle weights and compute the maximum number of paths in the graph and the minimum number of paths to reach all edges.

3. The graph in Figure 2.10 was used as an example for prime test paths. Add appropriate edge labels to the graph, then derive and simplify the path expressions. Next add edge weights of 1 for non-cycle edges and 5 for cycle edges. Then compute the maximum number of paths in the graph and the minimum number of paths to reach all edges. This graph has 25 prime paths. Briefly discuss the number of prime paths with the maximum number of paths and consider the effect of varying the cycle weight on the maximum number of paths.

4. Section 2.5 presented four different versions of a FSM for Stutter. Derive and simplify the path expressions for each of the four variations, then compute the maximum number of paths and the minimum number of paths to reach all edges in each. Discuss how the different numbers affect testing.

5. Perform complementary operations analysis on the graph in Figure 2.32. Assume complementary operators of **open** and **close**.

6. Derive and simplify the path expressions for the activity graph in Figure 2.42. The only loop in that graph has a bound of 3 tries. Use that to compute the maximum number of paths and the minimum number of paths to reach all edges. Discuss the relationship between the scenarios for that graph and the terms in the path expression.

7. Answer questions (a)–(c) for the graph defined by the following sets:
   - $N = \{1, 2, 3, 4, 5, 6, 7, 8, 9, 10\}$
   - $N_0 = \{1\}$
   - $N_f = \{10\}$
   - $E = \{(1, 2, a), (2, 3, b), (2, 4, c), (3, 5, d), (4, 5, e), (5, 6, f), (5, 7, g), (6, 6, h$
     $(1 - 4)), (6, 10, i), (7, 8, j), (8, 8, k(0 - 3)), (8, 9, l), (9, 7, m(2 - 5)), (9, 10, n)\}$

   (a) Draw the graph.

   (b) What is the maximum number of paths through the graph?

   (c) What is the approximate minimum number of paths through the graph?

2.8 BIBLIOGRAPHIC NOTES

During the research for this book, one thing that became abundantly clear is that this field has had a significant amount of parallel discovery of the same techniques by people working independently. Some individuals have discovered various aspects of the same technique, which was subsequently polished into very pretty test criteria. Others have invented the same techniques, but based them on different types of graphs or used different names. Thus, ascribing credit for software testing criteria is a perilous task. We do our best, but claim only that the bibliographic notes in this book are starting points for further study in the literature.

The research into covering graphs seems to have started with generating tests from finite state machines (FSMs), which has a long and rich history. Some of the earliest papers were in the 1970s [77, 164, 170, 232, 290]. The primary focus of most of these papers was on using FSMs to generate tests for telecommunication systems that were defined with standard finite automata, although much of the work pertained to general graphs. The control flow graph seems to have been invented (or should it be termed "discovered"?) by Legard in 1975 [204]. In papers published in 1975, Huang [170] suggested covering each edge in the FSM, and Howden [164] suggested covering complete trips through the FSM, but without looping. In 1976, McCabe [232] suggested the same idea on control flow graphs as the primary application of his cyclomatic complexity metric. In 1976, Pimont and Rault [290] suggested covering pairs of edges, or "switches," a technique that they referred to as "switch-testing," and which has been also called "switch cover." In 1978, Chow [77] suggested generating a spanning tree from a FSM and then basing test sequences on paths through this tree. He also generalized the idea of a switch to "n-switch," which are sequences of n edges. Fujiwara et al. [130] referred to Chow's approach with the term "W-method," and developed the "partial" W-method (the "Wp-method"). They also attributed the idea of switches to Chow's paper instead of Pimont and Rault's. The idea of covering pairs of edges was rediscovered in the 1990s. The British Computer Society Standard for Software Component Testing called it *two-trip* [317] and Offutt et al. [272], called it *transition-pair*.

Other test generation methods based on FSMs include tour [251], the distinguished sequence method [137], and unique input-output method [307]. Their objectives are to detect output errors based on state transitions driven by inputs. FSM-based test generation has been used to test a variety of applications including lexical analyzers, real-time process control software, protocols, data processing, and telephony. One early realization when developing this book is that the criteria for covering FSMs are not substantially different from criteria for other graphs.

This book has introduced the explicit inclusion of node coverage requirements in edge coverage requirements (the "up to" clause). This inclusion is not necessary for typical control flow graphs, where, indeed, subsumption of node coverage by edge coverage is often presented as a basic theorem, but it may be required for graphs derived from other artifacts.

Several later papers focused on automatic test data generation to cover structural elements in the program [39, 41, 80, 101, 117, 166, 190, 191, 267, 295]. Much of this work was based on the analysis techniques of symbolic evaluation [62, 83, 93, 101, 116, 164], and slicing [328, 339]. Some of these ideas are discussed in Chapter 6.

The problem of handling loops has plagued graph-based criteria from the beginning. It seems obvious that we want to cover paths, but loops create infinite numbers of paths. In Howden's 1975 paper [164], he specifically addressed loops by covering complete paths "without looping," and Chow's 1978 suggestion to use spanning trees was an explicit attempt to avoid having to execute loops [77]. Binder's book [33] used the technique from Chow's paper, but changed the name to *round trip*, which is the name used in this book.

Another early suggestion was based on testing loop free programs [66], which is certainly interesting from a theoretical view, but not particularly practical.

White and Wiszniewski [348] suggested limiting the number of loops that need to be executed based on specific patterns. Weyuker, Weiss, and Hamlet tried to choose specific loops to test based on data definitions and uses [345].

The notion of *subpath sets* was developed by Offutt et al. [178, 265] to support inter-class path testing and is essentially equivalent to tours with detours as presented here. The ideas of touring, sidetrips and detours were introduced by Ammann, Offutt and Huang [17].

The earliest reference we have found on data flow testing was a technical report in 1974 by Osterweil and Fosdick [282]. This technical report was followed by a 1976 paper in *ACM Computing Surveys* [122], *along with an almost simultaneous publication by Herman in the Australian Computer Journal* [158]. The seminal data flow analysis procedure (without reference to testing) was due to Allen and Cocke [13].

Other fundamental and theoretical references are by Laski and Korel in 1983 [201], who suggested executing paths from definitions to uses, Rapps and Weyuker in 1985 [297], who defined criteria and introduced terms such as All-Defs and All-Uses, and Frankl and Weyuker in 1988 [128]. These papers refined and clarified the idea of data flow testing, and are the basis of the presentation in this text. Stated in the language in this text, [128] requires direct tours for the All-du-Paths Coverage, but allows sidetrips for All-Defs coverage and All-Uses coverage. This text allows sidetrips (or not) for all of the data flow criteria. The pattern matching example used in this text has been employed in the literature for decades; as far as we know, Frankl and Weyuker [128] were the first to use the example for illustrating data flow coverage.

Forman also suggested a way to detect data flow anomalies without running the program [121].

Some detailed problems with data flow testing have been recurring. These include the application of data flow when paths between definitions and uses cannot be executed [127], and handling pointers and arrays [267, 345].

The method of defining data flow criteria in terms of sets of du-paths is original to this book, as is the explicit suggestion for best-effort touring.

Many papers present empirical studies of various aspects of data flow testing. One of the earliest was by Clarke, Podgurski, Richardson, and Zeil, who compared some of the different criteria [82]. Comparisons with mutation testing (introduced in Chapter 5) started with Mathur in 1991 [228], which was followed by Mathur and Wong [230], Wong and Mathur [357], Offutt, Pan, Tewary, and Zhang [274], and Frankl, Weiss, and Hu [125]. Comparisons of data flow with other test criteria have been published by Frankl and Weiss [124], Hutchins, Foster, Goradia, and Ostrand [172], and Frankl and Deng [123].

A number of tools have also been built by researchers to support data flow testing. Most worked by taking a program and tests as inputs, and deciding whether one or more data flow criteria have been satisfied (a *recognizer*). Frankl, Weiss, and Weyuker built ASSET in the mid 1980s [126], Girgis and Woodward built a tool to implement both data flow and mutation testing in the mid 1980s [134], and Laski built STAD in the late 1980s [200]. Researchers at Bellcore developed the ATAC data flow tool for C programs in the early 1990s [161, 162], and the first tool that included a test data generator for data flow criteria was built by Offutt, Jin, and Pan in the late 1990s [267].

Coupling was first discussed as a design metric by Constantine and Yourdon [88], and its use for testing was introduced implicitly by Harrold, Soffa, and Rothermel [152, 154] and explicitly by Jin and Offutt [178], who introduced the use of *first-uses* and *last-defs*.

Kim, Hong, Cho, Bae, and Cha used a graph-based approach to generate tests from UML state diagrams [186].

The USA's Federal Aviation Authority (FAA) has recognized the increased importance of modularity and integration testing by imposing requirements on structural coverage analysis of software that "the analysis should confirm the data coupling and control coupling between the code components" [305], p. 33, section 6.4.4.2.

Data flow testing has also been applied to integration testing by Harrold and Soffa [154], Harrold and Rothermel [152], and Jin and Offutt [178]. This work focused on class-level integration issues, but did not address inheritance or polymorphism. Data flow testing has been applied to inheritance and polymorphism in object-oriented software by Alexander and Offutt [11, 10, 12], and Buy, Orso, and Pezze [60, 281]. Gallagher and Offutt modeled classes as interacting state machines, and tested concurrency and communication issues among them [132].

SCR was first discussed by Henninger [157], and its use in model checking and testing was introduced by Atlee [20].

Constructing tests from UML diagrams is a more recent development, though relatively straightforward. It was first suggested by Abdurazik and Offutt [2, 264], and soon followed by Briand and Labiche [45].

The mechanisms for turning finite automata into regular expressions are standard fare in CS theory classes. As far as we know, Beizer [29] was the first to note the utility of these transformations in the testing context.

NOTES

1 By way of example, typical control flow graphs have very few, if any, syntactically unreachable nodes, but call graphs, especially for object-oriented programs, often do.

2 Our mathematician readers might notice that this definition is constructive in that it defines what is in the set TR, but does not actually bound the set. It is certainly our intention that TR contains no other elements.

3 The reader might wonder why NOTFOUND fails to appear in the set $use(2)$. The reason, as explained in Section 2.3.2 is that the use is *local*.

4 The reader is cautioned that despite the names of the criteria, All-Defs and All-Uses are not complementary criteria with respect to how they tread definitions and uses. Specifically, one does *not* arrive at All-Uses by replacing the notion of "def" with that of "use" in All-Defs. The reader might find it helpful to note that while All-Defs focuses on definitions, All-Uses focuses on def-use *pairs*. While one could argue that the naming convention is misleading, and that a name such as "All-Pairs" might be preferable to All-Uses, the authors elected to stick with the standard usage in the dataflow literature.

5 This is a bit of an overstatement, and, as usual, the culprit is infeasibility. Specifically, consider a du-path with respect to variable x that can only be toured with a sidetrip. Further, suppose that there are two possible sidetrips, one of which is def-clear with respect to x, and one of which is not. The relevant test path from the All-du-Paths test set necessarily tours the former sidetrip, where as the corresponding test path from the prime path test set is free to tour the latter side trip. Our opinion is that in most situations it is reasonable for the test engineer to ignore this special case and simply proceed with prime path coverage.

6 As in previous chapters, we explicitly leave out concurrency, so concurrent forks and joins are not considered.

7 Mathematicians who have studied abstract algebra will recognize that these tables define another algebra.

3
Logic Coverage

This chapter introduces test criteria based on logical expressions. While logic coverage criteria have been known for a long time, their use has been steadily growing in recent years. One cause for their use in practice has been their incorporation in standards such as those accepted by the US Federal Aviation Administration (FAA) for safety critical avionics software in commercial aircraft. As in Chapter 2, we start with a sound theoretical foundation for logic predicates and clauses with the goal of making the subsequent testing criteria simpler. As before, we take a generic view of the structures and criteria, then discuss how logic expressions can be derived from various software artifacts, including code, specifications, and finite state machines.

Readers who are already familiar with some of the common criteria may have difficulty recognizing them at first. This is because we introduce a generic collection of test criteria, and thus choose names that best help articulate all of the criteria. That is, we are abstracting a number of existing criteria that are closely related, yet use conflicting terminology.

3.1 OVERVIEW: LOGIC PREDICATES AND CLAUSES

We formalize logical expressions in a common mathematical way. A *predicate* is an expression that evaluates to a boolean value, and is our topmost structure. A simple example is: $((a > b) \lor C) \land p(x)$. Predicates may contain boolean variables, non-boolean variables that are compared with the comparator operators $\{>, <, =, \geq, \leq, \neq\}$, and function calls. The internal structure is created by the logical operators:

- $\neg$ – the *negation* operator
- $\land$ – the *and* operator
- $\lor$ – the *or* operator
- $\rightarrow$ – the *implication* operator
- $\oplus$ – the *exclusive or* operator
- $\leftrightarrow$ – the *equivalence* operator

Some of these operators ($\oplus$, $\rightarrow$, $\leftrightarrow$) may seem unusual for readers with a bias toward source code, but they turn out to be common in some specification languages and very handy in our purposes. Short circuit versions of the *and* and *or* operators are also sometimes useful and will be addressed when necessary. We adopt a typical precedence, which, from highest to lowest, matches the order listed above. When the order might not be obvious, we use parentheses for clarity.

A *clause* is a predicate that does not contain any of the logical operators. For example, the predicate $(a = b) \vee C \wedge p(x)$ contains three clauses: a relational expression $(a = b)$, a boolean variable C and the function call $p(x)$. Because they may contain a structure of their own, relational expressions require special treatment.

A predicate may be written in a variety of logically equivalent ways. For example, the predicate $((a = b) \vee C) \wedge ((a = b) \vee p(x))$ is logically equivalent to the predicate given in the previous paragraph, but $((a = b) \wedge p(x)) \vee (C \wedge p(x))$ is not. The usual rules of boolean algebra (not reviewed here) may be used to convert boolean expressions into equivalent forms.

Logical expressions come from a variety of sources. The most familiar to most readers will probably be source code of a program. For example, the following if statement:

```
if ((a > b) || C) && (x < y)
    o.m();
else
    o.n();
```

will yield the expression $((a > b) \vee C) \wedge (x < y)$. Other sources of logical expressions include transitions in finite state machines. A transition such as: button2 = true (when gear = park) will yield the expression *gear = park $\wedge$ button2 = true*. Similarly, a precondition in a specification such as "pre: stack Not full AND object reference parameter not null" will result in a logical expression such as $\neg$ *stackFull()* $\wedge$ *newObj $\neq$ null*.

In the material prior to Section 3.6 we treat logical expressions according to their semantic meanings, not their syntax. As a consequence, a given logical expression yields the same test requirements for a given coverage criterion no matter which form of the logic expression is used.

EXERCISES
Section 3.1.

1. List all the clauses for the predicate below:
   $(((f <= g) \wedge (X > 0)) \vee (M \wedge (e < d + c))$
2. Write the predicate (only the predicate) to represent the requirement: "List all the wireless mice that either retail for more than \$100 or for which the store has more than 20 items. Also list non-wireless mice that retail for more than \$50."

3.2 LOGIC EXPRESSION COVERAGE CRITERIA

Clauses and predicates are used to introduce a variety of coverage criteria. Let P be a set of predicates and C be a set of clauses in the predicates in P. For each predicate $p \in P$, let C_p be the clauses in p, that is, $C_p = \{c | c \in p\}$. C is the union of the clauses in each predicate in P, that is, $C = \bigcup_{p \in P} C_p$.

CRITERION **3.12 Predicate Coverage (PC):** *For each $p \in P$, TR contains two requirements: p evaluates to true, and p evaluates to false.*

The graph version of predicate coverage was introduced in Chapter 2 as edge coverage; this is where the graph coverage criteria overlap the logic expression coverage criteria. For control flow graphs where P is the set of predicates associated with branches, predicate coverage and edge coverage are the same. For the predicate given above, $((a > b) \vee C) \wedge p(x)$, two tests that satisfy predicate coverage are $(a = 5, b = 4, C = true, p(x) = true)$ and $(a = 5, b = 6, C = false, p(x) = false)$.

An obvious failing of this criterion is that the individual clauses are not always exercised. Predicate coverage for the above clause could also be satisfied with the two tests $(a = 5, b = 4, C = true, p(x) = true)$ and $(a = 5, b = 4, C = true, p(x) = false)$, in which the first two clauses never have the value *false*! To rectify this problem, we move to the clause level.

CRITERION **3.13 Clause Coverage (CC):** *For each $c \in C$, TR contains two requirements: c evaluates to true, and c evaluates to false.*

Our predicate $((a > b) \vee C) \wedge p(x)$ requires different values to satisfy CC. Clause coverage requires that $(a > b) = true$ and *false*, $C = true$ and *false*, and $p(x) = true$ and *false*. These requirements can be satisfied with two tests: $((a = 5, b = 4), (C = true), p(x) = true)$ and $((a = 5, b = 6), (C = false), p(x) = false)$.

Clause coverage does not subsume predicate coverage, and predicate coverage does not subsume clause coverage, as we show with the predicate $p = a \vee b$. The clauses C are $\{a, b\}$. The four test inputs that enumerate the combinations of logical values for the clauses:

	a	b	$a \vee b$
1	T	T	T
2	T	F	T
3	F	T	T
4	F	F	F

Consider two test sets, each with a pair of test inputs. Test set $T_{23} = \{2, 3\}$ satisfies clause coverage, but not predicate coverage, because p is never false. Conversely, test set $T_{24} = \{2, 4\}$ satisfies predicate coverage, but not clause coverage, because b is never true. These two test sets demonstrate that neither predicate coverage nor clause coverage subsumes the other.

From the testing perspective, we would certainly like a coverage criterion that tests individual clauses and that also tests the predicate. The most direct approach to rectify this problem is to try all combinations of clauses:

CRITERION **3.14 Combinatorial Coverage (CoC):**   *For each $p \in P$, TR has test requirements for the clauses in C_p to evaluate to each possible combination of truth values.*

Combinatorial coverage has also been called multiple condition coverage. For the predicate $(a \vee b) \wedge c$, the complete truth table contains eight elements:

	a	b	c	$(a \vee b) \wedge c$
1	T	T	T	T
2	T	T	F	F
3	T	F	T	T
4	T	F	F	F
5	F	T	T	T
6	F	T	F	F
7	F	F	T	F
8	F	F	F	F

A predicate p with n independent clauses has 2^n possible assignments of truth values. Thus combinatorial coverage is unwieldy at best, and impractical for predicates with more than a few clauses. What we need are criteria that capture the effect of each clause, but do so in a reasonable number of tests. These observations lead, after some thought,[1] to a powerful collection of test criteria that are based on the notion of making individual clauses "active" as defined in the next subsection. Specifically, we check to see that if we vary a clause in a situation where the clause should affect the predicate, then, in fact, the clause does affect the predicate. Later we turn to the complementary problem of checking to see that if we vary a clause in a situation where it should *not* affect the predicate, then it, in fact, does not affect the predicate.

3.2.1 Active Clause Coverage

The lack of subsumption between clause and predicate coverage is unfortunate, but clause and predicate coverage have deeper problems. Specifically, when we introduce tests at the clause level, we want also to have an effect on the predicate. The key notion is that of *determination*, the conditions under which a clause influences the outcome of a predicate. Although the formal definition is a bit messy, the basic idea is very simple: if you flip the clause, and the predicate changes value, then the clause determines the predicate. To distinguish the clause in which we are interested from the remaining clauses, we adopt the following convention. The *major* clause, c_i, is the clause on which we are focusing. All of the other clauses c_j, $j \neq i$, are *minor* clauses. Typically, to satisfy a given criterion, each clause is treated in turn as a major clause. Formally,

Definition 3.42 Determination: Given a major clause c_i in predicate p, we say that c_i *determines* p if the minor clauses $c_j \in p$, $j \neq i$ have values so that changing the truth value of c_i changes the truth value of p.

Note that this definition explicitly does **not** require that $c_i = p$. This issue has been left ambiguous by previous definitions, some of which require the predicate and the major clause to have the same value. This interpretation is not practical. When the negation operator is used, for example, if the predicate is $p = \neg a$, it becomes impossible for the major clause and the predicate to have the same value.

Consider the example above, where $p = a \vee b$. If b is false, then clause a determines p, because then the value of p is exactly the value of a. However if b is true, then a does not determine p, since p is true regardless of the value of a.

From the testing perspective, we would like to test each clause under circumstances where the clause determines the predicate. Consider this as putting different members of a team in charge of the team. We do not know if they can be effective leaders until they try. Consider again the predicate $p = a \vee b$. If we do not vary b under circumstances where b determines p, then we have no evidence that b is used correctly. For example, test set $T_{14} = \{TT, FF\}$, which satisfies both clause and predicate coverage, tests neither a nor b effectively.

In terms of criteria, we develop the notion of active clause coverage in a general way first with the definition below and then refine out the ambiguities in the definition to arrive at the resulting formal coverage criteria.

Definition 3.43 Active Clause Coverage (ACC): For each $p \in P$ and each major clause $c_i \in C_p$, choose minor clauses c_j, $j \neq i$ so that c_i determines p. TR has two requirements for each c_i: c_i evaluates to true and c_i evaluates to false.

For example, for $p = a \vee b$, we end up with a total of four requirements in TR, two for clause a and two for clause b. For clause a, a determines p if and only if b is false. So we have the two test requirements $\{(a = true, b = false), (a = false, b = false)\}$. For clause b, b determines p if and only if a is false. So we have the two test requirements $\{(a = false, b = true), (a = false, b = false)\}$. This is summarized in the partial truth table below (the values for the major clauses are in bold face).

	a	b
$c_i = a$	**T**	f
	F	f
$c_i = b$	f	**T**
	f	**F**

Two of these requirements are identical, so we end up with three distinct test requirements for active clause coverage for the predicate $a \vee b$, namely, $\{(a = true, b = false), (a = false, b = true), (a = false, b = false)\}$. Such overlap always happens, and it turns out that for a predicate with n clauses, $n + 1$ distinct test requirements, rather than the $2n$ one might expect, are sufficient to satisfy active clause coverage.

ACC is almost identical to the way early papers described another technique called MCDC. It turns out that this criterion has some ambiguity, which has led to a fair amount of confusion about how to interpret MCDC over the years. The most important question is whether the minor clauses c_j need to have the same values when the major clause c_i is true as when c_i is false. Resolving this ambiguity leads to three distinct and interesting flavors of ACC. For a simple predicate such as $p = a \vee b$, the three flavors turn out to be identical, but differences appear for more complex predicates. The most general flavor allows the minor clauses to have different values.

CRITERION **3.15 General Active Clause Coverage (GACC):** *For each $p \in P$ and each major clause $c_i \in C_p$, choose minor clauses c_j, $j \neq i$ so that c_i determines p. T R has two requirements for each c_i: c_i evaluates to true and c_i evaluates to false. The values chosen for the minor clauses c_j do* not *need to be the same when c_i is true as when c_i is false.*

Unfortunately, it turns out that GACC does not subsume predicate coverage, as the following example shows.

Consider the predicate $p = a \leftrightarrow b$. Clause a determines p for any assignment of truth values to b. So, when a is true, we choose b to be true as well, and when a is false, we choose b to be false as well. We make the same selections for clause b. We end up with only two test inputs: $\{TT, FF\}$. p evaluates to *true* for both of these cases, so predicate coverage is *not* achieved.

Many testing researchers have a strong feeling that ACC should subsume PC, thus the second flavor of ACC requires that p evaluates to true for one assignment of values to the major clause c_i, and false for the other. Note that c_i and p do not have to have the same values, as discussed with the definition for determination.

CRITERION **3.16 Correlated Active Clause Coverage (CACC):** *For each $p \in P$ and each major clause $c_i \in C_p$, choose minor clauses c_j, $j \neq i$ so that c_i determines p. T R has two requirements for each c_i: c_i evaluates to true and c_i evaluates to false. The values chosen for the minor clauses c_j must cause p to be true for one value of the major clause c_i and false for the other.*

So for the predicate $p = a \leftrightarrow b$ above, CACC can be satisfied with respect to clause a with the test set $\{TT, FT\}$ and with respect to clause b with the test set $\{TT, TF\}$. Merging these yields the CACC test set $\{TT, TF, FT\}$.

Consider the example $p = a \wedge (b \vee c)$. For a to determine the value of p, the expression $b \vee c$ must be true. This can be achieved in three ways: b true and c false, b false and c true, and both b and c true. So, it would be possible to satisfy CACC with respect to clause a with the two test inputs: $\{TTF, FFT\}$. Other choices are possible with respect to a. The following truth table helps enumerate them. The row numbers are taken from the complete truth table for the predicate given previously. Specifically, CACC can be satisfied for a by choosing one test requirement from rows 1, 2, and 3, and the second from rows 5, 6, and 7. Of course, nine possible ways exist to do this.

	a	b	c	$a \wedge (b \vee c)$
1	T	T	T	T
2	T	T	F	T
3	T	F	T	T
5	F	T	T	F
6	F	T	F	F
7	F	F	T	F

The final flavor forces the c_j to be identical for both assignments of truth values to c_i.

CRITERION **3.17 Restricted Active Clause Coverage (RACC):** *For each $p \in P$ and each major clause $c_i \in C_p$, choose minor clauses c_j, $j \neq i$ so that c_i determines p. TR has two requirements for each c_i: c_i evaluates to true and c_i evaluates to false. The values chosen for the minor clauses c_j must be the same when c_i is true as when c_i is false.*

For the example $p = a \wedge (b \vee c)$, only three of the nine sets of test requirements that satisfy CACC with respect to clause a will satisfy RACC with respect to clause a. In terms of the previously given complete truth table, row 2 can be paired with row 6, row 3 with row 7, or row 1 with row 5. Thus, instead of the nine ways to satisfy CACC, only three can satisfy RACC.

	a	b	c	$a \wedge (b \vee c)$
1	T	T	T	T
5	F	T	T	F
2	T	T	F	T
6	F	T	F	F
3	T	F	T	T
7	F	F	T	F

CACC versus RACC

Examples of satisfying a predicate for each of these three criteria are given later. One point that may not be immediately obvious is how CACC and RACC differ in practice.

It turns out that some logical expressions can be completely satisfied under CACC, but have infeasible test requirements under RACC. These expressions are a little subtle and only exist if dependency relationships exist among the clauses, that is, some combinations of values for the clauses are prohibited. Since this often happens in real programs, because program variables frequently depend upon one another, it is useful to consider such an example.

Consider a system with a valve that might be either open or closed, and several modes, two of which are "Operational" and "Standby." Assume the following two constraints:

1. The valve must be open in "Operational" and closed in all other modes.
2. The mode cannot be both "Operational" and "Standby" at the same time.

This leads to the following clause definitions:

a = *"The valve is closed"*
b = *"The system status is Operational"*
c = *"The system status is Standby"*

Suppose that a certain action can be taken only if the valve is closed and the system status is either in *Operational* or *Standby*. That is,

$$p = valve\ is\ closed\ AND\ (system\ status\ is\ Operational\ OR$$
$$system\ status\ is\ Standby)$$
$$= a \wedge (b \vee c)$$

This is exactly the predicate that was analyzed above. The constraints above can be formalized as

1 $\neg a \leftrightarrow b$
2 $\neg(b \wedge c)$

These constraints limit the feasible values in the truth table. As a reminder, the complete truth table for this predicate is

	a	b	c	$a \wedge (b \vee c))$	
1	T	T	T	T	violates constraints 1 & 2
2	T	T	F	T	violates constraint 1
3	T	F	T	T	
4	T	F	F	F	
5	F	T	T	F	violates constraint 2
6	F	T	F	F	
7	F	F	T	F	violates constraint 1
8	F	F	F	F	violates constraint 1

Recall that for a to determine the value of P, either b or c or both must be true. Constraint 1 rules out the rows where a and b have the same values, that is, rows 1, 2, 7, and 8. Constraint 2 rules out the rows where b and c are both true, that is, rows 1 and 5. Thus, the only feasible rows are 3, 4, and 6. Recall that CACC can be satisfied by choosing one from rows 1, 2, or 3 and one from rows 5, 6, or 7. But RACC requires one of the pairs 2 and 6, 3, and 7, or 1 and 5. Thus, RACC is infeasible for a in this predicate.

3.2.2 Inactive Clause Coverage

The Active Clause Coverage criteria focus on making sure the major clauses *do* affect their predicates. A complementary criterion to ACC ensures that changing a major clause that should *not* affect the predicate does not, in fact, affect the predicate.

Definition 3.44 Inactive Clause Coverage (ICC): For each $p \in P$ and each major clause $c_i \in C_p$, choose minor clauses c_j, $j \neq i$ so that c_i does *not* determine p. TR has four requirements for c_i under these circumstances: (1) c_i evaluates to true with p true, (2) c_i evaluates to false with p true, (3) c_i evaluates to true with p false, and (4) c_i evaluates to false with p false.

Although inactive clause coverage (ICC) has some of the same ambiguity as ACC does, only two distinct flavors can be defined, namely *general inactive clause coverage (GICC)* and *restricted inactive clause coverage (RICC)*. The notion of correlation is not relevant for Inactive Clause Coverage because c_i cannot correlate with p since c_i does not determine p. Also, predicate coverage is guaranteed, subject to feasibility, in all flavors due to the structure of the definition.

The following example illustrates the value of the inactive clause coverage criteria. Suppose you are testing the control software for a shutdown system in a reactor, and the specification states that the status of a particular valve (open vs. closed) is relevant to the reset operation in Normal mode, but not in Override mode. That is, the reset should perform identically in Override mode when the valve is open and when the valve is closed. The skeptical test engineer will want to test reset in Override mode for both positions of the valve, since a reasonable implementation mistake would be to take account the setting of the valve in all modes.

The formal versions of GICC and RICC are as follows.

CRITERION **3.18 General Inactive Clause Coverage (GICC):** *For each $p \in P$ and each major clause $c_i \in C_p$, choose minor clauses c_j, $j \neq i$ so that c_i does not determine p. TR has four requirements for c_i under these circumstances: (1) c_i evaluates to true with p true, (2) c_i evaluates to false with p true, (3) c_i evaluates to true with p false, and (4) c_i evaluates to false with p false. The values chosen for the minor clauses c_j may vary amongst the four cases.*

CRITERION **3.19 Restricted Inactive Clause Coverage (RICC):** *For each $p \in P$ and each major clause $c_i \in C_p$, choose minor clauses c_j, $j \neq i$ so that c_i does not determine p. TR has four requirements for c_i under these circumstances: (1) c_i evaluates to true with p true, (2) c_i evaluates to false with p true, (3) c_i evaluates to true with p false, and (4) c_i evaluates to false with p false. The values chosen for the minor clauses c_j must be the same in cases (1) and (2), and the values chosen for the minor clauses c_j must also be the same in cases (3) and (4).*

3.2.3 Infeasibility and Subsumption

A variety of technical issues complicate the Active Clause Coverage criteria. As with many criteria, the most important is the issue of infeasibility. Infeasibility is often a problem because clauses are sometimes related to one another. That is, choosing the truth value for one clause may affect the truth value for another clause. Consider, for example, a common loop structure, which assumes short circuit semantics:

```
while (i < n && a[i] != 0) {do something to a[i]}
```

The idea here is to avoid evaluating a[i] if i is out of range, and short circuit evaluation is not only assumed, but depended on. Clearly, it is not going to be possible to develop a test case where i < n is false and a[i] != 0 is true.

In principle, the issue of infeasibility for clause and predicate criteria is no different from that for graph criteria. In both cases, the solution is to satisfy test requirements that are feasible, and then decide how to treat infeasible test requirements.

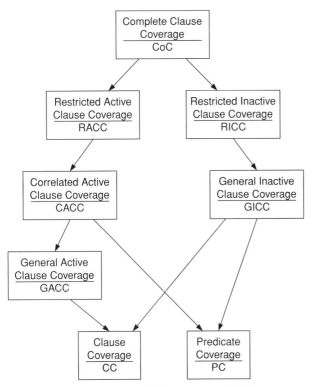

Figure 3.1. Subsumption relations among logic coverage criteria.

The simplest solution is to simply ignore infeasible requirements, which usually does not affect the quality of the tests.

However, a better solution for some infeasible test requirements is to consider the counterparts of the requirements in a subsumed coverage criterion. For example, if RACC coverage with respect to clause a in predicate p is infeasible (due to additional constraints between the clauses), but CACC coverage is feasible, then it makes sense to replace the infeasible RACC test requirements with the feasible CACC test requirements. This approach is similar to that of best-effort touring developed in the graph coverage chapter.

Figure 3.1 shows the subsumption relationships among the logic expression criteria. Note that the ICC criteria do not subsume any of the ACC criteria, and vice versa. The diagram assumes that infeasible test requirements are treated on a best effort basis, as explained above. Where such an approach does not result in feasible test requirements, the diagram assumes that the infeasible test requirements are ignored.

3.2.4 Making a Clause Determine a Predicate

So, how does one go about finding values for the minor clauses c_j so that the major clause c_i determines the value of p? The authors are aware of three different methods presented in the literature; we give a direct definitional approach here. Pointers to the other two, one of which is an algorithmic version of the definitional approach, are given in the bibliographic notes.

For a predicate p with clause (or boolean variable) c, let $p_{c=true}$ represent the predicate p with every occurrence of c replaced by *true* and $p_{c=false}$ be the predicate p with every occurrence of c replaced by *false*. For the rest of this development, we assume no duplicates (that is, p contains only one occurrence of c). Note that neither $p_{c=true}$ nor $p_{c=false}$ contains any occurrences of the clause c. Now we connect the two expressions with an exclusive or:

$$p_c = p_{c=true} \oplus p_{c=false}$$

It turns out that p_c describes the exact conditions under which the value of c determines that of p. That is, if values for the clauses in p_c are chosen so that p_c is true, then the truth value of c determines the truth value of p. If the clauses in p_c are chosen so that p_c evaluates to false, then the truth value of p is independent of the truth value of c. This is exactly what we need to implement the various flavors of active and inactive clause coverage.

As a first example, we try $p = a \lor b$. p_a is, by definition,

$$
\begin{aligned}
p_a &= p_{a=true} \oplus p_{a=false} \\
&= (true \lor b) \oplus (false \lor b) \\
&= true \oplus b \\
&= \neg b
\end{aligned}
$$

That is, for the major clause a to determine the predicate p, the only minor clause b must be false. This should make sense intuitively, since the value of a will have an effect on the value of p only if b is false. By symmetry, it is clear that p_b is $\neg a$.

If we change the predicate to $p = a \land b$, we get

$$
\begin{aligned}
p_a &= p_{a=true} \oplus p_{a=false} \\
&= (true \land b) \oplus (false \land b) \\
&= b \oplus false \\
&= b
\end{aligned}
$$

That is, we need $b = true$ to make a determine p. By a similar analysis, $p_b = a$.

The equivalence operator is a little less obvious and brings up an interesting point. Consider $p = a \leftrightarrow b$.

$$
\begin{aligned}
p_a &= p_{a=true} \oplus p_{a=false} \\
&= (true \leftrightarrow b) \oplus (false \leftrightarrow b) \\
&= b \oplus \neg b \\
&= true
\end{aligned}
$$

That is, for any value of b, a determines the value of p **without regard to the value for b**! This means that for a predicate p, such as this one, where the value of p_c is the constant true, the ICC criteria are infeasible with respect to c. Inactive clause coverage is likely to result in infeasible test requirements when applied to expressions that use the equivalence or exclusive-or operators.

A more general version of this conclusion can be drawn that applies to the ACC criteria as well. If a predicate p contains a clause c such that p_c evaluates to the constant false, the ACC criteria are infeasible with respect to c. The ultimate reason is that the clause in question is redundant; the predicate can be rewritten without it. While this may sound like a theoretical curiosity, it is actually a very useful result for testers. If a predicate contains a redundant clause, this is a very strong signal that something is wrong with the predicate!

Consider $p = a \land b \lor a \land \neg b$. This is really just the predicate $p = a$; b is irrelevant. Computing p_b, we get

$$
\begin{aligned}
p_b &= p_{b=true} \oplus p_{b=false} \\
&= (a \land true \lor a \land \neg true) \oplus (a \land false \lor a \land \neg false) \\
&= (a \lor false) \oplus (false \lor a) \\
&= a \oplus a \\
&= false
\end{aligned}
$$

so it is impossible for b to determine p.

We need to consider how to make clauses determine predicates for a couple of more complicated expressions. For the expression $p = a \land (b \lor c)$, we get

$$
\begin{aligned}
p_a &= p_{a=true} \oplus p_{a=false} \\
&= (true \land (b \lor c)) \oplus (false \land (b \lor c)) \\
&= (b \lor c) \oplus false \\
&= b \lor c.
\end{aligned}
$$

This example ends with an undetermined answer, which points out the key difference between CACC and RACC. Three choices of values make $b \lor c$ true, $(b = c = true)$, $(b = true, c = false)$, and $(b = false, c = true)$. For CACC, we could pick one pair of values when a is true and another when a is false. For RACC, we must choose the same pair for both values of a.

The derivation for b and equivalently for c is slightly more complicated:

$$
\begin{aligned}
p_b &= p_{b=true} \oplus p_{b=false} \\
&= (a \land (true \lor c)) \oplus (a \land (false \lor c)) \\
&= (a \land true) \oplus (a \land c) \\
&= a \oplus (a \land c) \\
&= a \land \neg c
\end{aligned}
$$

The last step in the simplification shown above may not be immediately obvious. If it is not, try constructing the truth table for $a \oplus (a \land c)$. The computation for p_c is equivalent and yields the solution $a \land \neg b$.

3.2.5 Finding Satisfying Values

The final step in applying the logic coverage criteria is to choose values that satisfy the criteria. This section shows how to generate values for one example; more cases are explored in the exercises and the application sections later in the chapter. The example is from the first section of the chapter:

$$
p = (a \lor b) \land c
$$

Finding values for predicate coverage is easy and was already shown in Section 3.2. Two test requirements are

$$
TR_{PC} = \{p = true, p = false\}
$$

and they can be satisfied with the following values for the clauses:

	a	b	c
$p = true$	t	t	t
$p = false$	t	t	f

To run the test cases, we need to refine these truth assignments to create values for clauses *a*, *b*, and *c*. Suppose that clauses *a*, *b*, and *c* were defined in terms of Java program variables as follows:

a	x < y, a relational expression for program variables x and y
b	done, a primitive boolean value
c	list.contains(str), for List and String objects

Thus, the complete expanded predicate is actually

$$p = (x < y \lor done) \land list.contains(str)$$

Then the following values for the program variables satisfy the test requirements for predicate coverage.

	a		b	c	
$p = true$	x=3	y=5	done = true	list=["Rat," "Cat," "Dog"]	str = "Cat"
$p = false$	x=0	y=7	done = true	list=["Red," "White"]	str = "Blue"

Note that the values for the program variables need not be the same in a particular test case if the goal is to set a clause to a particular value. For example, clause *a* is true in both tests, even though program variables *x* and *y* have different values.

Values to satisfy clause coverage were also shown in Section 3.2. Six test requirements are

$$TR_{CC} = \{a = true, a = false, b = true, b = false, c = true, c = false\}$$

and they can be satisfied with the following values for the clauses (blank cells represent "don't-care" values):

	a	b	c
$a = true$	t		
$a = false$	f		
$b = true$		t	
$b = false$		f	
$c = true$			t
$c = false$			f

Refining the truth assignments to create values for program variables *x*, *y*, *done*, *list*, and *str* is left as an exercise for the reader.

Before proceeding with the other criteria, we first choose values for minor clauses to ensure that the major clauses will determine the value of *p*. We gave a method of calculating p_a, p_b, and p_c earlier. The computations for this particular predicate p are left as an exercise. However, the results are

p_a	$\neg b \wedge c$
p_b	$\neg a \wedge c$
p_c	$a \vee b$

Now we can turn to the other clause coverage criteria. The first is combinatorial coverage, requiring all combinations of values for the clauses. In this case, we have eight test requirements, which can be satisfied with the following values:

	a	b	c	$(a \vee b) \wedge c$
1	t	t	t	t
2	t	t	f	f
3	t	f	t	t
4	t	f	f	f
5	f	t	t	t
6	f	t	f	f
7	f	f	t	f
8	f	f	f	f

Recall that general active clause coverage requires that each major clause be true and false and the minor clauses be such that the major clause determines the value of the predicate. Similarly to clause coverage, three pairs of test requirements can be defined:

$$TR_{GACC} = \{(a = true \wedge p_a, a = false \wedge p_a), (b = true \wedge p_b,$$
$$b = false \wedge p_b), (c = true \wedge p_c, c = false \wedge p_c)\}$$

The test requirements can be satisfied with the following values for the clauses. Note that these can be the same as with clause coverage with the exception that the blank cells from clause coverage are replaced with the values from the determination analysis. In the following (**partial** truth) table, values for major clauses are indicated with upper case letters in boldface.

	a	b	c	p
$a = true \wedge p_a$	**T**	f	t	t
$a = false \wedge p_a$	**F**	f	t	f
$b = true \wedge p_b$	f	**T**	t	t
$b = false \wedge p_b$	f	**F**	t	f
$c = true \wedge p_c$	t	f	**T**	t
$c = false \wedge p_c$	f	t	**F**	f

Note the duplication; the first and fifth rows are identical, and the second and fourth are identical. Thus, only four tests are needed to satisfy GACC.

A different way of looking at GACC considers all of the possible pairs of test inputs for each pair of test requirements. Recall that the active clause coverage criteria always generate test requirements in pairs, with one pair generated for each clause in the predicate under test. To identify these test inputs, we will use the row numbers from the truth table. Hence, the pair $(3, 7)$ represents the first two tests listed in the table above.

It turns out that $(3, 7)$ is the only pair that satisfies the GACC test requirements with respect to clause a (when a is major), and $(5, 7)$ is the only pair that satisfies the GACC test requirements with respect to clause b. For clause c, the situation is more interesting. Nine pairs satisfy the GACC test requirements for clause c, namely

$$\{(1, 2), (1, 4), (1, 6), (3, 2), (3, 4), (3, 6), (5, 2), (5, 4), (5, 6)\}$$

Recall that correlated active clause coverage requires that each major clause be true and false, the minor clauses be such that the major clause determines the value of the predicate, and the predicate must have both the value true and false. As with GACC, three pairs of test requirements can be defined: For clause a, the pair of test requirements is

$$a = true \land p_a \land p = x$$
$$a = false \land p_a \land p = \neg x$$

where x may be either true or false. The point is that p must have a different truth value in the two test cases. We leave the reader to write out the corresponding CACC test requirements with respect to b and c.

For our example predicate p, a careful examination of the pairs of test cases for GACC reveals that p takes on both truth values in each pair. Hence, GACC and CACC are the same for predicate p, and the same pairs of test inputs apply. In the exercises the reader will find predicates where a test pair that satisfies GACC with respect to some clause c turns out not to satisfy CACC with respect to c.

The situation for RACC is quite different, however, in the example p. Recall that restricted active clause coverage is the same as CACC except that it requires the values for the minor clauses c_j to be identical for both assignments of truth values to the major clause, c_i. For clause a, the pair of test requirements that RACC generates is

$$a = true \land p_a \land b = B \land c = C$$
$$a = false \land p_a \land b = B \land c = C$$

for some boolean constants B and C. An examination of the pairs given above for *GACC* reveals that with respect to clauses a and b, the pairs are the same. So pair $(3, 7)$ satisfies RACC with respect to clause a and pair $(5, 7)$ satisfies RACC with respect to b. However, with respect to c, only three of the pairs satisfy RACC, namely,

$$\{(1, 2), (3, 4), (5, 6)\}$$

This example does leave one question about the different flavors of the ACC criteria, namely, what is the practical difference among them? That is, beyond the subtle difference in the arithmetic, how do they affect practical testers? The real differences do not show up very often, but when they do they can be dramatic and quite annoying.

GACC does not require that predicate coverage be satisfied on the pair of tests for each clause, so use of that flavor may mean we do not test our program as thoroughly as we might like. In practical use, it is easy to construct examples where

GACC is satisfied but predicate coverage is not, when the predicates are very small (one or two terms), but difficult with three or more terms, since for one of the clauses, it is likely that the chosen GACC tests will also be CACC tests.

The restrictive nature of RACC, on the other hand, can sometimes make it hard to satisfy the criterion. This is particularly true when some combinations of clause values are infeasible. Assume that in the predicate used above, the semantics of the program effectively eliminate rows 2, 3, and 6 from the truth table. Then RACC cannot be satisfied with respect to clause *list.contains(str)* (that is, we have infeasible test requirements), but CACC can. The wise reader, (that is, if still awake) will by now realize that Correlated Active Clause Coverage is often the most practical flavor of ACC.

EXERCISES

Section 3.2.

Use predicates (1) through (10) to answer the following questions.

1. $p = a \wedge (\neg b \vee c)$
2. $p = a \vee (b \wedge c)$
3. $p = a \wedge b$
4. $p = a \rightarrow (b \rightarrow c)$
5. $p = a \oplus b$
6. $p = a \leftrightarrow (b \wedge c)$
7. $p = (a \vee b) \wedge (c \vee d)$
8. $p = (\neg a \wedge \neg b) \vee (a \wedge \neg c) \vee (\neg a \wedge c)$
9. $p = a \vee b \vee (c \wedge d)$
10. $p = (a \wedge b) \vee (b \wedge c) \vee (a \wedge c)$
    (a) Identify the clauses that go with predicate p.
    (b) Compute (and simplify) the conditions under which each of the clauses determines predicate p.
    (c) Write the complete truth table for all clauses. Label your rows starting from 1. Use the format in the example underneath the definition of combinatorial coverage in Section 3.2. That is, row 1 should be all clauses true. You should include columns for the conditions under which each clause determines the predicate, and also a column for the predicate itself.
    (d) Identify all pairs of rows from your table that satisfy general active clause coverage (GACC) with respect to each clause.
    (e) Identify all pairs of rows from your table that satisfy correlated active clause coverage (CACC) with respect to each clause.
    (f) Identify all pairs of rows from your table that satisfy restricted active clause coverage (RACC) with respect to each clause.
    (g) Identify all 4-tuples of rows from your table that satisfy general inactive clause coverage (GICC) with respect to each clause. Identify any infeasible GICC test requirements.
    (h) Identify all 4-tuples of rows from your table that satisfy restricted inactive clause coverage (RICC) with respect to each clause. Identify any infeasible RICC test requirements.

11. Refine the GACC, CACC, RACC, GICC, and RICC coverage criteria so that the constraints on the minor clauses are made more formal.
12. (**Challenging!**) Find a predicate and a set of additional constraints so that CACC is infeasible with respect to some clause, but GACC is feasible.

3.3 STRUCTURAL LOGIC COVERAGE OF PROGRAMS

As with graph coverage criteria, the logic coverage criteria apply to programs in a straightforward way. Predicates are derived directly from decision points in the programs (if, case, and loop statements). Although these criteria are difficult to apply when predicates have a large number of clauses, this is often not a problem with programs. The vast majority of predicates in programs have only one clause, and programmers tend to write predicates with a maximum of two or three clauses. It should be clear that when a predicate only has one clause, all of the logic coverage criteria collapse into the same criterion – predicate coverage.

The primary complexity of applying logic coverage to programs has more to do with reachability than with the criteria. That is, a logic coverage criterion imposes test requirements that are related to specific decision points (statements) in the program. Getting values that satisfy those requirements is only part of the problem; getting to the statement is sometimes more difficult. Two issues are associated with getting there. The first is simply that of reachability from Chapter 1; the test case must include values to reach the statement. In small programs (that is, most methods) this problem is not hard, but when applied within the context of an entire arbitrarily large program, satisfying reachability can be enormously complex. The values that satisfy reachability are prefix values in the test case.

The other part of "getting there" can be even harder. The test requirements are expressed in terms of program variables that may be defined locally to the unit or even the statement block being tested. Our test cases, on the other hand, can include values only for inputs to the program that we are testing. Therefore these *internal variables* have to be resolved to be in terms of the input variables. Although the values for the variables in the test requirements should ultimately be a function of the values of the input variables, this relationship may be arbitrarily complex. In fact, this *internal variable* problem is formally undecidable.

Consider an internal variable X that is derived from a table lookup, where the index to the table is determined by a complex function whose inputs are program inputs. To choose a particular value for X, the tester has to work backward from the statement where the decision appears, to the table where X was chosen, to the function, and finally to an input that would cause the function to compute the desired value. If the function includes randomness or is time sensitive, or if the input cannot be controlled by the tester, it may be impossible to satisfy the test requirement with certainty. This controllability problem has been explored in depth in the automatic test data generation literature and will not be discussed in detail here, except to note that this problem is a major reason why the use of program-level logic coverage criteria is usually limited to unit and module testing activities.

The example program in Figures 3.2 and 3.3 is used to illustrate logic coverage on programs.[2] The program is a simple triangle classification program called TriTyp. This program (or more accurately, the algorithm) has been used as an example in

```
 1  // Jeff Offutt--Java version Feb 2003
 2  // Classify triangles
 3  import java.io.*;
 4
 5  class trityp
 6  {
 7    private static String[] triTypes = { "", // Ignore 0.
 8          "scalene", "isosceles", "equilateral",
            "not a valid triangle"};
 9    private static String instructions = "This is the ancient
      TriTyp program.\nEnter three integers that represent the
      lengths of the sides of a triangle.\nThe triangle will be
      categorized as either scalene, isosceles, equilateral\n
      or invalid.\n";
10
11  public static void main (String[] argv)
12  { // Driver program for trityp
13    int A, B, C;
14    int T;
15
16    System.out.println (instructions);
17    System.out.println ("Enter side 1: ");
18    A = getN();
19    System.out.println ("Enter side 2: ");
20    B = getN();
21    System.out.println ("Enter side 3: ");
22    C = getN();
23    T = Triang (A, B, C);
24
25    System.out.println ("Result is: " + triTypes[T]);
26  }
27
28  // ===================================
29  // The main triangle classification method
30  private static int Triang (int Side1, int Side2, int Side3)
31  {
32    int triOut;
33
34    // triOut is output from the routine:
35    //    Triang = 1 if triangle is scalene
36    //    Triang = 2 if triangle is isosceles
37    //    Triang = 3 if triangle is equilateral
38    //    Triang = 4 if not a triangle
39
40    // After a quick confirmation that it's a valid
41    // triangle, detect any sides of equal length
42    if (Side1 <= 0 || Side2 <= 0 || Side3 <= 0)
43    {
44      triOut = 4;
45      return (triOut);
46    }
47
48    triOut = 0;
49    if (Side1 == Side2)
50      triOut = triOut + 1;
51    if (Side1 == Side3)
52      triOut = triOut + 2;
53    if (Side2 == Side3)
54      triOut = triOut + 3;
55    if (triOut == 0)
56    { // Confirm it's a valid triangle before declaring
57      // it to be scalene
58
```

Figure 3.2. TriTyp – Part A.

```
59     if (Side1+Side2 <= Side3 || Side2+Side3 <= Side1 ||
60         Side1+Side3 <= Side2)
61        triOut = 4;
62     else
63        triOut = 1;
64     return (triOut);
65   }
66
67   // Confirm it's a valid triangle before declaring
68   // it to be isosceles or equilateral
69
70   if (triOut > 3)
71      triOut = 3;
72   else if (triOut == 1 && Side1+Side2 > Side3)
73      triOut = 2;
74   else if (triOut == 2 && Side1+Side3 > Side2)
75      triOut = 2;
76   else if (triOut == 3 && Side2+Side3 > Side1)
77      triOut = 2;
78   else
79      triOut = 4;
80   return (triOut);
81 } // end Triang
82
83 // ===================================
84 // Read (or choose) an integer
85 private static int getN ()
86 {
87   int inputInt = 1;
88   BufferedReader in = new BufferedReader (new InputStreamReader (System.in));
89   String inStr;
90
91   try
92   {
93     inStr   = in.readLine ();
94     inputInt = Integer.parseInt(inStr);
95   }
96   catch (IOException e)
97   {
98     System.out.println ("Could not read input, choosing 1.");
99   }
100   catch (NumberFormatException e)
101   {
102     System.out.println ("Entry must be a number, choosing 1.");
103   }
104
105   return (inputInt);
106 } // end getN
107
108 } // end trityp class
```

Figure 3.3. TriTyp – Part B.

the testing literature for many years. As an example, it has several advantages: its purpose is relatively easy to understand, it is small enough to fit in a classroom exercise, and it has a very complicated logic structure that can illustrate most of the concepts. This version of TriTyp is written in Java and was compiled and tested with Sun's JDK Java 1.4.1. Line numbers have been added to allow us to refer to specific decision statements in the text.

Predicates are taken from decision points in the program, including if statements, case/switch statements, for loops, while loops, and do-until loops. This is illustrated with the Triang() method in the TriTyp program. Triang() has the following predicates (line numbers are shown on the left, and the else statements at lines 62 and 78 do not have their own predicates):

```
42: (Side1 <= 0 || Side2 <= 0 || Side3 <= 0)
49: (Side1 == Side2)
51: (Side1 == Side3)
53: (Side2 == Side3)
55: (triOut == 0)
59: (Side1+Side2 <= Side3 || Side2+Side3 <= Side1 ||
    Side1+Side3 <= Side2)
70: (triOut > 3)
72: (triOut == 1 && Side1+Side2 > Side3)
74: (triOut == 2 && Side1+Side3 > Side2)
76: (triOut == 3 && Side2+Side3 > Side1)
```

The TriTyp program has three inputs, which are read into variables A, B, and C in the main program method and then passed to the formal parameters Side1, Side2, and Side3 in Triang(). The rest of this section illustrates how to satisfy the logic coverage criteria on TriTyp. Before addressing the actual criteria, it is first necessary to analyze the predicates to find values that will reach the predicates (the reachability problem) and to understand how to assign particular values to the variable triOut (the internal variable problem).

In the Tables 3.1 through 3.3, Side1, Side2, and Side3 are abbreviated as S1, S2, and S3 to save space. First we consider reachability. The predicate on line 42 is

Table 3.1. Reachability for Triang predicates

```
42: True
49: P1 = (S1 > 0 && S2 > 0 && S3 > 0)
51: P1
53: P1
55: P1
59: P1 && (triOut == 0)
62: P1 && (triOut == 0)
    && (S1+S2 > S3) && (S2+S3 > S1) && (S1+S3 > S2)
70: P1 && (triOut != 0)
72: P1 && (triOut != 0) && (triOut <= 3)
74. P1 && (triOut !- 0) && (triOut <= 3)
    && ((triOut != 1) || (S1+S2 <= S3))
76: P1 && (triOut != 0) && (triOut <= 3)
    && ((triOut != 1) || (S1+S2 <= S3))
    && ((triOut != 2) || (S1+S3 <= S2))
78: P1 && (triOut != 0) && (triOut <= 3)
    && ((triOut != 1) || (S1+S2 <= S3))
    && ((triOut != 2) || (S1+S3 <= S2))
    && ((triOut != 3) || (S2+S3 <= S1))
```

always reached whenever Triang() is called, so its predicate is true, as shown in the first line of Table 3.1. Line 49 is reached only if the predicate on line 42 is false, so its reachability predicate is the inverse, $S1 > 0$ && $S2 > 0$ && $S3 > 0$. This predicate is given the label P1 and referred to in subsequent reachability predicates. The rest of the predicates are found in the similar manner, by negating the predicate on the previous edge.

Note that several predicates in Table 3.1 reference the variable triOut, which is a local (internal) variable assigned a value at lines 44, 48, 50, 52, 54, 61, 63, 71, 73, 75, 77, and 79. So the next step in generating tests is to discover how to assign specific values to triOut. At line 55, triOut has a value in the range (0..6) inclusive, as assigned in the previous statements. By applying the predicates in Table 3.1 and tracing the assignments, we can determine the following rules for triOut:

triOut	Rules for determining triOut
0	S1 != S2 && S1 != S3 && S2 != S3
1	S1 == S2 && S1 != S3 && S2 != S3
2	S1 != S2 && S1 == S3 && S2 != S3
3	S1 != S2 && S1 != S3 && S2 == S3
4	S1 == S2 && S1 != S3 && S2 == S3
5	S1 != S2 && S1 == S3 && S2 == S3
6	S1 == S2 && S1 == S3 && S2 == S3

The predicates for triOut equal to 4 and 5 are contradictions, so it cannot have those values after line 55. These values can be used to reduce and simplify the predicates in Table 3.1, resulting in the predicates shown in Table 3.2. These predicates

---

Table 3.2. Reachability for Triang predicates – reduced by solving for triOut

42: True
49: P1 = (S1 > 0 && S2 > 0 && S3 > 0)
51: P1
53: P1
55: P1
59: P1 && (S1 != S2 && S1 != S3 && S2 != S3)   (triOut == 0)
62: P1 && (S1 != S2 && S1 != S3 && S2 != S3)   (triOut == 0)
    && (S1+S2 > S3) && (S2+S3 > S1) && (S1+S3 > S2)
70: P1 && P2 = (S1 == S2 || S1 == S3 || S2 == S3)   (triOut != 0)
72: P1 && P2 && P3 = (S1!=S2 || S1!=S3 || S2!=S3)   (triOut <= 3)
74: P1 && P2 && P3 && (S1 != S2 || S1 + S2 <= S3)
76: P1 && P2 && P3 && (S1 != S2 || S1 + S2 <= S3)
    && ((S1 != S3) || (S1+S3 <= S2))
78: P1 && P2 && P3 && (S1 != S2 || S1 + S2 <= S3)
    && ((S1 != S3) || (S1+S3 <= S2))
    && ((S2 != S3) || (S2+S3 <= S1))

Table 3.3. Predicate coverage for Triang

		True				False			
	Predicate	A	B	C	EO	A	B	C	EO
p42:	$(S1 \leq 0 \vee S2 \leq 0 \vee S3 \leq 0)$	0	0	0	4	1	1	1	3
p49:	$(S1 == S2)$	1	1	1	3	1	2	2	2
p51:	$(S1 == S3)$	1	1	1	3	1	2	2	2
p53:	$(S2 == S3)$	1	1	1	3	2	1	2	2
p55:	$(triOut == 0)$	1	2	3	4	1	1	1	3
p59:	$(S1 + S2 \leq S3 \vee$ $S2 + S3 \leq S1 \vee$ $S1 + S3 \leq S2)$	1	2	3	4	2	3	4	1
p70:	$(triOut > 3)$	1	1	1	3	2	2	3	2
p72:	$(triOut == 1 \wedge S1 + S2 > S3)$	2	2	3	2	2	2	4	4
p74:	$(triOut == 2 \wedge S1 + S3 > S2)$	2	3	2	2	2	4	2	4
p76:	$(triOut == 3 \wedge S2 + S3 > S1)$	3	2	2	2	4	2	2	4

are beginning to look complicated, but they contain a lot of redundancy. Two more named formulas have been introduced, P2 = (S1 == S2 || S1 == S3 || S2 == S3) and P3 = (S1 != S2 || S1 != S3 || S2 != S3). Table 3.2 shows the predicates that will guarantee reachability for the given statement numbers. These are then used to find satisfying values for the logic criteria.

Finding values to satisfy **predicate coverage** for the predicate on line 42 in TriTyp is straightforward. Any one of the three variables can be given a value of 0 or less for the true case, and they all three have to be 1 or greater for the false case.

Predicates 49, 51, and 53 are similar. They are true if two of the sides have the same length and false if the values are of different lengths. Predicate 55 demonstrates the internal variable problem. *triOut* is an internal variable that has definitions on statements 48, 50, 52, and 54. Algebraic analysis can show that *triOut* is 0 only if neither of the predicates at lines 49, 51 or 53 is true. A semantic generalization of this analysis is that for *triOut* to be 0 (predicate 55 is true), all three sides have to have different lengths.

The other predicates are resolved in similar ways, with the internal variable *triOut* being resolved for values using the previous analysis. Values to satisfy predicate coverage are shown in Table 3.3. For each predicate, the inputs to guarantee the predicate be true and then false are given, along with the expected output (EO). It is generally safer to postpone choosing those values until reachability is determined.

It should be obvious from this example that predicate coverage on programs is simply another way to formulate the edge coverage criterion. It is not necessary to draw a graph for the logic criteria, but the control flow graph can help find values for reachability.

Previously we said that selection of values for "don't care" inputs should be postponed until reachability is determined. This is because of potential interactions with the requirements for reachability and the selection of values. That is, some inputs may be "don't care" for the test requirements, but may need specific values to reach

Table 3.4. Clause coverage for Triang

	Clause	True				False			
		A	**B**	**C**	**EO**	**A**	**B**	**C**	**EO**
p42:	$(S1 \leq 0)$	0	1	1	4	1	1	1	3
	$(S2 \leq 0)$	1	0	1	4	1	1	1	3
	$(S3 \leq 0)$	1	1	0	4	1	1	1	3
p59:	$(S1 + S2 \leq S3)$	2	3	6	4	2	3	4	1
	$(S2 + S3 \leq S1)$	6	2	3	4	2	3	4	1
	$(S1 + S3 \leq S2)$	2	6	3	4	2	3	4	1
p72:	$(triOut == 1)$	2	2	3	2	2	3	2	2
	$(S1 + S2 > S3)$	2	2	3	2	2	2	5	4
p74:	$(triOut == 2)$	2	3	2	2	3	2	2	2
	$(S1 + S3 > S2)$	2	3	2	2	2	5	2	4
p76:	$(triOut == 3)$	3	2	2	2	1	2	1	4
	$(S2 + S3 > S1)$	3	2	2	2	5	2	2	4

the decision. Thus, if we select values too early, it may become impossible to satisfy reachability.

The values needed to satisfy the other criteria are the same for the predicates that have only one clause (p49, p51, p53, p55, and p70). Thus, we consider **clause coverage** only for the predicates that have more than one clause.

The clauses for predicate 42 are simple, and simply require a value for one of the variables. The other values can be chosen arbitrarily. The other predicates are a bit more complicated, but again can be solved with simple algebra. Consider the first clause in predicate 59, $S1 + S2 \leq S3$. If we choose values for $S1$ and $S2$ as $(S1 = 2, S2 = 3)$, then $S1 + S2 = 5$, so $S3$ should be at least 5 for the true case. The same values can be used for $S1$ and $S2$ for the false case, and $S3$ can be 4. The first clause in predicate 72 has an additional complexity because it involves the internal variable $triOut$. The logic of $Triang()$ reveals that $triOut = 1$ if and only if $S1 = S2$, and neither $S1$ nor $S2$ equals $S3$. So the true case can be satisfied with $(2, 2, 3)$ and the false case can be satisfied by making the values of the variables different $(2, 3, 4)$.

Values to satisfy Clause Coverage are shown in Table 3.4.

Rather than going through all of the other criteria, we just focus on **correlated active clause coverage**. Because each predicate involves only one operator (|| or &&) the determination analysis is straightforward. For ||, the minor clauses must be false, and for &&, the minor clauses must be true. This example does bring up one additional complication. In p59, each clause is distinct, yet the individual clauses contain the same variables. This can sometimes make it difficult (and even impossible) to find values that satisfy CACC.

For example, consider the major clause $(S1 + S2 \leq S3)$. For it to determine the predicate, the two minor clauses $(S2 + S3 \leq S1)$ and $(S1 + S3 \leq S2)$ must both be false. If the test case $(0, 0, 0)$ is chosen to make $(S1 + S2 \leq S3)$ true, then all three clauses are true and $(S1 + S2 \leq S3)$ does not determine the predicate. (In the particular case of p59, however, because of the algebra of the requirements,

Table 3.5. Correlated active clause coverage for Triang

	Predicate	Clauses			A	B	C	EO
p42:	$(S1 \leq 0 \lor S2 \leq 0 \lor S3 \leq 0)$	T	f	f	0	1	1	4
		F	f	f	1	1	1	3
		f	T	f	1	0	1	4
		f	f	T	1	1	0	4
p59:	$(S1 + S2 \leq S3 \lor$	T	f	f	2	3	6	4
	$S2 + S3 \leq S1 \lor$	F	f	f	2	3	4	1
	$S1 + S3 \leq S2)$	f	T	f	6	2	3	4
		f	f	T	2	6	3	4
p72:	$(triOut == 1 \land S1 + S2 > S3)$	T	t	–	2	2	3	2
		F	t	–	2	3	3	2
		t	F	–	2	2	5	4
p74:	$(triOut == 2 \land S1 + S3 > S2)$	T	t	–	2	3	2	2
		F	t	–	2	3	3	2
		t	F	–	2	5	2	4
p76:	$(triOut == 3 \land S2 + S3 > S1)$	T	t	–	3	2	2	2
		F	t	–	3	6	3	4
		t	F	–	5	2	2	4

$(0, 0, 0)$ is the only test that has this problem.) Values to satisfy CACC are shown in Table 3.5.

3.3.1 Predicate Transformation Issues

ACC criteria are considered to be expensive for testers, and attempts have been made to reduce the cost. One approach is to rewrite the program to eliminate multiclause predicates, thus reducing the problem to branch testing. A conjecture is that the resulting tests will be equivalent to ACC. However, we explicitly advise against this approach for two reasons. One, the resulting rewritten program may have substantially more complicated control structure than the original (including repeated statements), thus endangering both reliability and maintainability. Second, as the following examples demonstrate, the transformed program may not require tests that are equivalent to the tests for ACC on the original program.

Consider the following program segment, where a and b are arbitrary boolean clauses and S1 and S2 are arbitrary statements. S1 and S2 could be single statements, block statements, or function calls.

```
if (a && b)
   S1;
else
   S2;
```

The CACC criterion requires the test specifications (t, t), (t, f), and (f, t) for the predicate $a \land b$. However, if the program segment is transformed into the following functionally equivalent structure:

```
if (a)
{
    if (b)
        S1;
    else
        S2;
}
else
    S2;
```

the predicate coverage criterion requires three tests: (t, t) to reach statement S1, (t, f) to reach the first occurrence of statement S2, and either (f, f) or (f, t) to reach the second occurrence of statement S2. Choosing (t, t), (t, f), and (f, f) means that our tests do **not** satisfy CACC in that they do not allow a to determine fully the predicate's value. Moreover, the duplication of S2 in the above example has been taught to be poor programming for years, because of the potential for mistakes when duplicating code.

A larger example reveals the flaw even more clearly. Consider the simple program segment

```
if ((a && b) || c)
    S1;
else
    S2;
```

A straightforward rewrite of this program fragment to remove the multiclause predicate results in this complicated ugliness:

```
if (a)
    if (b)
        if (c)
            S1;
        else
            S1;
    else
        if (c)
            S1;
        else
            S2;
else
    if (b)
        if (c)
            S1;
```

```
        else
          S2;
      else
        if (c)
          S1;
        else
          S2;
```

This fragment is cumbersome in the extreme, and likely to be error-prone. Applying the predicate coverage criterion to this would be equivalent to applying combinatorial coverage to the original predicate. A reasonably clever programmer (or good optimizing compiler) would simplify it as follows:

```
if (a)
  if (b)
    S1;
  else
    if (c)
      S1;
    else
      S2;
else
  if (c)
    S1;
  else
    S2;
```

This fragment is still much harder to understand than the original. Try to imagine a maintenance programmer trying to change this thing!

The following table illustrates truth assignments that can be used to satisfy CACC for the original program segment and predicate testing for the modified version. An 'X' under CACC or predicate indicates that truth assignment is used to satisfy the criterion for the appropriate program fragment. Clearly, predicate coverage on an equivalent program is not the same as CACC testing on the original. Predicate coverage on this modified program does not subsume CACC, and CACC does not subsume predicate coverage.

	a	b	c	$((a \wedge b) \vee c)$	CACC	Predicate
1	t	t	t	T		X
2	t	t	f	T	X	
3	t	f	t	T	X	X
4	t	f	f	F	X	X
5	f	t	t	T		X
6	f	t	f	F	X	
7	f	f	t	T		
8	f	f	f	F		X

EXERCISES
Section 3.3.

1. Answer the following questions for the method checkIt() below:

```
public static void checkIt (boolean a, boolean b, boolean c)
{
  if (a && (b || c))
  {
    System.out.println ("P is true");
  }
  else
  {
    System.out.println ("P isn't true");
  }
}
```

■ Transform *checkIt()* to *checkItExpand()*, a method where each *if* statement tests exactly one boolean variable. Instrument *checkItExpand()*
to record which edges are traversed. ("print" statements are fine for
this.)
■ Derive a GACC test set *T1* for *checkIt()*. Derive an edge coverage test set
T2 for *checkItExpand()*. Build *T2* so that it does **not** satisfy GACC on the
predicate in *checkIt()*.
■ Run both *T1* and *T2* on both *checkIt()* and *checkItExpand()*.

2. Answer the following questions for the method twoPred() below:

```
public String twoPred (int x, int y)
{
  boolean z;

  if (x < y)
    z = true;
  else
    z = false;

  if (z && x+y == 10)
    return "A";
  else
    return "B";
}
```

■ Identify test inputs for *twoPred()* that achieve Restricted Active Clause
Coverage (RACC).
■ Identify test inputs for *twoPred()* that achieve Restricted Inactive Clause
Coverage (RICC).

3. Answer the following questions for the program fragments below:

```
fragment P:            fragment Q:
  if (A || B || C)       if (A)
  {                      {
     m();                   m();
  }                         return;
  return;                }
                       if (B)
                       {
                          m();
                          return;
                       }
                       if (C)
                       {
                          m();
                       }
```

- Give a GACC test set for fragment P. (Note that GACC, CACC, and RACC yield identical test sets for this example.)
- Does the GACC test set for fragment P satisfy edge coverage on fragment Q?
- Write down an edge coverage test set for fragment Q. Make your test set include as few tests from the GACC test set as possible.

4. (**Challenging!**) For the TriTyp program, complete the test sets for the following coverage criteria by filling in the "don't care" values, ensuring reachability, and deriving the expected output. Download the program, compile it, and run it with your resulting test cases to verify correct outputs.
   - Predicate coverage (PC)
   - Clause coverage (CC)
   - Combinatorial coverage (CoC)
   - Correlated active clause coverage (CACC)
5. Repeat the prior exercise, but for the TestPat program in Chapter 2.
6. Repeat the prior exercise, but for the Quadratic program in Chapter 2.

3.4 SPECIFICATION-BASED LOGIC COVERAGE

Software specifications, both formal and informal, appear in a variety of forms and languages. They almost invariably include logical expressions, allowing the logic coverage criteria to be applied. We start by looking at their application to simple preconditions on methods.

Programmers often include preconditions as part of their methods. The preconditions are sometimes written as part of the design, and sometimes added later as documentation. Specification languages typically make preconditions explicit with the goal of analyzing the preconditions in the context of an invariant. A tester may consider developing the preconditions specifically as part of the testing process if preconditions do not exist. For a variety of reasons, including defensive programming and security, transforming preconditions into exceptions is common practice. In brief, preconditions are common and rich sources of predicates in specifications,

```
public static int cal (int month1, int day1, int month2,
                int day2, int year)
{
//**********************************************************
// Calculate the number of Days between the two given days in
// the same year.
// preconditions : day1 and day2 must be in same year
//           1 <= month1, month2 <= 12
//           1 <= day1, day2 <= 31
//           month1 <= month2
//           The range for year: 1 ... 10000
//**********************************************************
  int numDays;

  if (month2 == month1) // in the same month
    numDays = day2 - day1;
  else
  {
    // Skip month 0.
    int daysIn[] = {0, 31, 0, 31, 30, 31, 30, 31, 31, 30, 31, 30, 31};
    // Are we in a leap year?
    int m4 = year % 4;
    int m100 = year % 100;
    int m400 = year % 400;
    if ((m4 != 0) || ((m100 == 0) && (m400 != 0)))
      daysIn[2] = 28;
    else
      daysIn[2] = 29;

    // start with days in the two months
    numDays = day2 + (daysIn[month1] - day1);

    // add the days in the intervening months
    for (int i = month1 + 1; i <= month2-1; i++)
      numDays = daysIn[i] + numDays;
  }
  return (numDays);
}
```

Figure 3.4. Calendar method.

and so we focus on them here. Of course, other specification constructs, such as postconditions and invariants, also are rich sources of complex predicates.

Consider the cal method in Figure 3.4. The method lists explicit preconditions in natural language. These can be translated into predicate form as follows:

$$month1 >= 1 \land month1 <= 12 \land month2 >= 1 \land month2 <= 12 \land month1 <= month2$$
$$\land day1 >= 1 \land day1 <= 31 \land day2 >= 1 \land day2 <= 31 \land year >= 1 \land year <= 10000$$

The comment about $day1$ and $day2$ being in the same year can be safely ignored, because that prerequisite is enforced syntactically by the fact that only one parameter appears for $year$. It is probably also clear that these preconditions are not complete. Specifically, a day of 31 is valid only for some months. This requirement should be reflected in the specifications or in the program.

This predicate has a very simple structure. It has eleven clauses (which sounds like a lot!) but the only logical operator is "and." Satisfying predicate coverage for cal() is simple – all clauses need to be true for the true case and at least one clause needs to be false for the false case. So ($month1 = 4, month2 = 4, day1 = 12, day2 = 30, year = 1961$) satisfies the true case, and the false case is satisfied by violating the clause $month1 <= month2$, with ($month1 = 6, month2 = 4, day1 = 12, day2 = 30, year = 1961$). Clause coverage requires all clauses to be true and false.

Table 3.6. Correlated active clause coverage for cal() preconditions

	m1 ≥ 1	m1 ≤ 12	m2 ≥ 1	m2 ≤ 12	m1 ≤ m2	d1 ≥ 1	d1 ≤ 31	d2 ≥ 1	d2 ≤ 31	y ≥ 1	y ≤ 10000
1. m1 ≥ 1 = T	T	t	t	t	t	t	t	t	t	t	t
2. m1 ≥ 1 = F	F	t	t	t	t	t	t	t	t	t	t
3. m1 ≤ 12 = F	t	F	t	t	t	t	t	t	t	t	t
4. m2 ≥ 1 = F	t	t	F	t	t	t	t	t	t	t	t
5. m2 ≤ 12 = F	t	t	t	F	t	t	t	t	t	t	t
6. m1 ≤ m2 = F	t	t	t	t	F	t	t	t	t	t	t
7. d1 ≥ 1 = F	t	t	t	t	t	F	t	t	t	t	t
8. d1 ≤ 31 = F	t	t	t	t	t	t	F	t	t	t	t
9. d2 ≥ 1 = F	t	t	t	t	t	t	t	F	t	t	t
10. d2 ≤ 31 = F	t	t	t	t	t	t	t	t	F	t	t
11. y ≥ 1 = F	t	t	t	t	t	t	t	t	t	F	t
12. y ≤ 10000 = F	t	t	t	t	t	t	t	t	t	t	F

We might try to satisfy this requirement with only two tests, but some clauses are related and cannot both be false at the same time. For example, $month1$ cannot be less than 1 and greater than 12 at the same time. The true test for predicate coverage allows all clauses to be true, then we use the following tests to make each clause false: ($month1 = -1$, $month2 = -2$, $day1 = 0$, $day2 = 0$, $year = 0$) and ($month1 = 13$, $month2 = 14$, $day1 = 32$, $day2 = 32$, $year = 10500$).

We must first find how to make each clause determine the predicate to apply the ACC criteria. This turns out to be simple with disjunctive normal form predicates–all we have to do is make each minor clause true. To find the remaining tests, each other clause is made to be false in turn. Therefore, CACC (also RACC and GACC) is satisfied by the tests that are specified in Table 3.6. (To save space, we use abbreviations of the variable names.)

EXERCISES
Section 3.4.

Consider the remove() method from the Java Iterator interface. The remove() method has a complex precondition on the state of the Iterator, and the programmer can choose to detect violations of the precondition and report them as IllegalStateException.

1. Formalize the precondition.
2. Find (or write) an implementation of an Iterator. The Java Collection classes are a good place to search.
3. Develop and run CACC tests on the implementation.

3.5 LOGIC COVERAGE OF FINITE STATE MACHINES

Chapter 2 discussed the application of graph coverage criteria to finite state machines (FSMs). Recall that FSMs are graphs with nodes that represent states and edges that represent transitions. Each transition has a pre-state and a post-state. FSMs usually model behavior of the software and can be more or less formal and precise, depending on the needs and inclinations of the developers. This text views FSMs in the most generic way, as graphs. Differences in notations are considered only in terms of the effect they have on applying the criteria.

The most common way to apply logic coverage criteria to FSMs is to use logical expressions from the transitions as predicates. In the Elevator example in Chapter 2, the trigger and thus the predicate is $openButton = pressed$. Tests are created by applying the criteria from Section 3.2 to these predicates.

Consider the example in Figure 3.5. This FSM models the behavior of the memory seat in a car (Lexus 2003 ES300). The memory seat has two configurations for two separate drivers and controls the side mirrors (sideMirrors), the vertical height of the seat (seatBottom), the horizontal distance of the seat from the steering wheel (seatBack), and the lumbar support (lumbar). The intent is to remember the configurations so that the drivers can conveniently switch configurations with the press of a button. Each state in the figure has a number for efficient reference.

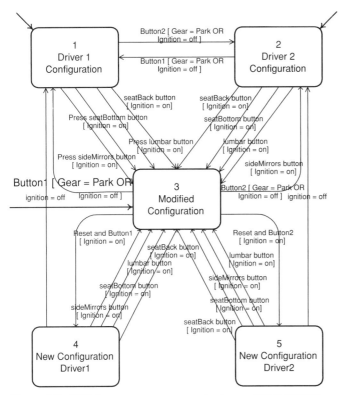

Figure 3.5. FSM for a memory car seat – Lexus 2003 ES300.

The initial state of the FSM is whichever configuration it was in when the system was last shut down, either Driver 1, Driver 2, or Modified Configuration. The drivers can modify the configuration by changing one of the four controls; changing the side mirrors, moving the seat backwards or forwards, raising or lowering the seat, or modifying the lumbar support (triggering events). These controls work only if the ignition is on (a guard). The driver can also change to the other configuration by pressing either Button1 or Button2 when the ignition is on. In these cases, the guards allow the configuration to be changed only if the Gear is in Park or the ignition is off. These are *safety constraints*, because it would be dangerous to allow the driver's seat to go flying around when the car is moving.

When the driver changes one of the controls, the memory seat is put into the modified configuration state. The new state can be saved by simultaneously pressing the Reset button and either Button1 or Button2 when the ignition is on. The new configuration is saved permanently when the ignition is turned off.

This type of FSM provides an effective model for testing software, although several issues must be understood and dealt with when creating predicates and then test values. Guards are not always explicitly listed as conjuncts, but they are conjuncts in effect and so should be combined with the triggers using the AND operator. In some specification languages, most notably SCR, the triggers actually imply two values. In SCR, if an event is labeled as triggering, it means that the value of the resulting expression must explicitly change. This implies two values, a before value and an

Table 3.7. Predicates from memory seat example

Pre-state	Post-state	Predicate
1	2	$Button2 \wedge (Gear = Park \vee ignition = off)$
1	3	$sideMirrors \wedge ignition = on$
1	3	$seatBottom \wedge ignition = on$
1	3	$lumbar \wedge ignition = on$
1	3	$seatBack \wedge ignition = on$
2	1	$Button1 \wedge (Gear = Park \vee ignition = off)$
2	3	$sideMirrors \wedge ignition = on$
2	3	$seatBottom \wedge ignition = on$
2	3	$lumbar \wedge ignition = on$
2	3	$seatBack \wedge ignition = on$
3	1	$Button1 \wedge (Gear = Park \vee ignition = off)$
3	2	$Button2 \wedge (Gear = Park \vee ignition = off)$
3	4	$Reset \wedge Button1 \wedge ignition = on$
3	5	$Reset \wedge Button2 \wedge ignition = on$
4	1	$ignition = off$
4	3	$sideMirrors \wedge ignition = on$
4	3	$seatBottom \wedge ignition = on$
4	3	$lumbar \wedge ignition = on$
4	3	$seatBack \wedge ignition = on$
5	2	$ignition = off$
5	3	$sideMirrors \wedge ignition = on$
5	3	$seatBottom \wedge ignition = on$
5	3	$lumbar \wedge ignition = on$
5	3	$seatBack \wedge ignition = on$

after value, and is modeled by introducing a new variable. For example, in the memory seat example, the transition from New Configuration Driver 1 to Driver 1 Configuration is taken when the ignition is turned off. If that is a triggering transition in the SCR sense, then the predicate needs to have two parts: $ignition = on \wedge$ $ignition' = off$. $ignition'$ is the after value.

The transitions from Modified Configuration to the two New Configuration states demonstrate another issue. The two buttons Reset and Button1 (or Button2) must be pressed **simultaneously**. In practical terms for this example, we would like to test for what happens when one button is pressed slightly prior to the other. Unfortunately, the mathematics of logical expressions used in this chapter do not have an explicit way to represent this requirement, thus it is not handled explicitly. The two buttons are connected in the predicate with the AND operator. In fact, this is a simple example of the general problem of timing, and needs to be addressed in the context of real-time software.

The predicates for the memory seat example are in Table 3.7 (using the state numbers from Figure 3.5).

The tests to satisfy the various criteria are fairly straightforward and are left to the exercises. Several issues must be addressed when choosing values for test cases. The first is that of reachability; the test case must include prefix values to reach the pre-state. For most FSMs, this is just a matter of finding a path from an initial state to the pre-state (using a depth first search), and the predicates associated with the transitions are solved to produce inputs. The memory seat example has three initial states, and the tester cannot control which one is entered because it depends on the state the system was in when it was last shut down. In this case, however, an obvious solution presents itself. We can begin every test by putting the Gear in park and pushing Button 1 (part of the prefix). If the system is in the Driver 2 or the Modified Configuration state, these inputs will cause the system to transition to the Driver 1 state. If the system is in the Driver 1 state, these inputs will have no effect. In all three cases, the system will effectively start in the Driver 1 state.

Some FSMs also have exit states that must be reached with postfix values. Finding these values is essentially the same as finding prefix values; that is, finding a path from the post-state to a final state. The memory seat example does not have an exit state, so this step can be skipped. We also need a way to see the results of the test case (verification values). This might be possible by giving an input to the program to print the current state, or causing some other output that is dependent on the state. The exact form and syntax this takes depends on the implementation, and so it cannot be finalized until the input-output behavior syntax of the software is designed.

One major advantage of this form of testing is determining the expected output. It is simply the post-state of the transition for the test case values that cause the transition to be true, and the pre-state for the test case values that cause the transition to be false (the system should remain in the current state). The only exception to this rule is that occasionally a false predicate might coincidentally be a true predicate for another transition, in which case the expected output should be the post-state of the alternate transition. This situation can be recognized automatically. Also, if a transition is from a state back to itself, then the pre-state and the post-state are the same and the expected output is the same whether the transition is true or false.

The final problem is that of converting a test case (composed of prefix values, test case values, postfix values, and expected output) into an executable test script. The potential problem here is that the variable assignments for the predicates must be converted into inputs to the software. This has been called the *mapping problem* with FSMs and is analogous to the internal variable problem of Section 3.3. Sometimes this step is a simple syntactic rewriting of predicate assignments (Button1 to program input *button1*). Other times, the input values can be directly encoded as method calls and embedded into a program (for example, Button1 becomes *pressButton1()*). At other times, however, this problem is much greater and can involve turning seemingly small inputs at the FSM modeling level into long sequences of inputs or method calls. The exact situation depends on the software implementation; thus a general solution to this problem is elusive at best.

EXERCISES
Section 3.5.

1. For the Memory Seat finite state machine, complete the test sets for the following coverage criteria by satisfying the predicates, ensuring reachability, and computing the expected output.
   - Predicate coverage
   - Correlated active clause coverage
   - General inactive clause coverage

2. Redraw Figure 3.5 to have fewer transitions, but more clauses. Specifically, nodes 1, 2, 4, and 5 each has four transitions to node 3. Rewrite these transitions to have only one transition from each of nodes 1, 2, 4, and 5 to node 3, and the clauses are connected by ORs. Then derive tests to satisfy CACC for the resulting predicates. How do these tests compare with the tests derived from the original graph?

3. Consider the following deterministic finite state machine:

Current State	Condition	Next State
Idle	$a \vee b$	Active
Active	$a \wedge b$	Idle
Active	$\neg b$	WindDown
WindDown	a	Idle

(a) Draw the finite state machine.

(b) This machine does not specify which conditions cause a state to transition back to itself. However, these conditions can be derived from the existing conditions. Derive the conditions under which each state will transition back to itself.

(c) Find CACC tests for each transition from the Active state.

4. Pick a household appliance such as a watch, calculator, microwave, VCR, clock-radio, or programmable thermostat. Draw the FSM that represents your appliance's behavior. Derive tests to satisfy predicate coverage, correlated active clause coverage, and general inactive clause coverage.

5. Implement the memory seat FSM. Design an appropriate input language to your implementation and turn the tests derived for question 1 into test scripts. Run the tests.

3.6 DISJUNCTIVE NORMAL FORM CRITERIA

In this section, we revisit the testing of boolean expressions. Instead of focusing on each clause by itself, we look at the structure of the predicate as expressed in a disjunctive normal form (DNF) representation.

A *literal* is a clause or the negation of a clause. A *term* is a set of literals connected by logical ANDs. A *Disjunctive Normal Form (DNF)* predicate is a set of terms connected by logical ORs. Terms in DNF predicates are also called *implicants*, because if a term is true, the entire predicate is also true.

For example, this predicate is in disjunctive normal form:

$$(a \wedge \neg c) \vee (b \wedge \neg c)$$

but this (equivalent) one is not:

$$(a \vee b) \wedge \neg c$$

In general, the DNF representation of a predicate is not unique. For example, the above predicate can be rewritten in the following DNF form:

$$(a \wedge b \wedge \neg c) \vee (a \wedge \neg b \wedge \neg c) \vee (\neg a \wedge b \wedge \neg c)$$

In this section, we follow convention for DNF representations and use adjacency for the $\land$ operator and an overstrike for the negation operator. This approach makes the sometimes long expressions easier to read. So, the last DNF predicate above will be written

$$ab\bar{c} \lor a\bar{b}\bar{c} \lor \bar{a}b\bar{c}$$

For our purposes, the interesting thing about the DNF representations is the test criteria that go with them. One way of testing with respect to DNF representations is to assign values to clauses so that each implicant in the DNF representation is satisfied on at least one test. Notice that all of these tests result in the predicate evaluating to true, causing the problem that we never test the false case. We address this problem by formulating a DNF expression for the negation of the predicate in question, and evaluating tests for the negated predicate with the same coverage criteria used for the predicate itself. These ideas are enough to define our first DNF coverage criterion:

CRITERION **3.20 Implicant Coverage (IC):** *Given DNF representations of a predicate f and its negation $\bar{f}$, for each implicant in f and $\bar{f}$, TR contains the requirement that the implicant evaluate to true.*

As an example of IC, consider the following DNF expression for a predicate f in three clauses.

$$f(a,\, b,\, c) \,=\, ab \lor b\bar{c}$$

Its negation can be computed as follows:

$$\begin{aligned}
\bar{f}(a,\, b,\, c) &= \overline{ab \lor b\bar{c}} \\
&= \overline{ab} \land \overline{b\bar{c}} \\
&= (\bar{a} \lor \bar{b}) \land (\bar{b} \lor c) \\
&= \bar{a}\bar{b} \lor \bar{a}c \lor \overline{bb} \lor \bar{b}c \\
&= (\bar{a}\bar{b} \lor \overline{bb}) \lor \bar{b}c \lor \bar{a}c \\
&= (\bar{b} \lor \bar{b}c) \lor \bar{a}c \\
&= \bar{b} \lor \bar{a}c
\end{aligned}$$

Collectively, f and $\bar{f}$ have a total of four implicants:

$$\{ab,\, b\bar{c},\, \bar{b},\, \bar{a}c\}$$

An obvious but simple way to generate tests for these four implicants would be to choose one test for each. However, they can be satisfied with fewer tests. Consider the following table, which indicates the truth assignments required for each of the four implicants.

	a	b	c		
1) ab	T	T		a	b
2) $b\bar{c}$		T	F	b	$\bar{c}$
3) $\bar{b}$		F		$\bar{b}$	
4) $\bar{a}c$	F		T	$\bar{a}$	c

The first and second row can be satisfied simultaneously, as can the third and fourth. Thus only two tests are needed to satisfy IC for this example:

$$T_1 = \{TTF, FFT\}$$

Note that IC subsumes predicate coverage, but will not necessarily subsume any of the ACC criteria.

A problem with IC is that tests might be chosen so that a single test satisfies multiple implicants. Indeed, this is how the two element test set T_1 above was chosen. Although this lets testers minimize the size of test suites, it is a bad thing from the perspective of testing the unique contributions that each implicant might bring to a predicate. Thus we introduce a method to force a kind of "independence" of the implicant.

The first step is to obtain a DNF form where each implicant can be satisfied without satisfying any other implicant. Fortunately, standard approaches already exist that can be used. A *proper subterm* of an implicant is an implicant with one or more subterms removed. For example, proper subterms of abc are ab and b. A *prime implicant* is an implicant such that no proper subterm of the implicant is also an implicant of the same predicate. That is, in a prime implicant, it is not possible to remove a term without changing the value of the predicate. For example, in the following reformulation of the previous example

$$f(a, b, c) = abc \vee ab\bar{c} \vee b\bar{c}$$

abc is not a prime implicant, because a proper subterm, namely ab, is an implicant. $ab\bar{c}$ is not a prime implicant either, because the proper subterm ab is an implicant, as is the proper subterm $b\bar{c}$.

We need one additional notion. An implicant is *redundant* if it can be omitted without changing the value of the predicate. As an example, the formula

$$f(a, b, c) = ab \vee ac \vee b\bar{c}$$

has three prime implicants, but the first one, ab, is redundant. A DNF representation is *minimal* if every implicant is prime and no implicant is redundant. Minimal DNF representations can be computed algebraically or by hand with Karnaugh maps, as discussed in a subsequent section.

With the above definitions, we can assume that we have a minimal DNF representation of a predicate. Given a minimal DNF representation for f, a *unique true point* with respect to the ith implicant is an assignment of truth values such that the ith implicant is true and all other implicants are false. It should be noted that if it is infeasible to make all of the "other" implicants false, then the implicant is redundant, violating our assumption that f is in minimal DNF form. The notion of unique true points allows a new criterion to be defined, *unique true point coverage (UTPC)*:

CRITERION **3.21 Unique True Point Coverage (UTPC):**   *Given minimal DNF representations of a predicate f and its negation $\bar{f}$, TR contains a unique true point for each implicant in f and each implicant in $\bar{f}$.*

To return to our previous example:

$$f(a, b, c) = ab \vee b\bar{c}$$
$$\bar{f}(a, b, c) = \bar{b} \vee \bar{a}c$$

Both the f and $\bar{f}$ representations are minimal DNF representations. The following table shows the required assignments to the clauses a, b, and c to satisfy each implicant:

	a	b	c
ab	T	T	
$b\bar{c}$		T	F
$\bar{b}$		F	
$\bar{a}c$	F		T

The truth assignments to the remaining clauses must be such that no other implicants are true. For the first implicant, ab, c must be true or the second implicant will be true. For the second implicant, $b\bar{c}$, a must take the value false. For the third implicant, $\bar{b}$, there are three choices for unique true points: $\{FFF, TFF, TFT\}$. We have shown the first choice in the table below. Finally, for the fourth implicant, $\bar{a}c$, b must take the value true. The following table summarizes the discussion:

	a	b	c
ab	T	T	t
$b\bar{c}$	f	T	F
$\bar{b}$	f	F	f
$\bar{a}c$	F	t	T

Thus, the following test set satisfies UTPC:

$$T_2 = \{TTT, FTF, FFF, FTT\}$$

Although IC is relatively weak, UTPC is a fairly powerful coverage criterion. It is interesting to note that none of the active or inactive clause coverage criteria subsume UTPC. This can be seen by considering a simple counting argument. The DNF representation for a predicate with n clauses may have up to 2^{n-1} prime implicants in a minimal DNF representation. Hence, UTPC can require up to an exponential number of tests, which is more than the linear number $(n + 1)$ required by the clause coverage criteria. The potential exponential explosion does not automatically disqualify UTPC from practical consideration. For many predicates, UTPC generates a modest number of tests. One way of looking at this is that UTPC produces as many tests as the DNF representation of a predicate demands. In other words, more complex DNF representations demand more test cases.

UTPC does not subsume the active clause coverage criteria. A counterexample can be seen as follows. Consider the predicate

$$f(a, b, c) = ac \vee b\bar{c}$$
$$\bar{f}(a, b, c) = \bar{a}c \vee \bar{b}\bar{c}$$

A possible UTPC test set is

$$T_3 = \{TTT, TTF, FFT, FFF\}$$

The conditions under which c determines the value of f compute to $a \oplus b$. Notice that in all of the tests in T_3, a and b have the same value, and therefore $a \oplus b$ always evaluates to false. In other words, in this test set, c never determines the value of f. Hence, UTPC does not even subsume GACC, let alone CACC or RACC.

The literature contains a number of other DNF coverage criteria. The motivation for these coverage criteria is their ability to detect certain categories of faults. We already have a definition for unique true points. We need a corresponding definition for near false points to articulate these additional criteria. Given a DNF representation of a predicate f, a *near false point* for f with respect to clause c in implicant i is an assignment of truth values such that f is false, but if c is negated and all other clauses are left as is, i (and hence f) evaluates to true. For example, if f is

$$f(a, b, c, d) = ab \lor cd$$

then the near false points are $FTFF$, $FTFT$, $FTTF$ for clause a in the implicant ab, and $TFFF$, $TFFT$, $TFTF$ for clause b in the implicant ab. Corresponding unique true point and near false point pair coverage (CUTPNFP) is defined as follows:

> CRITERION **3.22 Corresponding Unique True Point and Near False Point Pair Coverage (CUTPNFP):** *Given a minimal DNF representation of a predicate f, for each clause c in each implicant i, TR contains a unique true point for i and a near false point for c in i such that the two points differ only in the truth value of c.*

By way of example, for

$$f(a, b, c, d) = ab \lor cd$$

if we consider clause a in the implicant ab, we can choose one of three unique true points, namely, $TTFF$, $TTFT$, $TTTF$, and pair each, respectively, with the corresponding near false points $FTFF$, $FTFT$, $FTTF$. So, for example, we could choose the first pair, $TTFF$, $FTFF$, to satisfy CUTPNFP with respect to clause a in implicant ab. Likewise, we could choose the pair $TTFF$, $TFFF$ to satisfy CUTPNFP with respect to clause b in implicant ab, the pair $FFTT$, $FFFT$ to satisfy CUTPNFP with respect to clause c in implicant cd, and the pair $FFTT$, $FFTF$ to satisfy CUTPNFP with respect to clause d in implicant cd, The resulting CUTPNFP set is

$$(TTFF, FFTT, FTFF, TFFF, FFFT, FFTF)$$

Note that the first two tests are unique true points, and the remaining four are corresponding near false points.

Table 3.8 defines a set of syntactic faults on predicates in DNF form.[3] Figure 3.6 gives a detection relationship between the types of faults in 3.8. Specifically, if a test set is guaranteed to detect a given type of fault, then the test set is also guaranteed to detect the types of faults "downstream" from that fault. Note that ENF is a particularly easy fault to catch – any test detects it.

As an example of relating the DNF coverage criteria to the fault classes, consider the UTPC criterion in the context of TOF faults. UTPC effectively detects TOF

Table 3.8. DNF fault classes

Fault	Description
Expression Negation Fault (ENF)	Expression wrongly implemented as its negation: e.g. $f = ab + c$ written as $f' = \overline{ab + c}$
Term Negation Fault (TNF)	A term is wrongly implemented as its negation: e.g. $f = ab + c$ written as $f' = \overline{ab} + c$
Term Omission Fault (TOF)	A term is wrongly omitted: e.g. $f = ab + c$ written as $f' = ab$
Literal Negation Fault (LNF)	A literal is wrongly implemented as its negation: e.g. $f = ab + c$ written as $f' = a\bar{b} + c$
Literal Reference Fault (LRF)	A literal is wrongly replaced by another literal: e.g. $f = ab + bcd$ written as $f' = ad + bcd$
Literal Omission Fault (LOF)	A literal is wrongly omitted: e.g. $f = ab + c$ written as $f' = a + c$
Literal Insertion Fault (LIF)	A literal is wrongly added to a term: e.g. $f = ab + c$ written as $f' = ab + \bar{b}c$
Operator Reference Fault (ORF+)	An 'Or' is wrongly replaced by 'And': e.g. $f = ab + c$ written as $f' = abc$
Operator Reference Fault (ORF*)	An 'And' is wrongly replaced by 'Or': e.g. $f = ab + c$ written as $f' = a + b + c$

faults. Note that UTPC demands a unique true point from the omitted implicant. Since the true point is unique, no other implicant will coincidentally yield the correct truth value on that test. Hence, the implementation will produce the negation of the desired truth value on the test, thereby revealing the TOF fault. Given the detection relationships in Figure 3.6, we can infer that UTPC also detects ORF+, LNF, TNF, and ENF faults. As another example, CUTPNFP effectively detects LOF faults. The reason why is that for every clause c in term i, CUTPNFP demands an unique true point and a near false point. These two tests differ only in the value of the clause c. Hence if the literal mentioning c is wrongly deleted in the implementation, both of these tests will produce the same truth value, thereby revealing the fault. Given the detection relationships in Figure 3.6, we can infer that CUTPNFP also detects ORF*, LNF, TNF, and ENF faults. In addition, although CUTPNFP does not subsume UTPC, CUTPNFP also detects the faults that UTPC detects.

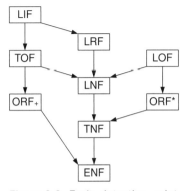

Figure 3.6. Fault detection relationships.

CUTPNFP does not necessarily detect LIF faults, but it does subsume RACC. For other detection relations we refer the reader to the literature, where other, yet more powerful (and expensive!) criteria are defined, some of which do indeed detect LIF.

Karnaugh Maps

In this section, we review Karnaugh maps, which are exceedingly useful for producing DNF representations for predicates with a modest number of clauses.

A Karnaugh map is a tabular representation of a predicate with the special property that groupings of adjacent table entries correspond to simple DNF representations. Karnaugh maps are useful for predicates of up to four or five clauses; beyond that, they become cumbersome. A Karnaugh map for a predicate in four clauses is given below:

	ab 00	01	11	10
cd 00			1	
01			1	
11	1	1	1	1
10			1	

Karnaugh map table for the predicate "$ab \vee cd$".

For now, suppose that entries in the table are restricted to truth values. Truth values can be assigned in 2^{2^n} possible ways to the 2^n entries in a table for n clauses. So, the four clauses represented in the table above have 2^4 or 16 entries, and $2^{16} = 65,536$ possible functions. The reader will be relieved to know that we will not enumerate all of these in the text. Notice the labeling of truth values along the columns and rows. In particular, notice that any pair of adjacent cells differ in the truth value of exactly one clause. It might help to think of the edges of the Karnaugh map as being connected as well, so that the top and bottom rows are adjacent, as are the left and right columns (that is, a toroidal mapping from 2-space to 3-space).

The particular function represented in the Karnaugh map above can be spelled out in full:

$$ab\bar{c}\bar{d} \vee ab\bar{c}d \vee abcd \vee abc\bar{d} \vee \bar{a}bcd \vee \bar{a}bcd \vee a\bar{b}cd$$

The expression simplifies to

$$ab \vee cd$$

The simplification can be read off the Karnaugh map by grouping together adjacent cells into rectangles of size 2^k for some $k > 0$ and forming rectangles of size 1 for cells with no adjacent cells. Overlaps among the groupings are fine. We give an example in three clauses to illustrate. Consider the following Karnaugh map:

	a, b 00	01	11	10
c 0		1	1	
1	1		1	1

Four rectangles of size 2 can be extracted from this graph. They are the functions $b\bar{c}$, ab, ac, and $\bar{b}c$, and are represented by the following Karnaugh maps:

		a, b		
	00	01	11	10
c 0		1	1	
1				

		a, b		
	00	01	11	10
c 0			1	
1			1	

		a, b		
	00	01	11	10
c 0				
1			1	1

		a, b		
	00	01	11	10
c 0				
1	1			1

At first, the last of these might be a bit hard to see as a rectangle, but remember that the Karnaugh map is joined at the edges, left and right, as well as top and bottom. We could write the original function out as the disjunction of these four Karnaugh maps, each of which gives a prime implicant, but notice that the second, representing ab, is, in fact, redundant with the other three implicants, since all of its entries are covered by another of the Karnaugh maps. The resulting minimal DNF expression is

$$f = b\bar{c} \vee ac \vee \bar{b}c$$

One can also note that all of the entries of ac are covered by other Karnaugh maps, so ac is redundant with the remaining three implicants. So a different minimal DNF representation is

$$f = b\bar{c} \vee ab \vee \bar{b}c$$

Negations in DNF form are also easy to pull from a Karnaugh map. Consider again the function f given above. Negating f yields the Karnaugh map:

		a, b		
	00	01	11	10
c 0	1			1
1		1		

Here, the three cells in the Karnaugh map can be covered with two rectangles, one of size 2, and the other of size 1. The resulting nonredundant, prime implicant formulation is

$$\bar{f} = \bar{b}\bar{c} \vee \bar{a}bc$$

Karnaugh maps are extremely convenient notations to derive test sets for many of the logic coverage criteria. For example, consider again the predicate $ab \vee cd$. Unique true points are simply true points covered by a single rectangle. Hence, of all the true points in $ab \vee cd$, all but $TTTT$ are unique true points. Near false points for any given true point are simply those false points that are immediately adjacent in the Karnaugh map. To determine UTPC tests, one simply takes the Karnaugh maps for f and $\bar{f}$ and, for each implicant, picks a cell covered only by that implicant. For CUTPNFP, one pairs up near false points with unique true points, being careful to obtain a pairing for each clause in f. Pairing of true points with near false points is also an easy way to develop RACC tests. Note that for RACC tests, it does not matter if the true points are unique or not.

EXERCISES
Section 3.6.

Use functions (1) through (4) to answer the following questions.

1. $f = ab\bar{c} + \bar{a}b\bar{c}$
2. $f = \bar{a}\bar{b}\bar{c}\bar{d} + abcd$
3. $f = ab + a\bar{b}c + \bar{a}\bar{b}c$
4. $f = \bar{a}\bar{c}\bar{d} + \bar{c}d + bcd$
   (a) Draw the Karnaugh maps for f and $\bar{f}$.
   (b) Find the nonredundant prime implicant representation for f and $\bar{f}$.
   (c) Give a test set that satisfies implicant coverage (IC) for f.
   (d) Give a test set that satisfies unique true point coverage (UTPC) for f.
   (e) Give a test set that satisfies Corresponding unique true point and near false point pair coverage (CUTPNFP) for f.
5 Use the following predicates to answer questions (a) through (e). In the questions, "simplest" means "fewest number of variable references."
   ■ $W = (B \wedge \neg C \wedge \neg D)$
   ■ $X = (B \wedge D) \vee (\neg B \neg D)$
   ■ $Y = (A \wedge B)$
   ■ $Z = (\neg B \wedge D)$
   (a) Draw the Karnaugh map for the predicates. Put AB on the top and CD on the side. Label each cell with W, X, Y, and/or Z as appropriate.
   (b) Write the simplest expression that describes all cells that have more than one definition.
   (c) Write the simplest expression that describes all cells that have no definitions.
   (d) Write the simplest expression that describes $X \vee Z$.
   (e) Give a test set for expression X that uses each prime implicant once.

6 Develop a counterexample to show that CUTPNFP does not subsume UPIC. Hint: You might wish to start with the expression given in the text, $f = ab + cd$.

3.7 BIBLIOGRAPHIC NOTES

The active clause criteria seem to have their beginnings in Myers' 1979 book [249]. A more accessible paper is by Zhu [367]. He defined decision and condition coverage, which Chilenski and Miller later used as a conceptual basis for MCDC [73, 305]. The definitions as originally given correspond to GACC in this book and did not address whether minor clauses had to have the same value for both values of the major clause. Chilenski also emphasized that the abbreviation should be "MCDC," not "MC/DC," and he has never put the '/' in the middle [72]. Most members of the aviation community interpreted MCDC to mean that the values of the minor clauses had to be the same, an interpretation that is called "unique-cause MCDC" [72]. Unique-cause MCDC corresponds to our RACC. More recently, the FAA has accepted the view that the minor clauses can differ, which is called "masking MCDC" [74]. Masking MCDC corresponds to our CACC. Our previous paper [17] clarified the definitions in the form used in this book and introduced the term "CACC."

The inactive clause criteria are adapted from the RC/DC method of Vilkomir and Bowen [332].

The result that the *internal variable* problem is formally undecidable is from Offutt's PhD dissertation [101, 262]. The problem is of primary importance in the automatic test data generation literature [36, 39, 101, 102, 150, 176, 179, 190, 191, 243, 295, 267].

Jasper et al. presented techniques for generating tests to satisfy MCDC [177]. They took the definition of MCDC from Chilenski and Miller's paper with the "default" interpretation that the minor clauses must be the same for both values of the major clauses. They went on to modify the interpretation so that if two clauses are coupled, which implies it is impossible to satisfy determination for both, the two clauses are allowed to have different values for the minor clauses. The fact that different values are allowed only when clauses are coupled puts their interpretation of MCDC between the RACC and CACC of this book.

Weyuker, Goradia, and Singh presented techniques for generating test data for software specifications that are limited to boolean variables [342]. The techniques were compared in terms of the ability of the resulting test cases to kill mutants (introduced in Chapter 5) [99, 101]. The results were that their technique, which is closely related to MCDC, performed better than any of the other techniques. Weyuker et al. incorporated syntax as well as meaning into their criteria. They presented a notion called *meaningful impact*, which is related to the notion of determination, but which has a syntactic basis rather than a semantic one.

Kuhn investigated methods for generating tests to satisfy various decision-based criteria, including MCDC tests [194]. He used the definition from Chilenski and Miller [73, 305], and proposed the boolean derivative to satisfy MCDC. In effect, this interpreted MCDC in such a way to match CACC.

Dupuy and Leveson's 2000 paper evaluated MCDC experimentally [108]. They presented results from an empirical study that compared pure functional testing with functional testing augmented by MCDC. The experiment was performed during the testing of the attitude control software for the HETE-2 (High Energy Transient Explorer) scientific satellite. The definition of MCDC from their paper is the traditional definition given in the FAA report and Chilenski and Miller's paper: "Every point of entry and exit in the program has been invoked at least once, every condition in a decision in the program has taken on all possible outcomes at least once, and each condition has been shown to affect that decision outcome independently. A condition is shown to affect a decision's outcome independently by varying just that decision while holding fixed all other possible conditions."

Note the misstatement in last line: "varying just that decision" should be "varying just that condition." This does not say that the decision has a different value when the condition's value changes. "Holding fixed" can be assumed to imply that the minor clauses cannot change with different values for the major clause (that is, RACC, not CACC).

The full predicate method of Offutt, Liu, Abdurazik and Ammann [272] explicitly relaxes the requirement that the major clauses have the same value as the predicate. This is equivalent to CACC and almost the same as masking MCDC.

Jones and Harrold have developed a method for reducing the regression tests that were developed to satisfy MCDC [180]. They defined MCDC as follows: "MC/DC is a stricter form of decision (or branch) coverage.... MC/DC requires that each condition in a decision be shown by execution to independently affect the outcome of the decision." This is taken directly from Chilenski and Miller's original paper, and their interpretation of the definition is the same as CACC.

SCR was first discussed by Henninger [157] and its use in model checking and testing was introduced by Atlee [20, 21].

The method of determining p_c given in this book uses the boolean derivative developed by Akers [6]. Both Chilenski and Richey [74] and Kuhn [194] applied Akers's derivative to exactly the problem given in this chapter. The other methods are the pairs table method of Chilenski and Miller and the tree method, independently discovered by Chilenski and Richey [74] and Offutt et al. [272]. The tree method implements the boolean derivative method in a procedural way.

Ordered binary decision diagrams (OBDDs) offer another way of determining p_c. In particular, consider any OBDD in which clause c is ordered last. Then any path through the OBDD that reaches a node labeled c (there will be exactly zero, one, or two such nodes) is, in fact, an assignment of values to the other variables so that c determines p. Continuing the path on to the constants T and F yields a pair of tests satisfying $RACC$ with respect to c. Selecting two different paths that reach the same node labeled c, and then extending each so that one reaches T and the other reaches F yields a pair of tests that satisfy $CACC$, but not $RACC$, with respect to c. Finally, if two nodes are labeled c, then it is possible to satisfy $GACC$ but not $CACC$ with respect to c: Select paths to each of the two nodes labeled c, extend one path by choosing c true, and the other by choosing c false. Both paths will necessarily end up in the same node, namely, either T or F. ICC tests with respect to c can be derived by considering paths to T and F in the OBDD where the paths do not include variable c. The attractive aspect of using OBDDs to derive ACC or ICC tests is that a variety of existing tools can handle a relatively large number of clauses. The unattractive aspect is that for a predicate with N clauses, N different OBDDs for a given function are required, since the clause being attended to needs to be the last in the ordering. To the knowledge of the authors, the use of OBDDs to derive ACC or ICC tests does not appear in the literature.

Beizer's book [29] includes a chapter on DNF testing, including a variant of IC coverage for f, but not $\bar{f}$, and an extensive development of Karnaugh maps. We do not address criteria defined predicates expressed in conjunctive normal form (CNF). The reason is that every DNF coverage criteria has a dual in CNF. Kuhn [194] developed the first fault detection relations; this work was greatly expanded by Yu, Lau, and Chen, who developed much of the key material relating DNF coverage criteria to fault detecting ability. Two good papers to begin study of this topic are by Chen and Lau [63], which develops a variety of coverage criteria, including CUTPNFP, and Lau and Yu [202], which is the source for the fault class hierarchy shown in Figure 3.6. In personal communications, Greg Williams and Gary Kaminski provided the authors with valuable assistance in organizing and expanding the DNF fault detection material. Greg Williams also developed the counterexample to show that UTPC and the ACC criteria do not share a subsumption relation.

NOTES

1 In practice, this "thought" turned out to be the collective effort of many researchers, who published dozens of papers over a period of several decades.
2 Old hands at testing may recognize and even be tired of the triangle example. It is used as a teaching tool for the same reasons it has staying power in the literature: it's a familiar problem; the control structure is interesting enough to illustrate most issues; and it does not use language features that make this analysis really hard, such as loops and indirect references. This version of TriTyp is a bit overly complicated, but that does help illustrate the concepts.
3 The notion of mutation operators developed in the Chapter 5 is closely related to the notion of fault classes presented here.

4

Input Space Partitioning

In a very fundamental way, all testing is about choosing elements from the input space of the software being tested. The criteria presented previously can be viewed as defining ways to divide the input space according to the test requirements. The assumption is that any collection of values that satisfies the same test requirement will be "just as good." Input space partitioning takes that view in a much more direct way. The input *domain* is defined in terms of the possible values that the input parameters can have. The input parameters can be method parameters and global variables, objects representing current state, or user-level inputs to a program, depending on what kind of software artifact is being analyzed. The input domain is then partitioned into regions that are assumed to contain equally useful values from a testing perspective, and values are selected from each region.

This way of testing has several advantages. It is fairly easy to get started because it can be applied with no automation and very little training. The tester does not need to understand the implementation; everything is based on a description of the inputs. It is also simple to "tune" the technique to get more or fewer tests.

Consider an abstract partition q over some domain D. The partition q defines a set of equivalence classes, which we simply call *blocks*, B_q.[1] The blocks are pairwise disjoint, that is

$$b_i \cap b_j = \emptyset, i \neq j; b_i, b_j \in B_q$$

and together the blocks cover the domain D, that is

$$\bigcup_{b \in B_q} b = D$$

This is illustrated in Figure 4.1. The input domain D is partitioned into three blocks, b_1, b_2, and b_3. The partition defines the values contained in each block and is usually designed from knowledge of what the software is supposed to do.

The idea in partition coverage is that any test in a block is as good as any other for testing. Several partitions are sometimes considered together, which, if not done carefully, leads to a combinatorial explosion of test cases.

Input Domain D

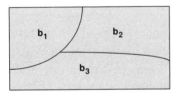

Figure 4.1. Partitioning of input domain D into three blocks.

A common way to apply input space partitioning is to start by considering the domain of each parameter separately, partitioning each domain's possible values into blocks, and then combining the variables for each parameter. Sometimes the parameters are considered completely independently, and sometimes they are considered in conjunction, usually by taking the semantics of the program into account. This process is called *input domain modeling* and the next section gives more details.

Each partition is usually based on some *characteristic C* of the program, the program's inputs, or the program's environment. Some possible characteristic examples are:

- Input X is null
- Order of file F (sorted, inverse sorted, arbitrary)
- Min separation distance of two aircraft

Each characteristic C allows the tester to define a partition. Formally, a partition *must* satisfy two properties:

1. The partition must cover the entire domain (completeness)
2. The blocks must not overlap (disjoint)

As an example, consider the characteristic "order of file F" mentioned above. This could be used to create the following (defective) partitioning:

- Order of file F
  - b_1 = Sorted in ascending order
  - b_2 = Sorted in descending order
  - b_3 = Arbitrary order

However, this is **not** a valid partitioning. Specifically, if the file is of length 0 or 1, then the file will belong in all three blocks. That is, the blocks are not disjoint. The easiest strategy to address this problem is to make sure that each characteristic addresses only one property. The problem above is that the notions of being sorted into ascending order and being sorted into descending order are lumped into the same characteristic. Splitting into two characteristics, namely sorted ascending and sorted descending, solves the problem. The result is the following (valid) partitioning of two characteristics.

- File F sorted ascending
  - b_1 = True
  - b_2 = False

- File *F* sorted descending
    - b_1 = True
    - b_2 = False

With these blocks, files of length 0 or 1 are in the True block for both characteristics.

The completeness and disjointness properties are formalized for pretty pragmatic reasons, and not just to be mathematically fashionable. Partitions that are not complete or disjoint probably reflect a lack of clarity in the rationale for the partition. In particular, if a partition actually encodes two or three rationales, the partition is likely to be quite messy, and it is also likely to violate either the completeness or the disjointness property (or both!). Identifying and correcting completeness or disjointness errors typically results in esthetically more pleasing partitions. Further, formally objectionable "partitions" cause unnecessary problems when generating tests, as discussed below. The rest of this chapter assumes that the partitions are both complete and disjoint.

4.1 INPUT DOMAIN MODELING

The first step in input domain modeling is identification of testable functions. Consider the TriTyp program from Chapter 3. TriTyp clearly has only one testable function with three parameters. The situation is more complex for Java class APIs. Each public method is typically a testable function that should be tested individually. However, the characteristics are often the same for several methods, so it helps to develop a common set of characteristics for the entire class and then develop specific tests for each method. Finally, large systems are certainly amenable to the input space partition approach, and such systems often supply complex functionality. Tools like UML use cases can be used to identify testable functions. Each use case is associated with a specific intended functionality of the system, so it is very likely that the use case designers have useful characteristics in mind that are relevant to developing test cases. For example, a "withdrawal" use case for an ATM identifies "withdrawing cash" as a testable function. Further, it suggests useful categories such as "Is Card Valid?" and "Relation of Withdrawal Policy to Withdrawal Request."

The second step is to identify all of the parameters that can affect the behavior of a given testable function. This step isn't particularly creative, but it is important to carry it out completely. In the simple case of testing a stateless method, the parameters are simply the formal parameters to the method. If the method has state, which is common in many object-oriented classes, then the state must be included as a parameter. For example, the insert(Comparable obj) method for a binary tree class behaves differently depending on whether or not obj is already in the tree. Hence, the current state of the tree needs to be explicitly identified as a parameter to the insert() method. In a slightly more complex example, a method find(String str) that finds the location of str in a file depends, obviously, on the particular file being searched. Hence, the test engineer explicitly identifies the file as a parameter to the find() method. Together, all of the parameters form the *input domain* of the function under test.

The third step, and the key creative engineering step, is modeling the input domain articulated in the prior step. An *input domain model* (*IDM*) represents the input space of the system under test in an abstract way. A test engineer describes the structure of the input domain in terms of input *characteristics*. The test engineer creates a *partition* for each characteristic. The partition is a set of *blocks*, each of which contains a set of *values*. From the perspective of that particular characteristic, the values in each block are considered equivalent.

A test input is a tuple of values, one for each parameter. By definition, the test input belongs to exactly one block from each characteristic. Thus, if we have even a modest number of characteristics, the number of possible combinations may be infeasible. In particular, adding another characteristic with *n* blocks increases the number of combinations by a factor of *n*. Hence, controlling the total number of combinations is a key feature of any practical approach to input domain testing. In our view, this is the job of the coverage criteria, which we address in Section 4.2.

Different testers will come up with different models, depending on creativity and experience. These differences create a potential for variance in the quality of the resulting tests. The structured method to support input domain modeling presented in this chapter can decrease this variance and increase the overall quality of the IDM.

Once the IDM is built and values are identified, some combinations of the values may be invalid. The IDM must include information to help the tester identify and avoid or remove invalid sub-combinations. The model needs a way to represent these restrictions. Constraints are discussed further in Section 4.3.

The next section provides two different approaches to input domain modeling. The *interface-based* approach develops characteristics directly from input parameters to the program under test. The *functionality-based* approach develops characteristics from a functional or behavioral view of the program under test. The tester must choose which approach to use. Once the IDM is developed, several coverage criteria are available to decide which combinations of values to use to test the software. These are discussed in Section 4.2.

4.1.1 Interface-Based Input Domain Modeling

The interface-based approach considers each particular parameter in isolation. This approach is almost mechanical to follow, but the resulting tests are surprisingly good.

An obvious strength of using the interface-based approach is that it is easy to identify characteristics. The fact that each characteristic limits itself to a single parameter also makes it easy to translate the abstract tests into executable test cases.

A weakness of this approach is that not all the information available to the test engineer will be reflected in the interface domain model. This means that the IDM may be incomplete and hence additional characteristics are needed.

Another weakness is that some parts of the functionality may depend on combinations of specific values of several interface parameters. In the interface-based approach each parameter is analyzed in isolation with the effect that important sub-combinations may be missed.

Consider the TriTyp program from Chapter 3. It has three integer parameters that represent the lengths of three sides of a triangle. In an interface-based IDM, Side1 will have a number of characteristics, as will Side2 and Side3. Since the three variables are all of the same type, the interface-based characteristics for each will likely be identical. For example, since Side1 is an integer, and zero is often a special value for integers, Relation of Side1 to zero is a reasonable interface-based characteristic.

4.1.2 Functionality-Based Input Domain Modeling

The idea of the functionality-based approach is to identify characteristics that correspond to the intended functionality of the system under test rather than using the actual interface. This allows the tester to incorporate some semantics or domain knowledge into the IDM.

Some members of the community believe that a functionality-based approach yields better test cases than the interface-based approach because the input domain models include more semantic information. Transferring more semantic information from the specification to the IDM makes it more likely to generate expected results for the test cases, an important goal.

Another important strength of the functionality-based approach is that the requirements are available before the software is implemented. This means that input domain modeling and test case generation can start early in development.

In the functionality-based approach, identifying characteristics and values may be far from trivial. If the system is large and complex, or the specifications are informal and incomplete, it can be very hard to design reasonable characteristics. The next section gives practical suggestions for designing characteristics.

The functionality-based approach also makes it harder to generate tests. The characteristics of the IDM often do not map to single parameters of the software interface. Translating the values into executable test cases is harder because constraints of a single IDM characteristic may affect multiple parameters in the interface.

Returning to the TriTyp program from Chapter 3, a functionality-based approach will recognize that instead of simply three integers, the input to the method is a triangle. This leads to the characteristic of a triangle, which can be partitioned into different types of triangles (as discussed below).

4.1.3 Identifying Characteristics

Identifying characteristics in an interface-based approach is simple. There is a mechanical translation from the parameters to characteristics. Developing a functionality-based IDM is more challenging.

Preconditions are excellent sources for functionality-based characteristics. They may be explicit or encoded in the software as exceptional behavior. Preconditions explicitly separate defined (or normal) behavior from undefined (or exceptional) behavior. For example, if a method choose() is supposed to select a value, it needs a precondition that a value must be available to select. A characteristic may be whether the value is available or not.

Postconditions are also good sources for characteristics. In the case of TriTyp, the different kinds of triangles are based on the postcondition of the method.

The test engineer should also look for other relationships between variables. These may be explicit or implicit. For example, a curious test engineer given a method m() with two object parameters x and y might wonder what happens if x and y point to the same object (aliasing), or to logically equal objects.

Another possible idea is to check for missing factors, that is, factors that may impact the execution but do not have an associated IDM parameter.

It is usually better to have many characteristics with few blocks than the reverse. It is also true that characteristics with small numbers of blocks are more likely to satisfy the disjointness and completeness properties.

Generally, it is preferable for the test engineer to use specifications or other documentation instead of program code to develop characteristics. The idea is that the tester should apply input space partitioning by using *domain knowledge* about the problem, not the implementation. However, in practice, the code may be all that is available. Overall, the more semantic information the test engineer can incorporate into characteristics, the better the resulting test set is likely to be.

The two approaches generally result in different IDM characteristics. The following method illustrates this difference:

```
public boolean findElement (List list, Object element)
// Effects: if list or element is null throw NullPointerException
//    else returns true if element is in the list, false otherwise
```

If the interface-based approach is used, the IDM will have characteristics for list and characteristics for element. For example, here are two interface-based characteristics for list, including blocks and values, which are discussed in detail in the next section:

- list is null
  - $b_1 = $ True
  - $b_2 = $ False

- list is empty
  - $b_1 = $ True
  - $b_2 = $ False

The functionality-based approach results in more complex IDM characteristics. As mentioned earlier, the functionality-based approach requires more thinking on the part of the test engineer, but can result in better tests. Two possibilities for the example are listed below, again including blocks and values.

- number of occurrences of element in list
  - $b_1 = 0$
  - $b_2 = 1$
  - $b_3 = $ More than 1

- element occurs first in list
  - $b_1 = $ True
  - $b_2 = $ False

4.1.4 Choosing Blocks and Values

After choosing characteristics, the test engineer partitions the domains of the characteristics into sets of values called *blocks*. A key issue in any partition approach is how partitions should be identified and how representative values should be selected from each block. This is another creative design step that allows the tester to tune the test process. More blocks will result in more tests, requiring more resources but possibly finding more faults. Fewer blocks will result in fewer tests, saving resources but possibly reducing test effectiveness. Several general strategies for identifying values are as follows:

- **Valid values**: Include at least one group of valid values.
- **Sub-partition**: A range of valid values can often be partitioned into sub-partitions, such that each sub-partition exercises a somewhat different part of the functionality.
- **Boundaries**: Values at or close to boundaries often cause problems.
- **Normal use**: If the operational profile focuses heavily on "normal use," the failure rate depends on values that are not boundary conditions.
- **Invalid values**: Include at least one group of invalid values.
- **Balance**: From a cost perspective, it may be cheap or even free to add more blocks to characteristics that have fewer blocks. In Section 4.2, we will see that the number of tests sometimes depends on the characteristic with the maximum number of blocks.
- **Missing partitions**: Check that the union of all blocks of a characteristic completely covers the input space of that characteristic.
- **Overlapping partitions**: Check that no value belongs to more than one block.

Special values can often be used. Consider a Java reference variable; null is typically a special case that needs to be treated differently from non null values. If the reference is to a container structure such as a Set or List, then whether the container is empty or not is often a useful characteristic.

Consider the TriTyp program from Chapter 3. It has three integer parameters that represent the lengths of three sides of a triangle. One common partitioning for an integer variable considers the relation of the variable's value to some special value in the testable function's domain, such as zero.

Table 4.1 shows a partitioning for the interface-based IDM for the TriTyp program. It has three characteristics, q_1, q_2, and q_3.

The first row in the table should be read as "Block $q_1.b_1$ is that Side 1 is greater than zero," "Block $q_1.b_2$ is that Side 1 is equal to zero," and "Block $q_1.b_3$ is that Side 1 is less than zero."

Table 4.1. First partitioning of TriTyp's inputs (interface-based)

Partition	b_1	b_2	b_3
q_1 = "Relation of Side 1 to 0"	greater than 0	equal to 0	less than 0
q_2 = "Relation of Side 2 to 0"	greater than 0	equal to 0	less than 0
q_3 = "Relation of Side 3 to 0"	greater than 0	equal to 0	less than 0

Table 4.2. Second partitioning of TriTyp's inputs (interface-based).

Partition	b_1	b_2	b_3	b_4
q_1 = "Length of Side 1"	greater than 1	equal to 1	equal to 0	less than 0
q_2 = "Length of Side 2"	greater than 1	equal to 1	equal to 0	less than 0
q_3 = "Length of Side 3"	greater than 1	equal to 1	equal to 0	less than 0

Consider the partition q_1 for Side 1. If one value is chosen from each block, the result is three tests. For example, we might choose Side 1 to have the value 7 in test 1, 0 in test 2, and -3 in test 3. Of course, we also need values for Side 2 and Side 3 of the triangle to complete the test case values. Notice that some of the blocks represent valid triangles and some represent invalid triangles. For example, no valid triangle can have a side of negative length.

It is easy to refine this categorization to get more fine grained testing if the budget allows. For example, more blocks can be created by separating inputs with value 1. This decision leads to a partitioning with four blocks, as shown in Table 4.2.

Notice that if the value for Side 1 were floating point rather than integer, the second categorization would **not** yield valid partitions. None of the blocks would include values between 0 and 1 (noninclusive), so the blocks would not cover the domain (not be complete). However, the domain D contains integers so the partitions are valid.

While partitioning, it is often useful for the tester to identify candidate values for each block to be used in testing. The reason to identify values now is that choosing specific values can help the test engineer think more concretely about the predicates that describe each block. While these values may not prove sufficient when refining test requirements to test cases, they do form a good starting point. Table 4.3 shows values that can satisfy the second partitioning.

The above partitioning is interface based and only uses syntactic information about the program (it has three integer inputs). A functionality-based approach can use the semantic information of the traditional geometric classification of triangles, as shown in Table 4.4.

Of course, the tester has to know what makes a triangle scalene, equilateral, isosceles, and invalid to choose possible values (this may be simple middle school geometry, but many of us have probably forgotten). An equilateral triangle is one in which all sides are the same length. An isosceles triangle is one in which at least two sides are the same length. A scalene triangle is any other valid triangle. This brings up a subtle problem, Table 4.4 does **not** form a valid partitioning. An equilateral triangle is also isosceles, thus we must first correct the partitions, as shown in Table 4.5.

Table 4.3. Possible values for blocks in the second partitioning in Table 4.2

Param	b_1	b_2	b_3	b_4
Side 1	2	1	0	-1
Side 2	2	1	0	-1
Side 3	2	1	0	-1

Table 4.4. Geometric partitioning of TriTyp's inputs (functionality-based)				
Partition	b_1	b_2	b_3	b_4
q_1 = "Geometric Classification"	scalene	isosceles	equilateral	invalid

Now values for Table 4.5 can be chosen as shown in Table 4.6. The triplets represent the three sides of the triangle.

A different approach to the equilateral/isosceles problem above is to break the characteristic Geometric Partitioning into four separate characteristics, namely Scalene, Isosceles, Equilateral, and Valid. The partition for each of these characteristics is boolean, and the fact that choosing Equilateral = true also means choosing Isosceles = true is then simply a constraint. Such an approach is highly recommended, and it invariably satisfies the disjointness and completeness properties.

4.1.5 Using More than One Input Domain Model

For a complex program it might be better to have several small IDMs than one large. This approach allows for a divide-and-conquer strategy when modeling characteristics and blocks. Another advantage with multiple IDMs for the same software is that it allows varying levels of coverage.

For instance, one IDM may contain only valid values and another IDM may contain invalid values to focus on error handling. The valid value IDM may be covered using a higher level of coverage. The invalid value IDM may use a lower level of coverage.

Multiple IDMs may be overlapping as long as the test cases generated make sense. However, overlapping IDMs are likely to have more constraints.

4.1.6 Checking the Input Domain Model

It is important to check the input domain model. In terms of characteristics, the test engineer should ask whether there is any information about how the function behaves that is not incorporated in some characteristics. This is necessarily an informal process.

The tester should also explicitly check each characteristic for the completeness and disjointness properties. The purpose of this check is to make sure that, for each characteristic, not only do the blocks cover the complete input space, but selecting a particular block implies excluding all other blocks in that characteristic.

If multiple IDMs are used, completeness should be relative to the portion of the input domain that is modeled in each IDM. When the tester is satisfied with the

Table 4.5. Correct geometric partitioning of TriTyp's inputs (functionality-based)				
Partition	b_1	b_2	b_3	b_4
q_1 = "Geometric Classification"	scalene	isosceles, not equilateral	equilateral	invalid

Table 4.6. Possible values for blocks in geometric partitioning in Table 4.5.

Param	b_1	b_2	b_3	b_4
Triangle	(4, 5, 6)	(3, 3, 4)	(3, 3, 3)	(3, 4, 8)

characteristics and their blocks, it is time to choose which combinations of values to test with and identify constraints among the blocks.

EXERCISES

Section 4.1.

1. Answer the following questions for the method search() below:

   ```
   public static int search (List list, Object element)
   // Effects: if list or element is null throw NullPointerException
   //    else if element is in the list, return an index
   //    of element in the list; else return -1
   //    for example, search ([3,3,1], 3) = either 0 or 1
   //       search ([1,7,5], 2) = -1
   ```

   Base your answer on the following characteristic partitioning:

   ```
   Characteristic: Location of element in list
       Block 1: element is first entry in list
       Block 2: element is last entry in list
       Block 3: element is in some position other than first or last
   ```

   (a) "Location of element in list" fails the disjointness property. Give an example that illustrates this.
   (b) "Location of element in list" fails the completeness property. Give an example that illustrates this.
   (c) Supply one or more new partitions that capture the intent of "Location of e in list" but do not suffer from completeness or disjointness problems.

2. Derive input space partitioning tests for the **GenericStack** class with the following method signatures:
   - public GenericStack ();
   - public void Push (Object X);
   - public Object Pop ();
   - public boolean IsEmt ();

   Assume the usual semantics for the stack. Try to keep your partitioning simple, choose a small number of partitions and blocks.
   (a) Define characteristics of inputs
   (b) Partition the characteristics into blocks
   (c) Define values for the blocks

4.2 COMBINATION STRATEGIES CRITERIA

The above description ignores an important question: "How should we consider multiple partitions at the same time?" This is the same as asking "What combination of blocks should we choose values from?" For example, we might wish to require a test case that satisfies block 1 from q_2 and block 3 from q_3. The most obvious choice is to choose all combinations. However, just like Combinatorial Coverage from previous chapters, using all combinations will be impractical when more than 2 or 3 partitions are defined.

> CRITERION 4.23 All Combinations Coverage (ACoC): *All combinations of blocks from all characteristics must be used.*

For example, if we have three partitions with blocks [A, B], [1, 2, 3], and [x, y], then ACoC will need the following twelve tests:

(A, 1, x)   (B, 1, x)
(A, 1, y)   (B, 1, y)
(A, 2, x)   (B, 2, x)
(A, 2, y)   (B, 2, y)
(A, 3, x)   (B, 3, x)
(A, 3, y)   (B, 3, y)

A test suite that satisfies ACoC will have a unique test for each combination of blocks for each partition. The number of tests will be the product of the number of blocks for each partition: $\prod_{i=1}^{Q}(B_i)$.

If we use a four block partition similar to q_2 for each of the three sides of the triangle, ACoC requires $4 * 4 * 4 = 64$ tests.

This is almost certainly more testing than is necessary, and will usually be economically impractical as well. Thus, as with paths and truth tables before, we must use some sort of coverage criterion to choose which combinations of blocks to pick values from.

The first, fundamental assumption is that different choices of values from the same block are equivalent from a testing perspective. That is, we need to take only one value from each block. Several *combination strategies* exist, which result in a collection of useful criteria. These combination strategies are illustrated with the TriTyp example, using the second categorization given in Table 4.2 and the values from Table 4.3.

The first combination strategy criterion is fairly straightforward and simply requires that we try each choice at least once.

> CRITERION 4.24 Each Choice Coverage (ECC): *One value from each block for each characteristic must be used in at least one test case.*

Given the above example of three partitions with blocks [A, B], [1, 2, 3], and [x, y], ECC can be satisfied in many ways, including the three tests $(A, 1, x), (B, 2, y)$, and $(A, 3, x)$.

Assume the program under test has Q parameters $q_1, q_2, \ldots, q_Q$, and each parameter q_i has B_i blocks. Then a test suite that satisfies ECC will have at least $Max_{i=1}^{Q} B_i$

values. The maximum number of blocks for the partitions for TriTyp is four, thus ECC requires at least four tests.

This criterion can be satisfied by choosing the tests {(2, 2, 2), (1, 1, 1), (0, 0, 0), (−1, −1, −1)} from Table 4.3. It does not take much thought to conclude that these are not very effective tests for this program. ECC leaves a lot of flexibility to the tester in terms of how to combine the test values, so it can be called a relatively "weak" criterion.

The weakness of ECC can be expressed as not requiring values to be combined with other values. A natural next step is to require explicit combinations of values, called *pair-wise*.

CRITERION **4.25 Pair-Wise Coverage (PWC):** *A value from each block for each characteristic must be combined with a value from every block for each other characteristic.*

Given the above example of three partitions with blocks [A, B], [1, 2, 3], and [x, y], then PWC will need sixteen tests to cover the following combinations:

(A, 1)	(B, 1)	(1, x)
(A, 2)	(B, 2)	(1, y)
(A, 3)	(B, 3)	(2, x)
(A, x)	(B, x)	(2, y)
(A, y)	(B, y)	(3, x)
		(3, y)

PWC allows the same test case to cover more than one unique pair of values. So the above combinations can be combined in several ways, including:

(A, 1, x)	(B, 1, y)
(A, 2, x)	(B, 2, y)
(A, 3, x)	(B, 3, y)
(A, −, y)	(B, −, x)

The tests with '−' mean that any block can be used.

A test suite that satisfies PWC will pair each value with each other value or have at least $(Max_{i=1}^{Q}(B_i)) * (Max_{j=1, j!=i}^{Q}(B_j))$ values. Each characteristic in TriTyp (Table 4.3) has four blocks; so at least 16 tests are required.

Several algorithms to satisfy PWC have been published and appropriate references are provided in the bibliography section of the chapter.

A natural extension to PWC is to require t values instead of pairs.

CRITERION **4.26 T-Wise Coverage (TWC):** *A value from each block for each group of t characteristics must be combined.*

If the value for T is chosen to be the number of partitions, Q, then TWC is equivalent to all combinations. A test suite that satisfies TWC will have at least $(Max_{i=1}^{q} B_i)^t$ values if the characteristics are all the same size. TWC is expensive in terms of the number of test cases, and experience suggests going beyond pair-wise (that is, $t = 2$) does not help much.

Both PWC and TWC combine values "blindly," without regard for which values are being combined. The next criterion strengthens ECC in a different way by bringing in a small but crucial piece of domain knowledge of the program; asking what is the most "important" block for each partition. This block is called the *base choice*.

CRITERION **4.27 Base Choice Coverage (BCC):** *A base choice block is chosen for each characteristic, and a base test is formed by using the base choice for each characteristic. Subsequent tests are chosen by holding all but one base choice constant and using each non-base choice in each other characteristic.*

Given the above example of three partitions with blocks [A, B], [1, 2, 3], and [x, y], suppose base choice blocks are 'A', '1' and 'x'. Then the base choice test is (A, 1, x), and the following additional tests would need to be used:

(B, 1, x)
(A, 2, x)
(A, 3, x)
(A, 1, y)

A test suite that satisfies BCC will have one base test, plus one test for each remaining block for each partition. This is a total of $1 + \sum_{i=1}^{Q}(B_i - 1)$. Each parameter for TriTyp has four blocks, thus BCC requires $1 + 3 + 3 + 3$ tests.

The base choice can be the simplest, the smallest, the first in some ordering, or the most likely from an end-user point of view. Combining more than one invalid value is usually not useful because the software often recognizes one value and negative effects of the others are masked. Which blocks are chosen for the base choices becomes a crucial step in test design that can greatly impact the resulting test. It is important that the tester document the strategy that was used so that further testing can reevaluate those decisions.

Following the strategy of choosing the most likely block for TriTyp, we chose "greater than 1" from Table 4.2 as the base choice block. Using the values from Table 4.3 gives the base test as (2, 2, 2). The remaining tests are created by varying each one of these in turn: $\{(2, 2, 1), (2, 2, 0), (2, 2, -1), (2, 1, 2), (2, 0, 2), (2, -1, 2), (1, 2, 2), (0, 2, 2), (-1, 2, 2)\}$.

Sometimes the tester may have trouble choosing a single base choice and may decide that multiple base choices are needed. This is formulated as follows:

CRITERION **4.28 Multiple Base Choice Coverage (MBCC):** *At least one, and possibly more, base choice blocks are chosen for each characteristic, and base tests are formed by using each base choice for each characteristic at least once. Subsequent tests are chosen by holding all but one base choice constant for each base test and using each non-base choice in each other characteristic.*

Assuming m_i base choices for each characteristic and a total of M base tests, MBCC requires $M + \sum_{i=1}^{Q}(M * (B_i - m_i))$ tests.

For example, we may choose to include two base choices for side 1 in TriTyp, "greater than 1" and "equal to 1." This would result in the two base tests (2, 2, 2) and (1, 2, 2). The formula above is thus evaluated with $M = 2$, $m_1 = 2$, and

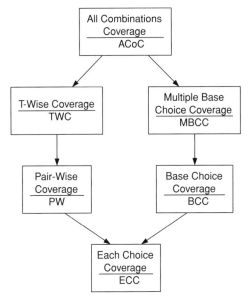

Figure 4.2. Subsumption relations among input space partitioning criteria.

$m_i = 1 \, \forall \, i, 1 < i \leq 3$. That is, $2 + (2*(4 - 2)) + (2*(4 - 1)) + (2*(4 - 1)) = 18$. The remaining tests are created by varying each one of these in turn. The MBCC criterion sometimes results in duplicate tests. For example, $(0, 2, 2)$ and $(-1, 2, 2)$ both appear twice for TriTyp. Duplicate test cases should, of course, be eliminated (which also makes the formula for the number of tests an upper bound).

Figure 4.2 shows the subsumption relationships among the input space partitioning combination strategy criteria.

EXERCISES

Section 4.2.

1. Enumerate all 64 tests to satisfy the All Combinations (ACoC) criterion for the second categorization of TriTyp's inputs in Table 4.2. Use the values in Table 4.3.
2. Enumerate all 16 tests to satisfy the pair-wise (PWC) criterion for the second categorization of TriTyp's inputs in Table 4.2. Use the values in Table 4.3.
3. Enumerate all 16 tests to satisfy the multiple base choice (MBCC) criterion for the second categorization of TriTyp's inputs in Table 4.2. Use the values in Table 4.3.
4. Answer the following questions for the method intersection() below:

```
public Set intersection (Set s1, Set s2)
    // Effects:  If s1 or s2 are null throw NullPointerException
    //    else return a (non null) Set equal to the intersection
    //    of Sets s1 and s2
```

Characteristic: Type of s1
- s1 = null
- s1 = {}
- s1 has at least one element

Characteristic: Relation between s1 and s2
- s1 and s2 represent the same set
- s1 is a subset of s2
- s2 is a subset of s1
- s1 and s2 do not have any elements in common

(a) Does the partition "Type of s1" satisfy the completeness property? If not, give a value for $s1$ that does not fit in any block.

(b) Does the partition "Type of s1" satisfy the disjointness property? If not, give a value for $s1$ that fits in more than one block.

(c) Does the partition "Relation between s1 and s2" satisfy the completeness property? If not, give a pair of values for $s1$ and $s2$ that does not fit in any block.

(d) Does the partition "Relation between s1 and s2" satisfy the disjointness property? If not, give a pair of values for $s1$ and $s2$ that fits in more than one block.

(e) If the "base choice" criterion were applied to the two partitions (exactly as written), how many test requirements would result?

5. Derive input space partitioning tests for the **BoundedQueue** class with the following signature:

- public BoundedQueue (int capacity);
- public void Enqueue (Object X);
- public Object Dequeue ();
- public boolean IsEmpty ();
- public boolean IsFull ();

Assume the usual semantics for a queue with a fixed, maximal capacity. Try to keep your partitioning simple–choose a small number of partitions and blocks.

(a) Identify all of the variables. Don't forget the state variables.

(b) Identify several characteristics that suggest partitions.

(c) Identify the blocks in the partition for each characteristic. Designate one block in each partition as the "Base" block.

(d) Define values for the blocks.

(e) Define a test set that satisfies base choice coverage (BCC).

6. Develop a set of characteristics and accompanying partitions for the pattern checking procedure (the method *pat()* in Figure 2.21 in Chapter 2).

(a) Develop tests to satisfy the base choice criterion. Your tests should have both inputs and expected outputs.

(b) Analyze your tests with respect to the data flow test sets developed in Chapter 2. How well does input space partitioning do?

Table 4.7. Examples of invalid block combinations

	Blocks			
Characteristics	**1**	**2**	**3**	**4**
A: length and contents	one element	more than one, unsorted	more than one, sorted	more than one, all identical
B: match	element not found	element found once	element found more than once	–

Invalid combinations: (A1, B3), (A4, B2)

4.3 CONSTRAINTS AMONG PARTITIONS

A subtle point about input space partitioning is that some combinations of blocks are infeasible. This must be documented in the IDM. For example, Table 4.7 shows an example based on the previously described boolean findElement (list, element) method. An IDM with two parameters A, that has four partitions, and B, that has three partitions, has been designed. Two of the partition combinations do not make sense and are thus invalid. In this example, these are represented as a list of invalid pairs of parameter partitions. In the general case other representations can be used, for example, a set of inequalities.

Constraints are relations between blocks from different characteristics. Two kinds of constraints appear. One kind says that a block from one characteristic cannot be combined with a block from another characteristic. The "less than zero" and "scalene" problem is an example of this kind of constraint. The other kind is the inverse; a block from one characteristic **must be** combined with a specific block from another characteristic. Although this sounds simple enough, identifying and satisfying the constraints when choosing values can be difficult.

How constraints are handled when values are selected depends on the coverage criterion chosen, and the decision is usually made when values are chosen. For the ACoC, PWC, and TWC criteria, the only reasonable option is to drop the infeasible pairs from consideration. For example, if PWC requires a particular pair that is not feasible, no amount of tinkering on the test engineer's part can make that requirement feasible. However, the situation is quite different for a criterion such as BCC. If a particular variation (for example, "less than zero" for "Relation of Side 1 to zero") conflicts with the base case (for example, "scalene" for "Geometric Classification"), then the obvious thing to do is change the offending choice for the base case so that the variation *is* feasible. In this case, "Geometric Classification" clearly needs to change to "invalid."

As another example, consider sorting an array. The input to our sort routine will be a variable length array of some arbitrary type. The output will have three parts: (1) a permutation of the input array, sorted in ascending order, (2) the largest value (max), and (3) the smallest value (min). We might consider the following characteristics:

- Length of array
- Type of elements

- Max value
- Min value
- Position of max value
- Position of min value

These characteristics can, in turn, reasonably result in the partitioning summarized as follows:

Length   {0, 1, 2..100, 101..MAXINT}
Type   {int, char, string, other}
Max   {≤ 0, 1, > 1, 'a', 'Z', 'b', ... , 'Y', blank, nonblank}
Min   { ··· }
Max pos {1, 2..Length-1, Length}
Min pos {1, 2..Length-1, Length}

The discerning reader will of course notice that not all combinations are possible. For example, if *Length* = 0, then nothing else matters. Also, some of the *Max* and *Min* values are available only if *Type* = *int*, and others if *Type* = *char*.

4.4 BIBLIOGRAPHIC NOTES

In the research literature, several testing methods have been described that are generally based on the model that the input space of the test object should be divided into subsets, with the assumption that all inputs in the same subset cause similar behavior. These are collectively called *partition testing* and include equivalence partitioning [249], boundary value analysis [249], category partition [283], and domain testing [29]. An extensive survey with examples was published by Grindal et al. [143].

The derivation of partitions and values started with Balcer, Hasling, and Ostrand's category partition method in 1988 [23, 283]. An alternate visualization is that of classification trees introduced by Grochtman, Grimm, and Wegener in 1993 [145, 146]. Classification trees organize the input space partitioning information into a tree structure. The first level nodes are the parameters and environment variables (characteristics); they may be recursively broken into sub-categories. Blocks appear as leaves in the tree and combinations are chosen by selecting among the leaves.

Chen et al. empirically identified common mistakes that testers made during input parameter-modeling [64]. Many of the concepts on input domain modeling in this chapter come from Grindal's PhD work [140, 142, 144]. Both Cohen et al. [84] and Yin et al. [363] suggest functionality oriented approaches to input parameter modeling. Functionality-oriented input parameter modeling was also implicitly used by Grindal et al. [141]. Two other IDM-related methods are Classification Trees [145] and a UML activity diagram based method [65]. Beizer [29], Malaiya [222], and Chen et al. [64] also address the problem of characteristic selection.

Grindal published an analytical/empirical comparison of different constraint-handling mechanisms [144].

Stocks and Carrington [320] provided a formal notion of specification-based testing that encompasses most approaches to input space partition testing. In particular, they addressed the problem of refining test frames (which we simply and informally call test requirements in this book) to test cases.

The each choice and base choice criteria were introduced by Ammann and Offutt in 1994 [16]. Cohen et al. [84] indicated that valid and invalid parameter values should be treated differently with respect to coverage. *Valid* values lie within the bounds of normal operation of the test object, and *invalid* values lie outside the normal operating range. Invalid values often result in an error message and the execution terminates. To avoid one invalid value masking another, Cohen et al. suggested that only one invalid value should be included in each test case.

Burroughs et al. [58] and Cohen et al. [84, 85, 86] suggested the heuristic pairwise coverage as part of the Automatic Efficient Test Generator (AETG). AETG also includes a variation on the base choice combination criterion. In AETG's version, called "default testing," the tester varies the values of one characteristic at a time while the other characteristics contain *some* default value. The term "default testing" was also used by Burr and Young [57], who described yet another variation of the base choices. In their version, all characteristics except one contain the default value, and the remaining characteristics contain a maximum or a minimum value. This variant will not necessarily satisfy "each choice coverage."

The Constrained Array Test System (CATS) tool for generating test cases was described by Sherwood [313] to satisfy pair-wise coverage. For programs with two or more characteristics, the in-parameter-order (IPO) combination strategy [205, 206, 322] generates a test suite that satisfies pair-wise coverage for the first two parameters (characteristic in our terminology). The test suite is then extended to satisfy pair-wise coverage for the first three parameters and continues for each additional parameter until all parameters are included.

Williams and Probert invented *T*-wise coverage [354]. A special case of T-wise coverage called *variable strength* was proposed by Cohen, Gibbons, Mugridge, and Colburn [87]. This strategy requires higher coverage among a subset of characteristics and lower coverage across the others. Assume for example a test problem with four parameters A, B, C, D. Variable strength may require 3-wise coverage for parameters B, C, D and 2-wise coverage for parameter A. Cohen, Gibbons, Mugridge, and Colburn [87] suggested using simulated annealing (SA) to generate test suites for T-wise coverage. Shiba, Tsuchiya, and Kikuno [314] proposed using a genetic algorithm (GA) to satisfy pair-wise coverage. The same paper also suggested using the ant colony algorithm (ACA).

Mandl suggested using orthogonal arrays to generate values for T-wise coverage [224]. This idea was further developed by Williams and Probert [353]. Covering arrays [352] is an extension of orthogonal arrays. A property of orthogonal arrays is that they are *balanced*, which means that each characteristic value occurs the same number of times in the test suite. If only T-wise (for instance pair-wise) coverage is desired, the balance property is unnecessary and will make the algorithm less efficient. In a covering array that satisfies T-wise coverage, each T-tuple occurs at least once but not necessarily the same number of times. Another problem with orthogonal arrays is that for some problem sizes we do not have enough orthogonal arrays to represent the entire problem. This problem is also avoided by using covering arrays.

Several papers have provided experiential and experimental results of using input space partitioning. Heller [156] uses a realistic example to show that testing all combinations of characteristic values is infeasible in practice. Heller concludes that we need to identify a subset of combinations of manageable size.

Kuhn and Reilly [195] investigated 365 error reports from two large real-life projects and discovered that pair-wise coverage was nearly as effective at finding faults as testing all combinations. More supporting data were given by Kuhn and Wallace [196].

Piwowarski, Ohba, and Caruso [291] describe how to apply code coverage successfully as a stopping criterion during functional testing. The authors formulated functional testing as the problem of selecting test cases from all combinations of values of the input parameters. Burr and Young [57] show that continually monitoring code coverage helps improve the input domain model. Initial experiments showed that ad hoc testing resulted in about 50% decision coverage, but by continually applying code coverage and refining the input domain models, decision coverage was increased to 84%.

Plenty of examples of applying input space partitioning in practice have been published. Dalal, Jain, Karunanithi, Leaton, Lott, Patton, and Horowitz [91, 92] report results from using the AETG tool. It was used to generate test cases for Bellcore's Intelligent Service Control Point, a rule-based system used to assign work requests to technicians, and a GUI window in a large application. Previously, Cohen, Dalal, Kajla, and Patton [85] demonstrated the use of AETG for screen testing, by testing the input fields for consistency and validity across a number of screens.

Burr and Young [57] also used the AETG tool to test a Nortel application that converts email messages from one format to another. Huller [171] used an IPO related algorithm to test ground systems for satellite communications.

Williams and Probert [353] demonstrated how input space partitioning can be used to organize configuration testing. Yilmaz, Cohen, and Porter [362] used covering arrays as a starting point for fault localization in complex configuration spaces.

Huller [171] showed that pair-wise configuration testing can save more than 60% in both cost and time compared to quasi-exhaustive testing. Brownlie, Prowse, and Phadke [50] compared the results of using orthogonal arrays (OA) on one version of a PMX/StarMAIL release with the results from conventional testing on a prior release. The authors estimated that 22% more faults would have been found if OA had been used on the first version.

Several studies have compared the number of tests generated. The number of tests varies when using nondeterministic algorithms. Several papers compared input space partitioning strategies that satisfy 2-wise or 3-wise coverage: IPO and AETG [205], OA and AETG [141], covering arrays (CA) and IPO [352], and AETG, IPO, SA, GA, and ACA [87, 314]. Most of them found very little difference.

Another way to compare algorithms is with respect to the execution time. Lei and Tai [206] showed that the time complexity of IPO is superior to that of AETG. Williams [352] reported that CA outperforms IPO by almost three orders of magnitude for the largest test problems in his study.

Grindal et al. [141] compared algorithms by the number of faults found. They found that BCC performs as well as AETG and OA despite fewer test cases.

Input space partitioning strategies can also be compared based on their code coverage. Cohen et al. [86] found that test suites generated by AETG for 2-wise coverage reach over 90% block coverage. Burr and Young [57] got similar results for AETG, getting 93% block coverage with 47 test cases, compared with 85% block coverage for a restricted version of BCC using 72 test cases.

NOTES

1 We choose to use blocks for simplicity. These are also sometimes called "partitions" in the literature.

5

Syntax-Based Testing

In previous chapters, we learned how to generate tests from graphs, logical expressions, and partitions of the input space. A fourth major source for test coverage criteria is syntactic descriptions of software artifacts. As with graphs and logical expressions, several types of artifacts can be used, including source and input requirements.

The essential characteristic of syntax-based testing is that a syntactic description such as a grammar or BNF is used. Chapters 2 and 3 discussed how to build graph models and logic models from artifacts such as the program, design descriptions, and specifications. Chapter 4 discussed how to build a model of the inputs based on some description of the input space. Then test criteria were applied to the models. With syntax-based testing, however, the syntax of the software artifact is used as the model and tests are created from the syntax.

5.1 SYNTAX-BASED COVERAGE CRITERIA

Syntax structures can be used for testing in several ways. We can use the syntax to generate artifacts that are valid (correct syntax), or artifacts that are invalid (incorrect syntax). Sometimes the structures we generate are test cases themselves, and sometimes they are used to help us find test cases. We explore these differences in the subsections of this chapter. As usual, we begin by defining general criteria on syntactic structures and then make them specific to specific artifacts.

5.1.1 BNF Coverage Criteria

It is very common in software engineering to use structures from automata theory to describe the syntax of software artifacts. Programming languages are described in BNF grammar notation, program behavior is described in finite state machines, and allowable inputs to programs are defined by grammars. Regular expressions and context free grammars are especially useful. Consider the regular expression:

$$(G \, s \, n \mid B \, t \, n)^*$$

The star is a "closure" operator that indicates zero or more occurrences of the expression it modifies. The vertical bar is the "choice" operator, and indicates either choice can be taken. Thus, this regular expression describes any sequence of "G s n" and "B t n." G and B may be commands to a program and s, t, and n may be arguments, method calls with parameters, or messages with values. The arguments s, t, and n can be literals, or represent a large set of values, for example, numbers or strings.

A test case can be a sequence of strings that satisfy the regular expression. For example, if the arguments are supposed to be numbers, the following may represent one test with four components, two separate tests, three separate tests, or four separate tests:

```
G 17 08.01.90
B 13 06.27.94
G 13 11.21.94
B 04 01.09.03
```

Although regular expressions are sometimes sufficient, a more expressive grammar is often used. The prior example can be refined into a grammar form as follows:

```
stream ::= action*
action ::= actG | actB
actG   ::= "G" s n
actB   ::= "B" t n
s      ::= digit^{1-3}
t      ::= digit^{1-3}
n      ::= digit^2 "." digit^2 "." digit^2
digit  ::= "0" | "1" | "2" | "3" | "4" | "5" | "6" | "7" | "8" | "9"
```

A grammar has a special symbol called the *start symbol*. In this case, the start symbol is stream. Symbols in the grammar are either *nonterminals*, which must be rewritten further, or *terminals*, for which no rewriting is possible. In the example, the symbols on the left of the ::= sign are all nonterminals, and everything in quotes is a terminal. Each possible rewriting of a given nonterminal is called a *production* or *rule*. In this grammar, a star superscript means zero or more, a plus superscript means one or more, a numeric superscript indicates the required number of repetitions, and a numeric range $(a - b)$ means there has to be at least a repetitions, and no more than b.

Grammars can be used in two ways. A *recognizer*, as defined in Chapter 1, decides whether a given string (or test case) is in the grammar. This is the classical automata theory problem of parsing, and automated tools (such as the venerable lex and yacc) make the construction of recognizers very easy. Recognizers are extremely useful in testing, because they make it possible to decide if a given test case is in a particular grammar or not. The other use of grammars is to build *generators*, also defined in Chapter 1. A generator derives a string of terminals from the grammar start symbol. In this case, the strings are test inputs. For example, the following derivation results in the test case above.

---

stream → action^*
          → **action action**^*
          → **actG** action^*
          → **G s n** action^*
          → G **digit^(1-3) digit^2 . digit^2 . digit^2** action^*
          → G **digitdigit digitdigit.digitdigit.digitdigit** action^*
          → G **14 08.01.90** action^*
          ⋮

The derivation proceeds by systematically replacing the next nonterminal (in this case, "action^*") with one of its productions. Derivation continues until all nonterminals have been rewritten and only terminal symbols remain. The key to testing is which derivations should be used, and this is how criteria are defined on grammars.

Although many test criteria could be defined, the most common and straightforward are *terminal symbol coverage* and *production coverage*.

CRITERION **5.29 Terminal Symbol Coverage (TSC):** *TR contains each terminal symbol t in the grammar G.*

CRITERION **5.30 Production Coverage (PDC):** *TR contains each production p in the grammar G.*

By now, it should be easy to see that PDC subsumes TSC (if we cover every production, we cover every terminal symbol). Some readers may also note that grammars and graphs have a natural relationship. Therefore, TSC and PDC can be rewritten to be equivalent to node coverage and edge coverage on the graph that represents the grammar. Of course, this means that the other graph-based coverage criteria can also be defined on grammars. To our knowledge, neither researchers nor practitioners have taken this step.

The only other related criterion defined here is the impractical one of deriving all possible strings in a graph.

CRITERION **5.31 Derivation Coverage (DC):** *TR contains every possible string that can be derived from the grammar G.*

The number of tests generated by TSC will be bounded by the number of terminal symbols. The stream BNF above has 13 terminal symbols: G, B, ., 0, 1, 2, 3, 4, 5, 6, 7, 8, 9. It has 18 productions (note the '|' symbol adds productions, so "action" has two productions and "digit" has 10). The number of derivations for DC depends on the details of the grammar, but generally can be infinite. If we ignore the first production in the stream BNF, we have a finite number of derivable strings. Two possible actions are (G and B), s and t each has a maximum of three digits with 10 choices, or 1000. The n nonterminal has three sets of two digits with 10 choices apiece, or 10^6. Altogether, the stream grammar can generate $2 * 1000 * 10^6 = 2,000,000,000$ strings. DC is of theoretical interest but is obviously impractical. (A point to remember the next time a tool salesperson or job applicant claims to have done "full string coverage" or "path coverage.")

TSC, PDC, and DC generate test cases that are members of the set of strings defined by the grammar. It is sometimes very helpful to generate test cases that are **not** in the grammar, which is addressed by the criteria in the next subsection.

EXERCISES
Section 5.1.1.

1. Consider how often the idea of covering nodes and edges pops up in software testing. Write a short essay to explain this.
2. Just as with graphs, it is possible to generate an infinite number of tests from a grammar. How and what makes this possible?

5.1.2 Mutation Testing

One of the interesting things that grammars do is describe what an input is *not*. We say that an input is *valid* if it is in the language specified by the grammar, and *invalid* otherwise. For example, it is quite common to require a program to reject malformed inputs, and this property should clearly be tested, since it is easy for programmers to forget it or get it wrong.

Thus, it is often useful to produce invalid strings from a grammar. It is also helpful in testing to use strings that are *valid* but that follow a different derivation from a preexisting string. Both of these strings are called *mutants*.[1] This can be done by mutating the grammar, then generating strings, or by mutating values during a production.

Mutation can be applied to various artifacts, as discussed in the following subsections. However, it has primarily been used as a program-based testing method, and much of the theory and many of the detailed concepts are specific to program-based mutation. Therefore, a lot more details appear in Section 5.2.2.

Mutation is always based on a set of "mutation operators," which are expressed with respect to a "ground" string.

Definition 5.45 Ground string: A string that is in the grammar.

Definition 5.46 Mutation Operator: A rule that specifies syntactic variations of strings generated from a grammar.

Definition 5.47 Mutant: The result of one application of a mutation operator.

Mutation operators are usually applied to ground strings, but can also be applied to a grammar, or dynamically during a derivation. The notion of a mutation operator is extremely general, and so a very important part of applying mutation to any artifact is the design of suitable mutation operators. A well designed set of operators can result in very powerful testing, but a poorly designed set can result in ineffective tests. For example, a commercial tool that "implements mutation" but that only changes predicates to *true* and *false* would simply be an expensive way to implement branch coverage.

We sometimes have a particular ground string in mind, and sometimes the ground string is simply the implicit result of not applying any mutation operators. For example, we care about the ground string when applying mutation to program statements. The ground string is the sequence of program statements in the program under test, and the mutants are slight syntactic variations of that program. We do not care about the ground string during invalid input testing, when the goal is to see if a program correctly responds to invalid inputs. The ground strings are valid inputs, and variants are the invalid inputs. For example, a valid input might be a transaction request from a correctly logged-in user. The invalid version might be the same transaction request from a user who is not logged in.

Consider the grammar in Section 5.1.1. If the first string shown, G 17 08.01.90, is taken as a ground string, two *valid* mutants may be

---

```
B 17 08.01.90
G 43 08.01.90
```

Two *invalid* mutants may be

```
12 17 08.01.90
G 23 08.01
```

When the ground string does not matter, mutants can be created directly from the grammar by modifying productions during a derivation, using a generator approach as introduced in the previous section. That is, if the ground strings are not of direct interest, they do not need to be explicitly generated.

When applying mutation operators, two issues often come up. First, should more than one mutation operator be applied at the same time to create one mutant? That is, should a mutated string contain one mutated element, or several? Common sense indicates no, and strong experimental and theoretical evidence has been found for mutating only one element at a time in program-based mutation. Another question is should every possible application of a mutation operator to a ground string be considered? This is usually done in program-based mutation. One theoretical reason is that program-based mutation subsumes a number of other test criteria, and if operators are not applied comprehensively, then that subsumption is lost. However, this is not always done when the ground string does not matter, for example, in the case of invalid input testing. This question is explored in more detail in the following application subsections.

Mutation operators have been designed for several programming languages, formal specification languages, BNF grammars, and at least one data definition language (XML). For a given artifact, the set of mutants is M and each mutant $m \in M$ will lead to a test requirement.

When a derivation is mutated to produce valid strings, the testing goal is to "kill" the mutants by causing the mutant to produce different output. More formally, given a mutant $m \in M$ for a derivation D and a test t, t is said to *kill m* if and only if the output of t on D is different from the output of t on m. The derivation D may be represented by the complete list of productions followed, or it may simply be represented by the final string. For example, in Section 5.2.2, the strings are programs or program components. Coverage is defined in terms of killing mutants.

CRITERION **5.32 Mutation Coverage (MC):** *For each mutant $m \in M$, TR contains exactly one requirement, to* kill *m*.

Thus, coverage in mutation equates to killing the mutants. The amount of coverage is usually written as a percent of mutants killed and called the *mutation score*.

When a grammar is mutated to produce invalid strings, the testing goal is to run the mutants to see if the behavior is correct. The coverage criterion is therefore simpler, as the mutation operators are the test requirements.

CRITERION **5.33 Mutation Operator Coverage (MOC):** *For each mutation operator, TR contains exactly one requirement, to create a mutated string m that is derived using the mutation operator.*

CRITERION **5.34 Mutation Production Coverage (MPC):** *For each mutation operator, and each production that the operator can be applied to, TR contains the requirement to create a mutated string from that production.*

The number of test requirements for mutation is somewhat difficult to quantify because it depends on the syntax of the artifact as well as the mutation operators. In most situations, mutation yields more test requirements than any other test criterion. Subsequent sections have more data on quantifying specific collections of mutation operators and more details are in the bibliographic notes.

Mutation testing is also difficult to apply by hand, and automation is more complicated than for most other criteria. As a result, mutation is widely considered a "high-end" test criterion, more effective than most but also more expensive. One common use of mutation is as a sort of "gold standard" in experimental studies for comparative evaluation of other test criteria.

EXERCISES

Section 5.1.2.

1. Define mutation score.
2. How is the mutation score related to coverage from Chapter 1?
3. Consider the stream BNF in Section 5.1.1 and the ground string "B 10 06.27.94." Give three valid and three invalid mutants of the string.

The rest of this chapter explores various forms of BNF and mutation testing. The table below summarizes the sections and the characteristics of the various flavors of syntax testing. Whether the use of syntax testing creates valid or invalid tests is noted for both BNF and mutation testing. For mutation testing, we also note whether a ground string is used, whether the mutants are tests or not, and whether mutants are killed.

	Program-based	Integration	Specification-based	Input space
BNF	5.2.1	5.3.1	5.4.1	5.5.1
Grammar	Programming languages	No known applications	Algebraic specifications	Input languages, including XML
Summary	Compiler testing			Input space testing
Mutation	5.2.2	5.3.2	5.4.2	5.5.2
Grammar	Programming languages	Programming languages	FSMs	Input languages, including XML
Summary	Mutates programs	Tests integration	Uses model-checking	Error checking
Ground?	Yes	Yes	Yes	No
Valid?	Yes, must compile	Yes, must compile	Yes	No
Tests?	Mutants are not tests	Mutants are not tests	Mutants are not tests	Mutants are tests
Killing?	Yes	Yes	Yes	No notion of killing
Notes	Strong and weak mutants. Subsumes many other techniques.	Includes object-oriented testing	Automatic detection of equivalent mutants	Sometimes the grammar is mutated, then strings are produced

5.2 PROGRAM-BASED GRAMMARS

As with most criteria, syntax-based testing criteria have been applied to programs more than other artifacts. The BNF coverage criteria have been used to generate programs to test compilers. Mutation testing has been applied to methods (unit testing) and to classes (integration testing). Application to classes is discussed in the next section.

5.2.1 BNF Grammars for Languages

The primary purpose of BNF testing for languages has been to generate test suites for compilers. As this is a very specialized application, we choose not to dwell on it in this book. The bibliographic notes section has pointers to the relevant, and rather old, literature.

5.2.2 Program-Based Mutation

Mutation was originally developed for programs and this section has significantly more depth than other sections in this chapter. Program-based mutation uses operators that are defined in terms of the grammar of a particular programming language. We start with a **ground string**, which is a program that is being tested. We then apply mutation operators to create mutants. These mutants must be compilable, so program-based mutation creates **valid** strings. The mutants are not tests, but are used to help us find tests.

Given a ground string program or method, a mutation-adequate test set distinguishes the program from a set of syntactic variations, or mutants, of that program. A simple example of a mutation operator for a program is the *Arithmetic Operation*

Original Method		With Embedded Mutants

int Min (int A, int B)
 {
   int minVal;
   minVal = A;
   if (B < A)
   {
     minVal = B;
   }
   return (minVal);
 } // end Min
	
	Δ1
	
	Δ2
	Δ3
	
	Δ4
	Δ5
	Δ6
		int Min (int A, int B)
		 {
		   int minVal;
		   minVal = A;
		   minVal = **B**;
		   if (B < A)
		   if (B > A)
		   if (B < **minVal**)
		   {
		     minVal = B;
		     Bomb();
		     minVal = **A**;
		     minVal = **failOnZero (B)**;
		   }
		   return (minVal);
		 } // end Min

Figure 5.1. Method Min and six mutants.

Mutation operator, which changes an assignment statement like "x = a + b" into a variety of possible alternatives, including "x = a - b", "x = a * b", and "x = a / b". Unless the assignment statement appears in a very strange program, it probably matters which arithmetic operator is used, and a decent test set should be able to distinguish among the various possibilities. It turns out that by careful selection of the mutation operators, a tester can develop very powerful test sets.

Mutation testing is used to help the user to strengthen the quality of test data iteratively. Test data are used to evaluate the ground program with the goal of causing each mutant to exhibit different behavior. When this happens, the mutant is considered *dead* and no longer needs to remain in the testing process since the fault that it represents will be detected by the same test that killed it. More importantly, the mutant has satisfied its requirement of identifying a useful test case.

A key to successful use of mutation is the mutation operators, which are designed for each programming, specification, or design language. In program-based mutation, invalid strings are syntactically illegal and would be caught by a compiler. These are called *stillborn* mutants and should not be generated. A *trivial* mutant can be killed by almost any test case. Some mutants are functionally *equivalent* to the original program. That is, they always produce the same output as the original program, so no test case can kill them. Equivalent mutants represent infeasible test requirements, as discussed in the previous chapters.

We refine the notion of killing and coverage for program-based mutation. These definitions are consistent with the previous section.

Definition 5.48 Killing Mutants: Given a mutant $m \in M$ for a ground string program P and a test t, t is said to *kill m* if and only if the output of t on P is different from the output of t on m.

As said in Section 5.1.2, it is hard to quantify the number of test requirements for mutation. In fact, it depends on the specific set of operators used and the language that the operators are applied to. One of the most widely used mutation systems was Mothra. It generated 44 mutants for the Fortran version of the Min() method in Figure 5.1. For most collections of operators, the number of program-based mutants is roughly proportional to the product of the number of references to variables times the number of variables that are declared ($O(Refs*Vars)$). The selective mutation approach mentioned below under "Designing Mutation Operators" eliminates the number of data objects so that the number of mutants is proportional to the number of variable references ($O(Refs)$). More details are in the bibliographic notes.

Program-based mutation has traditionally been applied to individual statements for unit level testing. Figure 5.1 contains a small Java method with six mutated lines (each preceded by the Δ symbol). Note that each mutated statement represents a separate program. The mutation operators are defined to satisfy one of two goals. One goal is to mimic typical programmer mistakes, thus trying to ensure that the tests can detect those mistakes. The other goal is to force the tester to create tests that have been found to effectively test software. In Figure 5.1, mutants 1, 3, and 5 replace one variable reference with another, mutant 2 changes a relational operator, and mutant 4 is a special mutation operator that causes a runtime failure as soon as the statement is reached. This forces every statement to be executed, thus getting statement or node coverage.

Mutant 6 looks unusual, as the operator is intended to force the tester to create an effective test. The *failOnZero*() method is a special mutation operator that causes a failure if the parameter is zero and does nothing if the parameter is not zero (it returns the value of the parameter). Thus, mutant 6 can be killed only if **B** has the value zero, which forces the tester to follow the time-tested heuristic of causing every variable and expression to have the value of zero.

One point that is sometimes confusing about mutation is how tests are created. When applying program-based mutation, the direct goal of the tester is to kill mutants; an indirect goal is to create good tests. Even less directly, the tester wants to find faults. Tests that kill mutants can be found by intuition, or if more rigor is needed, by analyzing the conditions under which a mutant will be killed.

The RIP fault/failure model was discussed in Section 1.2. Program-based mutations represent a software failure by a mutant, and reachability, infection, and propagation refer to reaching the mutant, the mutant causing the program state to be incorrect, and the eventual output of the program to be incorrect.

Weak mutation relaxes the definition of "killing" a mutant to include only reachability and infection, but **not** propagation. That is, weak mutation checks the internal state of the program immediately after execution of the mutated component (that is, after the expression, statement, or basic block). If the state is incorrect the mutant is killed. This is weaker than standard (or *strong*) mutation because an incorrect state does **not** always propagate to the output. That is, strong mutation may require more tests to satisfy coverage than weak mutation. Experimentation has shown that the difference is very small in most cases.

This difference can be formalized by refining the definition of killing mutants given previously.

> *Definition 5.49 Strongly Killing Mutants:* Given a mutant $m \in M$ for a program P and a test t, t is said to *strongly kill* m if and only if the output of t on P is different from the output of t on m.

CRITERION **5.35 Strong Mutation Coverage (SMC):** *For each $m \in M$, TR contains exactly one requirement, to strongly kill m.*

Definition 5.50 Weakly Killing Mutants: Given a mutant $m \in M$ that modifies a location l in a program P, and a test t, t is said to *weakly kill m* if and only if the state of the execution of P on t is different from the state of the execution of m immediately after l.

CRITERION **5.36 Weak Mutation Coverage (WMC):** *For each* $m \in M$, *TR contains exactly one requirement, to weakly kill m.*

Consider mutant 1 in Figure 5.1. The mutant is on the first statement, thus the reachability condition is always satisfied (*true*). In order to infect, the value of **B** must be different from the value of **A**, which is formalized as $(A \neq B)$. To propagate, the mutated version of **Min** must return an incorrect value. In this case, **Min** must return the value that was assigned in the first statement, which means that the statement inside the **if** block must **not** be executed. That is, $(B < A) = \textit{false}$. The complete test specification to kill mutant 1 is

> Reachability : *true*
> Infection : $A \neq B$
> Propagation : $(B < A) = \textit{false}$
> Full Test Specification : $\textit{true} \wedge (A \neq B) \wedge ((B < A) = \textit{false})$
> $\equiv (A \neq B) \wedge (B \geq A)$
> $\equiv (B > A)$

Thus, the test case value $(A = 5, B = 7)$ should cause mutant 1 to result in a failure. The original method will return the value 5 (A) but the mutated version returns 7.

Mutant 3 is an example of an equivalent mutant. Intuitively, **minVal** and **A** have the same value at that point in the program, so replacing one with the other has no effect. As with mutant 1, the reachability condition is *true*. The infection condition is $(B < A) \neq (B < minVal)$. However, dutiful analysis can reveal the assertion $(minVal = A)$, leading to the combined condition $((B < A) \neq (B < minVal)) \wedge (minVal = A)$. Simplifying by eliminating the inequality $\neq$ gives

$$(((B < A) \wedge (B \geq minVal)) \vee ((B \geq A) \wedge (B < minVal))) \wedge (minVal = A)$$

Rearranging the terms gives

$$(((A > B) \wedge (B \geq minVal)) \vee ((A \leq B) \wedge (B < minVal))) \wedge (minVal = A)$$

If $(A > B)$ and $(B \geq minVal)$, then by transitivity, $(A > minVal)$. Applying transitivity to both the first two disjuncts gives

$$((A > minVal) \vee (A < minVal)) \wedge (minVal = A)$$

Finally, the first disjunct can be reduced to a simple inequality, resulting in the following contradiction:

$$(A \neq minVal) \wedge (minVal = A)$$

The contradiction means that no values exist that can satisfy the conditions, thus the mutant is provably equivalent. In general, detecting equivalent mutants, just like detecting infeasible paths, is an undecidable problem. However, strategies such as algebraic manipulations and program slicing can detect some equivalent mutants.

As a final example, consider the following method, with one mutant shown embedded in statement 4:

```
1    boolean isEven (int X)
2    {
3        if (X < 0)
4            X = 0 - X;
Δ4           X = 0;
5        if (float) (X/2) == ((float) X) / 2.0
6            return (true);
7        else
8            return (false);
9    }
```

The reachability condition for mutant Δ4 is $(X < 0)$ and the infection condition is $(X \neq 0)$. If the test case X = -6 is given, then the value of X after statement 4 is executed is 6 and the value of X after the **mutated** version of statement 4 is executed is 0. Thus, this test satisfies reachability and infection, and the mutant will be killed under the weak mutation criterion. However, 6 and 0 are both even, so the decision starting on statement 5 will return true for both the mutated and nonmutated versions. That is, propagation is not satisfied, so test case X = -6 will not kill the mutant under the strong mutation criterion. The propagation condition for this mutant is that the number be odd. Thus, to satisfy the strong mutation criterion, we require $(X < 0) \wedge (X \neq 0) \wedge odd(X)$, which can be simplified to X is an odd, negative integer.

Testing Programs with Mutation

A test process gives a sequence of steps to follow to generate test cases. A single criterion may be used with many processes, and a test process may not even include a criterion. Choosing a test process for mutation is particularly difficult because mutation analysis is actually a way to measure the quality of the test cases and the actual testing of the software is a side effect. In practical terms, however, the software is tested, and tested well, or the test cases do not kill mutants. This point can best be understood by examining a typical mutation analysis process.

Figure 5.2 shows how mutation testing can be applied. The tester submits the program under test to an automated system, which starts by creating mutants. Optionally, those mutants are then analyzed by a heuristic that detects and eliminates as many equivalent mutants as possible.[2] A set of test cases is then generated automatically and executed first against the original program, and then the mutants. If the output of a mutant program differs from the original (correct) output, the mutant is marked as being dead and is considered to have been *strongly killed* by that test case. Dead mutants are not executed against subsequent test cases. Test cases that do not strongly kill at least one mutant are considered to be "ineffective" and eliminated, even though such test cases may weakly kill one or more mutants. This

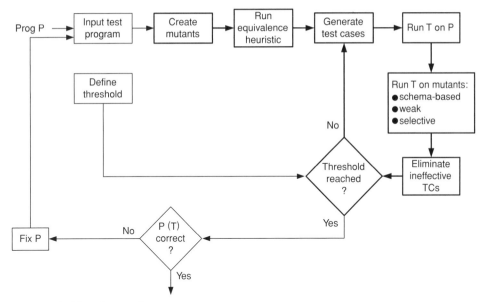

Figure 5.2. Mutation testing process.
Bold boxes represent steps that are automated; other boxes represent manual steps.

is because the requirement stated above requires the output (and not the internal state) to be different.

Once all test cases have been executed, coverage is computed as a mutation score. The mutation score is the ratio of dead mutants over the total number of non-equivalent mutants. If the mutation score reaches 1.00, that means all mutants have been detected. A test set that kills all the mutants is said to be *adequate* relative to the mutants.

A mutation score of 1.00 is usually impractical, so the tester defines a "threshold" value, which is a minimum acceptable mutation score. If the threshold has not been reached, then the process is repeated, each time generating test cases to target live mutants, until the threshold mutation score is reached. Up to this point, the process has been entirely automatic. To finish testing, the tester will examine expected output of the effective test cases, and fix the program if any faults are found. This leads to the fundamental premise of mutation testing: **In practice, if the software contains a fault, there will usually be a set of mutants that can only be killed by a test case that also detects that fault**.

Designing Mutation Operators

Mutation operators must be chosen for each language and although they overlap quite a bit, some differences are particular to the language, often depending on the language features. Researchers have designed mutation operators for various programming languages, including Fortran IV, COBOL, Fortran 77, C, C integration testing, Lisp, Ada, Java, and Java class relationships. Researchers have also designed Mutation operators for the formal specification language SMV (discussed in Section 5.4.2), and for XML messages (discussed in Section 5.5.2).

As a field, we have learned a lot about designing mutation operators over the years. Detailed lists of mutation operators for various languages are provided in the literature, as referenced in the bibliographic notes for this chapter. Mutation operators are generally designed either to mimic typical programmer mistakes, or to encourage testers to follow common testing heuristics. Operators that change relational operators or variable references are examples of operators that mimic typical programmer mistakes. The *failOnZero()* operator used in Figure 5.1 is an example of the latter design; the tester is encouraged to follow the common testing heuristic of "causing each expression to become zero."

When first designing mutation operators for a new language, it is reasonable to be "inclusive," that is, include as many operators as possible. However, this often results in a large number of mutation operators, and an even larger number of mutants. Researchers have devoted a lot of effort to trying to find ways to use fewer mutants and mutation operators. The two most common ways to have fewer mutants are (1) to randomly sample from the total number of mutants, and (2) to use mutation operators that are particularly effective.

The term *selective mutation* has been used to describe the strategy of using only mutation operators that are particularly effective. Effectiveness has been evaluated as follows: if tests that are created specifically to kill mutants created by mutation operator o_i also kill mutants created by mutation operator o_j with very high probability, then mutation operator o_i is more *effective* than o_j.

This notion can be extended to consider a collection of effective mutation operators as follows:

Definition 5.51 Effective Mutation Operators: If tests that are created specifically to kill mutants created by a collection of mutation operators $O = \{o_1, o_2, \ldots\}$ also kill mutants created by all remaining mutation operators with very high probability, then O defines an effective set of mutation operators.

Researchers have concluded that a collection of mutation operators that insert unary operators and that modify unary and binary operators will be **effective**. The actual research was done with Fortran 77 (the Mothra system), but the results are adapted to Java in this chapter. Corresponding operators can be defined for other languages. The operators defined below are used throughout the remainder of this chapter as the defining set of program-level mutation operators.

1. **ABS – Absolute Value Insertion**:

> Each arithmetic expression (and subexpression) is modified by the functions *abs()*, *negAbs()*, and *failOnZero()*.

abs() returns the absolute value of the expression and *negAbs()* returns the negative of the absolute value. *failOnZero()* tests whether the value of the expression is zero. If it is, the mutant is killed; otherwise, execution continues and the value of the expression is returned. This operator is designed specifically to force the tester to cause each numeric expression to have the value 0, a negative value, and a positive value. For example, the statement "x = 3 * a;" is mutated to create the following three statements:

```
x = 3 * abs (a);
x = 3 * - abs (a);
x = 3 * failOnZero (a);
```

2. *AOR – Arithmetic Operator Replacement*:

> Each occurrence of one of the arithmetic operators $+$, $-$, $*$, $/$, $**$, and $\%$ is replaced by each of the other operators. In addition, each is replaced by the special mutation operators *leftOp*, and *rightOp*.

leftOp returns the left operand (the right is ignored), *rightOp* returns the right operand, and *mod* computes the remainder when the left operand is divided by the right. For example, the statement "x = a + b;" is mutated to create the following seven statements:

```
x = a - b;
x = a * b;
x = a / b;
x = a ** b;
x = a;
x = b;
x = a % b;
```

3. *ROR – Relational Operator Replacement*:

> Each occurrence of one of the relational operators ($<$, $\leq$, $>$, $\geq$, $==$, $\neq$) is replaced by each of the other operators and by *falseOp* and *trueOp*.

falseOp always returns *false* and *trueOp* always returns *true*. For example, the statement "if (m > n)" is mutated to create the following seven statements:

```
if (m >= n)
if (m < n)
if (m <= n)
if (m == n)
if (m != n)
if (false)
if (true)
```

4. *COR – Conditional Operator Replacement*:

> Each occurrence of each logical operator (*and–&&, or–||, and with no conditional evaluation–&, or with no conditional evaluation–|, not equivalent –^*) is replaced by each of the other operators; in addition, each is replaced by *falseOp, trueOp, leftOp*, and *rightOp*.

leftOp returns the left operand (the right is ignored) and *rightOp* returns the right operand. *falseOp* always returns *false* and *trueOp* always returns *true*. For example, the statement "if (a && b)" is mutated to create the following eight statements:

```
if (a || b)
if (a & b)
if (a | b)
if (a ^ b)
if (false)
if (true)
```

    if (a)
    if (b)

5. *SOR – Shift Operator Replacement*:

> Each occurrence of one of the shift operators $<<$, $>>$, and $>>>$ is replaced by each of the other operators. In addition, each is replaced by the special mutation operator *leftOp*.

leftOp returns the left operand unshifted. For example, the statement "x = m << a;" is mutated to create the following three statements:

    x = m >> a;
    x = m >>> a;
    x = m;

6. *LOR – Logical Operator Replacement*:

> Each occurrence of each bitwise logical operator (*bitwise and* (&), *bitwise or* (|), and *exclusive or* (^)) is replaced by each of the other operators; in addition, each is replaced by *leftOp* and *rightOp*.

leftOp returns the left operand (the right is ignored) and *rightOp* returns the right operand. For example, the statement "x = m & n;" is mutated to create the following four statements:

    x = m | n;
    x = m ^ n;
    x = m;
    x = n;

7. *ASR – Assignment Operator Replacement*:

> Each occurrence of one of the assignment operators (=, +=, -=, *=, /=, %=, &=, |=, ^=, <<=, >>=, >>>=) is replaced by each of the other operators.

For example, the statement "x += 3;" is mutated to create the following ten statements:

    x -= 3;
    x *= 3;
    x /= 3;
    x %= 3;
    x &= 3;
    x |= 3;
    x ^= 3;
    x <<= 3;
    x >>= 3;
    x >>>= 3;

8. *UOI – Unary Operator Insertion*:

> Each unary operator (arithmetic +, arithmetic −, conditional !, logical ~) is inserted before each expression of the correct type.

For example, the statement "x = 3 * a;" is mutated to create the following four statements:

```
x = 3 * +a;
x = 3 * -a;
x = +3 * a;
x = -3 * a;
```

9. *UOD – Unary Operator Deletion*:

> Each unary operator (arithmetic +, arithmetic −, conditional !, logical ~) is deleted.

For example, the statement "if !(a > -b)" is mutated to create the following two statements:

```
if (a > -b)
if !(a > b)
```

Two other operators that are useful in examples are scalar variable replacement and the "bomb" operator. Scalar variable replacement results in a lot of mutants (V^2 if V is the number of variables), and it turns out that it is not necessary given the above operators. It is included here as a convenience for examples. The bomb operator results in only one mutant per statement, but it is also not necessary given the above operators.

10. *SVR – Scalar Variable Replacement*:

> Each variable reference is replaced by every other variable of the appropriate type that is declared in the current scope.

For example, the statement "x = a * b;" is mutated to create the following six statements:

```
x = a * a;
a = a * b;
x = x * b;
x = a * x;
x = b * b;
b = a * b;
```

11. *BSR—Bomb Statement Replacement*:

> Each statement is replaced by a special *Bomb*() function.

Bomb() signals a failure as soon as it is executed, thus requiring the tester to reach each statement. For example, the statement "x = a * b;" is mutated to create the following statement:

```
Bomb();
```

Subsumption of Other Test Criteria (*Advanced Topic*)

Mutation is widely considered the strongest test criterion in terms of finding the most faults. It is also the most expensive. This section shows that mutation subsumes a number of other coverage criteria. The proofs are developed by showing that specific mutation operators impose requirements that are identical to a specific coverage criterion. For each specific requirement defined by a criterion, a single mutant is created that can be killed only by test cases that satisfy the requirement. Therefore, the coverage criterion is satisfied if and only if the mutants associated with the requirements for the criterion are killed. In this case, the mutation operators that ensure coverage of a criterion are said to *yield* the criterion. If a criterion is yielded by one or more mutation operators, then mutation testing subsumes the criterion. Although mutation operators vary by language and mutation analysis tool, this section uses common operators that are used in most implementations. It is also possible to design mutation operators to force mutation to subsume other testing criteria. Further details are given in the bibliographic notes.

This type of proof has one subtle problem. The condition coverage criteria impose only a **local** requirement; for example, edge coverage requires that each branch in the program be executed. Mutation, on the other hand, imposes **global** requirements in addition to local requirements. That is, mutation also requires that the mutant program produce incorrect output. For edge coverage, some specific mutants can be killed only if each branch is executed **and** the final output of the mutant is incorrect. On the one hand, this means that mutation imposes stronger requirements than the condition coverage criteria. On the other hand, and somewhat perversely, this also means that sometimes a test set that satisfies a coverage criteria will not kill all the associated mutants. Thus, mutation as defined earlier will not strictly subsume the condition coverage criteria.

This problem is solved by basing the subsumptions on *weak mutation*. In terms of subsuming other coverage criteria, weak mutation only imposes the local requirements. In weak mutation, mutants that are **not** equivalent at the infection stage but **are** equivalent at the propagation stage (that is, an incorrect state is masked or repaired) are left in the set of test cases, so that edge coverage is subsumed. It is precisely the fact that such test cases are removed that strong mutation does not subsume edge coverage.

Thus, this section shows that the coverage criteria are subsumed by weak mutation, not strong mutation.

Subsumption is shown for graph coverage criteria from Chapter 2 and logic coverage criteria from Chapter 3. Some mutation operators only make sense for program source statements whereas others can apply to arbitrary structures such as logical expressions. For example, one common mutation operator is to replace statements with "bombs" that immediately cause the program to terminate execution or raise an exception. This mutation can only be defined for program statements. Another common mutation operator is to replace relational operators ($<$, $>$, etc.) with other relational operators (the ROR operator). This kind of relational operator replacement can be applied to any logical expression, including guards FSMs.

Node coverage requires each statement or basic block in the program to be executed. The mutation operator that replaces statements with "bombs" yields node coverage. To kill these mutants, we are required to find test cases that reach each

		(T T)	(T F)	(F T)	(F F)
	$a \wedge b$	T	F	F	F
1	$true \wedge b$	T	F	**T**	F
2	$false \wedge b$	**F**	F	F	F
3	$a \wedge true$	T	**T**	F	F
4	$a \wedge false$	**F**	F	F	F

Figure 5.3. Partial truth table for $(a \wedge b)$.

basic block. Since this is exactly the requirement of node coverage, this operator yields node coverage and mutation subsumes node coverage.

Edge coverage requires each edge in the control flow graph to be executed. A common mutation operator is to replace each predicate with both *true* and *false* (the ROR operator). To kill the *true* mutant, a test case must take the *false* branch, and to kill the *false* mutant, a test case must take the *true* branch. This operator forces each branch in the program to be executed, and thus it yields edge coverage and mutation subsumes edge coverage.

Clause coverage requires each clause to become both *true* and *false*. The ROR, COR, and LOR mutation operators will together replace each clause in each predicate with both *true* and *false*. To kill the *true* mutant, a test case must cause the clause (and also the full predicate) to be *false*, and to kill the *false* mutant, a test case must cause the clause (and also the full predicate) to be *true*. This is exactly the requirement for clause coverage. A simple way to illustrate this is with a modified form of a truth table.

Consider a predicate that has two clauses connected by an AND. Assume the predicate is $(a \wedge b)$, where a and b are arbitrary boolean-valued clauses. The partial truth table in Figure 5.3 shows $(a \wedge b)$ on the top line with the resulting value for each of the four combinations of values for a and b. Below the line are four mutations that replace each of a and b with *true* and *false*. To kill the mutants, the tester must choose an input (one of the four truth assignments on top of the table) that causes a result that is different from that of the original predicate. Consider mutant 1, $true \wedge b$. Mutant 1 has the same result as the original clause for three of the four truth assignments. Thus, to kill that mutant, the tester must use a test case input value that causes the truth assignment (F T), as shown in the box. Likewise, mutant 3, $a \wedge true$, can be killed only if the truth assignment (T F) is used. Thus, mutants 1 and 3 are killed if and only if clause coverage is satisfied, and the mutation operator yields clause coverage for this case. Note that mutants 2 and 4 are not needed to subsume clause coverage.

Although the proof technique of showing that mutation operators yield clause coverage on a case-by-case basis with the logical operators is straightforward and relatively easy to grasp, it is clumsy. More generally, assume a predicate p and a clause a, and the clause coverage requirements to test $p(a)$, which says that a must evaluate to both *true* and *false*. Consider the mutation $\Delta p(a \rightarrow true)$ (that is, the predicate where a is replaced by *true*). The only way to satisfy the infection condition for this mutant (and thus kill it) is to find a test case that causes a to take on the value of *false*. Likewise, the mutation $\Delta p(a \rightarrow false)$ can be killed only by a test case that causes a to take on the value of *true*. Thus, in the general case, the mutation operator that replaces clauses with *true* and *false* yield clause coverage and is subsumed by mutation.

Combinatorial coverage requires that the clauses in a predicate evaluate to each possible combination of truth values. In the general case combinatorial coverage has 2^N requirements for a predicate with N clauses. Since no single or combination of mutation operators produces 2^N mutants, it is easy to see that mutation cannot subsume COC.

Active clause coverage requires that each clause c in a predicate p evaluates to *true* and *false* **and** determines the value of p. The first version in Chapter 3, general active clause coverage allows the values for other clauses in p to have different values when c is true and c is false. It is simple to show that mutation subsumes general active clause coverage; in fact, we already have.

To kill the mutant $\Delta p(a \rightarrow true)$, we must satisfy the infection condition by **causing** $p(a \rightarrow true)$ **to have a different value from** $p(a)$, that is, a must determine p. Likewise, to kill $\Delta p(a \rightarrow false)$, $p(a \rightarrow false)$ must have a different result from $p(a)$, that is, a must determine p. Since this is exactly the requirement of GACC, this operator yields node coverage and mutation subsumes general active clause coverage. Note that this is only true if the incorrect value in the mutated program propagates to the end of the expression, which is one interpretation of weak mutation.

Neither correlated active clause coverage nor restricted active clause coverage are subsumed by mutation operators. The reason is that both CACC and RACC require pairs of tests to have certain properties. In the case of CACC, the property is that the predicate outcome be different on the two tests associated with a particular clause. In the case of RACC, the property is that the minor clauses have exactly the same values on the two tests associated with a particular clause. Since each mutant is killed (or not) by a single test case, (as opposed to a pair of test cases), mutation analysis, at least as traditionally defined, cannot subsume criteria that impose relationships between pairs of test cases.

Researchers have not determined whether mutation subsumes the inactive clause coverage criteria.

All-defs data flow coverage requires that each definition of a variable reach at least one use. That is, for each definition of a variable X on node n, there must be a definition-clear subpath for X from n to a node or an edge with a use of X. The argument for subsumption is a little complicated for All-defs, and unlike the other arguments, All-defs requires that strong mutation be used.

A common mutation operator is to delete statements with the goal of forcing each statement in the program to make an impact on the output.[3] To show subsumption of All-defs, we restrict our attention to statements that contain variable definitions. Assume that the statement s_i contains a definition of a variable x, and m_i is the mutant that deletes s_i ($\Delta s_i \rightarrow null$). To kill m_i under strong mutation, a test case t must (1) cause the mutated statement to be reached (reachability), (2) cause the execution state of the program after execution of s_i to be incorrect (infection), and (3) cause the final output of the program to be incorrect (propagation). Any test case that reaches s_i will cause an incorrect execution state, because the mutated version of s_i will not assign a value to x. For the final output of the mutant to be incorrect, two cases occur. First, if x is an output variable, t must have caused an execution of a subpath from the deleted definition of x to the output without an intervening definition (def-clear). Since the output is considered a use, this satisfies the criterion. Second, if x is not an output variable, then not defining x at s_i must result in an incorrect output state. This is possible only if x is used at some later point during execution without being redefined. Thus, t satisfies the all-defs criterion for the definition of x at s_i, and the mutation operator yields all-defs, ensuring that mutation subsumes all-defs.

It is possible to design a mutation operator specifically to subsume all-uses, but such an operator has never been published or used in any tool.

EXERCISES
Section 5.2.

1. Provide reachability conditions, infection conditions, propagation conditions, and test case values to kill mutants 2, 4, 5, and 6 in Figure 5.1.

2. Answer questions (a) through (d) for the mutant in the two methods, findVal() and sum().
   (a) If possible, find a test input that does **not** reach the mutant.
   (b) If possible, find a test input that satisfies reachability but **not infection** for the mutant.
   (c) If possible, find a test input that satisfies infection, but **not propagation** for the mutant.
   (d) If possible, find a test input that kills mutant m.

```
//Effects: If numbers null throw NullPointerException
//   else return LAST occurrence of val in numbers[]
//   If val not in numbers[] return -1
1. public static int findVal(int numbers[], int val)
2. {
3.    int findVal = -1;
4.
5.    for (int i=0; i<numbers.length; i++)
5'.// for (int i=(0+1); i<numbers.length; i++)
6.       if (numbers [i] == val)
7.          findVal = i;
8.    return (findVal);
9. }
```

```
//Effects: If x null throw NullPointerException
//   else return the sum of the values in x
1. public static int sum(int[] x)
2. {
3.    int s = 0;
4.    for (int i=0; i < x.length; i++) }
5.    {
6.       s = s + x[i];
6'.  // s = s - x[i]; //AOR
7.    }
8.    return s;
9. }
```

3. Refer to the TestPat program in Chapter 2 (Figure 2.21). Consider Mutant A and Mutant B given below:
   (a) If possible, find a test case that does **not reach** the mutants.
   (b) If possible, find a test input that satisfies reachability but **not infection** for the mutants.
   (c) If possible, find a test input that satisfies infection, but **not propagation** for the mutants.
   (d) If possible, find a test inputs that strongly kill the mutants.
   (a) while (isPat == false && isub + patternLen - 1 < subjectLen)
       while (isPat == false && isub + patternLen - 0 < subjectLen) // Mutant A
   (b) isPat = false;   // Inside the loops, not the declaration
       isPat = true;   // Mutant B

4. Why does it make sense to remove ineffective test cases?

5. Define 12 mutants for the following method *cal*() using the effective mutation operators given previously. Try to use each mutation operator at least once. Approximately how many mutants do you think there would be if all mutants for cal were created?

```
public static int cal (int month1, int day1, int month2, int day2, int year)
{
//*************************************************************
// Calculate the number of Days between the two given days in
// the same year.
// preconditions : day1 and day2 must be in same year
//                 1 <= month1, month2 <= 12
//                 1 <= day1, day2 <= 31
//                 month1 <= month2
//                 The range for year: 1 ... 10000
//*************************************************************
  int numDays;

    if (month2 == month1) // in the same month
      numDays = day2 - day1;
    else
    {
      // Skip month 0.
      int daysIn[] = {0, 31, 0, 31, 30, 31, 30, 31, 31, 30, 31, 30, 31};
      // Are we in a leap year?
      int m4 = year % 4;
      int m100 = year % 100;
      int m400 = year % 400;
      if ((m4 != 0) || ((m100 ==0) && (m400 != 0)))
        daysIn[2] = 28;
      else
        daysIn[2] = 29;

      // start with days in the two months
      numDays = day2 + (daysIn[month1] - day1);

      // add the days in the intervening months
      for (int i = month1 + 1; i <= month2-1; i++)
        numDays = daysIn[i] + numDays;
    }
    return (numDays);
}
```

6. Define 12 mutants for the following method *power*() using the effective mutation operators given previously. Try to use each mutation operator at least once. Approximately how many mutants do you think there would be if all mutants for *power*() were created?

```
public static int power (int left, int right)
{
///***********************************
// Raises Left to the power of Right
// precondition : Right >= 0
// postcondition: Returns Left**Right
///***********************************
   int rslt;
   rslt = Left;
   if (Right == 0)
   {
      rslt = 1;
   }
   else
   {
      for (int i = 2; i <= Right; i++)
         rslt = rslt * Left;
   }
   return (rslt);
}
```

7. The fundamental premise was stated as: "*In practice, if the software contains a fault, there will usually be a set of mutants that can be killed only by a test case that also detects that fault.*"
   (a) Give a brief argument **in support of** the fundamental mutation premise.
   (b) Give a brief argument **against** the fundamental mutation premise.
8. Try to design mutation operators that subsume combinatorial coverage. Why wouldn't we want such an operator?
9. Look online for the tool Jester, which is based on JUnit.[4] Based on your reading, evaluate Jester as a mutation-testing tool.
10. Download and install the Java mutation tool *muJava*: http://ise.gmu.edu/-~offutt/mujava/. Enclose the method *cal*() from the previous question inside a class, and use muJava to test *cal*(). Note that a test case is a method call to *cal*().
    (a) How many mutants are there?
    (b) How many test cases do you need to kill the mutants?
    (c) What mutation score were you able to achieve without analyzing for equivalent mutants?
    (d) How many equivalent mutants are there?

5.3 INTEGRATION AND OBJECT-ORIENTED TESTING

This book uses the term "integration testing" to refer to testing connections among separate program units. In Java, that involves testing the way classes, packages, and components are connected. This section uses the general term "component." This is also where features that are unique to object-oriented programming languages are tested, specifically, inheritance, polymorphism, and dynamic binding.

5.3.1 BNF Integration Testing

As far as we know, BNF testing has not been used at the integration level.

5.3.2 Integration Mutation

This section first discusses how mutation can be used for testing at the integration level without regard to object-oriented relationships, then how mutation can be used to test for problems involving inheritance, polymorphism, and dynamic binding.

Faults that can occur in the integration between two components usually depend on a mismatch of assumptions. For example, Chapter 1 discussed the Mars lander of September 1999, which crashed because a component sent a value in English units (miles) and the recipient component assumed the value was in kilometers. Whether such a flaw should be fixed by changing the caller, the callee, or both depends on the design specification of the program and possibly pragmatic issues such as which is easier to change.

Integration mutation (also called "interface mutation") works by creating mutations on the connections between components. Most mutations are around method calls, and both the calling (caller) and called (callee) method must be considered. Interface mutation operators do the following:

- Change a calling method by modifying the values that are sent to a called method.
- Change a calling method by modifying the call.
- Change a called method by modifying the values that enter and leave a method. This should include parameters as well as variables from a higher scope (class level, package, public, etc.).
- Change a called method by modifying statements that return from the method.

1. ***IPVR – Integration Parameter Variable Replacement***:

   > Each parameter in a method call is replaced by each other variable of compatible type in the scope of the method call.

   IPVR does not use variables of an incompatible type because they would be syntactically illegal (the compiler should catch them). In OO languages, this operator replaces primitive type variables as well as objects.

2. ***IUOI – Integration Unary Operator Insertion***:

   > Each expression in a method call is modified by inserting all possible unary operators in front and behind it.

   The unary operators vary by language and type. Java includes $++$ and $--$ as both prefix and postfix operators for numeric types.

3. ***IPEX – Integration Parameter Exchange***:

   > Each parameter in a method call is exchanged with each parameter of compatible type in that method call.

   For example, if a method call is max (a, b), a mutated method call of max (b, a) is created.

4. *IMCD – Integration Method Call Deletion*:

> Each method call is deleted. If the method returns a value and it is used in an expression, the method call is replaced with an appropriate constant value.

In Java, the default values should be used for methods that return values of primitive type. If the method returns an object, the method call should be replaced by a call to **new()** on the appropriate class.

5. *IREM – Integration Return Expression Modification*:

> Each expression in each return statement in a method is modified by applying the UOI and AOR operators from Section 5.2.2.

Object-Oriented Mutation Operators

Chapter 1 defined intra-method, inter-method, intra-class, and inter-class testing. Those mutation operators can be used at the inter-method level (between methods in the same class) and at the inter-class level (between methods in different classes). When testing at the inter-class level, testers also have to worry about faults in the use of inheritance and polymorphism. These are powerful language features that can solve difficult programming problems, but also introduce difficult testing problems.

Languages that include features for inheritance and polymorphism often also include features for information hiding and overloading. Thus, mutation operators to test those features are usually included with the OO operators, even though these are not usually considered to be essential to calling a language "object-oriented."

To understand how mutation testing is applied to such features, we need to examine the language features in depth. This is done in terms of Java; other OO languages tend to be similar but with some subtle differences.

Encapsulation is an abstraction mechanism to enforce information hiding, a design technique that frees clients of an abstraction from unnecessary dependence on design decisions in the implementation of the abstraction. Encapsulation allows objects to restrict access to their member variables and methods by other objects. Java supports four distinct access levels for member variables and methods: private, protected, public, and default (also called package). These access levels are poorly understood by many programmers, and often not carefully considered during design, so they are a rich source of faults. Table 5.1 summarizes these access levels. A *private* member is available only to the class in which it is defined. If access is not specified, the access level defaults to *package*, which allows access to classes in the same package, but **not** subclasses in other packages. A *protected* member is available

Table 5.1. Java's access levels

Specifier	Same class	Different class/ same package	Different package subclass	Different package non-subclass
private	Y	n	n	n
package	Y	Y	n	n
protected	Y	Y	Y	n
public	Y	Y	Y	Y

to the class itself, subclasses, and classes in the same package. A *public* member is available to any class in any inheritance hierarchy or package (the world).

Java does not support multiple class inheritance, so every class has only one immediate parent. A subclass inherits variables and methods from its parent and all of its ancestors, and can use them as defined, or override the methods or hide the variables. Subclasses can also explicitly use their parent's variables and methods using the keyword "super" (super.methodname();). Java's inheritance allows method overriding, variable hiding, and class constructors.

Method overriding allows a method in a subclass to have the same name, arguments and result type as a method in its parent. Overriding allows subclasses to redefine inherited methods. The child class method has the same signature, but a different implementation.

Variable hiding is achieved by defining a variable in a child class that has the same name and type of an inherited variable. This has the effect of hiding the inherited variable from the child class. This is a powerful feature, but it is also a potential source of errors.

Class constructors are not inherited in the same way other methods are. To use a constructor of the parent, we must explicitly call it using the *super* keyword. The call must be the first statement in the derived class constructor and the parameter list must match the parameters in the argument list of the parent constructor.

Java supports two versions of polymorphism, attributes and methods, both of which use dynamic binding. Each object has a *declared type* (the type in the declaration statement, that is, "*Parent P;*") and an *actual type* (the type in the instantiation statement, that is, "*P = new Child();,*" or the assignment statement, "*P = Pold;*"). The actual type can be the declared type or any type that is descended from the declared type.

A *polymorphic attribute* is an object reference that can take on various types. At any location in the program, the type of the object reference can be different in different executions. A *polymorphic method* can accept parameters of different types by having a parameter that is declared of type *Object*. Polymorphic methods are used to implement *type abstraction* (templates in C++ and generics in Ada).

Overloading is the use of the same name for different constructors or methods in the same class. They must have different *signatures*, or lists of arguments. Overloading is easily confused with overriding because the two mechanisms have similar names and semantics. Overloading occurs with two methods in the same class, whereas overriding occurs between a class and one of its descendants.

In Java, member variables and methods can be associated with the class rather than with individual objects. Members associated with a class are called *class* or *static variables* and *methods*. The Java run time system creates a single copy of a static variable the first time it encounters the class in which the variable is defined. All instances of that class share the same copy of the static variable. Static methods can operate only on static variables; they cannot access instance variables defined in the class. Unfortunately the terminology varies; we say *instance variables* are declared at the class level and are available to objects, *class variables* are declared with static, and *local variables* are declared within methods.

Mutation operators can be defined for all of these language features. The purpose of mutating them is to make sure that the programmer is using them correctly. One reason to be particularly concerned about the use of OO language features is because many programmers today have learned them "on the job," without having the opportunity to study the theoretical rules about how to use them appropriately.

Following are mutation operators for information hiding language features, inheritance, polymorphism and dynamic binding, method overloading, and classes.

1. *AMC – Access Modifier Change*:

> The access level for each instance variable and method is changed to other access levels.

The AMC operator helps testers generate tests that ensure that accessibility is correct. These mutants can be killed only if the new access level denies access to another class or allows access that causes a name conflict.

2. *HVD – Hiding Variable Deletion*:

> Each declaration of an overriding, or hiding variable is deleted.

This causes references to that variable to access the variable defined in the parent (or ancestor), which is a common programming mistake.

3. *HVI – Hiding Variable Insertion*:

> A declaration is added to hide the declaration of each variable declared in an ancestor.

These mutants can be killed only by test cases that can show that the reference to the overriding variable is incorrect.

4. *OMD – Overriding Method Deletion*:

> Each entire declaration of an overriding method is deleted.

References to the method will then use the parent's version. This ensures that the method invocation is to the intended method.

5. *OMM – Overridden Method Moving*:

> Each call to an overridden method is moved to the first and last statements of the method and up and down one statement.

Overriding methods in child classes often call the original method in the parent class, for example to modify a variable that is private to the parent. A common mistake to make is to call the parent's version at the wrong time, which can cause incorrect state behavior.

6. *OMR – Overridden Method Rename*:

> Renames the parent's versions of methods that are overridden in a subclass so that the overriding does not affect the parent's method.

The OMR operator is designed to check whether an overriding method causes problems with other methods. Consider a method $m()$ that calls another method $f()$, both in a class *List*. Further, assume that $m()$ is inherited without change in a child class *Stack*, but $f()$ is overridden in *Stack*. When $m()$ is called on an object of type *Stack*, it calls *Stack*'s version of $f()$ instead of *List*'s version. In this case, *Stack*'s version of $f()$ may have an interaction with the parent's version that has unintended consequences.

7. **SKD – Super Keyword Deletion**:

> Delete each occurrence of the *super* keyword.

After the change, the reference will be to the local version instead of the ancestor's version. The SKD operator is designed to ensure that hiding/hidden variables and overriding/overridden methods are used appropriately.

8. **PCD – Parent Constructor Deletion**:

> Each call to a *super* constructor is deleted.

The parent's (or ancestor's) default constructor will be used. To kill these mutants, it is necessary to find a test case for which the parent's default constructor creates an initial state that is incorrect.

9. **ATC – Actual Type Change**:

> The actual type of a new object is changed in the new() statement.

This causes the object reference to refer to an object of a type that is different from the original actual type. The new actual type must be in the same "type family" (a descendant) of the original actual type.

10. **DTC – Declared Type Change**:

> The declared type of each new object is changed in the declaration.

The new declared type must be an ancestor of the original type. The instantiation will still be valid (it will still be a descendant of the new declared type). To kill these mutants, a test case must cause the behavior of the object to be incorrect with the new declared type.

11. **PTC – Parameter Type Change**:

> The declared type of each parameter object is changed in the declaration.

This is the same as DTC except on parameters.

12. **RTC – Reference Type Change**:

> The right side objects of assignment statements are changed to refer to objects of a compatible type.

For example, if an Integer is assigned to a reference of type Object, the assignment may be changed to that of a String. Since both Integers and Strings are descended from Object, both can be assigned interchangeably.

13. **OMC – Overloading Method Change**:

> For each pair of methods that have the same name, the bodies are interchanged.

This ensure that overloaded methods are invoked appropriately.

14. **OMD – Overloading Method Deletion**:

> Each overloaded method declaration is deleted, one at a time.

The OMD operator ensures coverage of overloaded methods; that is, all the overloaded methods must be invoked at least once. If the mutant still works correctly without the deleted method, there may be an error in invoking one of the overloading methods; the incorrect method may be invoked or an incorrect parameter type conversion has occurred.

15. **AOC – *Argument Order Change***:

> The order of the arguments in method invocations is changed to be the same as that of another overloading method, if one exists.

This causes a different method to be called, thus checking for a common fault in the use of overloading.

16. **ANC – *Argument Number Change***:

> The number of the arguments in method invocations is changed to be the same as that of another overloading method, if one exists.

This helps ensure that the programmer did not invoke the wrong method. When new values need to be added, they are the constant default values of primitive types or the result of the default constructors for objects.

17. **TKD – this *Keyword Deletion***:

> Each occurrence of the keyword *this* is deleted.

Within a method body, uses of the keyword *this* refers to the current object if the member variable is hidden by a local variable or method parameter that has the same name. The TKD operator checks if the member variables are used correctly by replacing occurrences of "*this.X*" with "*X*."

18. **SMC – Static *Modifier Change***:

> Each instance of the *static* modifier is removed, and the *static* modifier is added to instance variables.

This operator validates use of instance and class variables.

19. **VID – *Variable Initialization Deletion***:

> Remove initialization of each member variable.

Instance variables can be initialized in the variable declaration and in constructors for the class. The VID operator removes the initializations so that member variables are initialized to the default values.

20. **DCD – *Default Constructor Delete***:

> Delete each declaration of default constructor (with no parameters).

This ensures that user-defined default constructors are implemented properly.

5.4 SPECIFICATION-BASED GRAMMARS

The general term "specification-based" is applied to languages that describe software in abstract terms. This includes formal specification languages such as Z, SMV, OCL, and informal specification languages and design notations such as statecharts, FSMs, and other UML diagram notations. Such languages are becoming more widely used, partly because of increased emphasis on software quality and partly because of the widespread use of the UML.

5.4.1 BNF Grammars

To our knowledge, terminal symbol coverage and production coverage have been applied to only one type of specification language: algebraic specifications. The idea is to treat an equation in an algebraic specification as a production rule in a grammar and then derive strings of method calls to cover the equations. As algebraic specifications are not widely used, this book does not discuss this topic.

5.4.2 Specification-Based Mutation

Mutation testing can also be a valuable method at the specification level. In fact, for certain types of specifications, mutation analysis is actually easier. We address specifications expressed as finite state machines in this section.

A finite state machine is essentially a graph G, as defined in Chapter 2, with a set of states (nodes), a set of initial states (initial nodes), and a transition relation (the set of edges). When finite state machines are used, sometimes the edges and nodes are explicitly identified, as in the typical bubble and arrow diagram. However, sometimes the finite state machine is more compactly described in the following way.

1. States are implicitly defined by declaring variables with limited ranges. The state space is then the Cartesian product of the ranges of the variables.
2. Initial states are defined by limiting the ranges of some or all of the variables.
3. Transitions are defined by rules that characterize the source and target of each transition.

The following example clarifies these ideas. We describe a machine with a simple syntax, and show the same machine with explicit enumerations of the states and transitions. Although this example is too small to show this point, the syntax version in SMV is typically *much* smaller than the graph version. In fact, since state space growth is combinatorial, it is quite easy to define finite state machines where the explicit version is far too long to write, even though the machine itself can be analyzed efficiently. Below is an example in the SMV language.

```
MODULE main
#define false 0
#define true 1

VAR
    x, y : boolean;

ASSIGN
    init (x) := false;
    init (y) := false;

    next (x) := case
    !x & y : true;
    !y     : true;
    x      : false;
```

```
    true   : x;
  esac;

  next (y) := case
    x & !y : false;
    x & y  : y;
    !x & y : false;
    true   : true;
  esac;
```

Two variables appear, each of which can have only two values (boolean), so the state space is of size $2 * 2 = 4$. One initial state is defined, in the two init statements under ASSIGN. The transition diagram is shown in Figure 5.4. Transition diagrams for SMV can be derived by mechanically following the specifications. Take a given state and decide what the next value for each variable is. For example, assume the above specification is in the state (*true, true*). The next value for *x* will be determined by the "x : false" statement. *x* is *true*, so its next value will be *false*. Likewise, *x & y* is true, so the next value of *y* will be its current value, or *true*. Thus, the state following (*true, true*) is (*false, true*). If multiple conditions in a case statement are true, the first one that is true is chosen. SMV has no "fall-through" semantics, such as one might find in a language such as C or Java.

Our context has two particularly important aspects of such a structure.

1. Finite state descriptions can capture system behavior at a very high level – suitable for communicating with the end user. Finite state machines are incredibly useful for the hardest part of testing, namely system testing.
2. The verification community has built powerful analysis tools for finite state machines. These tools are highly automated. Further, these tools produce explicit evidence, in the form of witnesses or counterexamples, for properties that do not hold in the finite state machine. These counterexamples can be interpreted as test cases. Thus, it is easier to automate test case generation from finite state machines than from program source.

Mutations and Test Cases
Mutating the syntax of state machine descriptions is very much like mutating program source. Mutation operators must be defined, and then they are applied to

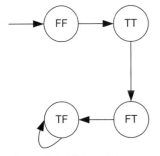

Figure 5.4. Finite state machine for SMV specification.

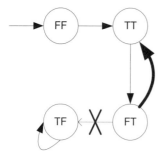

Figure 5.5. Mutated finite
state machine for SMV
specification.

the description. One example is the *Constant Replacement* operator, which replaces
each constant with other constants. Given the phrase !x & y : false in the next statement for y, replace it with !x & y : true. The finite state machine for this mutant is
shown in Figure 5.5. The new transition is drawn as an extra thick arrow and the
replaced transition is shown as a crossed-out dotted arrow.

Generating a test case to kill this mutant is a little different from program-based
mutation. We need a sequence of states that is allowed by the transition relation of
the original state machine, but not by the mutated state machine. Such a sequence
is precisely a test case that kills the mutant.

Finding a test to kill a mutant of a finite state machine expressed in SMV can be
automated using a *model checker*. A model checker takes two inputs. The first is a
finite state machine, described in a formal language such as SMV. The second is a
statement of some property, expressed in a *temporal logic*. We will not fully explain
temporal logic here, other than to say that such a logic can be used to express only
properties that are true "now," and also properties that will (or might) be true in
the future. The following is a simple temporal logic statement:

> The original expression, !x & y : false in this case, is **always** the same as the
> mutated expression, x | y : true.

For the given example, this statement is false with respect to a sequence of states
allowed by the original machine if and only if that sequence of states is rejected by
the mutant machine. In other words, such a sequence in question is a test case that
kills the mutant. If we add the following SMV statement to the above machine

SPEC AG (!x & y) $\longrightarrow$ AX(y = true)

The model checker will obligingly produce the desired test sequence:

```
/* state 1 */ { x  = 0, y  = 0 }
/* state 2 */ { x  = 1, y  = 1 }
/* state 3 */ { x  = 0, y  = 1 }
/* state 4 */ { x  = 1, y  = 0 }
```

Some mutated state machines are equivalent to the original machine. The model checker is exceptionally well adapted to deal with this. The key theoretical reason is that the model checker has a finite domain to work in, and hence the equivalent mutant problem is decidable (unlike with program code). In other words, if the model checker does not produce a counterexample, we *know* that the mutant is equivalent.

EXERCISES
Section 5.4.

1. (Challenging!) Find or write a small SMV specification and a corresponding Java implementation. Restate the program logic in SPEC assertions. Mutate the assertions systematically, and collect the traces from (nonequivalent) mutants. Use these traces to test the implementation.

5.5 INPUT SPACE GRAMMARS

One common use of grammars is to define the syntax of the inputs to a program, method, or software component formally. This section explains how to apply the criteria of this chapter to grammars that define the input space of a piece of software.

5.5.1 BNF Grammars

Section 5.1.1 of this chapter presented criteria on BNF grammars. One common use of a grammar is to define a precise syntax for the input of a program or method.

Consider a program that processes a sequence of deposits and debits, where each deposit is of the form deposit *account amount* and each debit is of the form debit *account amount*. The input structure of this program can be described with the regular expression:

(deposit *account amount*|debit *account amount*)*

This regular expression describes any sequence of deposits and debits. (The example in Section 5.1.1 is actually an abstract version of this example.)

The regular expression input description is still fairly abstract, in that it does not say anything about what an *account* or an *amount* looks like. We will refine those details later. One input that can be derived from this grammar is

```
deposit 739 $ 12.35
deposit 644 $ 12.35
debit 739 $ 19.22
```

It is easy to build a graph that captures the effect of regular expressions. Formally, these graphs are finite automata, either deterministic or nondeterministic. In either case, one can apply the coverage criteria from Chapter 2 directly.

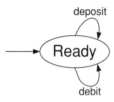

Figure 5.6. Finite state machine for bank example.

One possible graph for the above structure is shown in Figure 5.6. It contains one state (Ready) and two transitions that represent the two possible inputs. The input test example given above satisfies both the all nodes and all edges criteria for this graph.

Although regular expressions suffice for some programs, others require grammars. As grammars are more expressive than regular expressions we do not need to use both. The prior example specified in grammar form, with all of the details for *account* and *amount*, is

```
bank    ::= action*
action  ::= dep | deb
dep     ::= "deposit" account amount
deb     ::= "debit" account amount
account ::= digit³
amount  ::= "$" digit⁺ "." digit²
digit   ::= "0" | "1" | "2" | "3" | "4" | "5" | "6" | "7" | "8" | "9"
```

The graph for even this simple example is substantially larger once all details have been included. It is shown in Figure 5.7.

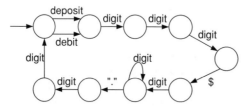

Figure 5.7. Finite state machine for bank example grammar.

A full derivation of the test case above begins as follows:

stream → action^*
   → **action action**^*
   → **dep** action^*
   → **deposit account amount** action^*
   → deposit **digit^3** amount action^*

$\rightarrow$ deposit **digit digit^2** amount action^*
$\rightarrow$ deposit **7** digit^2 amount action^*
$\rightarrow$ deposit 7 **digit digit** amount action^*
$\rightarrow$ deposit 7**3** digit amount action^*
$\rightarrow$ deposit 73**9** amount action^*
$\rightarrow$ deposit 739 **\$ digit^+ . digit^2** action^*
$\rightarrow$ deposit 739 \$ **digit^2** . digit^2 action^*
$\rightarrow$ deposit 739 \$ **digit digit** . digit^2 action^*
$\rightarrow$ deposit 739 \$**1** digit . digit^2 action^*
$\rightarrow$ deposit 739 \$1**2**. digit^2 action^*
$\rightarrow$ deposit 739 \$12. digit^2 action^*
$\rightarrow$ deposit 739 \$12. **digit digit** action^*
$\rightarrow$ deposit 739 \$12.**3** digit action^*
$\rightarrow$ deposit 739 \$12.3**5** action^*

$\vdots$

Deriving tests from this grammar proceeds by systematically replacing the next nonterminal (action) with one of its productions. The exercises below ask for complete tests to satisfy terminal symbol coverage and production coverage.

Of course, it often happens that an informal description of the input syntax is available, but not a formal grammar. This means that the test engineer is left with the engineering task of formally describing the input syntax. This process is **extremely** valuable and will often expose ambiguities and omissions in the requirements and software. Thus, this step should be carried out early in development, definitely before implementation and preferably before design. Once defined, it is sometimes helpful to use the grammar directly in the program for execution-time input validation.

XML Example

A language for describing inputs that is quickly gaining popularity is the *eXtensible Markup Language (XML)*. The most common use of XML is in web applications and web services, but XML's structure is generic enough to be useful in many contexts. XML is a language for describing, encoding and transmitting data. All XML "messages" (also sometimes called "documents") are in plain text and use a syntax similar to HTML. XML comes with a built-in language for describing the input messages in the form of a grammar, called *schemas*.

Like HTML, XML uses *tags*, which are textual descriptions of data enclosed in angle brackets ('<' and '>'). All XML messages must be *well formed*, that is, have a single document element with other elements properly nested under it, and every tag must have a corresponding closing tag. A simple example XML message for books is shown in Figure 5.8. This example is used to illustrate the use of BNF testing on software that uses XML messages. The example lists two books. The tag names ("books," "book," "ISBN," etc.) should be self descriptive and the XML message forms an overall hierarchy.

XML documents can be constrained by grammar definitions written in *XML Schemas*. Figure 5.9 shows a schema for books. The schema says that a "books"

```
<?xml version="1.0" encoding="UTF-8"?>
<!--Sample XML file for books-->
<books xmlns:xsi="http://www.w3.org/2001/XMLSchema-instance"
  xsi:noNamespaceSchemaLocation="C:\Books\books.xsd">
 <book>
   <ISBN>0471043281</ISBN>
   <title>The Art of Software Testing</title>
   <author>Glen Myers</author>
   <publisher>Wiley</publisher>
   <price>50.00</price>
   <year>1979</year>
 </book>
 <book>
   <ISBN>0442206720</ISBN>
   <title>Software Testing Techniques</title>
   <author>Boris Beizer</author>
   <publisher>Van Nostrand Reinhold, Inc</publisher>
   <price>75.00</price>
   <year>1990</year>
 </book>
</books>
```

Figure 5.8. Simple XML message for books.

XML message can contain an unbounded number of "book" tags. The "book" tags contain six pieces of information. Three, "title," "author," and "publisher," are simple strings. One, "price," is of type decimal (numeric), has two digits after the decimal point and the lowest value is 0. Two data elements, "ISBN" and "year," are types that are defined later in the schema. The type "yearType" is an integer with four digits, and "isbnType" can have up to 10 numeric characters. Each book must have a title, author, publisher, price, and year, and ISBN is optional.

Given an XML schema, the criteria defined in Section 5.1.1 can be used to derive XML messages that serve as test inputs. Following the production coverage criteria would result in two XML messages for this simple schema, one that includes an ISBN and one that does not.

5.5.2 Mutation for Input Grammars

It is quite common to require a program to reject malformed inputs, and this property should definitely be tested. It is the kind of thing that slips past the attention of implementors who are focused on making a program do what it is supposed to do.

Do invalid inputs really matter? From the perspective of program correctness, invalid inputs are simply those outside the precondition of a specified function. Formally speaking, a software implementation of that function can exhibit any behavior on inputs that do not satisfy the precondition. This includes failure to terminate, run time exceptions, and "bus error, core dumps."

However, the correctness of the intended functionality is only part of the story. From a practical perspective, invalid inputs sometimes matter a great deal because they hold the key to unintended functionality. For example, unhandled invalid inputs often represent security vulnerabilities, allowing a malicious party to break the software. Invalid inputs often cause the software to behave in surprising ways, which malicious parties can use to their advantage. This is how the classic "buffer overflow attack" works. The key step in a buffer overflow attack is to provide an

```
<?xml version="1.0" encoding="UTF-8"?>
<xs:schema xmlns:xs="http://www.w3.org/2001/XMLSchema"
   elementFormDefault="qualified"
   attributeFormDefault="unqualified">
 <xs:element name="books">
  <xs:annotation>
   <xs:documentation>XML Schema for Books</xs:documentation>
  </xs:annotation>
  <xs:complexType>
   <xs:sequence>
    <xs:element name="book" maxOccurs="unbounded">
     <xs:complexType>
      <xs:sequence>
       <xs:element name="ISBN" type="xs:isbnType" minOccurs="0"/>
       <xs:element name="title" type="xs:string"/>
       <xs:element name="author" type="xs:string"/>
       <xs:element name="publisher" type="xs:string"/>
       <xs:element name="price" type="xs:decimal" fractionDigits="2" minInclusive="0"/>
       <xs:element name="year" type="yearType"/>
      </xs:sequence>
     </xs:complexType>
    </xs:element>
   </xs:sequence>
  </xs:complexType>
 </xs:element>

 <xs:simpleType name="yearType">
  <xs:restriction base="xs:int">
   <xs:totalDigits value="4"/>
  </xs:restriction>
 </xs:simpleType>
 <xs:simpleType name="isbnType">
  <xs:restriction base="xs:string">
   <xs:pattern value="[0-9]{10}"/>
  </xs:restriction>
 </xs:simpleType>
</xs:schema>
```

Figure 5.9. XML schema for books.

input that is too long to fit into the available buffer. Similarly, a key step in certain web browser attacks is to provide a string input that contains malicious HTML, Javascript, or SQL. Software should behave "reasonably" with invalid inputs. "Reasonable" behavior may not always be defined, but the test engineer is obliged to consider it anyway.

To support security as well as to evaluate the software's behavior, it is useful to produce test cases that contain invalid inputs. A common way to do this is to mutate a grammar. When mutating grammars, the mutants are the tests and we create valid and invalid strings. No ground string is used, so the notion of killing mutants does not apply to mutating grammars. Several mutation operators for grammars are defined below.

1. *Nonterminal Replacement*:

> Every nonterminal symbol in a production is replaced by other nonterminal symbols.

This is a very broad mutation operator that could result in many strings that are not only invalid, they are so far away from valid strings that they are useless for testing. If the grammar provides specific rules or syntactic restrictions, some nonterminal replacements can be avoided. This is analogous to avoiding compiler errors in program-based mutation. For example, some strings represent type structures and only nonterminals of the same or compatible type should be replaced.

The production dep ::= "deposit" account amount can be mutated to create the following productions:

dep ::= "deposit" amount amount
dep ::= "deposit" account digit

Which can result in the corresponding tests:

deposit $19.22 $12.35
deposit 739 1

2. *Terminal Replacement*:

> Every terminal symbol in a production is replaced by other terminal symbols.

Just as with nonterminal replacement, some terminal replacements may not be appropriate. Recognizing them depends on the particular grammar that is being mutated. For example, the production amount ::= "$" digit$^+$ "." digit^2 can be mutated to create the following three productions:

amount ::= "." digit$^+$ "." digit^2
amount ::= "$" digit$^+$ "$" digit^2
amount ::= "$" digit$^+$ "1" digit^2

Which can result in the corresponding tests:

deposit 739 .12.35
deposit 739 $12$35
deposit 739 $12135

3. *Terminal and Nonterminal Deletion*:

> Every terminal and nonterminal symbol in a production is deleted.

For example, the production dep ::= "deposit" account amount can be mutated to create the following three productions:

dep ::= account amount
dep ::= "deposit" amount
dep ::= "deposit" account

Which can result in the corresponding tests:

739 $12.35
deposit $12.35
deposit 739

4. ***Terminal and Nonterminal Duplication***:

> Every terminal and nonterminal symbol in a production is duplicated.

This is sometimes called the "stutter" operator. For example, the production dep ::= "deposit" account amount can be mutated to create the following three mutated productions:

```
dep ::= "deposit" "deposit" account amount
dep ::= "deposit" account account amount
dep ::= "deposit" account amount amount
```

Which can result in the corresponding tests:

```
deposit deposit 739 $12.35
deposit 739 739 $12.35
deposit 739 $12.35 $12.35
```

We have significantly more experience with program-based mutation operators than grammar-based operators, so this list should be treated as being much less definitive.

These mutation operators can be applied in either of two ways. One is to mutate the grammar and then generate inputs. The other is to use the correct grammar, but one time during each derivation apply a mutation operator to the production being used. The operators are typically applied during production, because the resulting inputs are usually "closer" to valid inputs than if the entire grammar is corrupted. This approach is used in the previous examples.

Just as with program-based mutation, some inputs from a mutated grammar rule are still in the grammar. The example above of changing the rule

> dep   ::= "deposit" account amount

to be

> dep   ::= "debit" account amount

yields an "equivalent" mutant. The resulting input, debit 739 $12.35, is a valid input, although the effects are (sadly) quite different for the customer. If the idea is to generate invalid inputs exclusively, some way must be found to screen out mutant inputs that are valid. Although this sounds much like the equivalence problem for programs, the difference is small but significant. Here the problem is solvable and can be solved by creating a recognizer from the grammar, and checking each string as it is produced.

Many programs are supposed to accept some, but not all, inputs from some larger language. For example, a Web application might restrict its inputs to a subset of HTML. In this case, we have two grammars: the full grammar, and a grammar for the subset. In this case, the most useful invalid tests to generate are those that are in the first grammar, but not in the second.

XML Example

Section 5.5.1 showed examples of generating tests in the form of XML messages from a schema grammar definition. It is also convenient to apply mutation to XML schemas to produce invalid messages. Some programs will use XML parsers that validate the messages against the grammar. If they do, it is likely that the software will usually behave correctly on invalid messages, but testers still need to verify this. If a validating parser is not used, this can be a rich source for programming mistakes. It is also fairly common for programs to use XML messages without having an explicit schema definition. In this case, it is very helpful for the test engineer to develop the schema as a first step to developing tests.

XML schemas have a rich collection of built-in datatypes, which come with a large number of *constraining facets*. In XML, *constraining facets* are used to restrict further the range of values. The example in Figure 5.9 uses several constraining facets, including *fractionDigits*, *minInclusive*, and *minOccurs*. This suggests further mutation operators for XML schemas that modify the **values** of facets. This can often result in a rich collection of tests for software that use inputs described with XML.

Given the following four lines in the books schema in Figure 5.9:

```
<xs:element name="ISBN" type="xs:isbnType" minOccurs="0"/>
<xs:element name="price" type="xs:decimal" fractionDigits="2" minInclusive="0"/>
<xs:totalDigits value="4"/>
<xs:pattern value="[0-9]{10}"/>
```

we might construct the mutants:

```
<xs:element name="ISBN" type="xs:isbnType" minOccurs="1"/>

<xs:element name="price" type="xs:decimal" fractionDigits="1" minInclusive="0"/>
<xs:element name="price" type="xs:decimal" fractionDigits="3" minInclusive="0"/>
<xs:element name="price" type="xs:decimal" fractionDigits="2" minInclusive="1"/>
<xs:element name="price" type="xs:decimal" fractionDigits="2" maxInclusive="0"/>

<xs:totalDigits value="5"/>
<xs:totalDigits value="0"/>

<xs:pattern value="[0-8]{10}"/>
<xs:pattern value="[1-9]{10}"/>
<xs:pattern value="[0-9]{9}"/>
```

EXERCISES

Section 5.5.

1. Generate tests to satisfy TSC for the bank example grammar based on the BNF in Section 5.5.1. Try **not** to satisfy PDC.
2. Generate tests to satisfy PDC for the bank example grammar.
3. Consider the following BNF with start symbol A:

```
A ::= B"@"C"."B
B ::= BL | L
C ::= B | B"."B
L ::= "a" | "b" | "c" | ... | "y" | "z"
```

and the following six possible test cases:

t1 = a@a.a
t2 = aa.bb@cc.dd
t3 = mm@pp
t4 = aaa@bb.cc.dd
t5 = bill
t6 = @x.y

For each of the six tests, (1) identify the test sequence as either "in" the BNF, and give a derivation, or (2) identify the test sequence as "out" of the BNF, and give a mutant derivation that results in that test. (Use only one mutation per test, and use it only one time per test).

4. Provide a BNF description of the inputs to the *cal()* method in the homework set for Section 5.2.2. Succinctly describe any requirements or constraints on the inputs that are hard to model with the BNF.

5. Answer questions (a) through (c) for the following grammar:

val   ::= number | val pair
number ::= digit$^+$
pair   ::= number op | number pair op
op   ::= "+" | "-" | "*" | "/"
digit   ::= "0" | "1" | "2" | "3" | "4" | "5" | "6" | "7" | "8" | "9"

Also consider the following mutation, which adds an additional rule to the grammar:

pair ::= number op | number pair op | op number

(a) Which of the following strings can be generated by the (unmutated) grammar?

42
4 2
4 + 2
4 2 +
4 2 7 - *
4 2 - 7 *
4 2 - 7 * +

(b) Find a string that is generated by the mutated grammar, but not by the original grammar.

(c) (*Challenging*) Find a string whose generation uses the new rule in the mutant grammar, but is also in the original grammar. Demonstrate your answer by giving the two relevant derivations.

6. Answer questions (a) and (b) for the following grammar.

phoneNumber::= exhangePart dash numberPart
exchangePart ::= special zeroOrSpecial other
numberPart   ::= ordinary^4
ordinary   ::= zero | special | other
zeroOrSpecial ::= zero | special

```
zero        ::= "0"
special     ::= "1" | "2"
other       ::= "3" | "4" | "5" | "6" | "7" | "8" | "9"
dash        ::= "-"
```

(a) Classify the following as either phoneNumbers (or not). For non-phone numbers, indicate the problem.

- 123-4567
- 012-3456
- 109-1212
- 346-9900
- 113-1111

(b) *Consider the following mutation of the grammar:*

exchangePart ::= special ordinary other

If possible, identify a string that appears in the mutated grammar but not in the original grammar, another string that is in the original but not the mutated, and a third string that is in both.

7. Java provides a package, *java.util.regex*, to manipulate regular expressions. Write a regular expression for URLs and then evaluate a set of URLs against your regular expression. This assignment involves programming, since input structure testing without automation is pointless.

(a) Write (or find) a regular expression for a URL. Your regular expression does not need to be so general that it accounts for every possible URL, but give your best effort (for example "*" will not be considered a good effort). You are strongly encouraged to do some web surfing to find some candidate regular expressions. One suggestion is to visit the *Regular Expression Library*.

(b) Collect a set of URLs from a small web site (such as a set of course web pages). Your set needs to contain at least 20 (different) URLs. Use the *java.util.regex* package to validate each URL against your regular expression.

(c) Construct a valid URL that is not valid with respect to your regular expression (and show this with the appropriate *java.util.regex call*). If you have done an outstanding job in part 1, explain why your regular expression does not have any such URLs.

8. Why is the equivalent mutant problem solvable for BNF grammars but not for program-based mutation? (Hint: The answer to this question is based on some fairly subtle theory.)

5.6 BIBLIOGRAPHIC NOTES

We trace the use of grammars for testing compilers back to Hanford [150], who motivated subsequent related work [26, 107, 176, 285, 294]. Maurer's Data Generation Language (DGL) tool [231] showed the applicability of grammar-based generation to many types of software, a theme echoed in detail by Beizer [29].

Legend has it that the first ideas of mutation analysis were postulated in 1971 in a class term paper by Richard Lipton. The first research papers were published by

Budd and Sayward [52], Hamlet [148], and DeMillo, Lipton, and Sayward [99] in the late 1970s; DeMillo, Lipton, and Sayward's paper [99] is generally cited as the seminal reference. Mutation has primarily been applied to software by creating mutant versions of the source, but has also been applied to formal software specifications.

The original analysis of the number of mutants was by Budd [53], who analyzed the number of mutants generated for a program and found it to be roughly proportional to the product of the number of variable references times the number of data objects ($O(Refs*Vars)$). A later analysis [5] claimed that the number of mutants is $O(Lines*Refs)$–assuming that the number of data objects in a program is proportional to the number of lines. This was reduced to $O(Lines*Lines)$ for most programs; this figure appears in most of the literature.

A statistical regression analysis of actual programs by Offutt et al. [269] showed that the number of lines did **not** contribute to the number of mutants, but that Budd's figure is accurate. The selective mutation approach mentioned under "Designing Mutation Operators" eliminates the number of data objects so that the number of mutants is proportional to the number of variable references ($O(Refs)$).

A variant of mutation that has been widely discussed is weak mutation [134, 167, 358, 271]. However, experimentation has shown that the difference is very small [163, 226, 271]. Mutation operators have been designed for various programming languages, including Fortran IV [19, 56], COBOL [151], Fortran 77 [101, 187], C [95], C integration testing [94], Lisp [55], Ada [40, 276], Java [185], and Java class relationships [219, 220].

Research proof-of-concept tools have been built for Fortran IV and 77, COBOL, C, Java, and Java class relationships. By far the most widely used tool is Mothra, a mutation system for Fortran 77 that was built in the mid 1980s at Georgia Tech. Mothra was built under the leadership of Rich DeMillo, with most of the design done by DeMillo and Offutt, and most of the implementation by Offutt and King, with help from Krauser and Spafford. In its heyday in the early 1990s, Mothra was installed at well over a hundred sites and the research that was done to build Mothra and that later used Mothra as a laboratory resulted in around half a dozen PhD dissertations and many dozens of papers. As far as we know, the only commercial tool that supports mutation is by the company Certess, in the chip design industry.

The coupling effect says that complex faults are coupled to simple faults in such a way that test data that detects all simple faults will detect most complex faults [99]. The coupling effect was supported empirically for programs in 1992 [263], and has shown to hold probabilistically for large classes of programs in 1995 [335]. Budd [51] discussed the concept of program neighborhoods. The neighborhood concept was used to present the competent programmer hypothesis [99]. The fundamental premise of mutation testing, as coined by Geist et al. [133] is: **in practice, if the software contains a fault, there will usually be a set of mutants that can be killed only by a test case that also detects that fault**.

The operation of replacing each statement with a "bomb" was called Statement ANalysis (SAN) in Mothra [187]. Mothra's Relational Operator Replacement (ROR) operator replaces each occurrence of a relational operator ($<, >, \leq, \geq, =, \neq$) with each other operator and the expression with *true* and *false*. The above subsumption proofs used only the latter operators. Mothra's Logical Connector Replacement (LCR) operator replaces each occurrence of one of the logical operators ($\wedge, \vee, \equiv, \neq$)

with each other operator and the entire expression with *true*, *false*, *leftop* and *rightop*. *leftop* and *rightop* are special mutation operators that return the left side and the right side, respectively, of a relational expression. The mutation operator that removes each statement in the program is called Statement DeLetion (SDL) in Mothra [187].

A number of authors [14, 15, 37, 298, 350] have used traces from model checkers to generate tests, including mutation based tests. The text from Huth and Ryan [173] provides a easily accessible introduction to model checking and discusses use of the SMV system.

One of the key technologies being used to transmit data among heterogeneous software components on the Web is the eXtensible Markup Language (XML) [1, 43]. Data-based mutation defines **generic classes** of mutation operators. These mutation operator classes are intended to work with different grammars. The current literature [203] cites operator classes that modify the length of value strings and determine whether or not a value is in a predefined set of values.

NOTES

1 There is no relationship between this use of mutation and genetic algorithms, except that both make an analogy to biological mutation. Mutation for testing predated genetic algorithms by a number of years.
2 Of course, since mutant detection is undecidable, a heuristic is the best option possible.
3 This goal is in some sense equivalent to the goal of forcing each clause in each predicate to make a difference.
4 Jester's web page is http://jester.sourceforge.net/

PART 3

Applying Criteria in Practice

6

Practical Considerations

The first five chapters of this book help practical testers fill up their "toolbox" with various test criteria. While studying test criteria in isolation is needed, one of the most difficult obstacles to a software organization moving to level 3 or 4 testing is integrating effective testing strategies into the overall software development process. This chapter discusses various issues involved with applying test criteria during software development. The overriding philosophy is *to think*: if the tester looks at this as a technical problem, and seeks technical solutions, he or she will usually find that the obstacles are not as large as they first seem.

6.1 REGRESSION TESTING

Regression testing is the process of re-testing software that has been modified. Regression testing constitutes the vast majority of testing effort in commercial software development and is an essential part of any viable software development process. Large components or systems tend to have large regression test suites. Even though many developers don't want to believe it (even when faced with indisputable evidence!), small changes to one part of a system often cause problems in distant parts of the system. Regression testing is used to find this kind of problem.

It is worth emphasizing that regression tests *must* be automated. Indeed, it could be said that unautomated regression testing is equivalent to no regression testing. A wide variety of commercially available tools are available. Capture/replay tools automate testing of programs that use graphical user interfaces. Version control software, already in use to manage different versions of a given system, effectively manages the test sets associated with each version. Scripting software manages the process of obtaining test inputs, executing the software, marshaling the outputs, comparing the actual and expected outputs, and generating test reports.

The aim of this section is to explain what kinds of tests ought to be in a regression test set, which regression tests to run, and how to respond to regression tests that fail. We treat each of these issues in turn. We direct the reader interested in detail on any of these topics to the bibliographic notes.

The test engineer faces a Goldilocks problem in determining which tests to include in a regression test set. Including every test set possible results in an unmanageably large regression test set. The result is that the test set cannot be run as often as changes are made to the software. For many development organizations, this period amounts to a day; regression tests run at night to evaluate software changed that day, with developers reviewing the results the following morning. If the regression tests do not finish in a timely manner, the development process is disrupted. It is well worth throwing money at this problem in terms of additional computational resources to execute the tests, but, at some point, the marginal advantage of adding a given test is not worth the marginal expenditure of the resources needed to execute it. On the other side, a set that is too small will not cover the functionality of the software sufficiently well, and too many faults will make it past the regression test set to the customer.

The prior paragraph does not actually say which tests are in the regression test set, just that the set has to be the right size. Some organizations have a policy that for each problem report that has come in from the field, a regression test exists that, in principle, detects the problem. The idea is that customers are more willing to be saddled with new problems than with the same problem over and over. The above approach has a certain charm from the perspective of traceability, in that each test chosen in this way has a concrete rationale.

The coverage criteria that form the heart of this book provide an excellent basis for evaluating regression test sets. For example, if node coverage in the form of method call coverage shows that some methods are never invoked, then it is a good idea to either decide that the method is dead code with respect that particular application, or include a test that results in a call to the method.

If one or more regression tests fail, the first step is to determine if the change to the software is faulty, or if the regression test set itself is broken. In either case, additional work is required. If no regression tests fail, there is still work to do. The reason is that a regression test set that is satisfactory for a given version of the software is not necessarily satisfactory for a subsequent version. Changes to software are often classified as *corrective*, *perfective*, *adaptive*, and *preventive*. All of these changes require regression testing. Even when the (desired) external functionality of the software does not change, the regression test set still needs to be reanalyzed to see if it is adequate. For example, preventive maintenance may result in wholesale internal restructuring of some components. If the criteria used to select the original regression tests were derived from the structure of the implementation, then it is unlikely that the test set will adequately cover the new implementation.

Evolving a regression test set as the associated software changes is a challenge. Changes to the external interface are particularly painful, since such a change can cause all tests to fail. For example, suppose that a particular input moves from one drop-down menu to another. The result is that the capture/playback aspect of executing each test case needs an update. Or suppose that the new version of the software generates an additional output. All of the expected results are now out of date, and need to be augmented. Clearly, automated support for maintaining test sets is just as crucial as automated support for executing the tests.

Adding a (small) number of tests to a regression test set is usually simple. The marginal cost of each additional test is typically quite small. Cumulatively, however, the test set can become unwieldy. Removing tests from a regression test set is a dicey proposition. Invariably, a fault will show up in the field that one of the removed tests would have found. Fortunately, the same criteria that guide the construction of a regression test set apply when deciding how to update the regression test set.

A different approach to limiting the amount of time needed to execute regression tests, and a focus of much of the attention in the research literature, is selecting only a subset of the regression tests. For example, if the execution of a given test case does not visit *anything* modified, then the test case has to perform the same both before and after the modification, and hence can be safely omitted. Selection techniques include linear equations, symbolic execution, path analysis, data flow analysis, program dependence graphs, system dependence graphs, modification analysis, firewall definition, cluster identification, slicing, graph walks, and modified entity analysis. For example, as a reader of Chapter 2 might guess, data flow selection techniques choose tests only if they touch new, modified, or deleted DU pairs; other tests are omitted.

A selection technique is *inclusive* to the degree that it includes tests that are "modification-revealing." Unsafe techniques have inclusiveness of less than 100%. A technique is *precise* to the extent that it omits regression tests that are not modification-revealing. A technique is *efficient* to the degree that determining the appropriate subset of the regression test set is less computationally intensive than simply executing the omitted tests. Finally, a technique is *general* to the degree that applies to a wide variety of practical situations. To continue the example, the data flow approach to selecting regression tests is not necessarily either safe or precise, of polynomial complexity in certain program attributes, and requires, obviously, data flow information and program instrumentation at the data flow graph level. The bibliographic notes section contains pointers to further details on this work, including empirical evaluations.

6.2 INTEGRATION AND TESTING

Software is composed of many pieces of varying sizes. Individual programmers are often responsible for testing the lowest level components (classes, modules, and methods). After that, testing must be carried out in collaboration with software integration. Software can be integrated in many ways. This section discusses technical strategies that must be employed during testing. We do not try to catalog all of them from a process point of view.

Integration testing is the testing of incompatibilities and interfaces between otherwise correctly working components. That is, it is the testing needed to integrate subcomponents into a bigger working component. This is emphatically not the same as testing an already integrated component.

This chapter uses the term software "component" in a very broad sense: A *component* is a piece of a program that can be tested independently of the complete program or system. Thus, classes, modules, methods, packages, and even code fragments can be considered to be components.

Integration testing is often done with an incomplete system. The tester may be evaluating how only two of many components in the system work together, may be testing integration aspects before the full system is complete, or may be putting the system together piece by piece and evaluating how each new component fits with the previously integrated components.

6.2.1 Stubs and Drivers

When testing incomplete portions of software, developers and testers often need extra software components, sometimes called *scaffolding*. The two most common types of scaffolding are known as test stubs and test drivers. A *test stub* is a skeletal or special-purpose implementation of a software module, used to develop or test a component that calls the stub or otherwise depends on it. It replaces a called component. For OO programs, the XP community has developed a version of the stub called the mock. A *mock* is a special-purpose replacement class that includes behavior verification to check that a class under test made the correct calls to the mock. A *test driver* is a software component or test tool that replaces a component that takes care of the control and/or the calling of a software component.

One of the responsibilities of a test stub is to return values to the calling component. These values are seldom the same that the actual component being stubbed would return, or else we would not need the stub, but sometimes they must satisfy certain constraints.

The simplest action for a stub is to assign constant values to the outputs. More sophisticated approaches may be to return random values, values from a table lookup, or to let the user enter return values during execution. Test tools have included automated stubbing capabilities since the 1980s. More sophisticated tools discover methods that need to be stubbed, and ask the tester what kind of behavior the stub should have. Some tools collect instances of objects that have the correct return type and make these available as potential stub returns. As a default, this is a powerful approach that the test engineer need only override as necessary. It is possible to generate stubs automatically from formal specifications of the software components, but we are not aware of this functionality in available tools. Programmers also generate their own stubs when carrying out their own unit or module testing.

The simplest form of driver is a main() method for a class. Effective programmers often include a main() for every class, containing statements that carry out simple testing of the class. If the class is an ADT, the main() test driver will create some objects of the class, add values, retrieve values, and use the other operations on the class. Techniques from previous chapters, like sequencing constraints and state-based testing, can be implemented in the driver.

Test drivers can include hard-coded values or retrieve the values from an external source like the tester or a file. Tools exist to generate test drivers automatically. Both test driver and test stub generators are included in other test tools.

6.2.2 Class Integration Test Order

When integrating multiple components, it is important to decide in which order the classes or subsystems should be integrated and tested. Classes depend on each other in various ways. One class may use methods or variables defined in another, a class may inherit from another, or one class may aggregate objects of another class inside its data objects. If class A uses methods defined in class B, and B is not available, then we need stubs for those methods to test A. Therefore, it makes sense to test B first, then when A is tested we can use actual objects of B instead of stubs.

This is called the *class integration test order problem* (CITO), and the general goal is to integrate and test classes in the order that requires the least stubbing, as creating test stubs is considered to be a major cost of integration testing. If the dependencies among the classes have no cycles, the order of their integration is fairly simple. The classes that do not depend on any other classes are tested first. Then they are integrated with classes that depend only on them, and the new classes are tested. If the classes are represented as nodes in a "dependency graph," with edges representing dependencies, this approach follows a *topological sorting* of the graph.

The problem gets more complicated when the dependency graph has cycles, because we will eventually get to a class that depends on another class that has not yet been integrated and tested. This is when some sort of stubbing is required. For example, assume that class A uses methods in class B, B uses methods in class C, and C aggregates an object of class A. When this happens, the integration tester must "break the cycle" by choosing one class in the cycle to test first. The hope is to choose the class that results in the least extra work (primarily that of creating stubs).

Software designers may observe that class diagrams often have few if any cycles and in fact, most design textbooks strongly recommend against including cycles in designs. However, it is common to add classes and relationships as design progresses, for example, to improve performance or maintainability. As a result, class diagrams usually contain cycles by the end of low-level design or implementation, and practical testers have to solve the CITO problem.

The research literature proposes numerous solutions to the CITO problem. This is still an active research area and these solutions have not yet made it into commercial tools.

6.3 TEST PROCESS

Many organizations postpone all software testing activities to the end of development, after the implementation has started, or even after it has ended. By waiting until this late in the process, testing winds up being compressed, not enough resources (time and budget) remain, problems with previous stages have been solved by taking time and dollars from testing, and testers do not have enough time to plan for testing. Instead of planning and designing tests, the developers have time only to run tests, usually in an ad hoc manner. The key point is that the goal is to create high quality software, and the old adage that "quality cannot be tested in" is still very relevant. A tester cannot show up at the last minute and make a bad product good; high quality has to be part of the process from the beginning.

This section discusses how to integrate testing with development, where testing activities begin as soon as development activities begin, and are carried out in parallel with the development stages. Specific activities, including planning, active testing, and development-influencing activities, can be associated with each of the traditional lifecycle phases. These activities can be carried out by the developers or by separate test engineers, and can be associated with development stages within the confines of any specific development process. These testing activities allow the tester to detect and prevent faults throughout the software development process.

Projects that begin test activities after implementation is complete often produce very unreliable software. Wise testers (and testing level 4 organizations) incorporate a chain of test plans and procedures that begin in the first steps of software development, and proceed through all subsequent steps. By integrating software testing activities into all stages of the software development lifecycle, we can make dramatic improvements in the effectiveness and efficiency of testing, and impact the software development process in such a way that high quality software is more likely to be built.

Other textbooks and the research literature contain dozens of software processes (waterfall, spiral, evolutionary-prototyping, eXtreme programming, etc.). This section uses the following distinct stages without assuming any order or mapping them onto a specific process. Thus, the suggestions in this section can be adapted to whatever process is being used.

1. Requirements analysis and specification
2. System and software design
3. Intermediate design
4. Detailed design
5. Implementation
6. Integration
7. System deployment
8. Operation and maintenance

Any development process involves communication, comprehension, and transition of information among stages. Mistakes can be made during any stage, in the information handling, or in the transfer of the information from one stage to another. Integrating testing with the process is about trying to find errors at each stage as well as preventing these errors from propagating to other stages. Also, the integration of testing throughout the lifecycle provides a way to verify and trace consistencies among the stages. Testing should not be isolated into separate stages, but rather be on a parallel track that affects all stages.

Testing has different objectives during each stage, and these objectives are achieved in different ways. These sub-objectives of testing at each stage will then achieve the overall objective of ensuring high quality software. For most stages, the testing activities can be broken into three broad categories: *test actions* – testing the product or artifacts created at that stage; *test design* – using the development artifacts of that stage or testing artifacts from the previous stage to prepare to test the final software; and *test influence* – using development or test artifacts to influence future development stages.

6.3.1 Requirements Analysis and Specification

A software requirements and specifications document contains a complete description of the external behavior of the software system. It provides a way to

Table 6.1. Testing objectives and activities during requirements analysis and specification

Objectives	Activities
Ensure requirements are testable	Set up testing requirements
Ensure requirements are correct	■ testing criteria
Ensure requirements are complete	■ support software needed
Influence the software architecture	■ testing plans at each level
	■ build test prototypes
	Clarify requirement items and test criteria
	Develop project test plan

communicate with the other stages of the development, and defines the contents and boundary of the software system. Table 6.1 summarizes the major objectives and activities during requirements analysis and specification.

The major **test action goal** is to evaluate the requirements themselves. Each requirement should be evaluated to ensure it is correct, testable, and that the requirements together are complete. Many methods have been presented to do this, most commonly inspections and prototyping. These topics are well described elsewhere and are explicitly not covered in this book. A key point is that the requirements should be evaluated *before* design starts.

The major **test design goal** is to prepare for system testing and verification activities. Test requirements should be written to state testing criteria for the software system and high-level test plans should be developed to outline the testing strategy. The test plan should also include the scope and objectives for testing at each stage. This high-level test plan will be referenced in the later detailed test plans. The testing requirements should describe support software needed for testing at each stage. Testing requirements must be satisfied by later testing.

The major **test influence goal** is to influence the software architectural design. Project test plans and representative system test scenarios should be built to show that the system meets the requirements. The process of developing the test scenarios will often help detect ambiguous and inconsistent requirements specifications. The test scenarios will also provide feedback to the software architectural designers and help them develop a design that is easily testable.

6.3.2 System and Software Design

System and software design partitions the requirements into hardware or software systems and builds the overall system architecture. The software design should represent the software system functions so that they can be transformed into executable programs. Table 6.2 summarizes the major objectives and activities during system and software design.

The major **test action goal** is to verify the mapping between the requirements specification and the design. Any changes to the requirements specification should be reflected in the corresponding design changes. Testing at this stage should help validate the design and interface.

Table 6.2. Testing objectives and activities during system and software design

Objectives	Activities
Verify mapping between requirements specification and system design Ensure traceability and testability Influence interface design	Validate design and interface Design system tests Develop coverage criteria Design acceptance test plan Design usability test (if necessary)

The major **test design goal** is to prepare for acceptance and usability testing. An acceptance test plan is created that includes acceptance test requirements, test criteria, and a testing method. Also, requirements specifications and system design specifications should be kept traceable and testable for references and changes for the later stages. Testing at the system and software design stage also prepares for unit testing and integration testing by choosing coverage criteria from the previous chapters.

The major **test influence goal** is to influence the design of the user interface. Usability tests or an interface prototype should be designed to clarify the customer's interface desires. Usability testing is carried out when the user interface is an integral part of the system.

6.3.3 Intermediate Design

In intermediate design, the software system is broken into components and classes associated with each component. Design specifications are written for each component and class. Many problems in large software systems arise from component interface mismatches. The major **test action goal** is to avoid mismatches of interfaces. Table 6.3 summarizes the major objectives and activities during intermediate design.

The major **test design goal** is to prepare for unit testing, integration testing, and system testing by writing the test plans. The unit and integration test plans are refined at this level with information about interfaces and design decisions. To prepare for testing at the later stages, test support tools such as test drivers, stubs, and testing measurement tools should be acquired or built.

The major **test influence goal** is to influence detailed design. The class integration and test order (CITO) from Section 6.2.2 should be determined so as to have the proper effect on the detailed design.

Table 6.3. Testing objectives and activities during intermediate design

Objectives	Activities
Avoid mismatches of interfaces Prepare for unit testing	Specify system test cases Develop integration and unit test plans Build or collect test support tools Suggest ordering of class integration

Table 6.4. Testing objectives and activities during detailed design	
Objectives	**Activities**
Be ready to test when modules are ready	Create test cases (if unit) Build test specifications (if integration)

6.3.4 Detailed Design

At the detailed design stage, testers write subsystem specifications and pseudo-code for modules. Table 6.4 summarizes the major objectives and activities during detailed design. The major **test action goal** at the detailed design stage is to make sure that all test materials are ready for testing when the modules are written. Testers should prepare for both unit and integration testing. Testers must refine detailed test plans, generate test cases for unit testing, and write detailed test specifications for integration testing. The major **test influence goal** is to influence the implementation and unit and integration testing.

6.3.5 Implementation

At some point during software development, the "rubber hits the road" and the programmers start writing and compiling classes and methods. Table 6.5 summarizes the major objectives and activities during implementation.

The major **test action goal** is to perform effective and efficient unit testing. The effectiveness of unit testing is largely based on the testing criterion used and test data generated. Unit testing performed at this stage is as specified by the unit test plan, testing criteria, test cases, and test support tools that were made ready at the earlier stages. Unit test results and problems should be saved and reported properly for further processing. Designers and developers whose duties are becoming lighter at this point should be made available to help testers.

The major **test design goal** is to prepare for integration and system testing. The major **test influence goal** is that efficient unit testing can help ensure early integration and system testing. It is much cheaper and easier to find and fix bugs during unit testing!

Table 6.5. Testing objectives and activities during implementation	
Objectives	**Activities**
Efficient unit testing Automatic test data generation	Create test case values Conduct unit testing Report problems properly

Table 6.6. Testing objectives and activities during integration

Objectives	Activities
Efficient integration testing	Perform integration testing

6.3.6 Integration

The CITO problem, discussed in the previous section, is the major issue during software integration. Table 6.6 summarizes the major objectives and activities during integration.

The major **test action goal** is to perform integration testing. Integration and integration testing begin as soon as the needed components of an integrated subsystem pass unit testing. In practice, the CITO problem can be solved in a pragmatic way by integrating classes as soon as they are delivered from unit testing. Integration testing is concerned with finding errors that result from unexpected interactions among components.

6.3.7 System Deployment

Table 6.7 summarizes the major objectives and activities during system deployment. The major **test action goal** is to perform system testing, acceptance testing, and usability testing. System testing has the particular purpose to compare the software system to its original objectives, in particular, validating whether the software meets the functional and non-functional requirements. System testing test cases are developed from the system and project test plan from the requirements specification and software design phase according to criteria covered in previous chapters. Acceptance testing can be started as soon as system testing is completed. Acceptance testing ensures that the complete system satisfies the customers' needs, and should be done with their involvement. Test cases are derived from acceptance test plans and test data set up previously. Usability testing evaluates the user interface of the software. It should also be done with user involvement.

6.3.8 Operation and Maintenance

After the software is released (or delivered, or deployed, or whatever), users will occasionally find new problems or request new features. When the software is changed, it must be regression tested. Regression testing helps ensure that the

Table 6.7. Testing objectives and activities during system deployment

Objectives	Activities
Efficient system testing	Perform system testing
Efficient acceptance testing	Perform acceptance testing
Efficient usability testing	Perform usability testing

Table 6.8. Testing objectives and activities during operation and maintenance

Objectives	Activities
Efficient regression testing	Capture user problems
	Perform regression testing

updated software still possesses the functionality it had before the updates, as well as the new or modified functionality. Table 6.8 summarizes the major objectives and activities during operation and maintenance.

6.3.9 Summary

A key factor to instilling quality into a development process is based on individual professional ethics. Developers and testers alike can choose to **put quality first**. If the process is such that the tester does not know how to test it, then don't build it. This will sometimes result in conflicts with time-driven management, but even if you lose the argument, you will gain respect. It is important that developers begin test activities early. It also helps to take a stand against taking shortcuts. Almost all projects will eventually be faced with taking shortcuts that will ultimately reduce the quality of the software. Fight it! If you lose the argument you will gain respect: document your objections, vote with your feet, and don't be afraid to be right!

It is also essential that test artifacts be managed. A lack of organization is a sure recipe for failure. Put test artifacts under version control, make them easily available, and update them regularly. These artifacts include test design documents, tests, test results, and automated support. It is important to keep track of the criteria-based source of the tests, so when the source changes, it is possible to track which tests need to change.

6.4 TEST PLANS

A major emphasis for many organizations is documentation, including test plans and test plan reporting. Unfortunately, putting too much of a focus on documentation can lead to an environment where lots of meaningless reports are produced but nothing useful is done. That is why this book focuses on content, not form. The contents of a test plan are essentially how the tests were created, why the tests were created, and how they will be run.

Producing test plans, however, is an essential requirement for many organizations. Companies and customers often impose templates or outlines. Rather than surveying many different types of test plans, we look at the IEEE standard definition. Unfortunately, this is quite old (1983!), but it is still the most widely known. A quick search on the Web will supply you with more test plans and test plan outlines than you could ever use. ANSI/IEEE Standard 829-1983 describes a test plan as:

"A document describing the scope, approach, resources, and schedule of intended testing activities. It identifies test items, the features to be tested, the testing tasks, who will do each task, and any risks requiring contingency planning."

Several different general types of test plans are:

1. A *mission plan* tells "why." Usually only one mission plan appears per organization or group. Mission plans describe the reason that the organization exists, are typically very short (5–10 pages), and are the least detailed of all plans.
2. A *strategic plan* tells "what" and "when." Again, only one strategic plan usually is used per organization, although some organizations develop a strategic plan for each category of project. Strategic plans can say things such as "we will always do Edge Coverage during unit testing" and "Integration Testing will be driven by couplings." Strategic plans are more detailed and longer than mission plans, sometimes 20–50 pages or more. They are seldom detailed enough to be directly useful to practicing testers or developers.
3. A *tactical plan* tells "how" and "who." Most organizations use one overall tactical plan per product. Tactical plans are the most detailed of all plans, and are usually living documents. That is, a tactical plan may begin life as a table of contents, and be continually added to during the life of the product or product development. For example, a tactical test plan would specify how each individual unit will be tested.

Below are outlines of two sample test plans, provided as example only. The plans were derived from numerous samples that have been posted on the Web, so do not exactly represent a single organization. The first is for system testing and the second is a tactical plan for unit testing. Both are based on the IEEE 829-1983 standard.

1. Purpose
   The purpose of a **test plan** is to define the strategies, scope of testing, philosophy, test exit and entrance criteria, and test tools that will be used. The plan should also include management information such as resource allocations, staff assignments, and schedules.
2. Target Audience and Application
   (a) The test staff and quality assurance personnel must be able to understand and implement the test plan.
   (b) The quality assurance personnel must be able to analyze the results and make recommendations on the quality of the software under test to management.
   (c) The developers must be able to understand what functionalities will be tested and the conditions under which the tests are to be performed.
   (d) The marketing personnel must be able to understand with which configurations (hardware and software) the product was tested.
   (e) Managers must understand the schedule to the degree of when testing is to be performed and when it will be finished.
3. Deliverables
   The results of testing are the following deliverables:
   (a) Test cases, including input values and expected results
   (b) Test criteria satisfied
   (c) Problem reports (generated as a result of testing)
   (d) Test coverage analysis

4. Information Included

Each test plan should contain the following information. Note that this can (and often does) serve as the outline of the actual test plan, and can be tailored to most environments successfully.

(a) Introduction
(b) Test items
(c) Features tested
(d) Features not tested (per cycle)
(e) Test criteria, strategy and approach
   ■ Syntax
   ■ Description of functionality
   ■ Argument values for tests
   ■ Expected output
   ■ Specific exclusions
   ■ Dependencies
   ■ Test case success criteria
(f) Pass/fail standards
(g) Criteria for beginning testing
(h) Criteria for suspending test and requirements for restarting
(i) Test deliverables/status communications documents
(j) Hardware and software requirements
(k) Responsibilities for determining problem severity and correcting problems
(l) Staffing and training needs
(m) Test schedules
(n) Risks and contingencies
(o) Approvals

The above plan is in a very general and high level style. The next example is in a much more detailed style, and is more suited for tactical test plans for engineers.

1. Purpose

The purpose of the test plan is to describe the scope, approach, resources, and schedule of all testing activities. The plan should identify the items to be tested, the features to be tested, the testing tasks to be performed, the personnel responsible for each task, and the risks associated with this plan.

The test plan should be a dynamic document that can be used by testers, managers, and developers. The test plan should evolve as the project evolves. At the end of the project the test plan should document the activities and be the vehicle by which all parties sign indicating approval of the final product.

2. Outline

A test plan has the following structure:

(a) Test-plan identifier
(b) Introduction
(c) Test reference items
(d) Features that will be tested

(e) Features that will not be tested

(f) Approach to testing

(g) Criteria for pass/fail

(h) Criteria for suspending test and requirements for restarting

(i) Test deliverables

(j) Testing tasks

(k) Environmental needs

(l) Responsibilities

(m) Staffing and training needs

(n) Schedule

(o) Risks and contingencies

(p) Approvals

The sections are ordered in the sequence above. Additional sections may be included if necessary. If some or all of the content of a section is in another document, a reference to that document can be listed. The referenced material must be easily available. The following sections give details on the content of each section.

3. Test-Plan Identifier

Give a unique identifier (name) to this test plan.

4. Introduction

Give a description or purpose of the software, so that both the tester and the client are clear as to the purpose of the software and the approach to be taken in testing.

5. Test Reference Items

Identify items that are referred to by the tests, including their version/revision and dates. Supply references to the following documents, if available:

(a) Requirements specification

(b) Design specification

(c) Users guide

(d) Operations guide

(e) Installation guide

(f) Analysis diagrams, including data flow, etc.

(g) UML or other modeling documents

6. Features that Will Be Tested

Identify all features and feature combinations that need to be tested. Identify the test design that is associated with each feature and each combination of features.

7. Features that Will not Be Tested

Identify all features and significant combinations of features that will not be tested. Most importantly, state why.

8. Approach to Testing

For each major group of features or feature combinations, specify the approach that will ensure that these feature groups are adequately tested. Specify the major activities, criteria, and tools that will be used.

The approach should be described in enough detail to identify the major testing tasks and estimate how long each will take.

9. Criteria for Pass/Fail

   Specify the measure to be used to determine whether each test item has passed or failed testing. Will it be based on a criterion? The number of known faults?

10. Criteria for Suspending Testing and Requirements for Restarting

    In certain situations, testing must stop and the software sent back to the developers. Specify the criteria used to suspend all or any portion of the testing. Specify the activities that must be repeated to resume or restart testing activities.

11. Test Deliverables

    Identify the documents that should be included in the report. The following are candidate documents.

    (a) Test plan
    (b) Test design specifications
    (c) Test case specifications
    (d) Test process
    (e) Test logs
    (f) Test trouble reports
    (g) Test summary reports
    (h) Test input data and test output data (or where they are located)

12. Testing Tasks

    Identify the tasks necessary to prepare for and perform testing. Identify all dependencies among the tasks.

13. Environmental Needs

    Specify both the necessary and desired properties of the test environment. This specification should contain:

    (a) The physical characteristics of the facilities, including the hardware
    (b) Any communications and system software
    (c) The mode of usage (stand-alone, transient, web-based, etc.)
    (d) Any other software or supplies needed to run the test
    (e) Test tools needed
    (f) Any other testing needs (e.g., publications) and where to get them

14. Responsibilities

    Identify the groups responsible for all aspects of testing and correcting problems. In addition, identify the groups responsible for providing the test reference items identified and the environmental needs above.

15. Staffing and Training Needs

    Specify test staffing needs in terms of knowledge and skill. Identify training options when appropriate and necessary.

16. Schedule

    Include all test milestones identified in the software project schedule. Define any additional test milestones needed. Estimate the time required to do each testing task and specify the schedule for each testing task and test milestone.

17. Risks and Contingencies

    Identify any risky assumptions of the test plan. For example, specialized knowledge may be needed but not available. Specify contingency plans for each.

18. Approvals

Specify the names and titles of all persons who must approve this plan, and include space for them to sign and date the document.

6.5 IDENTIFYING CORRECT OUTPUTS

The main contribution of this book is set of coverage criteria for testing. But no matter what coverage criterion is used, sooner or later one wants to know whether a given program executes correctly on a given input. This is the *oracle* problem in software testing.

The oracle problem can be surprisingly difficult to solve, and so it helps to have a range of approaches available. This section describes several common approaches to the oracle problem.

6.5.1 Direct Verification of Outputs

If you are lucky, your program will come with a specification, and the specification will be clear as to what output accompanies a given input. For example, a *sort* program should produce a permutation of its input in a specified order.

Having a human evaluate the correctness of a given output is often effective, but is also expensive. Naturally, it is cheaper to automate this process. Automating direct verification of the output, when possible, is one of the best methods of checking program behavior. Below is an outline of a checker for sorting. Notice that the checking algorithm is *not* another sorting algorithm. It is not only different, it is not particularly simple. That is, writing output checkers can be hard.

```
Input: Structure S
    Make copy T of S
    Sort S
    // Verify S is a permutation of T
    Check S and T are of the same size
    For each object in S
        Check if object appears in S and T same number of times
    // Verify S is ordered
    For each index i but last in S
        Check if S[i] <= S[i+1]
```

Unfortunately, direct verification is not always possible. Consider a program that analyzes Petri nets, which are useful for modeling processes with state. One output of such analysis is the probability of being in any given state. It is difficult to look at a given probability and assert that it is correct – after all, it is just a number. How do you know if all of the digits are, in fact, the right ones? For Petri nets, the final probabilities cannot easily be related back to the input Petri net.

6.5.2 Redundant Computations

When direct verification is not applicable, redundant computations can be used instead. For example, to evaluate automatically the correctness of a *min* program, one could use another implementation of *min*–preferably a trustworthy or "gold" version. This initially appears to be a circularity; why should one trust one implementation more than another?

Let us formalize the process. Suppose that the program under test is labeled P, and $P(t)$ is the output of P on test t. A specification S of P also specifies an output $S(t)$, and we usually demand that $S(t) = P(t)$.[1] Suppose that S is, itself, executable, thereby allowing us to automate the output checking process. If S itself contains one or more faults, a common occurrence, $S(t)$ may very well be incorrect. If $P(t)$ is incorrect in exactly the same way, the failure of P goes undetected. If P fails in some way that is different from S on some test t, then the discrepancy will be investigated, with at least the possibility that the faults in both S and P will be discovered.

A potential problem is when P and S have faults that result in incorrect and identical (and hence unremarkable) outputs. Some authors have suggested that the oracle S should be developed independently of P to reduce this possibility. From a practical standpoint, such independent development is difficult to achieve.

Further, independent development is very unlikely to lead to independent failures. Both experimental evidence and theoretical arguments suggest that common failures occur at a rate substantially above what would be expected given an assumption of independence. The basic reason for this is that some inputs are "harder" than others to get right, and it is precisely these inputs that are the most likely to trigger common failures across multiple implementations.

Still, testing one implementation against another is an effective, practical technique for testing. In industry, the technique is implemented most often in regression testing, where the executable version of a specification S is simply the previous release of the software. Regression testing is extremely effective at identifying problems in software, and should be a standard part of any serious commercial software development activity.

Sometimes a problem might have different algorithms to solve it, and implementations of the different algorithms are excellent candidates for checking against each other, even though the common failure problem still remains. For example, consider searching algorithms. A binary search routine could easily be tested by comparing the result with a linear search.

6.5.3 Consistency Checks

An alternative to direct verification or redundant computations is consistency analysis. Consistency analysis is typically incomplete. Consider the Petri net example again. Given a putative probability, one can certainly say that if it is negative or larger than unity, then it is wrong. Consistency analysis can also be internal. Recall the RIP (reachability, infection, propagation) model for failures from Chapter 1. External checks can only examine the outputs, so the infection must propagate for the error to be detected.

Internal checks raise the possibility of identifying faulty behavior with only the first two (RI) properties. It is quite common for programmers to require certain relations to hold on internal structures. For example, an object representation might require that a given container never hold duplicate objects. Checking these "invariant" relations is an extremely effective way of finding faults. Programmers trained in developing software under the contract model can produce the code for such checking in the course of normal development. For object-oriented software, such checks are typically organized around object invariants – both on the abstraction of the object and on its representation – as well as object method preconditions and postconditions. Tools such as assertion facilities can efficiently turn such checks on during testing and turn them back off, if necessary for performance, during operation.

6.5.4 Data Redundancy

An extremely powerful method of evaluating correctness on a given input is to consider how the program behaves on other inputs. Consider a computation of the *sine* function. Given a computation $sin(x)$ for some input x, it is quite difficult to decide if the output is exactly right. Comparing to another implementation of *sine* is one possibility, but other techniques are possible. If *sine* is available, it is likely that *cosine* is as well, and it is an identity that $sin(x)^2 + cos(x)^2 = 1$, for all values of x.

This last check helps in many cases, but it doesn't help in the case where both $sin(x)$ and $cos(x)$ happen to be wrong in compensating ways. For example, if *cos* happens to be implemented with a call to *sin*, then we have not made much progress.

Still, identities are an extremely useful approach. Further, they often work with classes. For example, adding an element to a container and then removing the element from the container often has a well-defined effect on the container. For some containers, such as bags, the result is no change at all. For other containers, such as sets, the result might be no change, or it might be a change of one element, depending on whether the item was originally in the container.

Even more powerful are identities that use the same program, but on different inputs. Consider $sin(x)$ again. Another identity is $sin(a + b) = sin(a)cos(b) + cos(a)sin(b)$.[2] We have a relation on the inputs (namely, $a + b = x$) and a relation on the outputs ($sin(x)$ is a simple expression in terms of *sine* applied to a and b). Such checks can be repeated as often as desired with different random choices for the value of a. It turns out that even the most malicious implementor of a *sine* function has a vanishingly small chance of fooling such a check. This is truly powerful output checking!

This method applies, in its most powerful form, only to well-behaved mathematical functions such as *sine*. However, the approach applies to many other types of software. Consider an implementation of TCAS, the Traffic Collision and Avoidance System deployed on commercial aircraft. The function of this system is to give pilots guidance as to how best to avoid a potential collision. In the "vertical resolution" mode, the outputs of TCAS, or "resolution advisories," are either to stay level, to climb, or to descend.

TCAS is a complex system that considers many factors, including multiple recent positions of the various aircraft, the existence of complementary TCAS processing on other aircraft, proximity to the ground, and so on.

To apply the technique of data redundancy, suppose we rerun the TCAS software with slightly different positions for some or all of the aircraft. We would expect, in many cases, that the resolution advisory would not change. If the resolution advisory appeared to be unstable for some closely related inputs, we would have a strong indication that the pilot might not wish to place much confidence in the resolution advisory. Back in the laboratory, the TCAS engineers might want to pay special attention to such inputs – perhaps even regarding them as failures.

The technique illustrated with the TCAS software can be applied to any software where the input space has some notion of continuity. In any such system, it makes sense to speak of "nearby" inputs, and in many such systems, the output can be expected to vary in some piecewise continuous way.

6.6 BIBLIOGRAPHIC NOTES

Binder [33] has an excellent and detailed practical description of regression testing, in which he claimed that unautomated regression testing is equivalent to no regression testing. Rothermel and Harrold published the regression testing framework of inclusiveness, precision, efficiency, and generality [303], and evaluated a safe technique empirically [153]. Later papers by Li, Harman, and Hierons [208] and Xie and Notkin [361] are good places to start into the regression testing literature.

The notions of stubs and drivers have been around for decades. They were discussed in books as far back as the 1970s [88, 104, 165, 249]. Beizer pointed out that the creation of stubs can be error prone and costly [29]. Current tools such as JUnit use the term "mock" as a specialized form of a stub [27].

The first paper that defined the CITO problem was by Kung et al. [197]. They showed that when classes do not have any dependency cycles, deriving an integration order is equivalent to performing a topological sorting of classes based on their dependency graph – a well-known graph theory problem. In the presence of dependency cycles, they proposed a strategy of identifying strongly connected components (SCCs) and removing associations until no cycles remain. When there is more than one candidate for cycle breaking, Kung et al.'s approach chooses randomly.

Most researchers [197, 48, 321, 329] estimated the cost CITO by counting the number of test stubs that need to be created during integration testing. This method assumes that all stubs are equally difficult to write. Briand et al. pointed out that the cost of stubs is not constant and developed a genetic algorithm to solve the CITO problem [44]. Malloy et al. first tried to consider test stub complexity when estimating the testing effort [223].

Briand et al. showed that the complexity of stub construction for parent classes is induced by the likely construction of stubs for most of the inherited member functions [47]. Abdurazik and Offutt developed a new algorithm, based on coupling analysis, that uses more information about how the stubbed class couples with other classes to find a cheaper ordering [3].

Some good sources for details about test process and accepted definitions of terms are IEEE standards [175], BCS standards [317], books by Hetzel [160], DeMillo et al. [100], Kaner, Falk, and Nguyen [182], Dustin, Rashka, and Paul [109], and Copeland [90].

Weyuker [341] wrote an early essay identifying the oracle problem and various approaches to addressing it. Both Meyer [241] and Liskov [355] talk about how to articulate checkable assertions in the context of the contract model. Several commercial tools support assertion checking.

The notion of building multiple versions was championed in the fault-tolerance context by a number of authors, most vocally by Avizienis [22]. Limits on reliability for multiversion software were first explored experimentally by Knight and Leveson [188], then theoretically by Eckhardt and Lee [110] and Littlewood and Miller [214], and in a different context by Geist et al. [133]. Multiversion software actually works better for testing than for fault tolerance. If two versions of the program behave differently on the same inputs, then we know we have found a good test, and at least one of the versions is wrong. In particular, it is helpful to view regression testing as a multiversion testing arrangement.

Blum and Kannan [38] and Lipton [210] give theoretical treatments of data redundancy for certain mathematically well-defined problems; Ammann and Knight [18] provide a less powerful, but more widely applicable, approach.

NOTES

1 If S is *underdetermined*, then the requirement $S(t) = P(t)$ is not correct. Instead, S should be viewed as allowing a set of possible outputs, and the correctness constraint is that P produces one of them, namely $P(t) \in S(t)$.

2 If we wish, we can rewrite the $cos(x)$ calls to $sin(\pi/2 - x)$ calls, but this is not strictly necessary.

7

Engineering Criteria for Technologies

This chapter discusses how to engineer the criteria from Chapters 2 through 5 to be used with several different types of technologies. These technologies have come to prominence after much of the research literature in software testing, but are now very common and account for a large percentage of new applications being built. Sometimes we modify the criteria, and sometimes simply discuss how to build the models that the existing criteria can be applied to. Some of these technologies, such as Web applications and embedded software, tend to have extremely high reliability requirements. So testing is crucial to the success of the applications. The chapter explains what is different about these technologies from a testing viewpoint, and summarizes some of the existing approaches to testing software that uses the technologies.

Object-oriented technologies became prominent in the mid-1990s and researchers have spent quite a bit of time studying their unique problems. A number of issues with object-oriented software have been discussed in previous chapters, including various aspects of applying graph criteria in Chapter 2, integration mutation in Chapter 5 and the CITO problem in Chapter 6. This chapter looks into how the use of classes affects testing, and focuses on some challenges that researchers have only started addressing. Most of these solutions that have not yet made their way into automated tools. The most important of these challenges is testing for problems in the use of inheritance, polymorphism, and dynamic binding.

One of the most active areas in terms of technology as well as testing research is that of web applications and web services. Most web software is object-oriented in nature, but the Web allows some very interesting[1] structures that require testers to adapt their techniques and criteria. One interesting aspect of web applications and services is that they have to work **very well** – the environment is quite competitive and users will not tolerate failures. Web applications also have stringent security requirements, which is discussed in Chapter 9. Web applications are built with a particular type of graphical user interface, HTML running in a browser, but testing general GUIs brings in additional complexities. Some of the ideas in this chapter are still in the research and development stage, so may not be ready for practical use.

Finally, this chapter discusses some of the issues with testing real-time and embedded software. They are combined because many systems incorporate both. The amount of embedded software is growing very quickly as it pops up in all sorts of mechanical and electronic devices. Many of these systems also have safety critical requirements, a topic we defer until Chapter 9.

7.1 TESTING OBJECT-ORIENTED SOFTWARE

Object-oriented languages emphasize defining abstractions in the software. Abstractions such as abstract data types model concepts in an application domain. These abstractions are implemented in classes that represent user-defined types that have both state and behavior. This approach to abstraction has many benefits, but it also changes how testing needs to be carried out. The most important factor is that object-oriented software shifts much of the **complexity** of our software from algorithms in units and methods to how we connect software components. Thus, we need less emphasis on unit testing and more on integration testing.

Another factor is that the relationships in object-oriented components tend to be very complex. The compositional relationships of inheritance and aggregation, especially when combined with polymorphism, introduce new kinds of faults and require new methods for testing. This is because the way classes and components are integrated is different in object-oriented languages.

Object-oriented languages use *classes* (data abstraction), *inheritance, polymorphism*, and *dynamic binding* to support abstraction. New types created by inheritance are *descendants* of the existing type. A class *extends* its parent class if it introduces a new method name and does not override any methods in an ancestor class. (This new method is called an *extension* method.) A class *refines* the parent class if it provides new behavior not present in the overridden method, does not call the overridden method, and its behavior is semantically consistent with that of the overridden method.

Programmers use two types of inheritance, subtype and subclass. If class **B** uses *subtype* inheritance from class **A**, then it is possible to freely substitute any instance of class **B** for an instance of **A** and still satisfy an arbitrary client of class **A**. This is called the *substitution principle*. In other words, **B** has an "is-a" relationship with **A**. For example, a *chair* "is a" special case of a *furniture*. *Subclass* inheritance allows descendant classes to reuse methods and variables from ancestor classes without necessarily ensuring that instances of the descendants meet the specifications of the ancestor type. Although there has been intense discussion of which use of inheritance is appropriate, from a tester's perspective, professional programmers use both types. In the case of subtype inheritance, testers should focus on verifying that the substitution principle holds. The lack of firm guiding principles in subclass inheritance provides testers ample opportunities to find faults.

These abstractions have major effects on component integration. If class **B** inherits from class **A**, and both **A** and **B** define a method **m()**, then **m()** is called a *polymorphic method*. If an object **x** is *declared* to be of type **A** (in Java, "**A x;**"), then during execution **x** can have either the *actual* type **A** (from "**x = new A();**") or **B** (from "**x = new B();**"). When a call is made to a polymorphic method (for example, "**x.m();**"), which version is executed depends on the **current** actual type of the object. The collection of methods that can be executed is called the *polymorphic call set* (PCS). In this example, the PCS for **x.m()** is {**A::m()**, **B::m()**}.

7.1.1 Unique Issues with Testing OO Software

Several testing issues are unique to object-oriented software. Some researchers have claimed that traditional testing techniques are not as effective for object-oriented software and sometimes test the wrong things. Methods tend to be smaller and less complex, so path-based testing techniques may be less useful. As discussed previously, inheritance, polymorphism, and dynamic binding introduce special problems. The execution path is no longer based on the class's static declared type, but the dynamic type; and that is not known until execution.

When testing object-oriented software, a class is usually regarded as the basic unit of testing. This leads to four levels of testing classes.

1. *Intra-method testing*: Tests are constructed for individual methods (this is traditional unit testing)
2. *Inter-method testing*: Multiple methods within a class are tested in concert (this is traditional module testing)
3. *Intra-class testing*: Tests are constructed for a single class, usually as sequences of calls to methods within the class
4. *Inter-class testing*: More than one class is tested at the same time, usually to see how they interact (this is a type of integration testing)

Early research in object-oriented testing focused on the inter-method and intra-class levels. Later research focused on the testing of interactions between single classes and their users and system-level testing of OO software. Problems associated with inheritance, dynamic binding and polymorphism cannot be addressed at the inter-method or intra-class levels. These require multiple classes that are coupled through inheritance and polymorphism, that is, inter-class testing.

Most research in object-oriented testing has focused on one of two problems. One is the ordering in which classes should be integrated and tested. The CITO problem was discussed in Chapter 6. The other is developing techniques and coverage criteria for selecting tests. These coverage criteria are refinements of one or more of the criteria presented in the earlier chapters.

7.1.2 Types of Object-Oriented Faults

One of the hardest tasks for object-oriented software engineers is **visualizing** the interactions that can occur in the presence of inheritance, polymorphism, and dynamic binding. They are often very complex! This visualization assumes a class encapsulates state information in a collection of *state variables*, and has a set of behaviors that are implemented by methods that use those state variables.

As an example, consider the UML class diagram and code fragment shown in Figure 7.1. In the figure, V and X extend W, V overrides method m(), and X overrides methods m() and n(). The minuses ("–") indicate the attributes are private and the pluses ("+") indicate the attributes are non-private. The declared type of *o* is *W*, but at line 10, the actual type can be either *V* or *W*. Since *V*

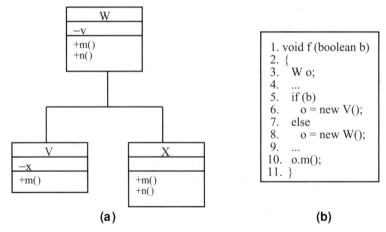

Figure 7.1. Example class hierarchy in UML.

overrides $m()$, which version of $m()$ is executed depends on the input flag to the method $f()$.

To illustrate problems from method overriding and polymorphism, consider the simple inheritance hierarchy shown on the left of Figure 7.2. The root class **A** contains four state variables and six methods. The state variables are *protected*, which means they are available to **A**'s descendents (**B** and **C**). **B** declares one state variable and three methods and **C** declares three methods. The arrows on the figure show the overriding: **B::h()** overrides **A::h()**, **B::i()** overrides **A::i()**, **C::i()** overrides **B::i()**, **C::j()** overrides **A::j()**, and **C::l()** overrides **A::l()**. The table on the right of Figure 7.2 shows the state variable definitions and uses for some of the methods in the hierarchy. The problem begins with a call to **A::d()**. This small example has

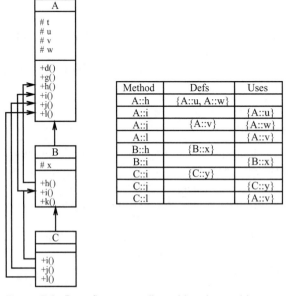

Method	Defs	Uses
A::h	{A::u, A::w}	
A::i		{A::u}
A::j	{A::v}	{A::w}
A::l		{A::v}
B::h	{B::x}	
B::i		{B::x}
C::i	{C::y}	
C::j		{C::y}
C::l		{A::v}

Figure 7.2. Data flow anomalies with polymorphism.

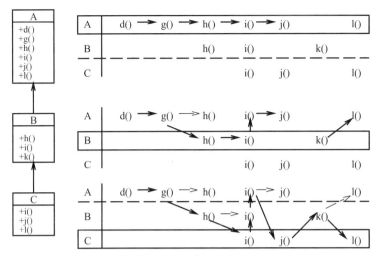

Figure 7.3. Calls to d() when object has various actual types.

some very complex interactions that potentially yield some very difficult problems to model, understand, test, and debug.

Suppose that an instance of **A** is bound to an object **o** (**o** = **new A();**), and a call is made through **o** to **A::d()** (**o.d()**), which calls **A::g()**, which calls **A::h()**, which calls **A::i()**, which finally calls **A::j()**. In this case, the variables **A::u** and **A::w** are first defined, then used in **A::i()** and **A::j()**, which poses no problems.

Now suppose that an instance of **B** is bound to **o** (**o** = **new B();**), and a call to **d()** is made (**o.d()**). This time **B**'s version of **h()** and **i()** are called, **A::u** and **A::w** are **not** given values, and thus the call to **A::j()** can result in a data flow anomaly!

Visualizing Polymorphism with the Yo-Yo Graph

Understanding which version of a method **will** be executed and which versions **can** be executed is very difficult for developers and testers alike. Execution can "bounce" up and down among levels of inheritance, which is called the yo-yo effect. The yo-yo *graph* is defined on an inheritance hierarchy that has a root and descendents. The graph shows all new, inherited, and overridden methods for each descendent. Method *calls* in the source are represented as arrows from caller to callee. Each class is given a *level* in the yo-yo graph that shows the actual calls made if an object has the actual type of that level. Bold arrows are actual calls and light arrows are calls that cannot be made due to overriding.

Consider the inheritance hierarchy from Figure 7.2. Assume that in **A**'s implementation, **d()** calls **g()**, **g()** calls **h()**, **h()** calls **i()**, and **i()** calls **j()**. Further, assume that in **B**'s implementation, **h()** calls **i()**, **i()** calls its parent's (that is, **A**'s) version of **i()**, and **k()** calls **l()**. Finally, assume that in **C**'s implementation, **i()** calls its parent's (this time **B**'s) version of **i()**, and **j()** calls **k()**.

Figure 7.3 is a yo-yo graph of this situation and illustrates the **actual** sequence of calls if a call is made to **d()** through an instance of actual type **A**, **B**, and **C**. The top level of the graph assumes that a call is made to method **d()** through an object of actual type **A**. This sequence of calls is simple and straightforward. The second level shows the situation is more complex when the object is of actual type **B**. When

Table 7.1. Faults and anomalies due to inheritance and polymorphism

Acronym	Fault/Anomaly
ITU	Inconsistent type use (context swapping)
SDA	State definition anomaly (possible post-condition violation)
SDIH	State definition inconsistency (due to state variable hiding)
SDI	State defined incorrectly (possible post-condition violation)
IISD	Indirect inconsistent state definition
ACB1	Anomalous construction behavior (1)
ACB2	Anomalous construction behavior (2)
IC	Incomplete construction
SVA	State visibility anomaly

g() calls **h()**, the version of **h()** defined in **B** is executed (the light dashed line from **A::g()** to **A::h()** emphasizes that **A::h()** is **not** executed). Then control continues to **B::i()**, **A::i()**, and then to **A::j()**.

When the object is of actual type **C**, we can see where the term "yo-yo" comes from. Control proceeds from **A::g()** to **B::h()** to **C::i()**, then back up through **B::i()** to **A::i()**, back to **C::j()**, back up to **B::k()**, and finally down to **C::l()**.

This example illustrates some of the complexities that can result in object-oriented programs due to method overriding and polymorphism. Along with this induced complexity comes more difficulty and effort required in testing.

Categories of Inheritance Faults and Anomalies

Inheritance helps developers be more creative, be more efficient, and reuse previously existing software components. Unfortunately, it also allows a number of anomalies and potential faults that anecdotal evidence has shown to be some of the most difficult problems to detect, diagnose, and correct. Table 7.1 summarizes the fault types that result from inheritance and polymorphism. Most apply to all programming languages, although the language that is used will affect details of how the faults look.

As pointed out above, object-oriented faults are different from faults in non-OO software. The following discussion assumes an anomaly or fault is manifested through polymorphism in a context that uses an instance of the ancestor. Thus, we assume that instances of descendant classes can be substituted for instances of the ancestor.

In an inconsistent type use fault (ITU) a descendant class does not override any inherited method. Thus, there can be no polymorphic behavior. Every instance of a descendant class C that is used when an instance of the ancestor T is expected can only behave exactly like an instance of T. That is, only methods of T can be used. Any additional methods specified in C are hidden since the instance of C is being used as if it is an instance of T. However, anomalous behavior is still possible. If an instance of C is used in multiple contexts (that is, through coercion, say first as a T, then as a C, then a T again), anomalous behavior can occur if C has extension methods. In this case, one or more of the extension methods can call a method of T or directly define a state variable inherited from T. Anomalous

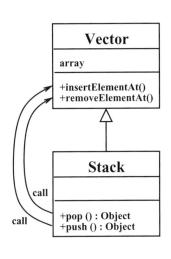

Method	CalledMethods
Vector::insertElementAt	
Vector::removeElementAt	
Stack::pop	Vector::removeElementAt
Stack::push	Vector::insertElementAt

State Variable Uses and Definitions		
Variable		Vector
Method		array
Vector::insertElementAt		d, u
Vector::removeElementAt		d, u
Stack::pop		d*, u*
Stack::push		d*, u*

Figure 7.4. ITU: Descendant with no overriding methods.

behavior will occur if either of these actions results in an inconsistent inherited state.

Figure 7.4 shows an example class hierarchy. Class *Vector* is a sequential data structure that supports direct access to its elements. Class *Stack* uses methods inherited from *Vector* to implement the stack. The top table summarizes the calls made by each method, and the bottom table summarizes the definitions and uses (represented as "d" and "u," respectively) of the state space of *Vector*.

The method *Stack::pop()* calls *Vector::removeElementAt()*, and *Stack::push()* calls *Vector::insertElementAt()*. These two classes clearly have different semantics. As long as an instance of *Stack* is used only as a *Stack*, there will not be any behavioral problems. Also, if the *Stack* instance is used only as a *Vector*, there will not be any behavioral problems. However, if the same object is sometimes used as a *Stack* and sometimes as a *Vector*, behavioral problems can occur.

The code fragment in Table 7.2 illustrates this problem. Three elements are pushed onto a *Stack s*, then the *Vector* method *g()* is called. Unfortunately, *g()* removes an element from the middle of the stack, which violates its semantics. Worse, the three pops after the call to *g()* no longer work. The fault is manifested when control reaches the first call to *Stack::pop()* at line 14. Here, the element removed from the stack is **not** the last element that was added, thus the stack integrity constraint will be violated. At the third call to *Stack::pop()*, the program will probably fail because the stack is empty.

In a **state definition anomaly fault (SDA)**, the state interactions of a descendant are not consistent with those of its ancestor. The refining methods implemented in the descendant should leave the ancestor in a state that is equivalent to the state that the ancestor's overridden methods would have left the ancestor in. For this to

Table 7.2. ITU: Code example showing inconsistent type usage

```
 1   public void f (Stack s)
 2   {
 3   String s1 = "s1";
 4   String s2 = "s2";
 5   String s3 = "s3";
 6   . . .
 7   s.push (s1);
 8   s.push (s2);
 9   s.push (s3);
10
11   g (s);
12
13   s.pop();
14   s.pop();
15   // Oops! The stack is empty!
16   s.pop();
17   . . .
18   }

19   public void g (Vector v)
20   {
21   // Remove the last element
22   v.removeElementAt (v.size()-1);
23   }
```

be true, the refining methods provided by the descendant must have the same state interactions as each public method that is overridden. From a data flow perspective, this means that the refining methods must provide definitions for the inherited state variables that are consistent with the definitions in the overridden method. If not, then a potential data flow anomaly exists. Whether or not an anomaly actually occurs depends upon the sequences of methods that are valid with respect to the ancestor.

Figure 7.5 shows an example class hierarchy and tables of definitions and uses. The parent is class W, and it has descendants X, and Y. W defines methods $m()$ and $n()$, each of which has the definitions and uses shown in the table. Assume that a valid method call sequence is $W::m()$ followed by $W::n()$. As the table of definitions and uses shows, $W::m()$ defines state variable $W::v$ and $W::n()$ uses it. Now consider the class X and its refining method $X::n()$. It also uses state variable $W::v$, which is consistent with the overridden method and with the method sequence given above. Thus far, there is no inconsistency in how X interacts with the state of W.

Now consider class Y and the method $Y::m()$, which overrides $W::n()$ through refinement. Observe that $Y::m()$ does not define $W::v$, as $W::m()$ does; but defines $Y::w$ instead. Now, a data flow anomaly exists with respect to the method sequence $m(); n()$ for the state variable $W::v$. When this sequence of methods is called on an instance of Y, $Y::w$ is defined first (because $Y::m()$ executes), but then $W::v$ is used by method $X::n()$. Thus, the assumption made in the implementation of $X::n()$

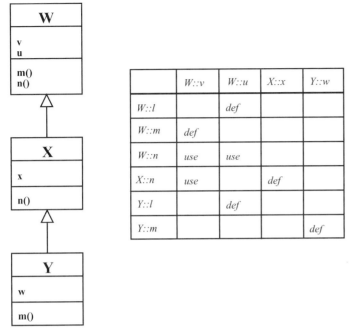

Figure 7.5. SDA, SDIH: State definition anomalies.

that $W::v$ is defined by a call to $m()$ prior to a call to $n()$ no longer holds, and a data flow anomaly has occurred. In this particular example, a failure occurs since there is no prior definition of $W::v$ when Y is the type of an instance being used. In general, the program might not fail at this point, but only create an incorrect state.

In a **state definition inconsistency due to state variable hiding fault (SDIH)**, introducing a local state variable can cause a data flow anomaly. If a local variable v is introduced to a class definition and the name of the variable is the same as an inherited variable v, the inherited variable is hidden from the scope of the descendant (unless explicitly qualified, as in $super.v$). A reference to v will refer to the descendant's v. This is not a problem if all inherited methods are overridden since no other method would be able to implicitly reference the inherited v. However, this pattern of inheritance is the exception rather than the rule. Some methods are usually not overridden. A data flow anomaly can exist if a method that normally defines the inherited v is overridden in a descendant when an inherited state variable is hidden by a local definition.

As an example, again consider the class hierarchy shown in Figure 7.5. Suppose the definition of class Y has the local state variable v that hides the inherited variable $W::v$. Further suppose method $Y::m()$ defines v, just as $W::m()$ defines $W::v$. Given the method sequence $m(); n()$, a data flow anomaly exists between W and Y with respect to $W::v$.

In a **state defined incorrectly fault (SDI)**, an overriding method defines the same state variable v that the overridden method defines. If the computation performed by the overriding method is not semantically equivalent to the computation of the overridden method with respect to v, then subsequent state dependent behavior in

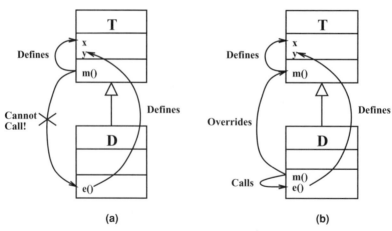

Figure 7.6. IISD: Example of indirect inconsistent state definition.

the ancestor can be affected, and the externally observed behavior of the descendant will be different from the ancestor. This is not a data flow anomaly, but it is a **potential** behavior anomaly.

In an **indirect inconsistent state definition fault (IISD)**, a descendant adds an extension method that defines an inherited state variable. For example, consider the class hierarchy shown in Figure 7.6(a), where Y specifies a state variable x and method $m()$, and the descendant D specifies method $e()$. Since $e()$ is an extension method, it cannot be directly called from an inherited method, ($T::m()$), because $e()$ is not visible to the inherited method. However, if an inherited method is overridden, the overriding method (such as $D::m()$ as depicted in Figure 7.6(b) can call $e()$ and introduce a data flow anomaly by having an effect on the state of the ancestor that is not semantically equivalent to the overridden method (e.g., with respect to the variable $T::y$ in the example). Whether an error occurs depends on which state variable is defined by $e()$, where $e()$ executes in the sequence of calls made by a client, and what state-dependent behavior the ancestor has on the variable defined by $e()$.

In an **anomalous construction behavior fault, version 1 (ACB1)**, the constructor of an ancestor class C calls a locally defined polymorphic method $f()$. Because $f()$ is polymorphic, a descendant class D can override it. If D does, then D's version of $f()$ will execute when the constructor of C calls $f()$, not the version defined by C. To see this, consider the class hierarchy shown in the left half of Figure 7.7. Class C's constructor calls $C::f()$. Class D contains the overriding method $D::f()$ that defines the local state variable $D::x$. There is no apparent interaction between D and C since $D::f()$ does not interact with the state of C. However, C interacts with D's state through the call that C's constructor makes to $C::f()$. In most common object-oriented languages (including Java and C-Sharp), constructor calls to polymorphic methods execute the method that is closest to the instance that is being created. For the class C in the hierarchy in Figure 7.7, the closest version of $f()$ to C is specified by C itself, and thus executes when an instance of C is being constructed. For D, the closest version is $D::f()$, which means that when an instance of D is being

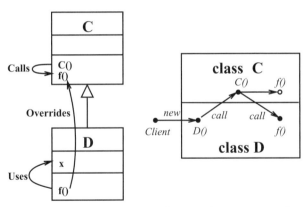

Figure 7.7. ACB1: Example of anomalous construction behavior.

constructed, the call made to $f()$ in C's constructor actually executes $D::f()$ instead of its own locally specified $f()$. This is illustrated by the partial yo-yo graph in the right half of Figure 7.7.

The result of the behavior shown in Figure 7.7 can be a data flow anomaly if $D::f()$ uses variables defined in the state space of D. Because of the order of construction, D's state space will not have been constructed. Whether or not an anomaly exists depends on if default initializations have been specified for the variables used by $f()$. Furthermore, a fault will likely occur if the assumptions or preconditions of $D::f()$ have not been satisfied prior to construction.

In an **anomalous construction behavior fault, version 2 (ACB2)**, the constructor of an ancestor class C calls a locally defined polymorphic method $f()$. A data flow anomaly can occur if $f()$ is overridden in a descendant class D and if that overriding method uses state variables inherited from C. The anomaly occurs if the state variables used by $D::f()$ have not been properly constructed by $C::f()$. This depends on the set of variables used by $D::f()$, the order in which the variables in the state of C are constructed, and the order in which $f()$ is called by C's constructor. Note that it is not generally possible for the programmer of class C to know in advance which version of $f()$ will actually execute, or on which state variables the executing version depends. Thus, invoking polymorphic method calls from constructors is unsafe and introduces non-determinism into the construction process. This is true of both ACB2 and ABC1.

In an **incomplete (failed) construction fault (IC)**, the object's initial state is undefined. In some programming languages, the value of the variables in the state space of a class before construction is undefined. This is true, for example, in C++ but not in Java. Constructors establish the initial state conditions and the state invariant for new instances of the class. To do so, the constructor will generally have statements that define every state variable. In some circumstances, again depending upon the programming language, default or other explicit initializations may be enough. In either case, by the time the constructor has finished, the state of the instance should be well defined. There are two ways for faults to occur. First, the construction process may have assigned an incorrect initial value to a particular state variable. Second,

Table 7.3. IC: Incomplete construction of state variable *fd*

```
1    Class abstract AbstractFile          14   Class SocketFile extends AbstractFile
2    {                                    15   {
3       FileHandle fd;                     16      public open()
4                                          17      {
5       abstract public open();            18         fd = new Socket ( ... );
6                                          19      }
7       public read() {fd.read ( ... ); }  20
8                                          21      public close()
9       public write() {fd.write ( ... ); } 22     {
10                                         23         fd.flush();
11      abstract public close();           24         fd.close();
12   }                                     25      }
                                           26   }
```

the initialization of a particular state variable may have been overlooked. In this case, there is a data flow anomaly between the constructor and each of the methods that will first use the variable after construction (and any other uses until a definition occurs).

An example of incomplete construction is shown by the code fragment in Table 7.3. Class *AbstractFile* contains the state variable *fd* that is not initialized by a constructor. The intent of the designer of *AbstractFile* is that a descendant class provide the definition of *fd* before it is used, which is done by method *open*() in the descendant class *SocketFile*. If any descendant that can be instantiated defines *fd*, and no method uses *fd* before the definition, there is no problem. However, a fault will occur if either of these conditions is not satisfied.

Observe that while the designer's intent is for a descendant to provide the necessary definition, a data flow anomaly exists within *AbstractFile* with respect to *fd* for methods *read*() and *write*(). Both of these methods use *fd*, and if either is called immediately after construction, a fault will occur. Note that this design introduces nondeterminism into *AbstractFile* since it is not known at design time what type of instance *fd* will be bound to, or if it will be bound at all. Suppose that the designer of *AbstractFile* also designed and implemented *SocketFile*, as also shown in Table 7.3. By doing so, the designer has ensured that the data flow anomaly that exists in *AbstractFile* is avoided by the design of *SocketFile*. However, this still does not eliminate the problem of nondeterminism and the introduction of faults since a new descendant can fail to provide the necessary definition.

In a **state visibility anomaly fault** (**SVA**), the state variables in an ancestor class A are declared private, and a polymorphic method $A::m()$ defines $A::v$. Suppose that B is a descendant of A, and C of B, as depicted in Figure 7.8(a). Further, C provides an overriding definition of $A::m()$ but B does not. Since $A::v$ has private visibility, it is not possible for $C::m()$ to properly interact with the state of A by directly defining $A::v$. Instead, $C::m()$ must call $A::m()$ to modify v. Now suppose that B also overrides m (Figure 7.8(b)). Then for $C::m()$ to properly define $A::v$, $C::m()$ must call $B::m()$, which in turn must call $A::m()$. Thus, $C::m()$ has no direct control over the data flow anomaly! In general, when private state variables are

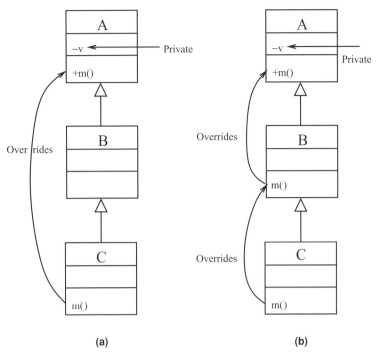

Figure 7.8. SVA: State visibility anomaly.

present, the only way to be sure to avoid a data flow anomaly is for every overriding method in a descendant to call the overridden method in its ancestor class. Failure to do so will quite possibly result in a fault in the state and behavior of A.

Testing Inheritance, Polymorphism and Dynamic Binding

Data flow testing can be applied to OO software by extending the concept of coupling from Chapter 2, section 2.4.2. Recall that a *coupling-def* is a last definition (*last-def*) in one method that can reach a first use, called a *coupling-use*, in another method. A *coupling path* between two program units is a path from a coupling-def to a coupling-use. The path must be def-clear.

In programs that use inheritance, polymorphism, and dynamic binding, identifying the definitions, uses and couplings is more complex, thus the semantics of the OO language features must be considered very carefully.

In the following definitions, o is an identifier whose type is a *reference to an instance* of an object, pointing to a memory location that contains an instance (value) of some type. The reference o can only refer to instances whose actual instantiated types are either the base type of o or a descendant of o's type. Thus, in the Java statement A o = new B();, o's base type, or *declared* type, is A and it's instantiated type, or *actual* type, is B. B must be a descendant of A.

Figure 7.9 shows a type family rooted at W. All members of a type family share some common behavior, as defined in the ancestors of each class. Every type definition by a class defines a type family. Members of the family include the base type of a hierarchy and all types that are descendants of that base type. Figure 7.9(b) shows the four type families defined by the hierarchy in Figure 7.9(a).

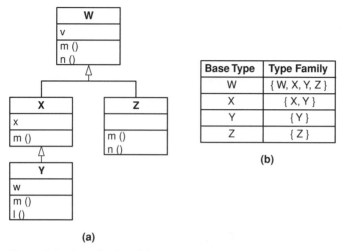

Figure 7.9. Sample class hierarchy (a) and associated type families (b).

The hardest part of data flow analysis of OO programs is the static nondeterminism that polymorphism and dynamic binding introduce. Polymorphism allows one call to refer to multiple methods, depending on the actual type of the object reference, and dynamic binding means that we cannot know which method is called until execution.

An object instance o is considered to be *defined* (assigned a value) when one of the state variables v of the object is defined. An *indirect definition*, or *i-def*, occurs when a method $m()$ defines v. Similarly, an *indirect use* (*i-use*) occurs when $m()$ references the value of v.

When finding the indirect definitions and uses that can occur at call sites through object references, we not only have to consider the syntactic call that is made, but the set of methods that can potentially execute, the *polymorphic call set* (PCS) defined previously. Luckily, **the set of potential methods is finite and can be determined statically**. This analysis uses the term satisfying set.

Definition 7.52 Satisfying Set: For a polymorphic call to method $m()$ through an object reference o, the set of methods that override $m()$, plus $m()$ itself.

Figure 7.10 is based on Figure 7.9. Assume that W includes a method *FactoryForW()* that returns an instance of W. Figure 7.10(a) shows a control flow fragment with an instance of W bound to o. This is a local definition of the object reference o that results from the call to the method *FactoryForW()*. The table in Figure 7.10(b) shows that $W.m()$ defines v, so an indirect definition occurs at node 2 through $o.m()$. Thus, any call to $m()$ with respect an instance of W bound to o results in an indirect definition of the state the object bound to o. There are no indirect uses by $m()$. The table in Figure 7.10(b) also shows all of the indirect definitions and uses that can occur for any instance that is a member of the type family defined by W. Node 3 contains no defs, but an *i-use* of v.

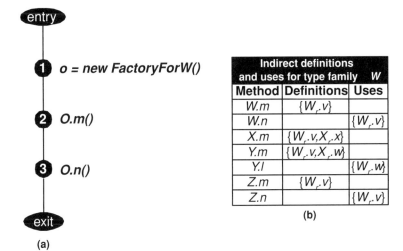

Figure 7.10. Control flow graph fragment (a) and associated definitions and uses (b).

The satisfying set for the call to $m()$ at node 2 is $\{W.m(), X.m(), Y.m(), Z.m()\}$ and the *i-def* set contains the following ordered pairs:

$$i\_def(2, o, m()) = \{(W.m(), \{W.v\}), (X.m(), \{W.v, X.x\}),$$
$$(Y.m(), \{W.v, Y.w\}), (Z.m(), \{W.v\})\}$$

Each pair of definitions and uses in Figure 7.10 indicates a satisfying method for a method and the set of state variables that the method defines. In this example, $X.m()$ defines state variables v from class W and x from X.

From Figure 7.10(b), the *i-use* set for node 2 is empty, as none of the satisfying methods for $m()$ reference any state variable. However, there are two methods that satisfy the call to $o.n()$ at node 3 that have nonempty *i-use* sets (but their *i-def* sets are empty), which yields the following *i-use* set:

$$i\_use\ (3, o, n()) = \{(W.n(), \{W.v\}), (Z.n(), \{W.v\})\}$$

Analyzing Polymorphic Paths

Def-use pairs and coupling paths are more complicated in object-oriented programs. In the following definitions, $m()$ is a method, V_m is the set of variables that are referenced by $m()$, and N_m the set of nodes in $m()$'s control flow graph. Also, *defs(i)* is the set of variables defined at node i and *uses(i)* is the set of variables used. *entry(m)* is the entry node of method $m()$, *exit(m)* is the exit node, *first(p)* is the first node in path p, and *last(p)* is the last node.

The following definitions handle the effects of inheritance and polymorphism. The set of classes that belong to the same type family specified by c is *family(c)*, where c is the base ancestor class. *type(m)* is the class that defines method $m()$ and *type(o)* is the class c that is the declared type of variable o. o must refer to an instance of a class that is in the type family of c. *state(c)* is the set of state variables for class c, either declared in c or inherited from an ancestor. *i-defs(m)* is the set of variables

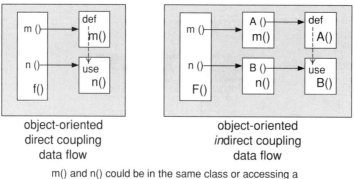

object-oriented
direct coupling
data flow

object-oriented
*in*direct coupling
data flow

m() and n() could be in the same class or accessing a
global or other non-local variable.

Figure 7.11. Def-use pairs in object-oriented software.

that are indirectly defined within $m()$ and *i-uses(m)* is the set of variables used by
$m()$.

A coupling sequence is a pair of nodes that call two methods in sequence; the first
method defines a variable and the second uses it. Both calls must be made through
the same instance object. The calling method is called the *coupling method* $f()$, and
it calls $m()$, the *antecedent method*, to define x, and $n()$, the *consequent method*, to
use x. This is illustrated in Figure 7.11 (repeated from Chapter 2). If the antecedent
or consequent method is the same as the coupling method, that is a special case that
is handled implicitly. If the antecedent or consequent method is called from another
method that is called by $f()$, this an *indirect data flow* (right side of Figure 7.11),
which we do not discuss.

The *control flow schematic* shown in Figure 7.12 illustrates the coupling method
calling both the antecedent and consequent methods. The schematic abstracts away
the details of the control flow graph and shows only nodes that are relevant to coupling analysis. The thin line segments represent control flow and the thicker lines
indicate control flow that is part of a coupling path. The line segments can represent
multiple sub-paths. A path may be annotated with a *transmission set* such as $[o, o.v]$,
which contains variables for which the path is definition-clear.

Assuming that the intervening sub-paths are def-clear with respect to the state
variable $o.v$, the path in Figure 7.12 from h to i to j to k and finally l forms a *transmission path* with respect to $o.v$. The object o is called the *context variable*.

Every coupling sequence $s_{j,k}$ has some state variables that are defined by the
antecedent method and then used by the consequent method. This set of variables
is the *coupling set* $\Theta^t_{s_{j,k}}$ of $s_{j,k}$ and is defined as the intersection of those variables
defined by $m()$ (an *indirect-def* or *i-def*) and used by $n()$ (an *indirect use* or *i-use*)
through the instance context provided by a context variable o that is bound to an
instance of t. Which versions of $m()$ and $n()$ execute is determined by the actual type
t of the instance bound to o. The members of the coupling set are called *coupling
variables*.

Coupling sequences require that there be at least one def-clear path between
each node in the sequence. Identifying these paths as parts of complete sequences of
nodes results in the set of *coupling paths*. A coupling path is considered to *transmit*
a def of a variable to a use.

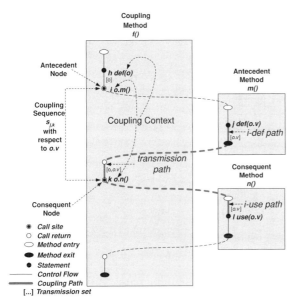

Figure 7.12. Control flow schematic for prototypical coupling sequence.

Each path consists of up to three sub-paths. The *indirect-def sub-path* is the portion of the coupling path that occurs in the antecedent method $m()$, extending from the last (indirect) definition of a coupling variable to the exit node of $m()$. The *indirect-use sub-path* is the portion of the consequent method $n()$ that extends from the entry node of $n()$ to the first (indirect) use of a coupling variable. The *transmission sub-path* is the portion of the coupling path in the coupling method that extends from the antecedent node to the consequent node, with the requirement that neither the value of the coupling variable nor the context variable is modified.

Each coupling sequence has a single set of coupling paths for each type of *coupling sub-path*. These sets are used to form coupling paths by matching together elements of each set. The set of coupling paths is formed by combining elements of the *indirect-def sub-path* set with an element from the *transmission sub-path* set, and then adding an element of the *indirect-use sub-path* set. The complete set of coupling paths is formed by taking the cross product of these sets.

To see the effects of inheritance and polymorphism on paths, consider the class diagram shown in Figure 7.13(a). The type family contains the classes A, B, and C. Class A defines methods $m()$ and $n()$ and state variables u and v. Class B defines method $l()$ and overrides A's version of $n()$. Likewise, C overrides A's version of $m()$. Definitions and uses for each of these methods are shown in Figure 7.13(b).

Figure 7.14 shows coupling paths for a method that uses the hierarchy in Figure 7.13(a). Figure 7.14(a) shows the declared type of the coupling variable o is A, and Figure 7.14(b) shows the antecedent and consequent methods when the actual type is also A. The coupling sequence $s_{j,k}$ extends from the node j where the antecedent method $m()$ is called to the call site of the consequent method at node k. As shown, the corresponding coupling set for $s_{j,k}$ when o is bound to an instance

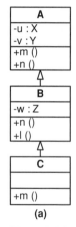

Method	Defs	Uses
A.m ()	{ A.u, A.v }	
A.n ()		{ A.v }
B.n ()		{ A.u }
B.l ()		{ A.v }
C.m ()	{ A.u }	

(b)

(a)

Figure 7.13. Sample class hierarchy and *def-use* table.

of A is $\Theta^A_{s_{j,k}} = \{A.v\}$. Thus, the set consists of the coupling paths for $s_{j,k}$ that extend from node e in $A.m()$ to the exit node of in $A.m()$, back to the consequent node k in the coupling method, and through the entry node of $A.n()$ to node g. There is no coupling path with respect to $A.u$ because $A.u$ does not appear in the coupling set for $A.m()$ and $A.n()$.

Now, consider the effect on the elements that comprise the set of coupling paths when o is bound to an instance of B, as shown in Figure 7.14(c). The coupling set for this case is different from when o was bound to an instance of A. This is because B provides an overriding method $B.n()$ that has a different use set than the overridden method $A.n()$. Thus, the coupling set is different with respect to the antecedent method $A.m()$ and the consequent method $B.n()$, yielding $\Theta^B_{s_{j,k}} = \{A.u\}$. In turn, this results in a different set of coupling paths. The set of coupling paths now extends from node f in $A.m()$ back through the call site at node k in the coupling method, and through the entry node of $B.n()$ to node g of $B.n()$.

Finally, Figure 7.14(c) shows the coupling sequence that results when o is bound to an instance of C. First, observe that execution of the node j in the coupling method results in the invocation of the antecedent method, which is now $C.m()$. Likewise, execution of node k results in the invocation of the consequent method $n()$. Since C does not override $m()$ and because C is a descendant of B, the version of $n()$ that is invoked is actually $B.n()$. Thus, the coupling set for $s_{j,k}$ is taken with respect to the antecedent method $C.m()$ and the consequent method $B.n()$, which yields $\Theta^C_{s_{j,k}} = \{A.u\}$. The corresponding coupling path set includes the paths that begin at node e in $C.m()$ and extend to the exit node of $C.m()$, then back to node j of the coupling method, and through the entry node of $B.n()$ to node g, also in $B.n()$.

Table 7.4 summarizes the coupling paths for the examples shown in Figure 7.14. Paths are represented as sequences of nodes. Each node is of the form *method(node)*, where *method* is the name of the method that contains the node, and *node* is the node identifier within the method. Note that the prefixes "call" or "return" are appended to the names of nodes that correspond to *call* or *return* sites.

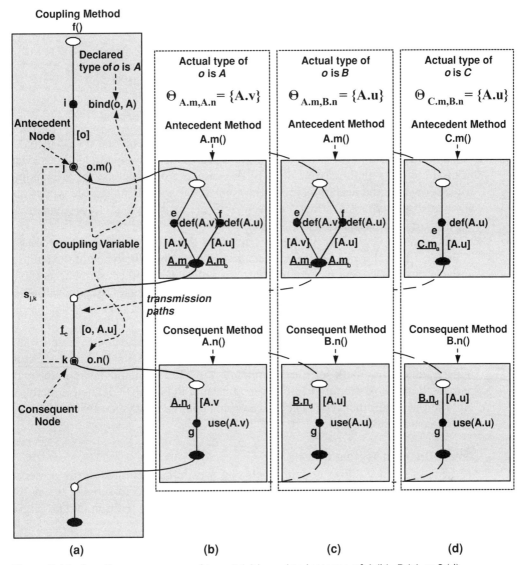

Figure 7.14. Coupling sequence: *o* of type *A* (a) bound to instance of *A* (b), *B* (c) or *C* (d).

To account for the possibility of polymorphic behavior at a call site, the definition of a coupling sequence must be amended to handle all methods that can execute. A *binding triple* for a coupling sequence contains the antecedent method *m*(), the consequent method *n*(), and the set of coupling variables that result from the binding of the context variable to an instance of a particular type. The triple matches a pair of methods *p*() and *q*() that can potentially execute as the result of executing the antecedent and consequent nodes *j* and *k*. Each may be from different classes that are members of the type family defined by *c*, provided that *p*() is an overriding method for *m*() or *q*() is an overriding method for *n*(). There will be exactly one binding triple for each class *d* ∈ *family*(*c*) that defines an overriding method for either *m*() or *n*().

Table 7.4. Summary of sample coupling paths.

Type	Coupling Path
A	$\langle A.m(e),\ A.m(exit),\ f(j.return),\ f(k.call),\ A.n(entry),\ A.n(g)\rangle$
B	$\langle A.m(e),\ A.m(exit),\ f(j.return),\ f(k.call),\ B.n(entry),\ B.n(t)\rangle$
C	$\langle C.m(s),\ C.m(exit),\ f(j.return),\ f(k.call),\ B.n(entry),\ B.n(t)\rangle$

A coupling sequence induces a set of binding triples. This set always includes the binding triple that corresponds to the antecedent and consequent methods, even when there is no method overriding. In this case, the only member of the binding triple set will be the declared type of the context variable, assuming the type is not abstract. If the type is abstract, an instance of the nearest concrete descendant to the declared type is used.

As an example, the set of binding triples for the coupling sequence $s_{j,k}$ shown in Figure 7.14 is shown in Table 7.5. The first column gives the type t of the context variable of $s_{j,k}$, the next two columns are the antecedent and consequent methods that execute for a particular t, and the final column gives the set of coupling variables induced when the context variable is bound to an instance of t. The type hierarchy corresponding to the coupling type t is shown in Figure 7.13.

The instance coupling paths above do not allow for polymorphic behavior when the actual type differs from the declared type. This requires that an instance coupling results in one path set for each member of the type family. The number of paths is limited by the number of overriding methods, either defined directly or inherited from another type. The polymorphic coupling paths are formed by considering each binding triple.

Object-Oriented Testing Criteria

The analysis above allows coupling defs and uses to be identified in the presence of inheritance and polymorphism. This information is used to support testing by adapting the data flow criteria from Chapter 2 to define sub-paths in OO programs that must be tested.

The data flow criteria in Chapter 2 are adapted for inheritance and polymorphism as follows. In the definitions, $f()$ represents a method being tested, $s_{j,k}$ is a coupling sequence in $f()$, where j and k are nodes in the control flow graph of $f()$, and $T_{s_{j,k}}$ represents a set of test cases created to satisfy $s_{j,k}$.

Table 7.5. Binding triples for coupling sequence from class hierarchy in Figure 7.13.

t	p	q	S
A	A.m()	A.n()	$\{A.v\}$
B	A.m()	B.n()	$\{A.u\}$
C	C.m()	B.n()	$\{A.u\}$

The first criterion is based on an assumption that each coupling sequence should be covered during integration testing. Accordingly, *All-Coupling-Sequences* requires that every coupling sequence in $f()$ be covered by at least one test case.

Definition 7.53 All-Coupling-Sequences (ACS): For every coupling sequence s_j in $f()$, there is at least one test case $t \in T_{s_{j,k}}$ such that there is a coupling path induced by $s_{j,k}$ that is a sub-path of the execution trace of $f(t)$.

ACS does not consider inheritance or polymorphism, so the next criterion includes instance contexts of calls. This is achieved by ensuring there is at least one test for every class that can provide an instance context for each coupling sequence. The idea is that the coupling sequence should be tested with every possible type substitution that can occur in a given coupling context.

Definition 7.54 All-Poly-Classes (APC): For every coupling sequence $s_{j,k}$ in method $f()$, and for every class in the family of types defined by the context of $s_{j,k}$, there is at least one test case t such that when $f()$ is executed using t, there is a path p in the set of coupling paths of $s_{j,k}$ that is a sub-path of the execution trace of $f(t)$.

The combination $(s_{j,k}, c)$ is feasible if and only if c is the same as the declared type of the context variable for $s_{j,k}$, or c is a child of the declared type and defines an overriding method for the antecedent or consequent method. That is, only classes that override the antecedent or consequent methods are considered.

APC requires that coupling sequences be covered but does not consider the state interactions that can occur when multiple coupling variables may be involved. Thus some definitions or uses of coupling variables may not be covered during testing.

The next criterion addresses these limitations by requiring that every last definition of a coupling variable v in an antecedent method of $s_{j,k}$ reaches every first use of v in a consequent method of $s_{j,k}$. Thus, there must be at least one test case that executes each feasible coupling path p with respect to each coupling variable v.

Definition 7.55 All-Coupling-Defs-Uses (ACDU): For every coupling variable v in each coupling $s_{j,k}$ of t, there is a coupling path p induced by $s_{j,k}$, such that p is a sub-path of the execution trace of $f(t)$ for at least one test case $t \in T_{s_{j,k}}$.

APC requires multiple instance contexts to be used, and ACDU requires definitions to reach uses. The final criterion merges these requirements. In addition to inheritance and polymorphism, the *All-Poly-Coupling-Defs-Uses* criterion requires that all coupling paths be executed for every member of the type family defined by the context of a coupling sequence.

Definition 7.56 All-Poly-Coupling-Defs-Uses (APCDU): For every coupling sequence $s_{j,k}$ in method $f()$, for every class in the family of types defined by the context of $s_{j,k}$, for every coupling variable v of $s_{j,k}$, for every node m that has a last definition of v and every node n that has a first use of v, there is at least one test case t such that when $f()$ is executed using t, there is a path p in the coupling paths of $s_{j,k}$ that is a sub-path of the trace of $f()$.

7.2 TESTING WEB APPLICATIONS AND WEB SERVICES

The use of the world wide Web to deploy software introduces a number of interesting issues for testers to solve. First, an essential difference is that of *deployment* – web applications are deployed on a web server, and made available to any client on the Internet by sending requests through the hypertext transfer protocol (HTTP). The stateless nature of HTTP and the distributed client/server structure creates a unique environment for applications to exist.

Web applications are accessible from virtually anywhere in the world. This factor alone creates a myriad of issues. There is the potential for a variety of users, and they can have different geographic locations, demographics, time zones, disabilities, languages, etc. Web applications are also very competitive, which imposes very high reliability requirements. Users expect web applications to work correctly every time, and if a web application does not, the users will look for a competing web application that does work. This makes testing crucial.

Web applications are also built in novel ways. First and foremost, they are composed of relatively small software components that are distributed (often across multiple computers), run concurrently, and share memory in novel ways, if at all. The HTTP is "stateless," which means that each request/response interaction from client to server and back is independent of the other. Therefore, any state in a web application must be explicitly managed by the software through technologies such as *cookies*, *session objects*, and offline storage such as databases.

Web applications are also created with a multitude of technologies, most fairly new. The technologies used include servlets, Java server pages, ASPs, C-sharp, Java, JavaBeans, XML, Javascript, Ajax, PHP, and many others. Testing the individual components is not much different from testing traditional software, but we are not sure how to test the interactions among these multiple technologies. Moreover, Web applications are usually composed of large numbers of small components that are integrated in novel ways.

The issues for testing can be divided into three broad categories:

1. Testing static hyper text web sites
2. Testing dynamic web applications
3. Testing web services

For this book, a *web page* contains HTML content that can be viewed in a single browser window. A web page may be stored as a static HTML file, or it may be dynamically generated by software such as a Java Server Page, Servlet, or Active Server Page. A *web site* is a collection of web pages and associated software elements that are related semantically by content and syntactically through links and other control mechanisms. A *static web page* is unvarying and the same to all users, and is usually stored as an HTML file on the server. A *dynamic web page* is created by a program on demand, and its contents and structure may be determined by previous inputs from the user, the state on the web server, and other inputs such as the location of the user, the user's browser, operating system, and even the time of day. A *web application* is a full software program that is deployed across the web. Users access web applications using HTTP requests and the user interface typically executes within a browser on the user's computer (HTML). A *test case* for a web application is described as a sequence of interactions between components on clients and servers. That is, they are paths of transitions through the web application.

7.2.1 Testing Static Hyper Text Web Sites

Early work in testing web sites focused on client-side validation and static server-side validation of links. An extensive listing of existing web test support tools is on a web site maintained by Hower.[2] Available commercial and free tools include link checking tools, HTML validators, capture/playback tools, security test tools, and load and performance stress tools.

These are all static validation and measurement tools. Such testing looks for dead links, that is, links to URLs that are no longer valid, and evaluates the navigation structure to look for invalid paths among pages and shortcuts that users may want.

A common way to model static web sites is as a graph, with web pages as nodes and links as edges. The graph can be built by starting with an introductory page, then recursively performing a breadth-first search of all links from that page. The resulting web site graph is then tested by traversing every edge in the graph (edge coverage).

7.2.2 Testing Dynamic Web Applications

One of many challenges with testing web applications is that the user interface (on the client) and most of the software (on the server) are separated. The tester usually does not have access to data, state, or source on the server. This section first discusses client-side testing strategies and their limitations, then server-side testing strategies that can be used when the tester has access to the implementation.

Client-Side Testing of Web Applications

Testing static hypertext links works well when all pages and links are statically encoded in HTML, but not when parts of the web site are created dynamically or include user inputs. We need some way to generate inputs for form fields. Generating a web site graph also becomes undecidable if some pages or links are only available after certain inputs are provided.

One method is to nondeterministically explore "action sequences," starting from a given URL. Data for form fields can be chosen from inputs pre-supplied by the testing.

Another method for generating input data is based on gathering data from previous users of a web application. This is called *user session data*. Most web servers either capture the data that users submit to web applications on the server, or their settings can be modified to gather the data. These data are collected in name-value pairs and used to generate test inputs.

Another approach to finding inputs is called *bypass testing*. Many web applications impose constraints on the inputs through HTML forms. These constraints come in two forms. Client-side script validation users small programs, usually written in JavaScript, that run on the client's computer and check the input data syntactically before sending it to the server. This is commonly used to ensure that required fields are filled out, numeric data fields only contain numbers, and the like. Another form uses explicit attributes associated with HTML form fields. For example, a text box can be set to only allow strings up to a preset maximum length, and the values from drop-down lists are preset to be the values contained in the HTML. Bypass testing creates inputs that intentionally violate these validation rules and constraints, then submits the inputs directly to the web application without letting the web page validate them.

A limitation of both these approaches comes from the fact that finding all the screens in a web application is undecidable. They rely on heuristic searches to try to identify all screens, but if some screens only appear when certain rare inputs are provided, it may be very difficult to find them. Server-side approaches may have the ability to look at program source, and therefore find more potential screens.

Server-Side Testing of Web Applications

Web software applications allow changes in the control of execution of the application that do not appear in traditional software. In traditional programs, the control flow is fully managed by the program, so the tester can only affect it through test inputs. Web applications do not have this same property. When executing web applications, users can *break* the normal control flow without alerting the "program controller." The model of program controller that is still taught in basic programming and operating system classes does not exactly apply to web applications because the flow of control is distributed across the client and one or more servers. Users can modify the expected control flow on the client by pressing the back or refresh buttons in the browser or by directly modifying the URL in the browser. These interactions introduce unanticipated changes in the execution flow, creating control paths cannot be represented with traditional techniques such as control flow graphs. Users can also directly affect data in unpredictable ways, for example, by modifying values of hidden form fields. Furthermore, changes in the client-side configuration may affect the behavior of web applications. For example, users can turn off cookies, which can cause subsequent operations to malfunction.

This analysis leads to a number of new connections, which we categorize as follows.

- Traditional *static links* are represented in HTML with the <A> tag.
- *Dynamic <A> links* make a request from a static web page to software components to execute some process. No form data is sent in the request, and the type of the HTTP request is always get.
- *Dynamic form links* make a request from a form in a static web page by sending data to software components that process the data, using a <FORM> tag. The type of HTTP request can be either get or post, as specified in the <method> attribute of the <FORM> tag. The data that is submitted via forms impacts the back-end processing, which is important for testing.

- *Dynamically created HTML* is created by web software components, which typically responds to the user with HTML documents. The contents of the HTML documents often depend on inputs, which complicates analysis.

- *State-dependent, dynamically created GUIs* are HTML pages whose contents and form are determined not just by inputs, but by part of the state on the server, such as the date or time, the user, database contents, or session information. The HTML documents can contain Javascript, which are of the web application program that execute on the client. They can also contain links, which determine the execution of the program. The Javascript and links may be different at different times, which is how different users see different programs.

- *Operational transitions* are introduced by the user outside of the control of the HTML or software. Operational transitions include use of the back button, the forward button, and URL rewriting. This type of transition is new to web software, very difficult to anticipate, and often leads to problems because they are difficult for programmers to anticipate.

- *Local software connections* are among back-end software components on the web server, such as method calls.

- *Off-site software connections* occur when web applications access software components that are available at a remote site. They can be accessed by sending calls or messages to software on another server, using HTTP or some other network protocol. This type of connection, while powerful, is difficult to analyze because the tester does not know much about the off-site software.

- *Dynamic connections* occur when new software components are installed dynamically during execution. Both the J2SE platform and .NET allow web application to detect and use the new components. This type of connection is especially difficult to evaluate because the components are not available until **after** the software is deployed.

The net result of these types of transitions is that traditional analysis structures such as control flow graphs, call graphs, data flow graphs, and data dependency graphs cannot accurately model web applications. That is, the program's *possible* flow of control cannot be known statically. These analysis structures are needed for testing, thus new techniques are needed to model web applications to support these activities.

An early attempt to develop tests for web applications tried to apply data flow analysis to web software components. Definition-use pairs can be split among client web pages and multiple server software components.

An *atomic section* is a section of HTML (possibly including scripting language routines such as JavaScript) that has the property that if part of the section is sent to a client, the entire section is. The atomic section allows web applications to be modeled in the same way that basic blocks and control flow graphs allow non-web applications to be modeled. Such graphs can then be used to implement the graph criteria in Chapter 2.

Thus far, these ideas have only appeared in the research literature, and have not made it to practical application.

7.2.3 Testing Web Services

Web services introduce a few more wrinkles for testers. Unfortunately, the term "web service" has not been standardized and the literature contains several different definitions, some of which conflict. The most common depend on particular technologies such as XML and the simple object access protocol (SOAP). This book will take a more generic approach. A *web service* is a distributed, modular application, whose components communicate by exchanging data in structured formats.

Testing web services is difficult because they are distributed applications with unusual runtime behaviors. The design and implementation details are not available, so testers need to use client-side testing. A single business process often involves multiple web services. Moreover, these multiple web services might be located on different servers, and belong to different companies. Web services interact by passing messages and data in structured ways, specifically with XML. Although technologies exist to verify syntactic aspects of the interactions, the problem of whether the two web services behave correctly with all possible messages is more difficult.

The goal of web service communication is to allow web services to be described, advertised, discovered and invoked through the Internet. This infrastructure uses several technologies to let web services function together. The *extensible markup language* (XML) is used to transmit messages and data. The *universal description, discovery and integration* (UDDI) specification is used to maintain directories of information about web services. These directories record information about web services, including location and requirements, in a format that other web services and applications can read. The *web services description language* (WSDL) is used to describe how to access web services and what operations they can perform. SOAP helps software transmit and receive XML messages over the Internet.

Research into testing web services has just begun and so far has centered on the messages. Inputs to web service components are XML messages that correspond to specific syntactic requirements. These requirements can be described in XML schemas, which provide a grammar-based description of the messages. Researchers are beginning to apply the syntax testing criteria in Chapter 5 to test web services.

7.3 TESTING GRAPHICAL USER INTERFACES

Graphical user interfaces (GUIs) account for half or more of the amount of source code in modern software systems. Yet there is very little help for testing this large amount of software. GUI testing falls into two categories. *Usability testing* refers to assessing how usable the interface is, using principles from user interface design. While usability testing is extremely important, it is out of the scope of this book. *Functional* testing refers to assessing whether the user interface works as intended.

Functional testing can be further broken down into four types. *GUI system testing* refers to performing system testing through the GUI. The only difference in GUI system testing other types of testing is in how to automate the tests. *Regression testing* refers to testing the UI after changes are made. The most common type of regression test tool is a capture-replay tool. Generally speaking, they *capture* some user inputs, *replay* them through the UI after changes have been made, and report the differences. Dozens of capture-replay tools are available on the market, the concept is fairly simple, so they is not discussed further in this chapter. *Input validation testing* tests how well the software recognizes and responds to invalid inputs. The techniques used for input validation testing are not particularly affected by using a graphical user interface as opposed to other types of interface, thus this topic is not discussed in this section. Finally, *GUI testing* refers to assessing how well the GUI works. The tester asks questions such as "Do all the UI controls work as intended?", "Does the software allow the user to navigate to all screens that the user would expect?", and "Are inappropriate navigations disallowed?".

7.3.1 Testing GUIs

One fairly obvious technique for testing GUIs is to use some sort of finite state machine model, then apply graph-based criteria from Chapter 2. Modeling a GUI as a state machine is fairly straightforward, as they are naturally event-based systems. Every user event (pushing a button, entering text, navigating to another screen) causes a transition to a new state. A path is a sequence of edges through the transitions, and represents one test case. An advantage of this approach is that the expected output is simply the final state that the test case input should arrive in. The problem with this approach is the possibility of state explosion; even small GUIs will have thousands of states and transitions.

The number of states can be reduced in one of several ways. *Variable finite state machines* reduce the number of abstract states by adding variables to the model. These models must be created by hand. Also, if these models are used for verification via an automated test oracle, effective mappings between the machine's abstract states and the GUI's concrete state need to be developed by hand.

A variation on the state-machine model for GUI test case generation partitions the state space into different machines based on user tasks. The tester identifies a user task (called a *responsibility*, that can be performed with the GUI. Each responsibility is converted to a *complete interaction sequence* (CIS). These are similar, but not exactly the same as the use cases in Chapter 2. Each CIS is a graph, and graph coverage criteria can be used to cover them. Although it is relatively simple to define the responsibilities, converting them into FSM models must be done by hand, which is a significant expense.

Another approach to testing GUIs relies on modeling the user behavior, specifically by mimicking *novice users*. The intuition is that expert users take short, direct paths through the GUI that are not particularly useful for testing. Novice users, on the other hand, take indirect paths that exercise the GUI in different ways. In this approach, an expert starts by generating a few sequences of inputs. These initial sequences are used to generate tests by applying genetic algorithms to modify them to look more like sequences created by novices.

A more recent compromise approach is based on an *event-flow* model through the GUI. The event flow model proceeds in two steps. First, each event is encoded in preconditions. *Preconditions* include the state in which the event can be executed and the *effects* of the event, that is, the state change that occurs as a result of the event. Second, the tester represents all possible sequences of events that can be executed on the GUI as a set of directed graphs. Third, preconditions and effects are used to generate tests by using a goal-directed approach. Because the expected outputs are the target states of the events, this allows test oracles to be automated created and checked. The directed graph model is used to generate tests that satisfy criteria in Chapter 2.

More details on how these methods can be applied can be found in the papers in the bibliographic section.

7.4 REAL-TIME SOFTWARE AND EMBEDDED SOFTWARE

Real-time software systems must respond to externally generated input stimuli within a finite and specified period. Real-time systems are often embedded and operate in the context of a larger engineering system, sometimes designed for a dedicated platform and application.

Real-time systems typically interact with other sub-systems and processes in the physical world. This is called the *environment* of the real-time system. For example, the environment of a real-time system that controls a robot arm includes items coming down a conveyor belt and messages from other robot control systems along the same production line. Real-time systems usually have explicit time constraints that specify the response time and temporal behavior of real-time systems. For example, a time constraint for a flight monitoring system can be that once landing permission is requested, a response must be provided within 30 seconds. A time constraint on the response time of a request is called a *deadline*. Time constraints come from the dynamic characteristics of the environment (movement, acceleration, etc.) or from design and safety decisions imposed by a system developer.

Timeliness refers to the ability of software to meet time constraints. For example, a time constraint for a flight monitoring system can be that once landing permission is requested, a response must be provided within 30 seconds. Faults in the software can lead to software timeliness violations and costly accidents. Thus testers need to detect violation of timing constraints.

Real-time systems are sometimes called *reactive* because they react to changes in their environment. These changes are recognized by *sensors*, and the system influences the environment through *actuators*. Since real-time systems control hardware that interacts closely with entities and people in the real world, they often need to be dependable.

A *real-time application* is defined by a set of tasks that implements a particular functionality for the real-time system. The execution environment of a real-time application is all the other software and hardware needed to make the system behave as intended, for example, real-time operating systems and I/O devices.

Two types of real-time tasks are commonly used. *Periodic* tasks are activated at a fixed frequency, thus all the points in time when such tasks are activated are known beforehand. For example, a task with a period of 4 time units will be activated at times 0, 4, 8, etc. *Aperiodic* tasks can be activated at any point in time. To achieve timeliness in a real-time system, aperiodic tasks must be specified with constraints on their activation pattern. When a constraint is present, the tasks are called *sporadic*. A common constraint is a *minimum inter-arrival time* between two consecutive task activations. Tasks may also have an *offset* that denotes the time before any instance may be activated.

Testers often want to know the *longest execution time* (the literature usually calls this "*worst-case.*" Unfortunately, this is very difficult to estimate, so a common goal in testing is to cause the software to execute as long as possible; hopefully reaching the worst-case execution time.

The *response time* of a real-time task is the time it takes from when it is activated until it finishes its execution. The response times of a set of concurrent tasks depend on the order in which they are scheduled to execute. This is called the *execution order* of tasks.

Issues with Testing Real-Time Systems

A landmark paper by Schütz described issues that need to be considered when testing real-time systems. In the context of real-time software, *observability* is the ability to monitor or log the behavior of a real-time system. Observability is usually increased by inserting *probes* that reveal information about the current state and internal state-changes in the system. A problem is that probes in real-time software can influence the temporal behavior of the system, so removing them can invalidate the test results. This problem is usually referred to as the *probe-effect*. The probe-effect problem is usually solved by leaving the probes in the software, but directing their output to a channel that consumes the same amount of resources but is inaccessible during operation.

A special type of probe is a built-in software (or hardware) component that monitors the activity in the system and then leave that component in the system. In systems with scarce computing resources, the probe-effect makes it desirable to keep the amount of logging to a minimum. This is fairly common in real-time embedded systems when the hardware is severely constrained (such as a spaceship).

Two related concepts are reproducibility and controllability. *Reproducibility* is when the system repeatedly exhibits identical behavior when stimulated with the same inputs. Reproducibility is a very desirable property for testing, particularly during regression testing and debugging.

It is very difficult to achieve reproducibility in real-time systems, especially in event-triggered and dynamically scheduled systems. This is because the actual behavior of a system depends on elements that have not been expressed explicitly as part of the systems input. For example, the response time of a task depends on the current load of the system, varying efficiency of hardware acceleration components, etc. These systems are nondeterministic. A high degree of controllability is typically required to effectively test nondeterministic software.

If the software under test is nondeterministic and has low controllability, testers must use statistical methods to ensure the validity of test results. This is usually done by executing the same test inputs many times to achieve statistically significant results. A minimum requirement on controllability is that a sequence of timed inputs can be repeatedly injected in the same way.

Timeliness Faults, Errors, and Failures

The term *timeliness fault* denotes a mistake in the implementation or configuration of a real-time application that may result in incorrect temporal behaviors. For example, a timeliness fault can be that a condition in a branch statement is wrong and causes a loop in a task to iterate more times than expected. Another example is when two tasks disturb each other (for example, via unprotected shared hardware and software resources) in a unanticipated way. Both these examples of timeliness faults may case some part of a task to execute longer than expected. Another type of timeliness fault occurs when the environment (or sensors and actuators) behaves differently than expected. For example, if an interrupt handling mechanism is subject to an unforeseen delay, then the internal inter-arrival time may become shorter than expected.

A *timeliness error* occurs when the system internally deviates from assumptions about its temporal behavior. This is similar when a non-real-time program has an internal state error. Timeliness errors are difficult to detect without extensive logging and precise knowledge about the internal behavior of the system. In addition, timeliness errors might only be detectable and lead to system level timeliness failures for specific execution orders.

A *timeliness failure* is a violation of a time constraint that can be observed externally. In a hard real-time system, this has some penalty or consequence for the continued operation of the overall system. Since time constraints typically are expressed with respect to the externally observable behavior of a system (or component), timeliness failures are often easy to detect.

Testing for Timeliness

Test criteria must be adapted to address timeliness because it is difficult to characterize a critical sequence of inputs without considering the effect on the set of active tasks and real-time protocols. However, the test criteria as presented in earlier chapters seldom use information about real-time design in test case generation, nor do they predict what execution orders may reveal faults in off-line assumptions.

Timeliness is traditionally analyzed and maintained using scheduling analysis techniques or timeliness is regulated online through admission control and contingency schemes. However, these techniques make assumptions about the tasks and activation patterns that must be correct for timeliness to be maintained. Further, a full schedulability analysis of non-trivial system models is complicated and requires specific rules to be followed by the run-time system. Testing for timeliness is more general; it applies to all system architectures and can be used to gain confidence in assumptions by systematically sampling among the execution orders that can lead to missed deadlines. However, only some of the possible execution orders reveal timeliness violations in the presence of timing faults. Therefore, the challenge is to find execution orders that will cause timeliness faults to result in failure.

Real-time testing often depends on formal models of the software. One approach is to describe the software with timed Petri nets. Then graph criteria such as edge or path coverage can be used to try to find test inputs that will violate timeliness constraints.

Another approach to modeling timeliness is to specify time constraints in a *constraint graph*, and specify the system under test using process algebra. Only constraints on the system inputs are considered.

Another approach specifies time constraints using a *clock region graph*. A timed automation specification of the system is then "flattened" to a conventional input output automation that is used to derive conformance tests for the implementation in each clock region.

Another modeling technique that is used for real-time systems is *temporal logic*. The elements of test cases are pairs of timed input and outputs. These pairs can be combined and shifted in time to create a large number of partial test cases;

the number of such pairs grows quickly with the size and constraints on the software.

Timed automata have also been used to verify sequences of timed action transitions. This approach uses a reachability analysis to determine what transitions to test; that is, a graph-based approach. This can suffer from state space explosion for large dynamic models. One way to ameliorate that problem is to use a sampling algorithm based on grid-automata and nondeterministic finite-state machines to reduce the test effort.

A non-formal model approach uses genetic algorithms. Data are gathered during execution of the real system and visualized for post analysis. Fitness of a test case is calculated based on its uniqueness and what exceptions are generated by the systems and test harness during test execution.

One approach to generating tests is to statically derive execution orders of a real-time system before it is put into operation. Each execution order is treated as a separate sequential program, and conventional test methods can be applied. This only works if all task activation times are fixed.

Most of the above approaches are based on graph criteria (Chapter 2) in one way or another. A different approach is based on mutation (Chapter 5). In mutation-based timeliness testing, potential faults are modeled as mutation operators. Mutants that have the potential to violate timeliness are identified, and test cases are constructed that try to kill the mutants.

Eight types of mutants have been defined. The **task set mutation operator** changes the points in time when a resource is taken. The **execution time mutation operator** increases or decreases the execution time of a task by a constant time delta. The **hold time shift mutation operator** changes the interval of time a resource is locked. The **lock time mutation operator** increases or decreases the time when a resource is locked. The **unlock time mutation operator** change when a resource is unlocked. The **precedence constraint mutation operator** adds or removes precedence constraint relations between pairs of tasks. The **inter-arrival time mutant operator** decreases the inter-arrival time between requests for a task execution by a constant time Δ. The **pattern offset mutation operator** changes the offset between two such patterns by a constant Δ time units. Test cases to kill timeliness mutants are created by model-checking and by genetic algorithms.

7.5 BIBLIOGRAPHIC NOTES

The bibliographic notes in this chapter follow the order of the sections above, object-oriented software, web applications, GUIS, and real-time and embedded software.

Good sources for building abstractions in object-oriented language are by Meyer [241], Liskov, Wing and Guttag [212, 213], and Firesmith [119]. Liskov, Wing and Guttag contributed the substitution principle. Discussions about whether the substitution principle should always be followed can be found by Lalonde and Pugh [199] and Taivalsaari [323].

Binder pointed out how OO relationships tend to be complex [35]. and Berard first articulated the differences in integration [31]. The connection between inheritance, polymorphism, dynamic binding and undecidability is due to Barbey [24].

Doong and Frankl [105] wrote a seminal paper on state-based object-oriented testing. The three class testing levels of *intra-method testing*, *inter-method testing*, and *intra-class testing* are due to Harrold and Rothermel [152]; Gallagher and Offutt [132] added *inter-class testing*.

Several papers focused on inter-method and intra-class testing [118, 152, 281, 315], testing interactions between classes and their users [284] and system-level testing [181].

The yo-yo graph was provided by Alexander and Offutt [266], and based on the discussion from Binder that execution can sometimes "bounce" up and down among levels of inheritance [35]. The categories of OO faults and anomalies are due to Alexander and Offutt [9, 266]. Most of the OO coupling and data flow test criteria were developed by Alexander as part of his thesis work [7, 10, 11].

The idea of using a graph to represent static web sites was initially proposed by Ricca and Tonella [300]. Kung et al. [198, 215] also developed a model to represent web sites as a graph, and provided preliminary definitions for developing tests based on the graph in terms of web page traversals. Their model includes static link transitions and focuses on the client side with only limited use of the server software. They define *intra-object* testing, where test paths are selected for the variables that have def-use chains within the object, *inter-object* testing, where test paths are selected for variables that have def-use chains across objects, and *inter-client* testing, where tests are derived from a reachability graph that is related to the data interactions among clients.

Benedikt, Freire, and Godefroid [30] initiated the idea of "action sequences" in a tool called VeriWeb. VeriWeb's testing is based on graphs where nodes are web pages and edges are explicit HTML links, and the size of the graphs is controlled by a pruning process.

Elbaum, Karre, and Rothermel [112, 113] proposed the idea of "user session data" to generate test cases for web applications.

Liu, Kung, Hsia, and Hsu [216] first tried to apply data flow analysis to web software components. The focus was on data interactions and their model did not incorporate dynamically generated web pages or operational transitions.

Bypass testing is due to Offutt, Wu, Du, and Huang [278]. The analysis about the connections in web applications in Section 7.2.2 is due to Offutt and Wu [359, 360]. They also introduced the concept of an atomic section.

Di Lucca and Di Penta [217] proposed testing sequences through a web application that incorporates some operational transitions, specifically focusing on the back and forward button transitions. Timewise, this paper is the first published work addressing operational transitions, although it postdates the earlier technical report by Offutt and Wu [359]. Di Lucca and Di Penta's model focused on the browser capabilities without considering the server-side software or dynamically generated web pages.

The use of syntax-based testing techniques to create XML messages as tests for web services components is due to Offutt and Wu [279, 280].

Nielson [253] provides an excellent overview of the importance of web usability in general and includes a discussion of usability testing.

Early work in using state-machine models to generate tests for GUIs are by Clarke [79], Chow [77], Esmiloglu [115], and Bernhard [32]. The variable finite state machine model is due to Shehady et al. [312].

The concept of partitioning the GUI state space into responsibilities is due to White et al. [346, 347]. The idea of modeling novice user behavior to generate tests is due to Kasik [183]. The event flow model has been extensively developed by Memon et al. [235, 236, 237, 238, 239, 240, 250].

The literature on testing real-time and embedded software is much smaller than some of the other topics in this book. The concepts presented in this chapter only introduce the topic. The following references are far from complete, but will help introduce the interested reader to the field.

General knowledge on real-time software systems and timeliness can be found in Young [364], Ramamrithaam [296], and Schütz [309]. Many of the issues in testing real-time systems were published by Schütz [310]. This probe-effect is due to Gait [131]. Timeliness was discussed by Verissimo and Kopetz [331].

The method of using Petri nets is due to Braberman et al. [42]. Cheung et al. [68] presented a framework for testing multimedia software, including temporal relations between tasks with "fuzzy" deadlines.

The framework for testing time constraints using constraint graphs and process algebras is due to Clarke and Lee [78].

The clock region graph approach is by Petitjean and Fochal [287]. Krichen and Tripakis [193] addressed limitations in applicability of previous client-side approaches and suggested a method for conformance testing using nondeterministic and partially observable models. Their testing criteria were inspired by Hessel et al. [159].

The temporal logic approach is due to Mandrioli et al. [225], who based their work on SanPietro et al. [308]. The timed automata approach is due to Cardell-Oliver and Glover [61]. Another automata-based approach was by En-Nouaary et al. [114], who introduced the sampling algorithm using grid-automata. Similarly, Nielsen and Skou [252] use a subclass of timed automata to specify real-time applications. Raymond et al. [299] presented a method to generate event sequences for reactive systems.

The genetic algorithm approach is due to Watkins et al. [337]. Morasca and Pezze [245] proposed a method for testing concurrent and real-time systems that uses high-level Petri nets for specification and implementation. The technique of statically deriving execution orders is due to Thane [326] and Pettersson and Thane [288]. Wegener et al. explored the capabilities of genetic algorithms for testing temporal properties of real-time tasks [338], attempting to create inputs that produced the worst and best-case execution times. The application of mutation to timeliness faults was by Nilsson [254, 255, 257, 256].

NOTES

1 Researchers interpret "interesting" to mean having fun problems to solve, but developers, especially managers, should interpret "interesting" as a threat to timely completion of a quality product.

2 The URL is http://www.softwareqatest.com/qatweb1.html

8

Building Testing Tools

Test criteria are used in several ways, but the most common way is to evaluate tests. That is, sets of test cases are evaluated by how well they cover a criterion. Applying criteria this way is prohibitively expensive, so automated coverage analysis tools are needed to support the tester. A *coverage analysis tool* accepts a test criterion, a program under test, and a collection of test cases, and computes the amount of coverage of the tests on the program under test. This chapter discusses the design techniques used in these tools. We do not discuss individual tools, although many are available. We also do not discuss the user interface issues, but focus on the core internal algorithms for measuring coverage.

8.1 INSTRUMENTATION FOR GRAPH AND LOGICAL EXPRESSION CRITERIA

The primary mechanism used to measure coverage is instrumentation. An *instrument* is additional program code that does not change the functional behavior of the program but collects some additional information. The instrument can affect the timing in a real-time system, and could also affect concurrency. Thus, such applications require special attention. Careful design can make instrumentation very efficient.

For test criteria coverage, the additional information is whether individual test requirements have been met. An initial example of instrumentation is shown in Figure 8.1. It illustrates a statement that is added to record if the body of an "if-block" has been reached.

8.1.1 Node and Edge Coverage

One of the simplest criteria to instrument for is node coverage. This method most obviously works with node coverage on program source, but the general idea works with arbitrary graphs. Each node in the graph is assigned a unique identifier number.

Original Function	**With Instrument**

public int min (A, B)
{
  int m = A;
  if (A > B)
  {
    m = B;
  }
  return (m);
}
	public int min (A, B)
	{
	  int m = A;
	  if (A > B)
	  {
	    Mark: "if body has been reached"
	    m = B;
	  }
	  return (m);
	}

Figure 8.1 Initial example of instrumentation.

An array is created that is indexed by the node numbers (called nodeCover []). Next, the following instrument is inserted at each node i: "nodeCover [i]++;."

It is important that the nodeCover[] array be "persistent," that is, it must be saved to disk after each test case. This allows results to be accumulated across multiple test cases. After some tests have been executed, every node i for which nodeCover[i] is zero has not been covered. If nodeCover[i] is not zero, its value represents the number of times node i was reached.

This process is shown in Figure 8.2. The nodeCover[] array must be read before execution starts and is shown on node 1 in the figure. Each node is annotated with the appropriate instrumentation ("nc" is used as an abbreviation for "nodeCover"). An automated coverage analysis tool can insert the instruments at the beginning

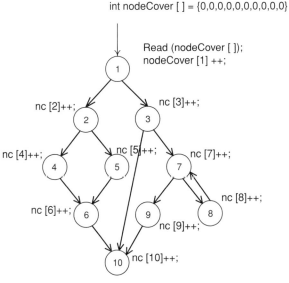

int nodeCover [ ] = {0,0,0,0,0,0,0,0,0,0}

Figure 8.2. Node coverage instrumentation.

int edgeCover [ ] = {0,0,0,0,0,0,0,0,0,0,0,0,0}

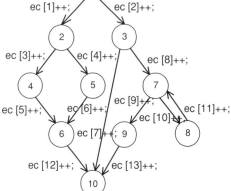

Figure 8.3. Edge coverage instrumentation.

of basic blocks or in front of individual statements. The latter is less accurate, but simpler to implement, so is fairly common in commercial tools. The instruments can also be inserted in the source code and then compiled separately, into executable files, or into intermediate forms such as Java ByteCode. Java Reflection could also be used to insert instrumentation, although we know of no tool that uses this technique.

Instrumenting for edge coverage is only slightly more complicated than for node coverage. Each edge in the graph is assigned a unique identifier number. An array is created that is indexed by the edge numbers (edgeCover []). Next the following instrument is inserted onto each edge i: "edgeCover[i]++;."

This process is illustrated in Figure 8.3. As with node coverage, the edgeCover[] array must be read before execution starts. Each edge in Figure 8.3 is annotated with "ec" as an abbreviation for "edgeCover." The instrumentation for some edges is sometimes omitted if coverage is implied by another. For example, in Figure 8.3, any test that causes edge 3 to be executed will also cause edge 5 to be executed.

Some structures do not explicitly represent all edges. For example, the following program source does not have a location for the instrumentation on the else edge:

```
if (isPrime)
{ // save it!
    primes[numPrimes] = curPrime;
    numPrimes++;
}
```

Therefore the else clause must be explicitly added to instrument for branch coverage:

```
if (isPrime)
{ // save it!
    primes[numPrimes] = curPrime;
    numPrimes++;
}
else
    edgeCover[5]++;
```

8.1.2 Data Flow Coverage

Data flow coverage is somewhat more complicated than node and edge coverage. The primary difference is that the criterion is based on two locations in the program: one for the definition and one for the use. As with node coverage, each node is assigned a unique number, but two arrays are used. Since edges can also contain uses, each edge must also be assigned a unique number. The technique is to use one array to keep track of definitions and another to keep track of uses.

At each location where variable x is defined, the statement "defCover[x] = i;" is added, where i is the node number. This means that defCover[x] will store the last location where x was defined. The second array keeps track of uses. For a variable x, useCover[] stores uses on a node or edge. For each node or edge i where a variable x is used, the statement "useCover[i, x, defCover[x]]++;" is added. The array location useCover[i, x, defCover[x]] indicates that x is used at node (or edge) i and the definition from node defCover[x] has reached the use at i.

Figure 8.4 illustrates instrumentation for All-uses. Variables x and y are defined (through parameter passing or assignments) at node 1 and y is redefined at node 2. Variable x is used at nodes 4 and 5 and y is used at node 6. If the path 1, 2,

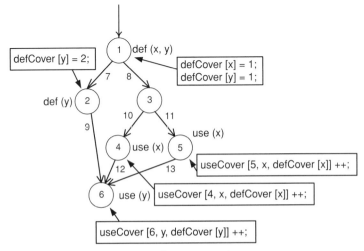

Figure 8.4. All uses coverage instrumentation.

6 is toured, then when the statement "useCover[6, y, defCover[y]]++;" at node 6 is reached, defCover[y] will be 2, and coverage of DU pair [2, 6] will be recorded. If, however, the path 1, 3, 4, 6 is toured, then defCover[y] will be 1 when node 6 is reached, so coverage of DU pair [1, 6] will be recorded.

All-uses instrumentation is a little hard to grasp at first. If in doubt, the reader should walk through a couple of simple examples to verify that the useCover[] array stores the needed information. After execution, the useCover[] array records zeros for DU pairs that have not been covered, and nonzero values for DU pairs that have been. Other analysis, not covered in this book, is required to determine which definitions can reach which uses, and which DU pairs have def-clear paths. Pairs of definitions and uses without def-clear paths between them will result in zero values in the useCover[] array.

8.1.3 Logic Coverage

We show how to instrument for just one of the logic coverage criteria from Chapter 3. The others are similar.

Instrumenting for the logic coverage criteria requires more instrumentation than structural or data flow instrumentation. The abstract view is whenever a predicate is reached, each clause in each predicate must be evaluated separately to determine which of the test requirements on the predicate have been satisfied. These evaluations are implemented in separate methods that mark special arrays to record which test requirements have been satisfied.

Consider the graph in Figure 8.5(a). The first predicate is (A && B) and it results in the test requirements (F, T), (T, T), and (T, F). Figure 8.5(b) gives the method that is called by the instrumented statement at node 1. It implements the predicate on the edge (1, 2) and marks the array CACCCover[] to indicate which test requirement has been satisfied.

The second predicate, C && (D || E), has three clauses and because of the "or" condition, some choices are possible in the test requirements. This is illustrated in Figure 8.5(c). Again the predicate is evaluated, one clause at a time, and the appropriate test requirement coverage is recorded. Note that CACCCover[5] is recorded in three different places. This represents the fact that one test requirement can be satisfied by one of three clause truth assignments.

A different approach to instrumenting for the ACC criteria is, for each predicate, simply to record the combination of truth values for each clause in that predicate. Such an approach is not appropriate if clauses have side effects, or if predicates rely on short circuit evaluation, such as testing an array index prior to dereferencing the array. However, the advantage of such an approach is that the analysis of satisfaction of the ACC criteria is separated from the code under instrumentation. Hence, the criteria analysis engine can be applied to ACC coverage data collected from any artifact.

8.2 BUILDING MUTATION TESTING TOOLS

Mutation was described in Chapter 5. It is widely regarded as the most difficult criterion to satisfy, and empirical studies have consistently found it to be stronger than

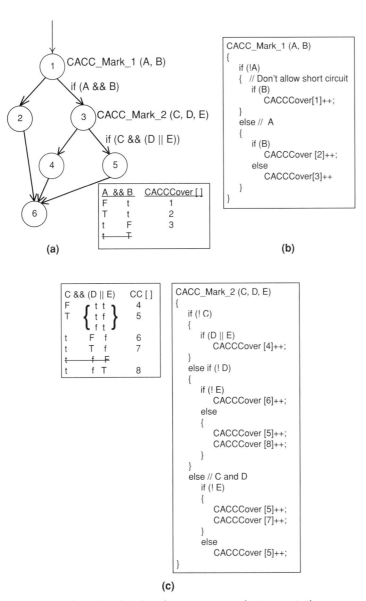

Figure 8.5. Correlated active clause coverage instrumentation.

other criteria in terms of the number of faults it can detect. It is also all but impossible to apply by hand; thus automation is a must. Not surprisingly, automating mutation is more complicated than automating other criteria. Simply adding instrumentation to the program does not work. The literature on building mutation testing systems is large, and we have lots of experience, at least in the research community. And luckily, changes in language design and advances in tools have made this kind of system much easier to build. This section explores issues with building mutation systems and explains how a mutation testing system can be built in a reasonably efficient manner.

The first thing to realize about a mutation testing system is that it is in large part a *language system*. Programs must be parsed, modified and executed. Please refer to Figure 5.2. To create mutants, the program must first be parsed, and the mutant creation engine must know the language. Likewise, the equivalence detector must be based on the semantics of the language. When the program is run ("Run T on P"), the system must recognize two possibilities that are usually abnormal behavior, but that are in fact normal behavior in mutation testing. If a mutant crashes, that's actually a good thing and the mutation system should mark the mutant as being dead. Similarly, if the mutant goes into an infinite loop, that also means the mutant has failed. The runtime system must handle both of these situations.

The first mutation systems were based on interpreting an intermediate form. This section presents the interpretation architecture, then points out the problems with that approach. The next solution is a compilation architecture, which brings in other problems. A compromise approach, schema-based mutation, is how a mutation tool should be built today.

8.2.1 The Interpretation Approach

In an interpretation architecture, a program under test is first parsed into an intermediate form. This is usually not a standard intermediate form that compilers use, but a special-purpose language designed specifically to support mutation. The create mutants component directly modifies the intermediate form to insert a mutant, and the mutation system includes a special-purpose interpreter. The interpreter can easily handle the bookkeeping when mutants are killed, and can respond to program failure. The usual way to handle infinite loops is first to run a test case on the original program, count the number of intermediate instructions executed, then run the test case on a mutant. If the mutant uses X times more intermediate instructions (X has usually been set at 10), then the mutant is assumed to be in an infinite loop and marked dead.

The interpretive approach has several advantages. Having full control of the execution environment is very helpful. Parsing the program and creating mutants is efficient. Creating mutants by making small changes to the intermediate form is simple and efficient. Individual mutants do not need to be stored on disk, only the rules for changing the intermediate form need to be saved.

A difficulty with this approach is that the mutation system must be a complete language system: parser, interpreter, and run-time execution engine. It is similar to building a compiler, but in many ways more complicated. Thus, building such a system is a significant investment. Another disadvantage is that they run fairly slowly; an interpreted program runs about 10 times slower than a compiled program. Researchers have found that it can take up to 30 minutes to run all mutants on a 30 line program.

8.2.2 The Separate Compilation Approach

The separate compilation approach tries to trade more up-front costs to save time on the backend. Each mutant is created as a complete program by modifying the source of the original program under test. Then each mutant is compiled, linked, and run.

This has the advantage of running mutants much faster than with the interpretive approach. However, it is more difficult to keep track of which mutants have been killed, and more difficult to handle run-time failures and infinite loops. The separate compilation approach can also suffer from a *compilation bottleneck*, particularly with large programs. This is also a problem with small programs that run very quickly, because the time to compile and link can be much greater than the time to execute. It is also difficult to apply weak mutation with the separate compilation approach.

8.2.3 The Schema-Based Approach

The "schema-based approach" was developed to solve the above problems. Instead of mutating an intermediate form, the MSG, short for Mutant Schema Generation, approach encodes all mutations into one source-level program, called a *metamutant*. The metamutant program is then compiled (once) with the same compiler used during development and is executed in the same operational environment at compiled-program speeds. Because mutation systems based on mutant schemata do not need to provide the entire run-time semantics and environment, they are significantly less complex and easier to build than interpretive systems, as well as more portable. Because of extra computation, MSG systems run slightly slower than compiler systems, but significantly faster than interpretive systems.

Let's look at how MSG works in more detail. A *program schema* is a template. A *partially interpreted program schema* syntactically resembles a program, but contains free identifiers that are called *abstract entities*. The abstract entities appear in place of some program variables, datatype identifiers, constants, and program statements. A schema is created through a process of *abstraction*. A schema can be *instantiated* to form a complete program by providing appropriate substitutions for the abstract entities.

For mutation, a mutant schema is created that uses abstract entities to represent elements in the program that are changed by mutants. A mutant schema has two components, a *metamutant* and a *metamethod set*, both of which are represented by syntactically valid (i.e., compilable) constructs.

As an example, consider the arithmetic operator replacement mutation operator (AOR). If the following statement appears in the program under test:

```
delta = newGuess - sqrt;
```

then it is mutated to create the following seven mutants:

```
delta = newGuess +  sqrt;
delta = newGuess *  sqrt;
delta = newGuess /  sqrt;
delta = newGuess ** sqrt;
delta = newGuess %  sqrt;
delta = newGuess;
delta = sqrt;
```

These mutations can be "generically" represented as

---

delta = newGuess *arithOp* sqrt;

---

where *arithOp* is a *metaoperator* abstract entity. This abstraction is implemented by using a metamethod:

---

delta = arithOp (newGuess, sqrt, 44);

The method arithOp() performs one arithmetic operation. The third argument, "44," represents the location in the program from where the metamethod is called. The metaprogram accepts a parameter that tells it which mutant to execute. The metamethod checks that global parameter, and if the mutant is an AOR mutant at location 44, it performs the appropriate arithmetic operation, otherwise it returns the original expression (newGuess - sqrt).

8.2.4 Using Java Reflection

An approach that takes advantage of a modern language feature to combine the interpretive and compiler-based approach uses *reflection*. Reflection allows a program to (1) access its internal structure and behavior, and (2) manipulate that structure, thereby modifying its behavior based on rules supplied by another program. Reflection is possible only in languages that support it, most notably Java and C-sharp. Both support reflection by allowing access to the intermediate form, that is, the Java bytecode. Reflection comes in three flavors. *Compile-time reflection* allows changes to be made when the program is compiled. *Load-time reflection* allows changes to be made when the program is loaded into the execution system (JVM with Java). *Run-time reflection* allows changes to be made when the program is executed.

Reflection is a natural way to implement mutation analysis for several reasons. First, it lets programmers extract information about a class by providing an object that represents a logical structure of the class definition. This means the mutation system does not have to parse the program. Second, it provides an API to modify the behavior of a program during execution. This can be used to create mutated versions of the program. Third, it allows objects to be instantiated and methods to be invoked dynamically. Finally, some of the OO operators cannot be implemented via MSG. For example, the hiding variable deletion (HVD) from Chapter 5 requires that declaration of variables that hide an ancestor's variable be deleted. This affects every reference to the variable and thus cannot be implemented in a mutant schema.

Java provides a built-in reflection capability with a dedicated API. This allows Java programs to perform functions such as asking for the class of a given object, finding the methods in that class, and invoking those methods. However, Java does not provide full reflective capabilities. Specifically, Java supports only *introspection*, which is the ability to introspect data structures, but does not directly support modification of the program behavior. Several reflection systems have been built and are available to support compile-time and load-time reflection. As of this writing, the technology for run-time reflection is still developing.

Bytecode translation is similar to reflection, but uses a different approach. Bytecode translation inspects and modifies the intermediate representation of Java programs, bytecode. Since it directly handles bytecode, it has some advantages over separate compilation and MSG approaches. First, it can process an off-the-shelf program or library that is supplied without source code. Second, it can run at load time, when the Java Virtual Machine loads a class file. Bytecode translation is not as efficient as run-time reflection, but presently the technology is more stable.

8.2.5 Implementing a Modern Mutation System

A modern mutation system would use a combination of MSG for mutants that do not affect the structure of the program, and reflection for mutants that do. Although still more complicated than instrumenting for statement or branch coverage, the amount of programming is significantly less than for interpretive systems. This is the approach taken by the muJava system mentioned in Chapter 5.

8.3 BIBLIOGRAPHIC NOTES

We were not able to find any published references for how to do instrumentation. However, researchers and tool builders have been using techniques such as what we have presented for many years.

PIMS [5, 52, 54, 211], an early mutation testing tool, pioneered the general process typically used in mutation testing of creating mutants (of Fortran IV programs), accepting test cases from the users, and then executing the test cases on the mutants to decide how many mutants were killed.

In 1987, this same process (of add test cases, run mutants, check results, and repeat) was adopted and extended in the Mothra mutation toolset [96, 101, 262, 268], which provided an integrated set of tools, each of which performed an individual, separate task to support mutation analysis and testing. Although other mutation testing tools have been developed since Mothra [95, 97, 220, 330], Mothra is likely the most widely known mutation testing system extant.

Many of the advances in mutation testing addressed the performance cost. They usually follow one of three strategies: *do fewer*, *do smarter*, or *do faster*.

The *do fewer* approaches try to run fewer mutant programs without incurring unacceptable information loss. Mutant sampling [4, 53, 356] uses a random sample of the mutants and is the simplest *do fewer* approach. A 10% sample of mutant programs, for example, was found to be only 16% less effective than a full set in ascertaining fault detection effectiveness. The effects of varying the sampling percentage from 10% to 40% in steps of 5% were later investigated by Wong [356]. An alternative sampling approach is proposed by Şahinoğlu and Spafford [106] that does not use samples of some *a priori* fixed size, but rather, based on a Bayesian sequential probability ratio test, selects mutant programs until sufficient evidence has been collected to determine that a statistically appropriate sample size has been reached.

Wong and Mathur suggested the idea of *selective mutation* as applying mutation only to the most critical mutation operators being used [230, 357]. This idea was later developed by Offutt et al. [269] who identified a set of selective operators for Fortran-77 with Mothra. Results showed that selective mutation provide almost the same test coverage as nonselective mutation. The operators presented in this Chapter are based on the selective approach.

The use of nonstandard computer architecture has been explored as a *do smarter* approach. This approach distributes the computational expense over several machines. Work has been done to adapt mutation analysis system to vector processors [229], SIMD machines [192], Hypercube (MIMD) machines [75, 275], and Network (MIMD) computers [365]. Because each mutant program is independent of all other mutant programs, communication costs are fairly low. At least one tool was able to achieve almost linear speedup for moderate sized program functions [275].

Weak mutation [167] is another *do smarter* approach. It is an approximation technique that compares the internal states of the mutant and original program immediately after execution of the mutated portion of the program. Experimentation has shown that weak mutation can generate tests that are almost as effective as tests generated with strong mutation, and that at least 50% and usually more of the execution time is saved. The Leonardo system [270, 271], which was implemented as part of Mothra, did two things. It implemented a working weak mutation system that could be compared easily with strong mutation, and evaluated the extent/firm concept by allowing comparisons to be made at four different locations after the mutated component: (1) after the first evaluation of the innermost expression surrounding the mutated symbol, (2) after the first execution of the mutated statement, (3) after the first execution of the basic block that contains the mutated statement, and (4) after **each** execution of the basic block that contains the mutated statement (execution stops as soon as an invalid state is detected).

In another "do smarter" approach, Fleyshgakker and Weiss describe algorithms that improve the run-time complexity of conventional mutation analysis systems at the expense of increased space complexity [120]. By intelligently storing state information, their techniques factor the expense of running a mutant over several related mutant executions and thereby lower the total computational costs.

In the *separate compilation* approach, each mutant is individually created, compiled, linked, and run. The Proteum system [95] is an example of the separate compilation approach. When mutant run times greatly exceed individual compilation/link times, a system based on such a strategy will execute 15–20 times faster than an interpretive system. When this condition is not met, however, a *compilation bottleneck* [75] may result.

To avoid compilation bottlenecks, DeMillo, Krauser, and Mathur developed a *compiler-integrated* program mutation scheme that avoids much of the overhead of the compilation bottleneck and yet is able to execute compiled code [97]. In this method, the program under test is compiled by a special compiler. As the compilation process proceeds, the effects of mutations are noted and *code patches* that represent these mutations are prepared. Execution of a particular mutant requires only that the appropriate code patch be applied prior to execution. Patching is inexpensive and the mutant executes at compiled speeds. However, crafting the special compiler needed turns out to be very expensive and difficult.

Untch developed a new execution model for mutation, the *m*utant *s*chema *g*eneration (MSG) method [330]. A *program schemata* is one complete, compilable, program that encode all mutants into one *metaprogram*. This is the current state of the art for mutation [277].

The OO mutation operators were designed to test the essential OO language features of inheritance, polymorphism, and dynamic binding [11, 219, 281]. The mutation operators used in muJava developed through several research papers by Kim, Clark, and McDermid [184, 185], Chevalley and Thévenod-Fosse [69, 71], Alexander et al. [8, 266], and Ma, Kwon, and Offutt [219, 220, 221]. MuJava uses OpenJava [324, 325] for compile-time reflection because it provides enough information to generate mutants and it is easy to use.

9

Challenges in Testing Software

We end this book with a discussion of three challenging areas in testing software. Although researchers have been interested in emergent properties for many years, the area, far from being "solved," continues to escalate in terms of importance for industry. Likewise, testability is attracting renewed attention due to characteristics of some of the newer software technologies. Finally, we suggest some directions for software testing in practice and in the research arena.

9.1 TESTING FOR EMERGENT PROPERTIES: SAFETY AND SECURITY

Testing for emergent properties presents special challenges. This section offers high level guidance for engineers faced with testing systems where safety and/or security play an important role.

Emergent properties arise as a result of collecting components together into a single system. They do not exist independently in any particular component. Safety and security are classic emergent properties in system design. For example, the overall safety of an airplane is not determined by the control software by itself, or the engines by themselves, or by any other component by itself. Certainly, the individual behavior of a given component may be extremely important with respect to overall safety, but, even so, the overall safety is determined by the interactions of all of these components when assembled into a complete airplane. In other words, an airplane engine is neither safe nor unsafe considered by itself because an airplane engine doesn't fly by itself. Only complete airplanes can fly, and hence only complete airplanes can be considered safe or unsafe with respect to flying. Likewise, the security of a web application is not determined by the security of a back-end database server by itself, or by a proxy server by itself, or by the cryptographic systems used by themselves, but by the interactions of all of these components.

Not only are systems where safety and/or security are important far more common than might first appear, they are becoming more common for a variety of technical and social reasons. For example, consider security for a system for controlling heating and air conditioning. A traditional system that can only be controlled through physical access cannot be compromised remotely. However, the ability to control several such systems from a central remote location clearly is cheaper, and using the Internet as the means of connecting such systems to a controller is an easy implementation. Unfortunately, such an approach also means that the system now has a nonzero risk of malicious attack from anywhere in the world. Further, if the developers of the central controller don't consider security during the initial design of the system, it is unlikely that the resulting product will be sufficiently secure, even if significant effort is put into security "upgrades" later.

More generally, there are three basic themes driving the pervasiveness of safety and security issues. The first, used in the example above, is *connectivity*. The Internet is everywhere, and there are powerful incentives for many applications to take advantage of "free" connectivity. The second is *complexity*. Networked, distributed software is hard to build well, and even harder to assess as being well built. The third reason is *extensibility*. Applications get ever more moving parts, some of which appear "on-the-fly," which means that they aren't even well-defined when a test engineer carries out an assessment.

It is important to distinguish testing safety and security functions from testing for safety or security. The former is, in principle, no different than testing any other sort of function. The latter focuses on undesirable, possibly malicious, behavior. For example, if a control system has an *emergency shutdown* feature, intended for use in situations an operator determines are hazardous, then this is a safety function, and the test engineer evaluates its functionality in the same way as any other system functionality. For an example in the security context, consider a function that authenticates a user with a id/password scheme. The test engineer assesses the authentication function in the same way as any other system functionality. In contrast, suppose there exist situations where the emergency shutdown should be invoked, but isn't. Or suppose that someone can become an authenticated user without invoking the authentication function. Upon reflection, the reader should realize that these two latter problems are *much* harder to address because they force the analyst to address the negative argument of showing that something bad thing won't happen, rather than the positive argument that something good will happen. These latter two examples illustrate the problem of testing for, respectively, safety and security, and this type of problem occupies our attention for the remainder of this section.

Roughly speaking, a system is *safe* if it reasonably free of unacceptable hazards, and a system is *secure* if it is reasonably robust with respect to malicious threats. The literature certainly offers valuable refinements on these rough definitions, but they are not appropriate for the level of material presented in this section. It is important to understand that insisting on completeness with respect to safety or security is hopeless. Rather, the process proceeds by identifying and ranking hazards and threats, choosing requirements that address these hazards and threats in a satisfactory way, and then selecting designs and implementations that promise to meet the requirements. Sometimes this process fails in the sense that it proves impossible to complete without unduly compromising safety or security. Arguably, such systems are better left unbuilt.

As everyone knows, the process outlined above is idealized and often not followed in practice. Unfortunately, the test engineer faced with the task of testing such a system will find it necessary to carry out the process anyway – or else have no idea what he or she is testing for or why. Worse, testing safety or security "into" a system after the fact is generally hopeless, precisely because of the emergent nature of these properties. Stated differently, the properties are not, by definition, in the components, and, if not provided for by design, will only be in the system by accident. Sadly, relying on blind luck rarely works out well.

Complicating matters is the difficult technical nature of many safety and security requirements. In the case of safety, quantitative requirements may be so stringent that they exceed the bounds of engineering practice. Consider the oft-cited requirement on safety critical software in commercial aircraft, namely a failure rate of 10^{-9} per 10 hour flight. Butler and Finelli wrote a great paper explaining why meeting such "ultra" requirements is infeasible, no matter what development and testing technology, current or future, is used. Instead of attempting to meet infeasible quantitative requirements, the common approach is to use qualitative "safety cases." Not surprisingly, such qualitative approaches rely heavily on sound development processes. Although the safety side is hard, the security side is harder, since it is complicated by the clever nature of human beings. Malicious human behavior is extremely hard to anticipate, much less thwart.

So, how does one go about testing such systems?

The first lesson to draw from the discussion above is that the test engineer has to have a clear idea of what to test for. Explicit documentation of safety and security requirements, along with links to the hazards and threats they address is crucial for making this determination. Some safety and security requirements are untestable. For example, consider the problem of "backdoor" code inserted during development. System testing has no chance of finding such code, because the malicious designer has so many options for choosing how to open the back door. In other words, spending testing resources on this threat is a poor expenditure of resources. Instead, the threat must be addressed through process, personnel practices, or inspections.

A more profitable place to spend testing resources is in probing assumptions underlying the safety and security model. Every design relies on such assumptions because the assumptions go all the way back to the ranking of hazards and threats. For example, designers of the Arianne 4 rocket design made assumptions about the positions, velocities, and accelerations that the rocket would experience early in flight, and these assumptions were used in the placement of exception handlers in the control code. These assumptions were valid for the Arianne 4, but, regrettably not for the Arianne 5, where much of the control software was reused. From a testing perspective, access to such assumptions is extremely valuable, which means that documenting these assumptions is a critical process.

Assumptions are a fertile source of tests for security as well. Consider the common issue of downloading software from a network onto a device. One strategy is to inform the user of the impending download (and its inherent risk), and allow the user to accept or decline. This strategy incorporates at least three assumptions: first, that users will be able to make an informed decision; second, that users will be willing to make an informed decision; and third, that it will be possible for the user to actually say "No." Many cell phones rely on the third assumption, but it is easily violated in an environment where the malicious adversary can query the user at a very high rate. Specifically, if a mobile phone has a virus on it that queries nearby mobile phones about downloading itself, and responds to "No" by immediately re-asking the question, then users are subject to a classic denial of service (DOS) attack, and may eventually click "Ok" out of frustration. The phone is then infected with the virus. Notice that the security problem here is not fixable, or even well defined, at the level of the component phone, but is instead a classic emergent aspect of the phone, the phone network, and the population of users, including malicious users. Further, addressing the problem requires a fundamental reassessment of the rules under which mobile phones should be allowed to interact with each other.

Reuse of software is a classic area where prior assumptions may be violated, and hence testing is appropriate. Consider web software. In a typical web application, business logic embedded in the web server protects back-end applications such as databases from malicious user inputs. But if the web application is redeployed to a web service, the web server may be removed, and the back-end applications are once again vulnerable.

9.1.1 Classes of Test Cases for Emergent Properties

The intent of the prior discussion is to describe some basic issues in testing emergent properties. Here we switch gears and provide some common strategies for selecting test cases.

1. **Develop misuse cases**. Use cases are a common modeling tool that enumerate expected usage of the software, typically during the requirements analysis phase. Misuse cases are the same, except they explore unintended usage. The requirements phase is the ideal time to consider such scenarios, since it is the correct place to eliminate or mitigate them.
2. **Identify assumptions and then devise test cases that violate them**. Even after misuse case analysis, assumptions of varying plausibility will be left over. As discussed above, testing these can be extremely productive.
3. **Identify configuration issues and design tests to check them**. Configuration issues, in which inconsistent versions of components are used to realize a system, is a ripe area for problems. Configuration tests tend to be oriented more to the development process than the product itself, except for the case where the components in a product are explicitly aware of their configuration data.
4. **Develop invalid input tests**. Invalid inputs are an extremely fertile area for security testing. Simple invalid input attacks such as buffer overflow and query injection attacks are responsible for a great many security breaches. Every time a system collects data from its environment, the data can violate assumptions about its size or content. Fortunately, generating test data to probe the limits on input data is easy to automate and well understood using the techniques developed in Chapter 5.

Another complicating factor in assessing safety and security is the difference between developers and users. Naturally, systems are built by developers, and hence it is developers who make provisions for system safety and system security. However, systems are employed by users, typically operations specialists and network administrators. Developers and users usually have very different skill sets, levels of training, and mental models of the application domain. Developers focus on software artifacts, particularly code. Conversely, users tend to be only vaguely aware that there is software in their systems, and instead focus on the abstractions suitable for their jobs. We need systems that are safe and secure, not only in theory when conceived by developers, but also in practice when employed by users. Hence, test engineers should bias their perspective toward the usage environment, as opposed to the development environment, when considering tests for safety and security.

9.2 SOFTWARE TESTABILITY

Software *testability* is an important notion distinct from software testing. In general, software testability is an estimate or measurement of a conditional probability, namely, assuming that a given software artifact contains a fault, how likely is it that testing will reveal that fault. We are all familiar with software development projects where, despite extensive testing, faults continue to be found. Testability gets to the core of how easy or hard it is for faults to escape detection – even from well-chosen test suites.

There are a variety of reasons to study testability. Given testability estimates for a set of software artifacts, the test engineer has a number of options:

1. For artifacts with low testability, the test engineer knows that testing alone is unlikely to result in a satisfactory job of verifying that the artifact meets his requirements, and so the test engineer can pursue alternative verification means. In the case of critical software, this might mean formal analysis. In more ordinary software, design or code reviews might be more appropriate.
2. Artifacts with low testability can be altered in a variety of ways that improve testability. Although we will defer the technical details until later in this section, any approach that improves testability will almost certainly be worth the investment.
3. The test engineer can proceed to test artifacts with high testability and be confident that the test results are accurate indicators of artifact quality.
4. In cases where testability is low and resistant to improvement, and where alternative means of verification are impractical, the test engineer has a solid argument to take to management that the artifact poses an undue amount of risk.

Various authors have proposed different approaches for tackling testability. Some authors have focused on software observability and software controllability as the key components of testability. We begin with a model of testability built on the fault, error, and failure model from Chapter 1.

We define testability in terms of three attributes of the RIP model from Chapter 1: reachability, infection, and propagation. We assume that if an artifact contains a fault, then that fault must exist at some location in the artifact. For the fault at a given location to result in a failure, three things must happen. First, execution must reach the location of the fault. Second, the execution of the fault must result in an infection of the program state, an error, at the given location. Finally, the error must propagate from the location to an output of the artifact. The *sensitivity* of a given location is simply the probability that reachability, infection, and propagation will all occur for that location.

Notice that we do not specify what a fault at a given location necessarily looks like. The reader might think it helpful to think of either average case or worst case behavior for all faults possible at that location. The *testability* of an artifact is defined as the minimum value of the sensitivity over all locations in the artifact.

To clarify the idea that sensitivities are probabilities, it is necessary to model inputs as being drawn from one or more *usage distributions*. In other words, we assume that test cases are sampled from some profile. In practice, defining usage distributions is quite easy to do, and such an approach to testing has numerous proponents; citations are available in the bibliographic notes section.

Given a distribution for selecting test inputs, measuring the reachability probability for any given location is a direct affair. Further, if the reachability probability for a given location is deemed to be too low, it is easy to change the input distribution to channel a larger fraction of the test inputs to that location. Stated more directly, the reachability attribute of testability is under the direct control of the test engineer. One way to think of this property is in terms of controllability. Software with low controllability will probably suffer from low reachability probabilities, no matter how the input distribution is skewed.

Estimating infection probabilities is a bit trickier, since it requires the adoption of both a fault model and an infection model, both of which must be suitable for the location in question. One choice is to use mutation analysis for the fault model, and measure infections by observing the effect of mutants on candidate program states.

Determining propagation probabilities also involves a certain amount of modeling. One choice is to use perturbation models to alter the program state at the location in question and then observe whether the infection persists to the outputs. One way to think of this property is in terms of observability. Software with low observability will probably suffer from low propagation. However, there are quite a few things that can be done to re-engineer code to have higher propagation.

First, there is the dimensionality of the output space to consider. For example, consider a method with a single boolean output. Such a method is prone to have low testability, if, for no other reason, than propagation from any infection is limited by the collapsing of the entire internal state to a single boolean output. The test engineer can interact with system designers to see if additional outputs are possible, thereby giving better access to the internal state, and hence better propagation.

Second, there is the notion of assertion checking. Assertion mechanisms are ideal for transforming internal state inconsistencies into observable events, typically via an exception mechanism. Designers can assist this process by providing extensive checks of internal states. Such checks need not be enabled during operational deployment; from the testability perspective, it is sufficient that they be enabled during testing only.

9.2.1 Testability for Common Technologies

Object-oriented software presents special challenges for testability. The chief reason is that objects encode state information in instance variables, and access to these instance variables is usually indirect. Consider the simple example of a stack. The method push(Object item) changes the state of the stack, perhaps by storing item in an instance variable Object[] elements. The method top() yields access to the most recent element in the stack, and so a push() followed immediately by a top() allows the test engineer to verify that the element returned by top() is indeed the most recent element. However, access to older elements is hidden; the typical stack interface does not, and should not, allow direct access to these elements. From an observability perspective, the stack interface is a problem for the test engineer. Most classes are far more complex than the stack class, so it should come as no great surprise that testability for object-oriented software tends to be low.

Inheritance compounds the lack of testability for object-oriented software. To continue the stack class example, suppose a sub-class logs the number of push() calls. To implement the sub-class, the typical programmer overrides the push() method to increment the log and then calls the superclass push() method to take care of the state change. Such modifications of classes are routine in object-oriented development. From the observability perspective, testability for the subclass suffers from the fact that some of the updated instance variables are not even in the sub-class being tested. In fact, it is quite likely that the developer of the subclass doesn't have access to the source code for the superclass.

To improve observability, there are two basic approaches. The first is to require developers to provide additional get methods that allow the test engineer access to the full state. Although this may be a reasonable approach in cases where extensive test sets are developed concurrently with, or even prior to, the class itself, it is quite likely that the test engineer will still end up having to test code where, for whatever reason, the software was not developed in accordance with testability guidelines.

A second approach is a tool approach that exploits something like the Java reflection mechanism to access internal variables, independent of whether source code is available. On the other hand, this approach suffers from the fact that interpreting the data values so captured is a nontrivial task for the test engineer.

Maintenance for tests is also an issue, since every time the developers change the implementation of a class, tests that access internal state of that class are unlikely to execute at all, let alone execute correctly.

Web applications pose a different set of challenges for testability. Again, both controllability and observability are likely to be extremely low for a typical web application. To appreciate the situation, consider the architecture of a typical web server, in which a proxy interacts with an individual client, a session manager oversees the entire pool of clients, application logic determines processing of client requests, and data flows in and out of a back-end database. From the client perspective, almost all of this infrastructure is intended to be invisible, hence accessing much of the state is impossible from the client. The server pieces are quite likely to be distributed, not only across multiple hardware platforms, but also across multiple corporate organizations. Bringing high testability to such an environment is still a research topic.

9.3 TEST CRITERIA AND THE FUTURE OF SOFTWARE TESTING

When the authors started their careers in the mid 1980s, the field of software engineering was very different from today. A huge difference can be expressed in terms of economics. In the 1980s, the economics of software engineering were such that the cost of applying high-end testing criteria usually exceeded the economic benefits.

This meant that software development organizations had very little incentive to test their software well.

This situation had a lot to do with how software was marketed and deployed. Most software came "bundled" on the computer – the cost of the software was included with the computer and customers had very few choices. Other software was purchased "shrink-wrapped," that is, it was bought in a sealed package and customers bought and paid for the software without having a chance to try it. Another major mechanism for marketing software was by "contract," where a customer contracted a supplier to provide some specific software. By far the biggest purchaser at this time was the US Government, led by the US Department of Defense. Although there have always been attempts to hold software suppliers accountable for quality, the system had numerous problems. From a broad brush point of view, when problems were found, the supplier could often get additional funding to repair the software. The fact that there are few standards for testing or quality assurance, and the requirements often changed frequently during development, made it very difficult to hold suppliers responsible for quality problems or cost overruns.

Of course, these points do not cover the entire field. We have always needed software that had to be highly reliable, such as safety-critical software. However, this part of the market was tiny in the 1980s and there was not enough critical mass to support tool vendors or widespread education in software testing.

The bottom line is that for much of our careers, the software market has been dominated by one supplier and one purchaser. This has resulted in a very noncompetitive market, and relatively little motivation for quality assurance or testing. That is, software testers have been "selling" techniques that are seldom needed.

On a more positive note, the field has dramatically changed. The software market is much larger; it is more competitive, there are significantly more users, and we are using software in many more applications. A major impetus for this change has been the development of the Web. The World Wide Web provides a different way to **deploy** software. Instead of buying a computer with software bundled inside, or buying a shrink-wrapped CD from a store, or hiring programmers to build custom-made software, users can now run software that is deployed on a server across the Web. This makes the market much more competitive – if users are unhappy with software on one web site, they can easily "vote with their mouse" by going to a different site. Another aspect of the Web is that more software is available to more users. Such a growth in the market brings a correspondingly increase in expectations. Highly educated, technically proficient, users will tolerate lots of problems. The "blue screen of death" presents a familiar situation to an engineer: the system went into an error state and we need to reboot. However, the excise tasks of rebooting and other compensating actions are not well received by the broader user community. When software is made available to billions of users who **did not explicitly purchase the software**, those users have very low tolerance for errors. How successful would Amazon or Netflix be if they sent the wrong product, sent the product to the wrong place, billed the customers incorrectly, or simply froze during use? Efficiency and time-to-market matter less on the Web and in E-Commerce applications. The success of Google relative to earlier search engines is a well-known examples of this fact, but it is true for many smaller businesses as well. As we say in our classes, on the Web "it is better to be late and better than early and worse."

There are other reasons why quality and reliability requirements continue to go up in software. In the 1980s we had a few embedded software applications. Most were high-end, special-purpose, and very expensive. The devices and the software were built by specialists, often in the military or avionics industry. We are now literally surrounded by embedded software. Companies who make mobile phones can view themselves not as vendors of phones, but as software companies who happen to put their software on a particular kind of device. Many other electronic devices include substantial software: PDAs, portable music players, cameras, watches, calculators, TV and Internet cable boxes, home wireless routers, home appliance remote controllers, garage door openers, refrigerators, and microwave ovens. Even the humble toaster now comes with software-controlled sensors. New cars are thick with sensors and software – doors that open automatically, sensors for airbags, automatic seat movement, sensors to detect when tire pressure is low, and automatic parking. All of this software has to work very well. When we embed software in an appliance, users expect the software to be **more reliable** than the appliance, not less.

Of course, the elephant in this particular room has become security. At one time, security was all about clever algorithms to encrypt data. Later security became a database problem, then a networking problem. Most software security vulnerabilities today are **due to software faults**. Software must be highly reliable to be secure, and any software that uses a network is vulnerable.

How can we develop software for these many applications that work as reliably as we need it to? One part of the answer is that software developers need more testing and more efficient testing. Most of the criteria and techniques in this book have been known for years. The time is ripe for these concepts to be taught in computer science and software engineering curriculum, incorporated into more and better quality software testing tools, and most importantly, adopted by industry.

9.3.1 Going Forward with Testing Research

This book presents a different way to look at software. Instead of considering software testing as being conducted differently with different criteria throughout the development process (that is, unit testing is different from module testing is different from integration testing is different from system testing), this book presents the view that test criteria are defined on four models of software (graphs, logical expressions, input spaces, and syntax), and the models can be developed from any software artifact. That is, a graph can be created from units (methods), from modules, from integration information, or from the system as a whole. Once the graph is created, the same criteria are used cover the graph, no matter where it came from.

This book presents a total of 36 criteria on the four structures. Many other, closely related, criteria appear in the literature, but were not included in this book because we felt they would be unlikely to be used in practice. Much of the testing research in the last 30 years has focused on inventing new test criteria. Our opinion is that the field does not need many more criteria. It does need several other things, however.

A continuing need will be research into engineering existing criteria for new technologies and situations. Chapter 7 illustrates this by showing how the criteria in Chapters 2 through 5 can be engineered to apply to object-oriented software, web applications, graphical user interfaces, and real-time, embedded software. Computing technology will continue to evolve, presenting new and interesting challenges to testing researchers. We hope that the criteria presentation in this book will provide a foundational basis for this kind of research.

A major problem for development managers is deciding which testing criteria to use. In fact, this question delays adoption of improved test technologies, particularly if the cost (real or perceived) of adoption is high. Each of Chapter 2 through 5 included a subsumption graph that indicated which criteria subsumed which other criteria. For example, if we have satisfied edge coverage on a graph, we have provably satisfied node coverage. This information is only part of the question, however, and a small part for practical software developers. Assuming "subsumes" means "better" in the sense of possibly finding more faults, a development manager wants to know "how much better?" and "how much more expensive?". Although dozens, and perhaps hundreds, of papers have been published presenting experimental comparisons of test criteria, we still are far from having enough knowledge to tell a development manager which criterion to use and when.

An expansion on this question is the question of how to compare test criteria that **cannot** be compared with subsumption. This kind of comparison must be experimental in nature, and almost certainly will need to be replicated. For example, data flow criteria (Chapter 2) and mutation criteria (Chapter 4) are incomparable with subsumption. Several papers were published in the 1990s that compared program mutation with one or more of the data flow criteria. Individually, none of the papers was convincing, yet taken together, they have convinced researchers that mutation testing will find more faults. However, none of this research looked at large-scale industrial software, and none had much useful information about cost (beyond the observation that mutation usually requires more tests).

Another major issue is how best to fully automate these criteria. Most of the early publications on individual criteria, and a lot of the followup papers included algorithms, tool development, and efficiency improvements. Chapter 8 provides an introduction to tool building but it is important to note that many of these concepts have not made it out of the research laboratory. Commercial test tools must be more robust, more efficient, and have much better user interfaces than research tools. Although companies have tried to sell criteria-based test tools for decades, it is only recently that companies such as Agitar and Certess have had commercial success. The earlier point that testing is become more crucial to the economic success of software companies should mean that the market for software test tools is in growth mode.

A significant problem with adopting any new technology in practice is how it affects the current development process. Making it easy for developers to integrate test techniques into their existing process is a key ingredient for success. If test tools can be integrated into compilers (as with early test tools such as dead code detection) or with IDEs like Eclipse (such as Agitar does), then the tools will become much more accessible to developers.

A major outstanding problem with automation is test data generation. Automatic test data generation has been a subject of research since the early days, but useful commercial tools are still few and far between. This is not because of lack of interest, but because it is a very hard problem. Some of the earliest research papers in software testing focused on automatic test data generation, but progress proved so difficult that most researchers diverted into more tractable problems. Some early work focused on randomly generating test inputs. While simpler to implement than other approaches, random test data generation has two problems. The first is that, as Dick Lipton said, "faults ain't fish." That is, faults are not distributed uniformly (randomly) through the program like fish in a school. Any programmer knows that faults tend to clump around troublesome portions of the program or difficult to define regions in the input space. The second problem with random test data generation is with structure data. It is easy to randomly generate numbers and characters, but when the data has some structure (addresses, product records, etc.), random generation becomes much harder.

The most complicated idea is to analyze program source and use detailed information about the software to automatically generate test data specifically to satisfy test criteria. The most common analysis method has been symbolic evaluation, often coupled with constraint representations and sometimes slicing. Some analysis techniques have been static and others dynamic. Solving the equations or constraints for actual input values has been done with exact solutions such as constraint solving (linear programming) and inexact special purpose heuristics. Significant problems with analysis-based techniques are the so-called "internal variable problem," loops, and indeterminate memory references such as pointers, arrays and aliases. The internal variable problem refers to the fact that we may have specific requirements on test inputs such as "*X must be greater than Y on line 5306*," yet X and Y are not inputs. Finding input values to indirectly control the values of X and Y has been troublesome. Dynamic analysis techniques are the most promising way to address these problems, however, these problems are why analysis-based techniques are mostly considered to apply to small structures such as program units.

The most recent automatic test data generation approach uses search techniques such as genetic algorithms. Search-based approaches have several advantages, including being easy to implement and being very flexible. They cannot use as much information as the analysis-based methods, and thus can get stuck on values that are hard to find. For example, if a search-based technique is used to achieve edge coverage on a method-level control flow graph, a predicate such as x+y = z presents difficulty for search-based techniques. This problem is compounded if several such predicates have to be satisfied to reach a portion of the method. For this reason, search-based techniques have so far achieved more success at the system level than the unit level.

9.4 BIBLIOGRAPHIC NOTES

An excellent, if slightly dated, place to start on software for safety critical systems is Leveson's book [207]. Butler and Finelli wrote a great article on the futility of assuring ultra high confidence levels in software via *any* means, including testing [59]. Heimdahl [155] presents a good state-of-the-art perspective on the challenges of safety in software intensive systems. McGraw [233] is a good current source for the many issues to consider in building secure software. For a somewhat older treatment, readers might wish to try Rubin [306]. Denning's book [103] is a classic, although it is out of print and hence harder to obtain.

Casting the testability problem in terms of controllability and observability comes originally from hardware testing; Friedman [129] and Binder [34] adapted it to software testing. Voas [333] developed the three part sensitivity model described in this chapter. Applying the testability model in conduction with random testing yields an interesting verification argument [334].

Other criteria that we chose to omit are cataloged in a recent book by Pezze and Young [289]. Other references can be found in the research papers cited in previous chapters.

A good start for how the Web changes the way software is viewed is a book by Powell [292]. Several authors have commented on the inadequacies of subsumption for practical use [149, 340, 344]. We know of four papers that compared data flow with mutation testing [125, 230, 267, 274]. Lots of other papers have appeared that empirically compared other test criteria [25, 49, 81, 123, 124, 135, 258, 302, 304, 311, 327].

Random automatic test data generation approaches date back to the mid-1970s [36, 176, 218, 243]. Older specification-based test data generation approaches use formal specifications [23, 76]; more recent approaches use model-based languages such as the UML [2, 46, 70]. Grammar-based test data generation approaches appeared more than 35 years ago and are currently being revived for XML-based software such as web services [150, 231, 248, 280]. Several researchers investigated how to use program analysis techniques for automatic test data generation [39, 80, 101, 102, 174, 190, 191, 267, 295, 342]. The use of search-based techniques, primarily genetic algorithms started with informally acquiring knowledge about tests [351] and has been refined since then [179, 234, 242].

List of Criteria

Criterion Name	Acronym	Page Defined
Chapter 4		
All Combinations Coverage	ACoC	160
Each Choice Coverage	ECC	160
Pair-Wise Coverage	PWC	161
T-wise Coverage	TWC	161
Base Choice Coverage	BCC	162
Multiple Base Choice Coverage	MBCC	162
Chapter 5		
Terminal Symbol Coverage	TSC	172
Production Coverage	PDC	172
Derivation Coverage	DC	172
Mutation Coverage	MC	175
Mutation Operator Coverage	MOC	175
Mutation Production Coverage	MPC	175
Strong Mutation Coverage	SMC	178
Weak Mutation Coverage	WMC	179

Bibliography

[1]   W3C #28. Extensible markup language (XML) 1.0 (second edition) – W3C recommendation, October 2000. http://www.w3.org/XML/#9802xml10.

[2]   Aynur Abdurazik and Jeff Offutt. Using UML collaboration diagrams for static checking and test generation. In *Third International Conference on the Unified Modeling Language (UML '00)*, pages 383–395, York, England, October 2000.

[3]   Aynur Abdurazik and Jeff Offutt. Coupling-based class integration and test order. In *Workshop on Automation of Software Test (AST 2006)*, pages 50–56, Shanghai, China, May 2006.

[4]   Alan T. Acree. *On Mutation*. PhD thesis, Georgia Institute of Technology, Atlanta, GA, 1980.

[5]   Alan T. Acree, Tim A. Budd, Richard A. DeMillo, Richard J. Lipton, and Fred G. Sayward. Mutation analysis. Technical report GIT-ICS-79/08, School of Information and Computer Science, Georgia Institute of Technology, Atlanta, GA, September 1979.

[6]   S. B. Akers. On a theory of boolean functions. *Journal Society Industrial Applied Mathematics*, 7(4):487–498, December 1959.

[7]   Roger T. Alexander. *Testing the Polymorphic Relationships of Object-oriented Programs*. PhD thesis, George Mason University, Fairfax, VA, 2001. Technical report ISE-TR-01-04, http://www.ise.gmu.edu/techrep/.

[8]   Roger T. Alexander, James M. Bieman, Sudipto Chosh, and Bixia Ji. Mutation of Java objects. In *13th International Symposium on Software Reliability Engineering*, pages 341–351, Annapolis, MD, November 2002. IEEE Computer Society Press.

[9]   Roger T. Alexander, James M. Bieman, and John Viega. Coping with Java programming stress. *IEEE Computer*, 33(4):30–38, 2000.

[10] Roger T. Alexander and Jeff Offutt. Analysis techniques for testing polymorphic relationships. In *Thirtieth International Conference on Technology of Object-Oriented Languages and Systems (TOOLS USA '99)*, pages 104–114, Santa Barbara, CA, August 1999.

[11] Roger T. Alexander and Jeff Offutt. Criteria for testing polymorphic relationships. In *11th International Symposium on Software Reliability Engineering*, pages 15–23, San Jose, CA, October 2000. IEEE Computer Society Press.

[12] Roger T. Alexander and Jeff Offutt. Coupling-based testing of O-O programs. *Journal of Universal Computer Science*, 10(4):391–427, April 2004. http://www.jucs.org/jucs_10_4/coupling_based_testing_of.

[13] F. E. Allen and J. Cocke. A program data flow analysis procedure. *Communications of the ACM*, 19(3):137–146, March 1976.

[14] Paul Ammann and Paul Black. A specification-based coverage metric to evaluate tests. In *4th IEEE International Symposium on High-Assurance Systems Engineering*, pages 239–248, Washington, DC, November 1999.

[15] Paul Ammann, Paul Black, and W. Majurski. Using model checking to generate tests from specifications. In *2nd International Conference on Formal Engineering Methods*, pages 46–54, Brisbane, Australia, December 1998.

[16] Paul Ammann and Jeff Offutt. Using formal methods to derive test frames in category-partition testing. In *Ninth Annual Conference on Computer Assurance (COMPASS 94)*, pages 69–80, Gaithersburg MD, June 1994. IEEE Computer Society Press.

[17] Paul Ammann, Jeff Offutt, and Hong Huang. Coverage criteria for logical expressions. In *14th International Symposium on Software Reliability Engineering*, pages 99–107, Denver, CO, November 2003. IEEE Computer Society Press.

[18] Paul E. Ammann and John C. Knight. Data diversity: An approach to software fault tolerance. *IEEE Transactions on Computers*, 37(4):418–425, April 1988.

[19] D. M. St. Andre. Pilot mutation system (PIMS) user's manual. Technical report GIT-ICS-79/04, Georgia Institute of Technology, April 1979.

[20] Jo M. Atlee. Native model-checking of SCR requirements. In *Fourth International SCR Workshop*, November 1994.

[21] Jo M. Atlee and John Gannon. State-based model checking of event-driven system requirements. *IEEE Transactions on Software Engineering*, 19(1):24–40, January 1993.

[22] Algirdas Avizienis. The n-version approach to fault-tolerant software. *IEEE Transactions on Software Engineering*, SE-11(12):1491–1501, December 1985.

[23] M. Balcer, W. Hasling, and T. Ostrand. Automatic generation of test scripts from formal test specifications. In *Third Symposium on Software Testing, Analysis, and Verification*, pages 210–218, Key West Florida, December 1989. ACM SIGSOFT 89.

[24] Stephane Barbey and Alfred Strohmeier. The problematics of testing object-oriented software. In *SQM'94 Second Conference on Software Quality Management*, volume 2, pages 411–426, Edinburgh, Scotland, UK, 1994.

[25] Vic R. Basili and Richard W. Selby. Comparing the effectiveness of software testing strategies. *IEEE Transactions on Software Engineering*, 13(12):1278–1296, December 1987.

[26] J. A. Bauer and A. B. Finger. Test plan generation using formal grammars. In *Fourth International Conference on Software Engineering*, pages 425–432, Munich, September 1979.

[27]   Erich Beck and Kent Gamma. JUnit: A cook's tour. *Java Report*, 4(5):27–38, May 1999.

[28]   Boris Beizer. *Software System Testing and Quality Assurance*. Van Nostrand, New York, 1984.

[29]   Boris Beizer. *Software Testing Techniques*. Van Nostrand Reinhold, New York, 2nd edition, 1990. ISBN 0-442-20672-0.

[30]   Michael Benedikt, Juliana Freire, and Patrice Godefroid. VeriWeb: Automatically testing dynamic Web sites. In *11th International World Wide Web Conference (WWW'2002) – Alternate Paper Tracks (WE-3 Web Testing and Maintenance)*, pages 654–668, Honolulu, HI, May 2002.

[31]   Edward V. Berard. *Essays on Object-Oriented Software Engineering*, volume 1. Prentice Hall, New York, 1993.

[32]   Philip J. Bernhard. A reduced test suite for protocol conformance testing. *ACM Transactions on Software Engineering and Methodology*, 3(3):201–220, July 1994.

[33]   Robert Binder. *Testing Object-oriented Systems*. Addison-Wesley, New York, 2000.

[34]   Robert V. Binder. Design for testability in object-oriented systems. *Communications of the ACM*, 37(9):87–101, September 1994.

[35]   Robert V. Binder. Testing object-oriented software: A survey. *Software Testing, Verification and Reliability*, 6(3/4):125–252, 1996.

[36]   D. L. Bird and C. U. Munoz. Automatic generation of random self-checking test cases. *IBM Systems Journal*, 22(3):229–345, 1983.

[37]   Paul Black, Vladim Okun, and Y. Yesha. Mutation operators for specifications. In *Fifteenth IEEE International Conference on Automated Software Engineering*, pages 81–88, September 2000.

[38]   Manuel Blum and Sampath Kannan. Designing programs that check their work. In *Twenty-First ACM Symposium on the Theory of Computing*, pages 86–97, 1989.

[39]   Juris Borzovs, Audris Kalniņš, and Inga Medvedis. Automatic construction of test sets: Practical approach. In *Lecture Notes in Computer Science, Vol. 502*, pages 360–432. Springer Verlag, 1991.

[40]   John H. Bowser. Reference manual for Ada mutant operators. Technical report GIT-SERC-88/02, Georgia Institute of Technology, February 1988.

[41]   R. S. Boyer, B. Elpas, and K. N. Levitt. Select – a formal system for testing and debugging programs by symbolic execution. In *International Conference on Reliable Software*, June 1975. SIGPLAN Notices, vol. 10, no. 6.

[42]   V. Braberman, M. Felder, and M. Marré. Testing timing behavior of real-time software. In *International Software Quality Week*, 1997.

[43]   T. Bray, J. Paoli, and C. M. Sperberg-McQueen. Extensible markup language (XML) 1.0. W3C recommendation, February 1998. http://www.w3.org/TR/REC-xml/.

[44]   Lionel Briand, J. Feng, and Yvan Labiche. Using genetic algorithms and coupling measures to devise optimal integration test orders. In *14th International Conference on Software Engineering and Knowledge Engineering*, pages 43–50, Ischia, Italy, 2002. IEEE Computer Society Press.

[45] Lionel Briand and Yvan Labiche. A UML-based approach to system testing. In *Fourth International Conference on the Unified Modeling Language (UML '01)*, pages 194–208, Toronto, Canada, October 2001.

[46] Lionel Briand and Yvan Labiche. A UML-based approach to system testing. *Software and Systems Modeling*, 1(1):10–42, 2002.

[47] Lionel Briand, Yvan Labiche, and Yihong Wang. Revisiting strategies for ordering class integration testing in the presence of dependency cycles. Technical report sce-01-02, Careleton University, 2001.

[48] Lionel Briand, Yvan Labiche, and Yihong Wang. An investigation of graph-based class integration test order strategies. *IEEE Transactions on Software Engineering*, 29(7):594–607, July 2003.

[49] Lionel Briand, Massimiliano Di Penta, and Y. Labiche. Assessing and improving state-based class testing: A series of experiments. *IEEE Transactions on Software Engineering*, 30(11):770–793, November 2004.

[50] R. Brownlie, J. Prowse, and M. S. Phadke. Robust testing of AT&T PMX/StarMAIL using OATS. *AT&T Technical Journal*, 71(3):41–47, May/June 1992.

[51] Tim Budd and Dana Angluin. Two notions of correctness and their relation to testing. *Acta Informatica*, 18(1):31–45, November 1982.

[52] Tim Budd and Fred Sayward. Users guide to the Pilot mutation system. Technical report 114, Department of Computer Science, Yale University, 1977.

[53] Tim A. Budd. *Mutation Analysis of Program Test Data*. PhD thesis, Yale University, New Haven, CT, 1980.

[54] Tim A. Budd, Richard A. DeMillo, Richard J. Lipton, and Fred G. Sayward. The design of a prototype mutation system for program testing. In *NCC, AFIPS Conference Record*, pages 623–627, 1978.

[55] Tim A. Budd and Richard J. Lipton. Proving Lisp programs using test data. In *Digest for the Workshop on Software Testing and Test Documentation*, pages 374–403, Ft. Lauderdale, FL, December 1978. IEEE Computer Society Press.

[56] Tim A. Budd, Richard J. Lipton, Richard A. DeMillo, and Fred G. Sayward. Mutation analysis. Technical report GIT-ICS-79/08, School of Information and Computer Science, Georgia Institute of Technology, Atlanta GA, April 1979.

[57] K. Burr and W. Young. Combinatorial test techniques: Table-based automation, test generation and code coverage. In *International Conference on Software Testing, Analysis, and Review (STAR'98)*, San Diego, CA, October 1998.

[58] K. Burroughs, A. Jain, and R. L. Erickson. Improved quality of protocol testing through techniques of experimental design. In *IEEE International Conference on Communications (Supercomm/ICC'94)*, pages 745–752, New Orleans, LA, May 1994. IEEE Computer Society Press.

[59] Ricky W. Butler and George B. Finelli. The infeasibility of quantifying the reliability of life-critical real-time software. *Software Engineering*, 19(1):3–12, 1993.

[60] Ugo Buy, Alessandro Orso, and Mauro Pezze. Automated testing of classes. In *2000 International Symposium on Software Testing, and Analysis (ISSTA '00)*, pages 39–48, Portland, OR, August 2000. IEEE Computer Society Press.

[61] R. Cardell-Oliver and T. Glover. A practical and complete algorithm for testing real-time systems. *Lecture Notes in Computer Science*, 1486:251–261, 1998.

[62] T. E. Cheatham, G. H. Holloway, and J. A. Townley. Symbolic evaluation and the analysis of programs. *IEEE Transactions on Software Engineering*, 5(4), July 1979.

[63] T. Y. Chen and M. F. Lau. Test case selection strategies based on boolean specifications. *Software Testing, Verification, and Reliability*, 11(3):165–180, June 2001.

[64] T. Y. Chen, P. L. Poon, S. F. Tang, and T. H. Tse. On the identification of categories and choices for specification-based test case generation. *Information and Software Technology*, 46(13):887–898, 2004.

[65] T. Y. Chen, S. F. Tang, P. L. Poon, and T. H. Tse. Identification of categories and choices in activity diagrams. In *Fifth International Conference on Quality Software (QSIC 2005)*, pages 55–63, Melbourne, Australia, September 2005. IEEE Computer Society Press.

[66] J. C. Cherniavsky. On finding test data sets for loop free programs. *Information Processing Letters*, 8(2):106–107, February 1979.

[67] J. C. Cherniavsky and C. H. Smith. A theory of program testing with applications. *Workshop on Software Testing*, pages 110–121, July 1986.

[68] Shing Chi Cheung, Samuel T. Chanson, and Zhendong Xu. Toward generic timing tests for distributed multimedia software systems. In *12th International Symposium on Software Reliability Engineering (ISSRE'01)*, page 210, Washington, DC, 2001. IEEE Computer Society Press.

[69] Philippe Chevalley. Applying mutation analysis for object-oriented programs using a reflective approach. In *8th Asia-Pacific Software Engineering Conference (APSEC 2001)*, Macau SAR, China, December 2001.

[70] Philippe Chevalley and Pascale Thévenod-Fosse. Automated generation of statistical test cases from UML state diagrams. In *Proc. of IEEE 25th Annual International Computer Software and Applications Conference (COMPSAC2001)*, Chicago, IL, October 2001.

[71] Philippe Chevalley and Pascale Thévenod-Fosse. A mutation analysis tool for Java programs. *Journal on Software Tools for Technology Transfer (STTT)*, September 2002.

[72] John J. Chilenski. Personal communication, March 2003.

[73] John J. Chilenski and Steven P. Miller. Applicability of modified condition/decision coverage to software testing. *Software Engineering Journal*, 9(5):193–200, September 1994.

[74] John J. Chilenski and L. A. Richey. Definition for a masking form of modified condition decision coverage (MCDC). Technical report, Boeing, Seattle, WA, 1997.

[75] Byoung-Ju Choi and Aditya Mathur. High-performance mutation testing. *Journal of Systems and Software*, 20(2):135–152, February 1993.

[76] N. Choquet. Test data generation using a prolog with constraints. In *Workshop on Software Testing*, pages 51–60, Banff, Alberta, July 1986. IEEE Computer Society Press.

[77] T. Chow. Testing software designs modeled by finite-state machines. *IEEE Transactions on Software Engineering*, SE-4(3):178–187, May 1978.

[78] D. Clarke and I. Lee. Automatic generation of tests for timing constraints from requirements. In *Third International Workshop on Object-Oriented Real-Time Dependable Systems*, Newport Beach, CA, February 1997.

[79] James M. Clarke. Automated test generation from a behavioral model. In *Software Quality Week Conference*, Brussels, Belgium, May 1998.

[80] Lori Clarke. A system to generate test data and symbolically execute programs. *IEEE Transactions on Software Engineering*, 2(3):215–222, September 1976.

[81] Lori Clarke, Andy Podgurski, Debra Richardson, and Steven Zeil. A comparison of data flow path selection criteria. In *Eighth International Conference on Software Engineering*, pages 244–251, London, UK, August 1985. IEEE Computer Society Press.

[82] Lori Clarke, Andy Podgurski, Debra Richardson, and Steven Zeil. A formal evaluation of data flow path selection criteria. *IEEE Transactions on Software Engineering*, 15:1318–1332, November 1989.

[83] Lori Clarke and Debra Richardson. Applications of symbolic evaluation. *Journal of Systems and Software*, 5(1):15–35, January 1985.

[84] David M. Cohen, Siddhartha R. Dalal, Michael L. Fredman, and Gardner C. Patton. The AETG system: An approach to testing based on combinatorial design. *IEEE Transactions on Software Engineering*, 23(7):437–444, July 1997.

[85] David M. Cohen, Siddhartha R. Dalal, A. Kajla, and Gardner C. Patton. The automatic efficient test generator (AETG) system. In *Fifth International Symposium on Software Reliability Engineering (ISSRE'94)*, pages 303–309, Los Alamitos, CA, November 1994. IEEE Computer Society Press.

[86] David M. Cohen, Siddhartha R. Dalal, Jesse Parelius, and Gardner C. Patton. The combinatorial design approach to automatic test generation. *IEEE Software*, pages 83–88, September 1996.

[87] M. B. Cohen, P. B. Gibbons, W. B. Mugridge, and C. J. Colburn. Constructing test cases for interaction testing. In *25th International Conference on Software Engineering, (ICSE'03)*, pages 38–48. IEEE Computer Society, May 2003.

[88] L. L. Constantine and E. Yourdon. *Structured Design*. Prentice-Hall, Englewood Cliffs, NJ, 1979.

[89] Alan Cooper. *About Face: The Essentials of User Interface Design*. Hungry Minds, New York, 1995.

[90] Lee Copeland. *A Practitioner's Guide to Software Test Design*. Artech House Publishers, Norwood, MA, 2003.

[91] S. R. Dalal, A. Jain, N. Karunanithi, J. M. Leaton, and C. M. Lott. Model-based testing of a highly programmable system. In *9th International Symposium in Software Engineering (ISSRE'98)*, pages 174–178, Paderborn, Germany, November 1998. IEEE Computer Society Press.

[92] S. R. Dalal, A. Jain, N. Karunanithi, J. M. Leaton, C. M. Lott, G. C. Patton, and B. M. Horowitz. Model-based testing in practice. In *21st International Conference on Software Engineering (ICSE'99)*, pages 285–294, Los Angeles, CA, May 1999. ACM Press.

[93] J. A. Darringer and J. C. King. Applications of symbolic execution to program testing. *IEEE Computer*, 11(4), April 1978.

[94]   Márcio Delamaro, José C. Maldonado, and Aditya P. Mathur. Interface muta-
        tion: An approach for integration testing. *IEEE Transactions on Software Engi-
        neering*, 27(3):228–247, March 2001.

[95]   Márcio E. Delamaro and José C. Maldonado. Proteum – A tool for the assess-
        ment of test adequacy for C programs. In *Conference on Performability in Com-
        puting Systems (PCS 96)*, pages 79–95, New Brunswick, NJ, July 1996.

[96]   Richard A. DeMillo, Dana S. Guindi, Kim N. King, W. Michael McCracken,
        and Jeff Offutt. An extended overview of the Mothra software testing en-
        vironment. In *Second Workshop on Software Testing, Verification, and Anal-
        ysis*, pages 142–151, Banff, Alberta, July 1988. IEEE Computer Society
        Press.

[97]   Richard A. DeMillo, Edward Krauser, and Aditya P. Mathur. Compiler-
        integrated program mutation. In *Fifteenth Annual Computer Software and Appli-
        cations Conference (COMPSAC '92)*, Tokyo, Japan, September 1991. Kogakuin
        University, IEEE Computer Society Press.

[98]   Richard A. DeMillo, Richard J. Lipton, and Alan J. Perlis. Social processes and
        proofs of theorems and programs. *Communications of the ACM*, 22(5), May
        1979.

[99]   Richard A. DeMillo, Richard J. Lipton, and Fred G. Sayward. Hints on test data
        selection: Help for the practicing programmer. *IEEE Computer*, 11(4):34–41,
        April 1978.

[100]   Richard A. DeMillo, W. Michael McCracken, Rhonda J. Martin, and John F.
        Passafiume. *Software Testing and Evaluation*. Benjamin/Cummings, Menlo Park,
        CA, 1987.

[101]   Richard A. DeMillo and Jeff Offutt. Constraint-based automatic test data gen-
        eration. *IEEE Transactions on Software Engineering*, 17(9):900–910, September
        1991.

[102]   Richard A. DeMillo and Jeff Offutt. Experimental results from an automatic
        test case generator. *ACM Transactions on Software Engineering Methodology*,
        2(2):109–127, April 1993.

[103]   Dorothy Denning. *Cryptography and Data Security*. Addison Wesley, New York,
        1982.

[104]   M. S. Deutsch. *Software Verification and Validation Realistic Project Approaches*.
        Prentice-Hall, Englewood Cliffs, NJ, 1982.

[105]   R. K. Doong and Phyllis G. Frankl. Case studies on testing object-oriented pro-
        grams. In *Fourth Symposium on Software Testing, Analysis, and Verification*,
        pages 165–177, Victoria, British Columbia, Canada, October 1991. IEEE Com-
        puter Society Press.

[106]   Mehmet Şahinoğlu and Eugene H. Spafford. A Bayes sequential statistical
        procedure for approving software products. In Wolfgang Ehrenberger, editor,
        The IFIP Conference on Approving Software Products (ASP–90), pages 43–56,
        Garmisch-Partenkirchen, Germany, September 1990. Elsevier/North Holland,
        New York.

[107]   A. G. Duncan and J. S. Hutchison. Using attributed grammars to test designs
        and implementations. In *Fifth International Conference on Software Engineering*,
        pages 170–178, San Diego, CA, March 1981.

[108]   Arnaud Dupuy and Nancy Leveson. An empirical evaluation of the MC/DC coverage criterion on the HETE-2 satellite software. In *Digital Aviations Systems Conference (DASC)*, October 2000.

[109]   Elfriede Dustin, Jeff Rashka, and John Paul. *Automated Software Testing: Introduction, Management, and Performance*. Addison-Wesley Professional, New York, 1999.

[110]   Dave E. Eckhardt Jr. and Larry D. Lee. Fundamental differences in the reliability of n-modular redundancy and n-version programming. *Journal of Systems and Software*, 8(4):313–318, September 1988.

[111]   Alan Edelman. The mathematics of the Pentium division bug. *SIAM Review*, 39:54–67, March 1997. http://www.siam.org/journals/sirev/39-1/29395.html.

[112]   Sebastian Elbaum, Srikanth Karre, and Gregg Rothermel. Improving Web application testing with user session data. In *25th International Conference on Software Engineering*, pages 49–59, Portland, OR, May 2003. IEEE Computer Society Press.

[113]   Sebastian Elbaum, Gregg Rothermel, Srikanth Karre, and Marc Fisher. Leveraging user-session data to support web application testing. *IEEE Transactions on Software Engineering*, 31(3):187–202, March 2005.

[114]   R. En-Nouaary, Khendek F. Dssouli, and A. Elqortobi. Timed test case generation based on a state characterization technique. In *Proceeding of the 19th IEEE Real-Time Systems Symposium (RTSS98)*, Madrid, Spain, December 1998.

[115]   Sadik Esmelioglu and Larry Apfelbaum. Automated test generation, execution, and reporting. In *Pacific Northwest Software Quality Conference*. IEEE Press, October 1997.

[116]   R. E. Fairley. An experimental program testing facility. *IEEE Transactions on Software Engineering*, SE-1:350–3571, December 1975.

[117]   Roger Ferguson and Bogdan Korel. The chaining approach for software test data generation. *ACM Transactions on Software Engineering Methodology*, 5(1):63–86, January 1996.

[118]   S. P. Fiedler. Object-oriented unit testing. *Hewlett-Packard Journal*, 40(2):69–74, April 1989.

[119]   Donald G. Firesmith. Testing object-oriented software. In *Testing Object-Oriented Languages and Systems (TOOLS)*, March 1993.

[120]   Vladimir N. Fleyshgakker and Stewart N. Weiss. Efficient mutation analysis: A new approach. In *International Symposium on Software Testing and Analysis (ISSTA 94)*, pages 185–195, Seattle, WA, August 17–19 1994. ACM SIGSOFT, ACM Press.

[121]   I. R. Forman. An algebra for data flow anomaly detection. In *Seventh International Conference on Software Engineering*, pages 278–286. Orlando, FL, March 1984. IEEE Computer Society Press.

[122]   L. D. Fosdick and L. J. Osterweil. Data flow analysis in software reliability. *ACM Computing Surveys*, 8(3):305–330, September 1976.

[123]   Phyllis G. Frankl and Yuetang Deng. Comparison of delivered reliability of branch, data flow and operational testing: A case study. In *2000 International Symposium on Software Testing, and Analysis (ISSTA '00)*, pages 124–134, Portland, OR, August 2000. IEEE Computer Society Press.

[124] Phyllis G. Frankl and Stewart N. Weiss. An experimental comparison of the effectiveness of branch testing and data flow testing. *IEEE Transactions on Software Engineering*, 19(8):774–787, August 1993.

[125] Phyllis G. Frankl, Stewart N. Weiss, and C. Hu. All-uses versus mutation testing: An experimental comparison of effectiveness. *Journal of Systems and Software*, 38(3):235–253, 1997.

[126] Phyllis G. Frankl, Stewart N. Weiss, and Elaine J. Weyuker. ASSET: A system to select and evaluate tests. In *Conference on Software Tools*, New York, April 1985. IEEE Computer Society Press.

[127] Phyllis G. Frankl and Elaine J. Weyuker. Data flow testing in the presence of unexecutable paths. In *Workshop on Software Testing*, pages 4–13, Banff, Alberta, July 1986. IEEE Computer Society Press.

[128] Phyllis G. Frankl and Elaine J. Weyuker. An applicable family of data flow testing criteria. *IEEE Transactions on Software Engineering*, 14(10):1483–1498, October 1988.

[129] Roy S. Freedman. Testability of software components. *IEEE Transactions on Software Engineering*, 17(6):553–564, June 1991.

[130] S. Fujiwara, G. Bochman, F. Khendek, M. Amalou, and A. Ghedasmi. Test selection based on finite state models. *IEEE Transactions on Software Engineering*, 17(6):591–603, June 1991.

[131] J. Gait. A probe effect in concurrent programs. *Software – Practice and Experience*, 16(3):225–233, March 1986.

[132] Leonard Gallagher, Jeff Offutt, and Tony Cincotta. Integration testing of object-oriented components using finite state machines. *Software Testing, Verification, and Reliability*, 17(1):215–266, January 2007.

[133] Robert Geist, Jeff Offutt, and Fred Harris. Estimation and enhancement of real-time software reliability through mutation analysis. *IEEE Transactions on Computers*, 41(5):550–558, May 1992. Special issue on Fault-Tolerant Computing.

[134] M. R. Girgis and M. R. Woodward. An integrated system for program testing using weak mutation and data flow analysis. In *Eighth International Conference on Software Engineering*, pages 313–319, London, UK, August 1985. IEEE Computer Society Press.

[135] M. R. Girgis and M. R. Woodward. An experimental comparison of the error exposing ability of program testing criteria. In *Workshop on Software Testing*, pages 64–73. Banff, Canada, July 1986. IEEE Computer Society Press.

[136] A. Goldberg, T. C. Wang, and D. Zimmerman. Applications of feasible path analysis to program testing. In *1994 International Symposium on Software Testing, and Analysis*, pages 80–94, Seattle, WA, August 1994.

[137] G. Gonenc. A method for the design of fault-detection experiments. *IEEE Transactions on Computers*, C-19:155–558, June 1970.

[138] J. B. Goodenough and S. L. Gerhart. Toward a theory of test data selection. *IEEE Transactions on Software Engineering*, 1(2), June 1975.

[139] J. S. Gourlay. A mathematical framework for the investigation of testing. *IEEE Transactions on Software Engineering*, 9(6):686–709, November 1983.

[140] Mats Grindal. *Evaluation of Combination Strategies for Practical Testing*. PhD thesis, Skövde University / Linköping University, Skövde Sweden, 2007.

[141]   Mats Grindal, Birgitta Lindström, Jeff Offutt, and Sten F. Andler. An evaluation of combination testing strategies. *Empirical Software Engineering*, 11(4):583–611, December 2006.

[142]   Mats Grindal and Jeff Offutt. Input parameter modeling for combination strategies. In *IASTED International Conference on Software Engineering (SE 2007)*, Innsbruck, Austria, February 2007. ACTA Press.

[143]   Mats Grindal, Jeff Offutt, and Sten F. Andler. Combination testing strategies: A survey. *Software Testing, Verification, and Reliability*, 15(2):97–133, September 2005.

[144]   Mats Grindal, Jeff Offutt, and Jonas Mellin. Conflict management when using combination strategies for software testing. In *Australian Software Engineering Conference (ASWEC 2007)*, pages 255–264, Melbourne, Australia, April 2007.

[145]   Matthias Grochtmann and Klaus Grimm. Classification trees for partition testing. *Software Testing, Verification, and Reliability*, 3(2):63–82, 1993.

[146]   Matthias Grochtmann, Klaus Grimm, and J. Wegener. Tool-supported test case design for black-box testing by means of the classification-tree editor. In *1st European International Conference on Software Testing Analysis & Review (EuroSTAR 1993)*, pages 169–176, London, UK, October 1993.

[147]   Richard Hamlet. Reliability theory of program testing. *Acta Informatica*, pages 31–43, 1981.

[148]   Richard G. Hamlet. Testing programs with the aid of a compiler. *IEEE Transactions on Software Engineering*, 3(4):279–290, July 1977.

[149]   Richard G. Hamlet and Richard Taylor. Partition testing does not inspire confidence. *IEEE Transactions on Software Engineering*, 16(12):1402–1411, December 1990.

[150]   K. V. Hanford. Automatic generation of test cases. *IBM Systems Journal*, 4:242–257, 1970.

[151]   Jim M. Hanks. Testing cobol programs by mutation: Volume I – Introduction to the CMS.1 system, Volume II – CMS.1 system documentation. Technical report GIT-ICS-80/04, Georgia Institute of Technology, February 1980.

[152]   Mary Jean Harrold and Gregg Rothermel. Performing data flow testing on classes. In *Symposium on Foundations of Software Engineering*, pages 154–163, New Orleans, LA, December 1994. ACM SIGSOFT.

[153]   Mary Jean Harrold and Gregg Rothermel. Empirical studies of a safe regression test selection technque. *IEEE Transactions on Software Engineering*, 24(6):401–419, June 1998.

[154]   Mary Jean Harrold and Mary Lou Soffa. Selecting and using data for integration testing. *IEEE Software*, 8(2):58–65, March 1991.

[155]   Mats E. Heimdahl. Safety and software intensive systems: Challenges old and new. In *International Conference on Software Engineering: Future of Software Engineering*, pages 137–152, May 2007.

[156]   E. Heller. Using design of experiment structures to generate software test cases. In *12th International Conference on Testing Computer Software*, pages 33–41, New York, 1995. ACM.

[157] K. Henninger. Specifiying software requirements for complex systems: New techniques and their applications. *IEEE Transactions on Software Engineering*, SE-6(1):2–12, January 1980.

[158] P. Herman. A data flow analysis approach to program testing. *Australian Computer Journal*, 8(3):92–96, November 1976.

[159] A. Hessel, K. Larsen, B. Nielsen, and A Skou. Time optimal real-time test case generation using UPPAAL. In *Workshop on Formal Approaches to Testing of Software (FATES)*, Montreal, October 2003.

[160] Bill Hetzel. *The Complete Guide to Software Testing*. Wiley-QED, second edition, 1988.

[161] J. Robert Horgan and Saul London. Data flow coverage and the C language. In *Fourth Symposium on Software Testing, Analysis, and Verification*, pages 87–97, Victoria, British Columbia, Canada, October 1991. IEEE Computer Society Press.

[162] J. Robert Horgan and Saul London. ATAC: A data flow coverage testing tool for C. In *Symposium of Quality Software Development Tools*, pages 2–10, New Orleans, LA, May 1992. IEEE Computer Society Press.

[163] J. Robert Horgan and Aditya P. Mathur. Weak mutation is probably strong mutation. Technical report SERC-TR-83-P, Software Engineering Research Center, Purdue University, West Lafayette, IN, December 1990.

[164] Willam E. Howden. Methodology for the generation of program test data. *IEEE Transactions on Software Engineering*, SE-24, May 1975.

[165] Willam E. Howden. Reliability of the path analysis testing strategy. *IEEE Transactions on Software Engineering*, 2(3):208–215, September 1976.

[166] Willam E. Howden. Symbolic testing and the DISSECT symbolic evaluation system. *IEEE Transactions on Software Engineering*, 3(4), July 1977.

[167] Willam E. Howden. Weak mutation testing and completeness of test sets. *IEEE Transactions on Software Engineering*, 8(4):371–379, July 1982.

[168] Willam E. Howden. The theory and practice of function testing. *IEEE Software*, 2(5), September 1985.

[169] William E. Howden. *Functional Program Testing and Analysis*. McGraw-Hill, New York, 1987.

[170] J. C. Huang. An approach to program testing. *ACM Computing Surveys*, 7(3):113–128, September 1975.

[171] J, Huller. Reducing time to market with combinatorial design method testing. In *10th Annual International Council on Systems Engineering (INCOSE'00)*, Minneapolis, MN, July 2000.

[172] M. Hutchins, H. Foster, T. Goradia, and T. Ostrand. Experiments on the effectiveness of dataflow- and controlflow-based test adequacy criteria. In *Sixteenth International Conference on Software Engineering*, pages 191–200, Sorrento, Italy, May 1994. IEEE Computer Society Press.

[173] Michael Huth and Mark D. Ryan. *Logic in Computer Science: Modelling and Reasoning About Systems*. Cambridge University Press, Cambridge, UK, 2000.

[174]   G. Hwang, K. Tai, and T. Hunag. Reachability testing: An approach to testing concurrent software. *International Journal of Software Engineering and Knowledge Engineering*, 5(4), December 1995.

[175]   IEEE. *IEEE Standard Glossary of Software Engineering Terminology*. ANSI/ IEEE Std 610.12-1990, 1996.

[176]   D. C. Ince. The automatic generation of test data. *Computer Journal*, 30(1):63–69, 1987.

[177]   R. Jasper, M. Brennan, K. Williamson, B. Currier, and D. Zimmerman. Test data generation and feasible path analysis. In *1994 International Symposium on Software Testing, and Analysis*, pages 95–107, Seattle, WA, August 1994.

[178]   Zhenyi Jin and Jeff Offutt. Coupling-based criteria for integration testing. *Software Testing, Verification, and Reliability*, 8(3):133–154, September 1998.

[179]   B. F. Jones, D. E. Eyres, and H. H. Sthamer. A strategy for using genetic algorithms to automate branch and fault-based testing. *Computer Journal*, 41(2):98–107, 1998.

[180]   J. A. Jones and Mary Jean Harrold. Test-suite reduction and prioritizaion for modified condition/decision coverage. *IEEE Transactions on Software Engineering*, 29(3):195–209, March 2003.

[181]   Paul C. Jorgensen and Carl Erickson. Object-oriented integration testing. *Communications of the ACM*, 37(9):30–38, 1994.

[182]   Cem Kaner, Jack Falk, and Hung Q. Nguyen. *Testing Computer Software*. John Wiley and Sons, New York NY, second edition, 1999.

[183]   David J. Kasik and Harry G. George. Toward automatic generation of novice user test scripts. In *Conference on Human Factors in Computing Systems: Common Ground*, pages 244–251, New York, April 1996.

[184]   Sun-Woo Kim, John Clark, and John McDermid. Assessing test set adequacy for object-oriented programs using class mutation. In *of Symposium on Software Technology (SoST'99)*, pages 72–83, September 1999.

[185]   Sunwoo Kim, John A. Clark, and John A. McDermid. Investigating the effectiveness of object-oriented strategies with the mutation method. In *Mutation 2000: Mutation Testing in the Twentieth and the Twenty First Centuries*, pages 4–100, San Jose, CA, October 2000. Special issue of the *Journal of Software Testing, Verification, and Reliability*, December 2001.

[186]   Y. G. Kim, H. S. Hong, S. M. Cho, D. H. Bae, and S. D. Cha. Test cases generation from UML state diagrams. *IEE Proceedings – Software*, 146(4):187–192, August 1999.

[187]   Kim N. King and Jeff Offutt. A Fortran language system for mutation-based software testing. *Software – Practice and Experience*, 21(7):685–718, July 1991.

[188]   John C. Knight and Nancy G. Leveson. An experimental evaluation of the assumption of independence in multiversion programming. *IEEE Transactions on Software Engineering*, SE-12(1):96–109, January 1986.

[189]   Charles Knutson and Sam Carmichael. Safety first: Avoiding software mishaps, November 2000. http://www.embedded.com/2000/0011/0011feat1.htm.

[190]   Bogdan Korel. Automated software test data generation. *IEEE Transactions on Software Engineering*, 16(8):870–879, August 1990.

[191]   Bogdan Korel. Dynamic method for software test data generation. *Software Testing, Verification, and Reliability*, 2(4):203–213, 1992.

[192]   Edward W. Krauser, Aditya P. Mathur, and Vernon Rego. High performance testing on SIMD machines. In *Second Workshop on Software Testing, Verification, and Analysis*, pages 171–177, Banff, Alberta, July 1988. IEEE Computer Society Press.

[193]   M. Krichen and S. Tripakis. Black-box conformance testing for real-time systems. In *The SPIN'04 Workshop on Model-Checking Software*, Barcelona, Spain, 2004.

[194]   D. R. Kuhn. Fault classes and error detection capability of specification-based testing. *ACM Transactions on Software Engineering Methodology*, 8(4):411–424, October 1999.

[195]   D. R. Kuhn and M. J. Reilly. An investigation of the applicability of design of experiments to software testing. In *27th NASA/IEE Software Engineering Workshop*, NASA Goodard Space Flight Center, MD, December 2002. NASA/IEEE.

[196]   D. R. Kuhn, D. R. Wallace, and A. M. Gallo Jr. Software fault interactions and implications for software testing. *IEEE Transactions on Software Engineering*, 30(6):418–421, June 2004.

[197]   D. Kung, J. Gao, Pei Hsia, Y. Toyoshima, and C. Chen. A test strategy for object-oriented programs. In *19th Computer Software and Applications Conference (COMPSAC '95)*, pages 239–244, Dallas, TX, August 1995. IEEE Computer Society Press.

[198]   D. Kung, C. H. Liu, and P. Hsia. An object-oriented Web test model for testing Web applications. In *IEEE 24th Annual International Computer Software and Applications Conference (COMPSAC2000)*, pages 537–542, Taipei, Taiwan, October 2000.

[199]   W. LaLonde and J. Pugh. Subclassing != subtyping != is-a. *Journal of Object Oriented Programming*, 3(5): 57–62, January 1991.

[200]   Janusz Laski. Data flow testing in STAD. *Journal of Systems and Software*, 12:3–14, 1990.

[201]   Janusz Laski and Bogdan Korel. A data flow oriented program testing strategy. *IEEE Transactions on Software Engineering*, 9(3):347–354, May 1983.

[202]   M. F. Lau and Y. T. Yu. An extended fault class hierarchy for specification-based testing. *ACM Transactions on Software Engineering Methodology*, 14(3):247–276, July 2005.

[203]   Suet Chun Lee and Jeff Offutt. Generating test cases for XML-based web component interactions using mutation analysis. In *12th International Symposium on Software Reliability Engineering*, pages 200–209, Hong Kong, China, November 2001. IEEE Computer Society Press.

[204]   H. Legard and M. Marcotty. A generalogy of control structures. *Communications of the ACM*, 18:629–639, November 1975.

[205]   Yu Lei and K. C. Tai. In-parameter-order: A test generation strategy for pairwise testing. In *Third IEEE High Assurance Systems Engineering Symposium*, pages 254–261, November 1998. IEEE Computer Society Press.

[206] Yu Lei and K. C. Tai. A test generation strategy for pairwise testing. Technical Report TR-2001-03, Department of Computer Science, North Carolina State University, Raleigh, 2001.

[207] Nancy G. Leveson. *Safeware: System Safety and Computers*. Addison-Wesley, Reading, MA, 1995.

[208] Zhang Li, Mark Harman, and Rob M. Hierons. Meta-heuristic search algorithms for regression test case prioritization. *IEEE Transactions on Software Engineering*, 33(4):225–237, April 2007.

[209] J. L. Lions. Ariane 5 flight 501 failure: Report by the inquiry board, July 1996. http://sunnyday.mit.edu/accidents/Ariane5accidentreport.html.

[210] Richard Lipton. New directions in testing. In *Distributed Computing and Cryptography, DIMACS Series in Discrete Mathematics and Theoretical Computer Science*, volume 2, pages 191–202, Providence, RI, 1991.

[211] Richard J. Lipton and Fred G. Sayward. The status of research on program mutation. In *Digest for the Workshop on Software Testing and Test Documentation*, pages 355–373, December 1978.

[212] Barbara Liskov and John Guttag. *Program Development in Java: Abstraction, Specification, and Object-Oriented Design*. Addison Wesley, New York, 2001.

[213] Barbara H. Liskov and Jeannette M. Wing. A behavioral notion of subtyping. *ACM Transactions on Programming Languages and Systems*, 16(1):1811–1841, November 1994.

[214] B. Littlewood and D. R. Miller. Conceptual modeling of coincident failures in multiversion software. *IEEE Transactions on Software Engineering*, 15(12):1596–1614, December 1989.

[215] C. H. Liu, D. Kung, P. Hsia, and C. T. Hsu. Structural testing of Web applications. In *11th International Symposium on Software Reliability Engineering*, pages 84–96, San Jose, CA, October 2000. IEEE Computer Society Press.

[216] C. H. Liu, D. C. Kung, P. Hsia, and C. T. Hsu. An object-based data flow testing approach for Web applications. *International Journal of Software Engineering and Knowledge Engineering*, 11(2):157–179, 2001.

[217] Giuseppe A. Di Lucca and Massimiliano Di Penta. Considering browser interaction in web application testing. In *5th International Workshop on Web Site Evolution (WSE 2003)*, pages 74–84, Amsterdam, The Netherlands, September 2003. IEEE Computer Society Press.

[218] Stephen F. Lundstrom. Adaptive random data generation for computer software testing. In *National Computer Conference*, pages 505–511, 1978.

[219] Yu-Seung Ma, Yong-Rae Kwon, and Jeff Offutt. Inter-class mutation operators for Java. In *13th International Symposium on Software Reliability Engineering*, pages 352–363, Annapolis, MD, November 2002. IEEE Computer Society Press.

[220] Yu-Seung Ma, Jeff Offutt, and Yong-Rae Kwon. Mujava : An automated class mutation system. *Software Testing, Verification, and Reliability*, 15(2):97–133, June 2005.

[221] Yu-Seung Ma, Jeff Offutt, and Yong-Rae Kwon. mujava home page. online, 2005. http://ise.gmu.edu/ offutt/mujava/, http://salmosa.kaist.ac.kr/LAB/MuJava/, last access April 2006.

[222] Yashwant K. Malaiya. Antirandom testing: Getting the most out of black-box testing. In *International Symposium on Software Reliability Engineering (IS-SRE'95)*, pages 86–95, Toulouse, France, October 1995.

[223] Brian A. Malloy, Peter J. Clarke, and Errol L. Lloyd. A parameterized cost model to order classes for class-based testing of C++ applications. In *14th International Symposium on Software Reliability Engineering*, Denver, CO, 2003. IEEE Computer Society Press.

[224] Robert Mandl. Orthogonal latin squares: An application of experiment design to compiler testing. *Communications of the ACM*, 28(10):1054–1058, October 1985.

[225] D. Mandrioli, S. Morasca, and A. Morzenti. Generating test cases for real-time systems from logic specifications. *ACM Transactions on Computer Systems*, 4(13):365–398, Nov. 1995.

[226] Brian Marick. The weak mutation hypothesis. In *Fourth Symposium on Software Testing, Analysis, and Verification*, pages 190–199, Victoria, British Columbia, Canada, October 1991. IEEE Computer Society Press.

[227] Brian Marick. *The Craft of Software Testing: Subsystem Testing, Including Object-Based and Object-Oriented Testing*. Prentice-Hall, Englewood Cliffs, New Jersey, 1995.

[228] Aditya P. Mathur. On the relative strengths of data flow and mutation based test adequacy criteria. In *Sixth Annual Pacific Northwest Software Quality Conference*, Portland, OR, Lawrence and Craig, 1991.

[229] Aditya P. Mathur and Edward W. Krauser. Mutant unification for improved vectorization. Technical report SERC-TR-14-P, Software Engineering Research Center, Purdue University, West Lafayette, IN, April 1988.

[230] Aditya P. Mathur and W. Eric Wong. An empirical comparison of data flow and mutation-based test adequacy criteria. *Software Testing, Verification, and Reliability*, 4(1):9–31, March 1994.

[231] P. M. Maurer. Generating test data with enhanced context-free grammars. *IEEE Software*, 7(4):50–55, July 1990.

[232] T. J. McCabe. A complexity measure. *IEEE Transactions on Software Engineering*, 2(4):308–320, December 1976.

[233] Gary McGraw. *Software Security: Building Security In*. Addison-Wesley, New York, 2006.

[234] Phil McMinn. Search-based software test data generation: A survey. *Software Testing, Verification, and Reliability*, 13(2):105–156, June 2004.

[235] Atif M. Memon, Martha E. Pollack, and Mary Lou Soffa. Using a goal-driven approach to generate test cases for GUIs. In *21st International Conference on Software Engineering*, pages 257–266, May 1999.

[236] Atif M. Memon, Martha E. Pollack, and Mary Lou Soffa. Automated test oracles for GUIs. In *ACM SIGSOFT 8th International Symposium on the Foundations of Software Engineering (FSE-8)*, pages 30–39, New York, November 2000.

[237] Atif M. Memon, Martha E. Pollack, and Mary Lou Soffa. Hierarchical GUI test case generation using automated planning. *IEEE Transactions on Software Engineering*, 27(2):144–155, February 2001.

[238] Atif M. Memon and Mary Lou Soffa. Regression testing of GUIs. In *9th European Software Engineering Conference (ESEC) and 11th ACM SIGSOFT International Symposium on the Foundations of Software Engineering (FSE-11)*, pages 118–127, September 2003.

[239] Atif M. Memon, Mary Lou Soffa, and Martha E. Pollack. Coverage criteria for GUI testing. In *8th European Software Engineering Conference (ESEC) and 9th ACM SIGSOFT International Symposium on the Foundations of Software Engineering (FSE-9)*, pages 256–267, September 2001.

[240] Atif M. Memon and Qing Xie. Empirical evaluation of the fault-detection effectiveness of smoke regression test cases for GUI-based software. In *The International Conference on Software Maintenance 2004 (ICSM'04)*, pages 8–17, Washington, DC, September 2004.

[241] Bertrand Meyer. *Object-Oriented Software Construction*. Prentice Hall, Upper Saddle River, NJ, second edition, 1997.

[242] C. C. Michael, G. McGraw, and M. A. Schatz. Generating software test data by evolution. *IEEE Transactions on Software Engineering*, 27(12):1085–1110, December 2001.

[243] E. F. Miller and R. A. Melton. Automated generation of testcase datasets. In *International Conference on Reliable Software*, pages 51–58, April 1975.

[244] Cleve Moler. A tale of two numbers. *SIAM News*, 28(1), January 1995.

[245] S. Morasca and Mauro Pezze. Using high level Petri-nets for testing concurrent and real-time systems. *Real-Time Systems: Theory and Applications*, pages 119–131. Amsterdam, North-Holland, 1990.

[246] Larry J. Morell. *A Theory of Error-Based Testing*. PhD thesis, University of Maryland, College Park, MD, 1984. Technical Report TR-1395.

[247] Larry J. Morell. A theory of fault-based testing. *IEEE Transactions on Software Engineering*, 16(8):844–857, August 1990.

[248] Carlos Urias Munoz. An approach to software product testing. *IEEE Transactions on Software Engineering*, 14(11):1589–1595, November 1988.

[249] Glenford Myers. *The Art of Software Testing*. John Wiley and Sons, New York, 1979.

[250] Adithya Nagarajan and Atif M. Memon. Refactoring using event-based profiling. In *First International Workshop on REFactoring: Achievements, Challenges, Effects (REFACE)*, Victoria, British Columbia, November 2003.

[251] S. Naito and M. Tsunoyama. Fault detection for sequential machines by transition tours. In *Fault Tolerant Computing Systems*, pages 238–243. IEEE Computer Society Press, 1981.

[252] B. Nielsen and A. Skou. Automated test generation from timed automata. In *21st IEEE Real-Time Systems Symposium*, Walt Disney World, Orlando, FL, 2000. IEEE Computer Society Press.

[253] Jacok Nielsen. *Designing Web Usability*. New Riders Publishing, Indianapolis, IN, 2000.

[254] Robert Nilsson. *Automatic Timeliness Testing of Dynamic Real-Time Systems*. PhD thesis, Skövde University/Linköping University, Skövde Sweden, 2006.

[255]   Robert Nilsson and Jeff Offutt. Automated testing of timeliness : A case study. In *Second Workshop on Automation of Software Test (AST 2007)*, Minneapolis, MN, May 2007.

[256]   Robert Nilsson, Jeff Offutt, and Sten F. Andler. Mutation-based testing criteria for timeliness. In *28th Annual International Computer Software and Applications Conference (COMPSAC 2004)*, pages 306–312, Hong Kong, September 2004.

[257]   Robert Nilsson, Jeff Offutt, and Jonas Mellin. Test case generation for mutation-based testing of timeliness. In *2nd International Workshop on Model Based Testing*, pages 102–121, Vienna, Austria, March 2006.

[258]   S. C. Ntafos. An evaluation of required element testing strategies. In *Seventh International Conference on Software Engineering*, pages 250–256, Orlando FL, March 1984. IEEE Computer Society Press.

[259]   Bashar Nuseibeh. Who dunnit? *IEEE Software*, 14:15–16, May/June 1997.

[260]   Department of Defense. *DOD-STD-2167A: Defense System Software Development*. Department of Defense, February 1988.

[261]   Department of Defense. *MIL-STD-498: Software Development and Documentation*. Department of Defense, December 1994.

[262]   Jeff Offutt. *Automatic Test Data Generation*. PhD thesis, Georgia Institute of Technology, Atlanta, GA, 1988. Technical report GIT-ICS 88/28.

[263]   Jeff Offutt. Investigations of the software testing coupling effect. *ACM Transactions on Software Engineering Methodology*, 1(1):3–18, January 1992.

[264]   Jeff Offutt and Aynur Abdurazik. Generating tests from UML specifications. In *Second IEEE International Conference on the Unified Modeling Language (UML99)*, pages 416–429, Fort Collins, CO, October 1999. Springer-Verlag Lecture Notes in Computer Science Volume 1723.

[265]   Jeff Offutt, Aynur Abdurazik, and Roger T. Alexander. An analysis tool for coupling-based integration testing. In *The Sixth IEEE International Conference on Engineering of Complex Computer Systems (ICECCS '00)*, pages 172–178, Tokyo, Japan, September 2000. IEEE Computer Society Press.

[266]   Jeff Offutt, Roger Alexander, Ye Wu, Quansheng Xiao, and Chuck Hutchinson. A fault model for subtype inheritance and polymorphism. In *12th International Symposium on Software Reliability Engineering*, pages 84–93, Hong Kong, China, November 2001. IEEE Computer Society Press.

[267]   Jeff Offutt, Zhenyi Jin, and Jie Pan. The dynamic domain reduction approach to test data generation. *Software – Practice and Experience*, 29(2):167–193, January 1999.

[268]   Jeff Offutt and Kim N. King. A Fortran 77 interpreter for mutation analysis. In *1987 Symposium on Interpreters and Interpretive Techniques*, pages 177–188, St. Paul MN, June 1987. ACM SIGPLAN.

[269]   Jeff Offutt, Ammei Lee, Gregg Rothermel, Roland Untch, and Christian Zapf. An experimental determination of sufficient mutation operators. *ACM Transactions on Software Engineering Methodology*, 5(2):99–118, April 1996.

[270]   Jeff Offutt and Stephen D. Lee. How strong is weak mutation? In *Fourth Symposium on Software Testing, Analysis, and Verification*, pages 200–213, Victoria, British Columbia, Canada, October 1991. IEEE Computer Society Press.

[271] Jeff Offutt and Stephen D. Lee. An empirical evaluation of weak mutation. *IEEE Transactions on Software Engineering*, 20(5):337–344, May 1994.

[272] Jeff Offutt, Shaoying Liu, Aynur Abdurazik, and Paul Ammann. Generating test data from state-based specifications. *Software Testing, Verification, and Reliability*, 13(1):25–53, March 2003.

[273] Jeff Offutt and Jie Pan. Detecting equivalent mutants and the feasible path problem. *Software Testing, Verification, and Reliability*, 7(3):165–192, September 1997.

[274] Jeff Offutt, Jie Pan, Kanupriya Tewary, and Tong Zhang. An experimental evaluation of data flow and mutation testing. *Software – Practice and Experience*, 26(2):165–176, February 1996.

[275] Jeff Offutt, Roy Pargas, Scott V. Fichter, and P. Khambekar. Mutation testing of software using a MIMD computer. In *1992 International Conference on Parallel Processing*, pages II257–266, Chicago, August 1992.

[276] Jeff Offutt, Jeffrey Payne, and Jeffrey M. Voas. Mutation operators for Ada. Technical report ISSE-TR-96-09, Department of Information and Software Systems Engineering, George Mason University, Fairfax, VA, March 1996. http://www.ise.gmu.edu/techrep/.

[277] Jeff Offutt and Roland Untch. Mutation 2000: Uniting the orthogonal. In *Mutation 2000: Mutation Testing in the Twentieth and the Twenty First Centuries*, pages 45–55, San Jose, CA, October 2000.

[278] Jeff Offutt, Ye Wu, Xiaochen Du, and Hong Huang. Bypass testing of web applications. In *15th International Symposium on Software Reliability Engineering*, pages 187–197, Saint-Malo, Bretagne, France, November 2004. IEEE Computer Society Press.

[279] Jeff Offutt and Wuzhi Xu. Generating test cases for web services using data perturbation. In *Workshop on Testing, Analysis and Verification of Web Services*, Boston, MA, July 2004. ACM SIGSoft.

[280] Jeff Offutt and Wuzhi Xu. Testing web services by XML perturbation. In *16th International Symposium on Software Reliability Engineering*, Chicago, IL, November 2005. IEEE Computer Society Press.

[281] Alex Orso and Mauro Pezze. Integration testing of procedural object oriented programs with polymorphism. In *Sixteenth International Conference on Testing Computer Software*, pages 103–114, Washington, DC, June 1999. ACM SIGSOFT.

[282] L. J. Osterweil and L. D. Fosdick. Data flow analysis as an aid in documentation, assertion generation, validation, and error detection. Technical report CU-CS-055-74, Department of Computer Science, University of Colorado, Boulder, CO, September 1974.

[283] T. J. Ostrand and M. J. Balcer. The category-partition method for specifying and generating functional tests. *Communications of the ACM*, 31(6):676–686, June 1988.

[284] Jan Overbeck. *Integration Testing for Object-Oriented Software*. PhD dissertation, Vienna University of Technology, 1994.

[285] A. J. Payne. A formalised technique for expressing compiler exercisers. *SIGLPAN Notices*, 13(1):59–69, January 1978.

[286] Ivars Peterson. Pentium bug revisited, May 1997. http://www.maa.org/mathland/mathland_5_12.html.

[287] E. Petitjean and H. Fochal. A realistic architecture for timed testing. In *Fifth IEEE International Conference on Engineering of Complex Computer Systems*, Las Vegas, October 1999.

[288] A. Pettersson and H. Thane. Testing of multi-tasking real-time systems with critical sections. In *Proceedings of Ninth International Conference on Real-Time Computing Systems and Applications (RTCSA'03)*, Tainan City, Taiwan, February 2003.

[289] Mauro Pezze and Michal Young. *Software Testing and Analysis: Process, Principles, and Techniques*. Wiley, Hoboken, NJ, 2008.

[290] S. Pimont and J. C. Rault. A software reliability assessment based on a structural behavioral analysis of programs. In *Second International Conference on Software Engineering*, San Francisco, CA, October 1976.

[291] P. Piwowarski, M. Ohba, and J. Caruso. Coverage measure experience during function test. In *14th International Conference on Software Engineering (ICSE'93)*, pages 287–301, Los Alamitos, CA, May 1993. ACM.

[292] T. A. Powell. *Web Site Engineering: Beyond Web Page Design*. Prentice-Hall, Englewood Cliffs, NJ, 2000.

[293] R. E. Prather. Theory of program testing – an overview. *Bell System Technical Journal*, 62(10):3073–3105, December 1983.

[294] Paul Purdom. A sentence generator for testing parsers. *BIT*, 12:366–375, 1972.

[295] C. V. Ramamoorthy, S. F. Ho, and W. T. Chen. On the automated generation of program test data. *IEEE Transactions on Software Engineering*, 2(4):293–300, December 1976.

[296] K. Ramamritham. The origin of time constraints. In *First International Workshop on Active and Real-Time Database Systems (ARTDB 1995)*, pages 50–62, Skövde, Sweden, June 1995. Springer, New York, 1995.

[297] S. Rapps and Elaine J. Weyuker. Selecting software test data using data flow information. *IEEE Transactions on Software Engineering*, 11(4):367–375, April 1985.

[298] S. Rayadurgam and M. P. E. Heimdahl. Coverage based test-case generation using model checkers. In *8th IEEE International Conference and Workshop on the Engineering of Computer Based Systems*, pages 83–91, April 2001.

[299] Pascal Raymond, Xavier Nicollin, Nicolas Halbwachs, and Daniel Weber. Automatic testing of reactive systems. In *Proceeding of the 19th IEEE Real-Time Systems Symposium (RTSS98)*, 1998.

[300] F. Ricca and P. Tonella. Analysis and testing of Web applications. In *23rd International Conference on Software Engineering (ICSE '01)*, pages 25–34, Toronto, CA, May 2001.

[301] Marc Roper. *Software Testing*. International Software Quality Assurance Series. McGraw-Hill, New York, 1994.

[302] Dave Rosenblum and Gregg Rothermel. A comparative study of regression test selection techniques. In *IEEE Computer Society 2nd International Workshop on*

Empirical Studies of Software Maintenance, pages 89–94, Bari, Italy, October 1997. IEEE Computer Society Press.

[303] Gregg Rothermel and Mary Jean Harrold. Analyzing regression test selection techniques. *IEEE Transactions on Software Engineering*, 22(8):529–551, August 1996.

[304] J. Rowland and Y. Zuyuan. Experimental comparison of three system test strategies preliminary report. In *Third Symposium on Software Testing, Analysis, and Verification*, pages 141–149, Key West, FL, December 1989. ACM SIGSOFT 89.

[305] RTCA-DO-178B. Software considerations in airborne systems and equipment certification, December 1992.

[306] Avi D. Rubin. *White-Hat Secuirty Arsenal: Tackling the Threats*. Addison-Wesley, New York, 2001.

[307] K. Sabnani and A. Dahbura. A protocol testing procedure. *Computer Networks and ISDN Systems*, 14(4):285–297, 1988.

[308] P. SanPietro, A. Morzenti, and S. Morasca. Generation of execution sequences for modular time critical systems. *IEEE Transactions on Software Engineering*, 26(2):128–149, February 2000.

[309] W. Schütz. *The Testability of Distributed Real-Time Systems*. Kluwer Academic Publishers, Norwell, MA, 1993.

[310] W. Schütz. Fundamental issues in testing distributed real-time systems. *Real-Time Systems*, 7(2):129–157, September 1994.

[311] Richard W. Selby. Combining software testing strategies: An empirical evaluation. In *Workshop on Software Testing*, pages 82–90, Banff, Alberta, July 1986. IEEE Computer Society Press.

[312] Richard K. Shehady and Daniel P. Siewiorek. A method to automate user interface testing using variable finite state machines. In *27th International Symposium on Fault-Tolerant Computing (FTCS'97)*, pages 80–88, Washington, Brussels, Tokyo, June 1997.

[313] G. Sherwood. Effective testing of factor combinations. In *Third International Conference on Software Testing, Analysis, and Review (STAR94)*, Washington, DC, May 1994. Software Quality Engineering.

[314] T. Shiba, T. Tsuchiya, and T. Kikuno. Using artificial life techniques to generate test cases for combinatorial testing. In *28th Annual International Computer Software and Applications Conference (COMPSAC'04)*, pages 72–77, Hong Kong, China, September 2004. IEEE Computer Society Press.

[315] M. D. Smith and D. J. Robson. Object-oriented programming: The problems of validation. In *6th International Conference on Software Maintenance*, pages 272–282, Los Alamitos, CA, 1990. IEEE Computer Society Press.

[316] Ian Sommerville. *Software Engineering*. Addison-Wesley, New York, 6th edition, 2001.

[317] British Computer Society Specialist Interest Group in Software Testing. *Standard for Software Component Testing, Working Draft 3.3*. British Computer Society, 1997. http://www.rmcs.cranfield.ac.uk/~cised/sreid/BCS_SIG/.

[318] W. P. Stevens, G. J. Myers, and L. L. Constantine. Structured design. *IBM Systems Journal*, 13(2):115–139, 1974.

[319]   Phil Stocks and Dave Carrington. Test templates: A specification-based testing framework. In *Fifteenth International Conference on Software Engineering*, pages 405–414, Baltimore, MD, May 1993.

[320]   Phil Stocks and Dave Carrington. A framework for specification-based testing. *IEEE Transactions on Software Engineering*, 22(11):777–793, November 1996.

[321]   K. C. Tai and F. J. Daniels. Test order for inter-class integration testing of object-oriented software. In *The Twenty-First Annual International Computer Software and Applications Conference (COMPSAC '97)*, pages 602–607, Santa Barbara, CA, 1997. IEEE Computer Society.

[322]   K. C. Tai and Yu Lei. A test generation strategy for pairwise testing. *IEEE Transactions on Software Engineering*, 28(1):109–111, January 2002.

[323]   Antero Taivalsaari. On the notion of inheritance. *ACM Computing Surveys*, 28(3):438–479, September 1996.

[324]   M. Tatsubori. OpenJava WWW page. Tokyo Institute of Technology, Chiba Shigeru Group, 2002. http://www.csg.is.titech.ac.jp/~mich/openjava/ (accessed May 2004).

[325]   M. Tatsubori, S. Chiba, M.-O. Killijian, and K. Itano. OpenJava: A class-based macro system for Java. *Reflection and Software Engineering*, LNCS 1826:117–133, June 2000.

[326]   H. Thane. *Monitoring, Testing and Debugging of Distributed Real-Time Systems*. PhD thesis, Royal Institute of Technology, KTH, Stockholm, Sweden, 2000.

[327]   P. Thévenod-Fosse, H. Waeselynck, and Y. Crouzet. An experimental study on software structural testing: Deterministic versus random input generation. In *Fault-Tolerant Computing: The Twenty-First International Symposium*, pages 410–417, Montreal, Canada, June 1991. IEEE Computer Society Press.

[328]   F. Tip. A survey of program slicing techniques. Technical report CS-R-9438, Computer Science/Department of Software Technology, Centrum voor Wiskunde en Informatica, 1994.

[329]   Yves Le Traon, Thierry Jéron, Jean-Marc Jézéquel, and Pierre Morel. Efficient object-oriented integration and regression testing. *IEEE Transactions on Reliability*, 49(1):12–25, March 2000.

[330]   Roland H. Untch, Jeff Offutt, and Mary Jean Harrold. Mutation analysis using program schemata. In *1993 International Symposium on Software Testing, and Analysis*, pages 139–148, Cambridge, MA, June 1993.

[331]   P. Verissimo and H. Kopetz. Design of distributed real-time systems. In S. Mullender, editor, *Distributed Systems*, pages 511–530. Addison-Wesley, New York, 1993.

[332]   S. A. Vilkomir and J. P. Bowen. Reinforced condition/decision coverage (RC/DC): A new criterion for software testing. In *ZB2002: 2nd International Conference of Z and B Users*, pages 295–313, Grenoble, France, January 2002. Springer-Verlag, LNCS 2272.

[333]   Jeffrey M. Voas. Pie: A dynamic failure-based technique. *IEEE Transactions on Software Engineering*, 18(8):717–727, August 1992.

[334]   Jeffrey M. Voas and Keith W. Miller. Software testability: The new verification. *IEEE Software*, 12(3):553–563, May 1995.

[335]   K. S. How Tai Wah. Fault coupling in finite bijective functions. *Software Testing, Verification, and Reliability*, 5(1):3–47, March 1995.

[336]   K. S. How Tai Wah. A theoretical study of fault coupling. *Software Testing, Verification, and Reliability*, 10(1):3–46, March 2000.

[337]   A. Watkins, D. Berndt, K. Aebischer, J. Fisher, and L. Johnson. Breeding software test cases for complex systems. In *37th Annual Hawaii International Conference on System Sciences (HICSS'04) – Track 9*, page 90303.3, Washington, DC, USA, 2004. IEEE Computer Society Press.

[338]   J. Wegener, H. H. Sthammer, B. F. Jones, and D. E. Eyres. Testing real-time systems using genetic algorithms. *Software Quality Journal*, 6(2):127–135, 1997.

[339]   Mark Weiser. Program slicing. *IEEE Transactions on Software Engineering*, SE-10(4):352–357, July 1984.

[340]   Steward N. Weiss. What to compare when comparing test data adequacy criteria. *ACM SIGSOFT Notes*, 14(6):42–49, October 1989.

[341]   Elaine Weyuker. The oracle assumption of program testing. In *Thirteenth International Conference on System Sciences*, pages 44–49, Honolulu, HI, January 1980.

[342]   Elaine Weyuker, Thomas Goradia, and A. Singh. Automatically generating test data from a boolean specification. *IEEE Transactions on Software Engineering*, 20(5):353–363, May 1994.

[343]   Elaine J. Weyuker and Thomas J. Ostrand. Theories of program testing and the application of revealing subdomains. *IEEE Transactions on Software Engineering*, 6(3):236–246, May 1980.

[344]   Elaine J. Weyuker, Stewart N. Weiss, and Richard G. Hamlet. Comparison of program testing strategies. In *Fourth Symposium on Software Testing, Analysis, and Verification*, pages 1–10, Victoria, British Columbia, Canada, October 1991. IEEE Computer Society Press.

[345]   Elaine J. Weyuker, Stewart N. Weiss, and Richard G. Hamlet. Data flow-based adequacy analysis for languages with pointers. In *Fourth Symposium on Software Testing, Analysis, and Verification*, pages 74–86, Victoria, British Columbia, Canada, October 1991. IEEE Computer Society Press.

[346]   Lee White and Husain Almezen. Generating test cases for GUI responsibilities using complete interaction sequences. In *9th International Symposium on Software Reliability Engineering*, pages 110–121, October 2000.

[347]   Lee White, Husain Almezen, and Nasser Alzeidi. User-based testing of GUI sequences and their interaction. In *10th International Symposium on Software Reliability Engineering*, pages 54–63, November 2001.

[348]   Lee White and Bogdan Wiszniewski. Path testing of computer programs with loops using a tool for simple loop patterns. *Software – Practice and Experience*, 21(10):1075–1102, October 1991.

[349]   Lee J. White. Software testing and verification. In Marshall C. Yovits, editor, *Advances in Computers*, volume 26, pages 335–390. Academic Press, New York, 1987.

[350]   Duminda Wijesekera, Lingya Sun, Paul Ammann, and Gordon Fraser. Relating counterexamples to test cases in CTL model checking specifications. In *A-MOST*

'07: Third ACM Workshop on the Advances in Model-Based Testing, co-located with ISSTA 2007, London, UK, July 2007.

[351] Christian Wild, Steven Zeil, and Gao Feng. Employing accumulated knowledge to refine test descriptions. *Software Testing, Verification, and Reliability*, July 2(2): 53–68, 1992.

[352] Alan W. Williams. Determination of test configurations for pair-wise interaction coverage. In *13th International Conference on the Testing of Communicating Systems (TestCom 2000)*, pages 59–74, Ottawa, Canada, August 2000.

[353] Alan W. Williams and Robert L. Probert. A practical strategy for testing pair-wise coverage of network interfaces. In *7th International Symposium on Software Reliability Engineering (ISSRE96)*, White Plains, New York, November 1996.

[354] Alan W. Williams and Robert L. Probert. A measure for component interaction test coverage. In *ACSI/IEEE International Conference on Computer Systems and Applications (AICCSA 2001)*, pages 304–311, Beirut, Lebanon, June 2001.

[355] Barbara Liskov with John Guttag. *Program Development in Java: Abstraction, Specification, and Object-Oriented Design*. Addison-Wesley, New York, 2001.

[356] W. Eric Wong. *On Mutation and Data Flow*. PhD thesis, Purdue University, December 1993. (Also Technical Report SERC-TR-149-P, Software Engineering Research Center, Purdue University, West Lafayette, IN).

[357] W. Eric Wong and Aditya P. Mathur. Fault detection effectiveness of mutation and data flow testing. *Software Quality Journal*, 4(1):69–83, March 1995.

[358] M. R. Woodward and K. Halewood. From weak to strong, dead or alive? An analysis of some mutation testing issues. In *Second Workshop on Software Testing, Verification, and Analysis*, pages 152–158, Banff Alberta, July 1988. IEEE Computer Society Press.

[359] Ye Wu and Jeff Offutt. Modeling and testing Web-based applications. Technical report ISE-TR-02-08, Department of Information and Software Engineering, George Mason University, Fairfax, VA, July 2002. http://www.ise.gmu.edu/techrep/.

[360] Ye Wu, Jeff Offutt, and Xiaochen Du. Modeling and testing of dynamic aspects of Web applications. Technical report ISE-TR-04-01, Department of Information and Software Engineering, George Mason University, Fairfax, VA, July 2004. http://www.ise.gmu.edu/techrep/.

[361] Tao Xie and Dave Notkin. Checking inside the black box: Regression testing by comparing value spectra. *IEEE Transactions on Software Engineering*, 31(10):869–883, October 2005.

[362] C. Yilmaz, M. B. Cohen, and A. Porter. Covering arrays for efficient fault characterization in complex configuration spaces. In *ACM SIGSOFT International Symposium on Software Testing and Analysis (ISSTA 2004)*, pages 45–54, Boston, MA, July 2004. ACM Software Engineering Notes.

[363] H. Yin, Z. Lebne-Dengel, and Y. K. Malaiya. Automatic test generation using checkpoint encoding and antirandom testing. Technical Report CS-97-116, Colorado State University, 1997.

[364] S. J. Young. *Real-Time Languages: Design and Development*. Ellis Horwood, Chichester, UK, 1982.

[365]   Christian N. Zapf. Medusamothra – A distributed interpreter for the mothra mutation testing system. M.S. thesis, Clemson University, Clemson, SC, August 1993.

[366]   Hong Zhu. A formal analysis of the subsume relation between software test adequacy criteria. *IEEE Transactions on Software Engineering*, 22(4):248–255, April 1996.

[367]   Hong Zhu, Patrick A. V. Hall, and John H. R. May. Software unit test coverage and adequacy. *ACM Computing Surveys*, 29(4):366–427, December 1997.

Index

active clause coverage (ACC)
  ambiguity, 108–109
  definition, 108
activity diagram , 89–90
All-Coupling-Defs-Uses (ACDU), 255
All-Coupling-Sequences (ACS), 255
All-Poly-Classes (APC), 255
All-Poly-Coupling-Defs-Uses (APCDU), 256
ANSI/IEEE Standard, 225
architectural design, 6
Ariane rocket, 8
automatic test data generation, 289–290

basic block, 28, 52–55, 178, 186, 259, 270, 278
  definition, 52
best effort touring, *see* tour, best effort
black-box testing
  definition, 21
block, 150, 153
bottom-up testing
  definition, 22
bypass testing, 258

characteristic, 151, 153
  examples, 151, 152, 155
  functionality-based, 153–155, 158
  interface-based, 153–157
CITO, *see* class integration test order
class integration test order, 218–219, 222, 237
  definition, 219
clause
  definition, 105
combination strategy, 160
component, 6, 11, 65, 73, 191–192, 217–218,
    236–237, 256–260
  definition, 217
concurrency, 268
connector, 6
control flow graph, 259
controllability, 120, 263, 284–286
  definition, 14
coupling path, 247–256

coupling sequence, 250–256
coverage analysis tool, 269
  definition, 268
coverage criterion
  definition, 17
coverage level
  definition, 18
criteria
  ACoC, 160, 163
  ADC, 48, 50, 70, 79, 102
  ADUPC, 48–51, 70, 102, 103
  AUC, 48–51, 70, 79, 102, 271–272
  BCC, 162–163
  CACC, 109–111, 113, 115, 118–119, 126–129,
      133, 134, 142, 147–148, 188, 272
  CC, 106, 113, 116–117, 126, 132, 187
  CoC, 107, 113, 117
  CPC, 36, 50
  CRTC, 36, 50
  CUTPNFP, 113, 142–149
  DC, 172
  EC, 34, 50–51, 54, 65–66, 79, 90, 96, 101, 172,
      187, 268–271
  ECC, 160–161, 163
  EPC, 35, 50, 79
  GACC, 109, 113, 117–119, 134, 142, 147, 148,
      188
  GICC, 112
  IC, 113, 139–141, 149
  MBCC, 162–163
  MC, 175
  MOC, 175
  MPC, 175
  NC, 33–35, 50, 54, 65–67, 78, 87, 90, 96, 101, 172,
      186, 268–271
  PC, 106–109, 112, 113, 115, 116, 118–120, 125,
      128–129, 132, 134, 140
  PDC, 172
  PPC, 35–36, 39, 50–51
  PWC, 161, 163
  RACC, 110–111, 113, 115, 118–119, 134, 142,
      144, 146–148, 188

319